PENGUIN BUSINESS
RAHUL BAJAJ

Gita Piramal is one of India's foremost business historians, researchers and bestselling authors. Her previous books include *Business Maharajas* and *Business Legends*. A former journalist, Piramal has contributed for several decades to various international and Indian publications, including the UK's *Financial Times* and the *Economic Times*. She also founded The Smart Manager, a pioneering management magazine, and has served as a board member of some of India's best-known companies, including the Bajaj Group companies.

Piramal is a senior associate fellow at Somerville College, University of Oxford, and holds a BA and MA in history, and a PhD in business history, all from Bombay University.

RAHUL BAJAJ

An Extraordinary Life

Gita Piramal

BUSINESS
An imprint of Penguin Random House

PENGUIN BUSINESS

USA | Canada | UK | Ireland | Australia
New Zealand | India | South Africa | China

Penguin Business is part of the Penguin Random House group of companies
whose addresses can be found at global.penguinrandomhouse.com

Published by Penguin Random House India Pvt. Ltd
4th Floor, Capital Tower 1, MG Road,
Gurugram 122 002, Haryana, India

First published in Penguin Business by Penguin Random House India 2022

10 9 8 7 6 5 4 3 2 1

This book is a work of non-fiction. The views and opinions expressed
in the book are those of the author only and do not reflect or
represent the views and opinions held by any other person.
This book is based on a variety of sources including published materials
and research, conducted by the author, and on interviews and interactions
of the author with the persons mentioned in the manuscript. It reflects the
author's own understanding and conception of such materials and/or
can be verified by research. All persons within the book are actual
individuals and the names and characteristics of some individuals
have been changed to respect their privacy. The objective of this book
is not to hurt any sentiments or be biased in favour of or against any
particular person, political party, region, caste, society, gender,
creed, nation or religion.

ISBN 9780143460480

Typeset in Adobe Garamond Pro by MAP Systems, Bengaluru, India

www.penguin.co.in

For

AMARTYA & AGASTYA

my two little gurus

Contents

Contents

'Integrity and character matter.
Without them, no amount of ability can get you anywhere.
In addition, you need courage—courage to make
difficult decisions, and courage to oppose something
if your conscience tells you that you are right.'

—Rahul Bajaj

Foreword

Rakesh Mohan

Gita Piramal has done a great service to the country in penning this biography of Rahul Bajaj. It is an intimate, affectionate and comprehensive narrative of Rahul's life which can only be done by someone as skilled as Gita in capturing the captivating stories of India's leading business families as they have emerged and grown since Independence. She has the advantage of being an insider, both as a member of one of India's older and successful business families herself, and as a non-executive director on the apex boards of the Bajaj group. Given her familiarity with her subject at both the personal and professional levels, this narrative could easily have descended into hagiography, which Gita has avoided successfully. In reading this book we slowly come to know Rahul Bajaj, warts and all, as he evolved from being an indifferent school and college student to becoming one of the tallest Indian business leaders in both a literal and figurative sense! His presence in any setting has been larger than life.

Among Indian business leaders, Rahul had an exceptional upbringing which probably shaped his outlook on life, business and family alike. His grandfather, Jamnalal Bajaj, was among Gandhi's earliest colleagues and friends after his return from South Africa; his father, Kamalnayan Bajaj, followed suit and lived in the Wardha

Ashram in Maharashtra through much of his life; and his mother, Savitri, was active in the freedom struggle, including the suffering of jail terms. Consequently, Rahul grew up in a traditional Marwari business family but imbued with the Gandhian ethics of truth, austerity, honesty, kindness and respect for others along with an overall sense of duty, which he has endeavoured to transmit to his children. As one goes through this volume, one begins to understand Rahul's evolution as a person, ethical business leader, son, father and patriarch. He has always spoken truth to power regardless of the regime in power and exhibited his independence despite intolerable business and personal pressures at different times. When he agreed to be a member of Parliament, he insisted on standing as an independent candidate rather than joining any particular political party.

Through his sagacious leadership during the licence-permit raj he built Bajaj Auto brick by brick into the two-wheeler leader that it became. He, of course, benefited greatly, like others, from the command-and-control regime where he could dominate a limited market through the production of the limited number of scooters that he was allowed, without any innovation throughout the period. But Vespa became the most loved Indian brand: a symbol of the Indian middle class arriving at the market. Although he was the leader of the so-called Bombay Club protesting the 1991 major economic reforms, unlike some of his colleagues, he benefited greatly from these reforms and took his company to greater heights taking advantage of all the new opportunities presenting themselves with the opening of the country's domestic markets and competition. He has been among the foremost Indian business leaders who promoted India internationally, particularly through his participation and leadership of the World Economic Forum in Davos and promotion of the annual India economic summits. In fact, I first met him at the 1990 Davos meeting, which began a lifelong professional friendship ever since.

He has also been among the movers and shakers of the Confederation of Indian Industry (CII) as it evolved from its origins as Association of Indian Engineering Industry (AIEI), through its transformation as Confederation of Engineering Industry (CEI) and final emergence as the leading Indian business organization with a predominant international outlook. Despite his own initial reservations on the speed of liberalization in the 1990s, he helped CII play a very significant role in supporting the government's efforts in carrying the country through its major economic transformation over almost twenty-five years. He is essentially an institution builder devoted to furthering the broad interests of the country at home and abroad.

What are some of his shortcomings that Gita has described over different parts of the book? He was slow in seeing the transformation in consumer preferences moving away from scooters to motorcycles but he listened to the next generation and, once he was convinced, moved full speed ahead in making Bajaj Auto a powerhouse in that segment as well in the face of stiff competition. Similarly, it would appear that he has exhibited insufficient interest in promoting technology and research in his companies: perhaps understandable given the very protected market that his company grew up in with ten-year-long queues for the coveted Vespa. Once again, he seems to have listened to the next generation and Bajaj Auto is reportedly displaying much greater interest in this aspect of business development as well. Finally, like other busy business leaders, he neglected his growing family in their early years, according to his own telling, but has made up for it in recent years.

Gita is at her best in chronicling Rahul's evolution as a patriarch and his increasing devotion to his extended family, as illustrated by the touching heartfelt tributes of his children and grandchildren at the end of the book. This has helped in engineering smooth succession planning for the next phase of the expanding Bajaj business empire. This has not been without its problems, but he has succeeded in making adequate space and potential for growth for different members of his extended family. In order to be given leadership positions in the expanding Bajaj group, each of them had to demonstrate their business acumen: nothing was given to them on a platter. As he slowly eased himself out of active management, he listened more and more to the next generation as they persuaded him to diversify the Bajaj group towards the financial sector in both insurance and non-bank financing, with each arm emerging as private sector leaders in their respective segments.

One can hope that, with the ethical upbringing of the whole Bajaj family, also imbued with the practice of hard work, the next generation will continue to be inspired by the example set by their patriarch.

I also hope that this labour of love compiled by Gita will be widely read and serve as a beacon for the practice of dynamic and ethical business, responsible leadership and demonstration of the importance of family in our lives.

Introduction

Successful leaders can be viewed through several prisms. And so is the case with Rahul Bajaj. There are many reasons to study a life as extraordinary as his. As a friend, journalist, author, board member and business historian, I have had the opportunity to observe his exceptional journey at close quarters. Not only did he build the world's most valuable two-wheeler company, he followed it up by laying the foundation for a financial sector powerhouse. I have wanted to document this story, and share it with the wider world, for a long time.

I believe Rahul's life story can inspire different generations of readers, whether a young MBA student, a seasoned entrepreneur, a mid-career professional or simply someone who would like to know this fascinating person a bit better. So I would like to invite you, my dear reader, to look at his journey through three key prisms.

First, the lens of leadership. To my mind, Rahul exemplifies leadership as it is taught in business school, yet is often so elusive in the actual corporate world itself. He is a visionary and clear on strategy, is decisive, action-oriented and execution-driven, and excellent with people and in building teams. What makes him distinctive are his convictions, and his ability to speak out and to defend his beliefs. Ultimately, this is the true hallmark of leadership.

Second, his journey captures the intricate and inseparable relationship between business, government and society. Over a period of more than six decades, he symbolizes the evolution of this relationship in India. This book is as much a story of the Bajaj Group of companies, as it is a tale of Indian industry, government and society relationships during these years. Historians, I think, will find this book helpful. But lessons from history apply to all of us. Given that we live in a world where environmental, social and governance concerns are increasingly important to investors and other stakeholders, I hope that these lessons will resonate with readers from a diverse range of backgrounds.

Finally, the prism of sustainability and the value of leaving a lasting legacy. Many young entrepreneurs today are motivated by billion-dollar valuations and relatively quick exits. That is certainly a tempting path. Yet Rahul's journey is testimony to a life of perseverance and purpose, towards value creation with a horizon that spans multiple generations. If you, dear reader, want to examine your life, your career or your business with a long-term perspective, I believe there is no better place to start than right here.

A word on nomenclature: Throughout the book, Rahul Bajaj is simply referred to as 'Bajaj', whereas all other Bajaj family members are referred to by their first name. I would also like to say a word on the book's structure. Each chapter in this book describes an important event in Rahul's life. In order to explain the event in its entirety, the chapters occasionally overlap in time and hence the book is not written in a traditional, linear chronology. Instead, each chapter can be read on its own as a vignette. All chapters collectively serve as a comprehensive account of his history.

Welcome to a life well-lived.

Gita Piramal

The Bajaj Family Tree

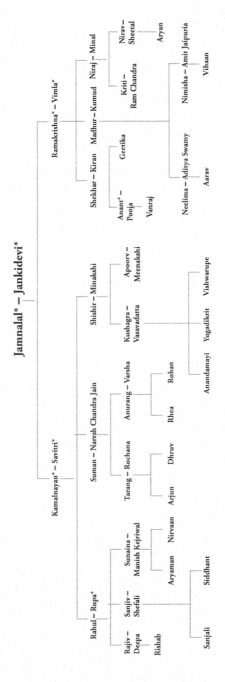

Jamnalal* – Jankidevi*

Kamalnayan* – Savitri*

Ramakrishna* – Vimla*

Rahul – Rupa*

Rajiv – Deepa

Rishab

Sanjiv – Shefali

Sunaina – Manish Kejriwal

Aryaman   Nirvaan

Sanjali   Siddhant

Suman – Naresh Chandra Jain

Tarang – Rochana

Arjun   Dhruv

Anurang – Varsha

Rhea   Rohan

Anandamayi   Yugadikrit   Vishwarupe

Shishir – Minakshi

Kushagra – Vasavadatta

Apoorv – Meenakshi

Shekhar – Kiran

Anant* – Pooja

Vanraj

Geetika

Madhur – Kumud

Niraj – Minal

Kriti – Ram Chandra

Nirav – Sheetal

Aryan

Neelima – Aditya Swamy

Aarav

Nimisha – Amit Jaipuria

Vihaan

*deceased

xix

1

11 August 1942

Savitri, Bajaj and Kamalnayan.

Images courtesy of Bajaj Archives

The six-year-old boy looked up at the face in front of him. '*Aap hamari ma ho?*—Are you our mother?' Tears rolled down Savitri's cheeks.

Bajaj was four years old when Savitri was taken away. The Quit India movement was launched on 9 August 1942 in Mumbai. On 11 August, a crowd gathered at Gandhi Chowk. Two young men were hit, one fatally, in the police firing. The encounter propelled Bajaj's mother into active politics. Savitri describes the event in her autobiography, *God's Plan Works*:

> 'His old parents were sent for. Their wailing was more than one could stand. Even after 47 years, I can still recall the scene vividly. How brave the father was, how courageous. I do not know his name or even much about him; but I remember the words uttered by him then, standing next to the dead body of his son—"I am proud that my son has died for his country (in Marathi) " . . .'
>
> 'At that moment my heart stirred as nothing had in my life. I decided to join the movement. A timid person like me was transformed. . . . 9th August is my birthdate too. I was just 22 years old and I felt that I was re-born that day, I too had to take part in this fight against imperialism. I wrote to my father, in Calcutta, that night—asking him to send somebody for my son Rahul and daughter Suman—aged four and three.'
>
> 'If they were with my parents, I would not worry about them. In Wardha, things were unsettled. One did not know what was going to happen and who would be arrested next. The whole Bajaj family was involved in the Quit India movement, while my parents were not actively involved in politics. In a few days the children went to Calcutta to be with my parents. I remember I did not feel the parting so much. My heart and mind were engrossed in the present issues.'

The Bajaj family were at the forefront of the Independence movement. Bajaj, from infancy, became used to members of his family suddenly disappearing. As he grew older, he would learn and accept that they were in jail for good reason. Savitri was incarcerated for thirteen months and ten days in Wardha, Nagpur and Jubbulpore prisons. Released, she could not walk. Other family members had longer and harsher terms. But it's still tough dealing with a mom's absence for two years.

2

Matchmaker, Matchmaker, Make Me a Match:[1] 1938–46

Left to right: Suman, Savitri, Kamalnayan and Bajaj.

---

[1] Extracts from Savitri Bajaj's autobiography, *God's Plan Works,* and a collection of her writings, '*I write as I feel*'.

Jamnalal, Bajaj's grandfather, was a tall, handsome man with a straight back (even if the grainy image in the last chapter of this book does not appear to match these words). On 9 January 1915, twenty-six-year-old Jamnalal arrived at the pier of the almost ready Gateway of India. He and a small group of like-minded businessmen boarded a ferry to take them to the S.S. *Arabia*. Mohandas Karamchand Gandhi was back in India after twenty-one years in South Africa.

The vibe between the two men was instant and the friendship energizing. After a few spells in jail, the Dandi March among other activities, in 1933 Gandhi arrived in Wardha, Bajaj's hometown. Jamnalal donated a piece of land. The Sevagram Ashram was up and running by April 1936. Leafing through Gandhi's diaries, beyond the politicking, Gandhi apparently enjoyed matchmaking. Until his assassination, Gandhi vetted every potential male or female candidate for membership to the Bajaj clan.

Jamnalal's favourite hunting ground for mates for his five children was Calcutta,[2] the centre of Marwari wealth and glamour. Towering above them all was the firm of Tarachand Ghanshyamdas founded by Bhagoti Ram Poddar in the mid-1750s.

'The Poddar business empire had branches at the major seaports in Bombay and Calcutta, on the river ports along the Ganges, and throughout the opium- and cotton-growing areas,' describes historian Thomas Timberg. 'The firm took deposits, gave loans, engaged in the wholesale trade of commodities, transferred funds for clients to distant cities, cashed bills of trade, insured shipments, and speculated on commodity futures when the opportunity arose.' It was banker to the royal families of Jaipur, Bikaner and Hyderabad. The grandfathers of both Ghanshyam Das Birla and Lakshmi Mittal trained in Poddar's Calcutta head office, Kaligodam, on Mullik Street in Burrabazar.

World War I would play a critical shadow role in the dynamics of Tarachand Ghanshyamdas and its owners. A kerosene and oil bonanza opened in India. 'Stick to Tarachand Ghanshyamdas,' advised the US Trade Consul to visiting American businessmen. 'When business is done through a strong guarantee broker, there is little danger to the seller, as the former pays the bill if the buyer does

---

[2] See Bajaj Family Tree.

not.' At this point, it was impossible to think the managing agency could collapse.

As a potential windfall opened, Lakshmanprasad and Radhakrishna[3] expeditiously moved from Mathura, the family's home base, to Calcutta. 'Grandfather was successful in getting the Burmah Shell agencies for kerosene for the whole of India,' recalls Savitri in her memoir. 'There were roughly 300 to 400 branches spread all over the country with head offices in Calcutta, Bombay, Madras and Karachi.' When Shaw Wallace came calling, Tarachand Ghanshyamdas was able to guarantee oil and fertilizer imports across undivided India. Post-Independence, Tarachand Ghanshyamdas would be dissolved on 3 March 1958.

After Radhakrishna's death in 1916, with all three sisters married, the next generation continued to live in No. 10 Central Avenue as a joint family of four brothers—Raghunathprasad, Jankiprasad, Lakshmanprasad and Hanumanprasad. The fraternal threads began to fray.

'Father had a big family of five children,' explained Savitri. 'My eldest uncle had no offspring, the second uncle a daughter, and the youngest was married only a few years back. One brother with a large family was a thorn in the flesh. In the joint family system, a much larger expenditure for one brother could not be tolerated. My mother was made unhappy and there was inner discontent and discord in daily living.'

Lakshmanprasad rented a house on Hastings Road in Alipore, a tony British enclave, and he, his wife Urmila, sons Mahavir and Jagdish and daughters Savitri, Vimla and Lalita moved out of No. 10. The idea of migrating to England intensified. Could the Tarachand Ghanshyamdas links to British firms open up business possibilities, mused Lakshmanprasad.

In the 1930s he took his family to England, hoping to settle there. He hired an English governess for the little ones, placed the older ones in a school in Letchworth village in Hertfordshire, and rented a modest country house near the school. As a freshman and then sophomore at Calcutta's Presidency College, Lakshmanprasad used to enjoy Bengali plays, tennis, football and rowing.

---

[3] Savitri Bajaj's uncles.

As his children developed, he inducted them in his hobbies.
Savitri learnt to row regatta-style, knock a tennis ball, and dress
up for balls and masquerades—rather useful skills in an English
school. 'Savitri became a product of two worlds—the British and
the nationalists,' described Russi M. Lala. 'She was brought up by a
father who was perhaps the most pro-British Marwari businessman.'

'The plans to stay in England did not materialize,' records Savitri,
'mainly due to two reasons. One was unforeseen financial problems.
The second was homesickness. As months passed, my father missed
his familiar life, friends, and relations. In a new land, it is not easy
to make friends and settle into a life totally different from Indian
ways.' The downhearted Poddars returned to Alipore, unexcited or
oblivious to the Second Round Table Conference discussions taking
place in London[4] attended by Gandhi and G.D. Birla.

Oh, Calcutta!

Back in Calcutta, the big question was, is twelve-year-old Savitri
too old and too unusual to be accepted as a daughter-in-law?
Technically, Savitri had been betrothed at age four to a well-known
local Marwari family. The boy's side were fine to go ahead with the
marriage. It was the bride who bolted. 'We returned all the jewellery
given to me eight years back. My would-have-been father-in-law
was deeply hurt,' she admitted. 'Most Marwari ladies in those days
observed purdah and led a socially restricted life.'

Savitri continued to reject potential suitors. Her mother
stopped taking her to community events. Kamalnayan Bajaj's name
popped up.

'Father must have heard about Jamnalalji and his background,'
figured Savitri. 'There was not too much money there, but the
restrictions of an orthodox family would be absent. On his next visit
to Calcutta, Jamnalalji came to see me. His son was in Ceylon for his
studies. Kamalnayan was to return in a few weeks.'

'Kamal was the first son in Bachhraji's family after three
generations,' wrote Jankidevi Bajaj in her autobiography, *My*

[4] Three Round Conferences took place in the UK: first: 12 November 1930–19 January
1931; second: 7 September 1931–1 December 1931 and third: 17 November 1932–24
December 1932.

Life's Journey. 'Savitri was extremely good looking and I was rather inclined to say yes. She was very skinny and I wondered if she could bear children. The Poddar family was keen and Bapu[5] agreed to the proposal. The Poddars wanted to organise a grand wedding and expected a huge participation from our family. However, on Bapuji's advice, only fifteen of us travelled to Calcutta.'

'*Khadi* was of course the chosen attire,' continues Jankidevi. 'Savitri wanted to wear a *zari*-laden *saree*. We ordered this specially from the Charkha Sangh, who wove a *khadi saree* with *zari*. The bride's family tailored a few *khadi* outfits for Kamalnayan such as a silk shirt and an embroidered turban. They met us at the station before Calcutta and wished for Kamalnayan to alight the train in this wedding attire. But he was content wearing his white *khadi kurta, dhoti*, cap and a saffron shawl. He continued to wear these for the ceremony.'

'We received a very warm welcome at Calcutta station,' continues Jankidevi. 'The bride's family were disappointed to see only fifteen people emerge from the train. They had made arrangements to welcome an entourage. We reached Calcutta in the morning and the wedding got underway at 6 p.m. We were to return the next day. Birlaji[6] wanted to host a celebratory party at his house. After the post-wedding festivities at Birlaji's place, Savitri's family wanted to shower our family with gifts. We politely declined to accept them. We had stopped following these rituals. Finally, we agreed to five pairs of clothes for the groom. Kamalnayan accepted only one single rupee as a gesture of goodwill. We were not interested in finding out what gifts Savitri brought along with her as part of her trousseau.'

Kamalnayan and Savitri married on 30 June 1937. 'There are no photographs of my marriage ceremony,' writes Savitri wistfully, 'as nobody remembered to call the waiting photographer. Next day, of course, we had some studio photos taken.'

It's a Boy!

'From Wardha, we were supposed to go for our honeymoon. It was just a dream,' Savitri writes in *God's Plan Works*. 'Kamalnayan and

---

[5] Mohandas Karamchand Gandhi.
[6] Ghanshyam Das Birla.

I had barely ten weeks together when he had to return to Cambridge. It was earlier understood that after marriage I would accompany him to England. But I started expecting my first baby, and considering my condition, I was not allowed to go. I was terribly disappointed. After marriage, to be parted again so soon and for such a long time was sheer torture.'

'My in-laws hoped that I should stay on in Wardha and have the baby there. I was glad to return to my parents. During the October Puja holiday, my parents took my sisters and brothers to Ranchi, a hill station near Calcutta. For the spring festival of Holi, my father-in-law came to Ranchi for a few days. My brothers and sisters and I threw coloured water on him and made him ride a donkey. He managed to balance on a bicycle. He was very sporting and mixed with my family so well! He became very fond of my sister Vimla. Nine years later Vimla would marry Kamalnayan's younger brother Ramkrishna.'

Bonny and healthy Rahul was born on 10 June 1938. But 'it was a protracted and difficult birth and I was lucky to be in my mother's care and get the best medical attention at home,' wrote Savitri. Kamalnayan returned from London a month later and dashed to Calcutta to see his firstborn.

The family of three left Calcutta for Wardha in time for the mid-December 1938 Congress Working Committee. In Sevagram, Gandhi was ready with a draft policy for the Indian states. 'One day there was a hue and cry for Kamalnayan,' wrote Savitri. 'He was wanted immediately by Bapuji. He became a little apprehensive by the frantic call and immediately left to see Bapuji at Sevagram. "Have you done anything about Savitri's home and seen to her comforts?" Kamalnayan heaved a sigh of relief! He explained the changes. Bapuji was happy and satisfied. He felt personally responsible for me as an adopted grandfather who had approved me as a daughter-in-law of Jamnalalji.'

'Jawaharlalji[7] came to see and bless my son,' remembers Savitri, 'I asked him to suggest a name for him. Panditji immediately said "Rahul". Rahul was not a common name those days. Madalsaji rushed out of the room, collected some sweets, rushed back and distributed

---

[7] Jawaharlal Nehru.

them to Panditji and others. The name proved lucky for him, and of course for all of us.' Savitri was soon expecting her second child. Suman arrived on 6 August 1939 and Shishir on 10 December 1947.

Mussoorie

The year 1944 saw Savitri released from Jubbulpore prison. Her father scooped her up. The first pitstop: Wardha. 'From the station, up the ramp, I was carried on a chair till the car. I half covered my face with my saree . . . to see Jamnalalji's daughter-in-law under such conditions saddened the coolies, ticket collectors and others on the platform,' wrote Savitri. 'After a few days, father took me to Mussoorie, a hill station in the foothills of the Garhwal Himalayan range. My father's house in Calcutta was requisitioned during the war years but he still had a garden cottage in Mathura. For the hot summer months, he rented the Rani of Kalsia's house in Mussoorie.'

Four coolies appeared with a hand-pulled rickshaw to carry home Savitri, Rahul and Suman. 'My darlings sat with me. They were dressed identically in closed-collar woollen coats and pants. Brothers Mahavir and Jagdish, bhabhis, sisters—my whole family waited anxiously to see us.'

As she stepped down from the rickshaw, memories flooded Savitri. The clan had celebrated Jagdish's wedding in Mussoorie in July 1942. 'I was hesitant to go to my brother's wedding as my father-in-law[8] had recently died in February, and I did not wish to leave Mataji alone,' recalled Savitri, 'but Mataji was very kind and persuaded me to go to Mussoorie for the wedding with both Rahul and Suman.' Kamalnayan, as the eldest son, automatically became the family's karta at age twenty-seven. Bare weeks later, Savitri was back in Wardha, and the Gandhi Chowk shooting took place.

While in jail Savitri's weight dropped to under 33 kg. Surrounded by her family and children, Savitri found peace and normality. Kamalnayan arrived. The circle was complete. 'The next year, Kamalnayan rented a separate house for us. We would climb down from our house to my parent's house in under four minutes. In winter, we would go to the Poddar house in Mathura. Three years

---

[8] Jamnalal Bajaj.

I spent like this. I regained my health and returned to Bombay. Rahul and Suman had to be admitted to schools.'

'Kamalnayan was inclined towards a Hindi medium education. I was sure that English education was essential for higher studies and other spheres of life,' wrote Savitri. 'My husband did not insist. I had to admit them in a lesser school in the beginning. Later, Rahul got admission to the Cathedral Boys' School and Suman to the Cathedral Girls' School.' 'Subsequently, if I remember correctly, from 1965 Cathedral became a co-ed school,' shares Bajaj.

During Bajaj's childhood, Kamalnayan was scarcely at home. 'My father was a distant figure,' he recalls. 'My mother influenced me the most. She shaped my frame of mind.' At one point, Bajaj's parents separated but a chance meeting on an overnight train to Bombay brought them back together. 'When her husband fell ill, she travelled daily to his home to look after him. After some days, he invited her to rejoin him and they remained united until he passed away in 1972,' described fellow writer, Russi M. Lala.

Suman

'My early childhood was growing up with bhaiya[9] in Mussoorie, Calcutta, Ranchi, Mathura and Wardha,' remembers Suman Jain, Bajaj's sister. 'Those were beautiful and nostalgic days when family members gave us a lot of time, attention and love. Some holidays stand out: dacoit-infested Rajasthan by car, Kashmir in houseboats. Panditji, our tutor from Mathura, travelled with us to all these places so that our basic studies were not neglected.'

'Bhaiya was good at studies and very naughty. He would tease me and play pranks. My mother once pointed out to me that he was pinching me when we were being photographed. I was given a sweet so I would not cry. Later, as I grew older, I was the beneficiary as I would get his toys as compensation!'

'Panditji told us stories from the Mahabharat and the Ramayana, and introduced us to story books, and put some good values in us,' shares Suman. 'Both Rahul and I are very fond of reading. I remember Rahul once walking on the parapet of a bridge. Poor Panditji was really scared. We spent a lot of time when very young in

---

[9] Rahul Bajaj.

Mussoorie with our Calcutta grandparents and mother, sometimes for six months at a time.'

'We also went to Africa for three months with Kakasaheb Kalelkar[10] and our parents,' continues Suman. 'Nehruji wanted informal ambassadors to judge the situation there. Appasaheb Pant was then our ambassador. We went by ship to Mombasa. Rahul used to send me to father who would be playing bridge, to ask permission to have ginger ale. I disliked aerated water, but like a fool, I would go to Kakaji[11] who never refused me, and Rahul used to gulp both the bottles of the aerated stuff.'

'We both had great fun in Africa, Uganda, Tanzania and Kenya. We went where the cannibals lived. A truck, a jeep and gun-wielding guards were, of course, with us. We visited the Masai village. They were very tall and seemed to be gentle folk. They had sharp eyes and would spot a herd coming before our binoculars would spot the buffaloes. We saw a lot of wild game and Kakaji would make us sit on either side of the car as bhaiya would keep troubling me. Lots of functions took place and as our parents were busy, we used to have snacks and tea with heaps of sugar with no one to check us. People would spoil us.'

'We spent a lot of time in Wardha. We learnt to bicycle. Panditji and sometimes Dadiji[12] would join us in our class of two. Even then, Bhaiya would trouble me. So, my parents introduced a punishment for him. If I screamed "*cheez zupt*", I could take one of his toys. It was like an electric shock for him. We used to get many toys from our Calcutta relatives, and I had many duplicate toys. Our Wardha relatives never thought of giving us toys: they were busy doing work for the freedom movement. My father gave me a beautiful watch. Rahul was furious as he knew I could not read the time. I was given twenty-four hours to learn or surrender the watch!'

'Later we moved to Mumbai. Both of us schooled at Cathedral, I in the girls' section, Bhaiya in the boys. We used to go to movies together. Ice cream cones were a novelty. We each would have one

---

[10] Kakasaheb Kalelkar: member of the Rajya Sabha from 1952 to 1964, president of the Backward Classes Commission in 1953, established Gandhi Vidyapith, Vedchhi in 1967 and served as its vice-chancellor.
[11] Kamalnayan.
[12] Jankidevi Bajaj.

cone when we entered, one during the interval, and the last one when going home. Growing up, he was always there for me—loving, forthright, fair-minded and helpful. Not every sibling can boast of having a big brother like him.'

Adds aunt Chandramukhi Poddar in *Dear Rahul*,[13] 'The fondest memory I have is the image of little you and small Suman clad in pants, stuffed in cotton wool, looking like cute igloos. You were so naughty and would pinch Suman in passing and make her cry. Nanaji would say, "Suman *sara din roheti roheti hai*" and you would have that wicked smile on your face—"*maza aaya*". Later, Jijaji[14] sent you to Kolkata to study and you came to stay with us. I received a lot of affection from you. In your growing years, you turned into a gracious and considerate boy, endearing yourself towards all. I became extremely fond of you.'

'Bhaiya was a good student and I was not, but in my school final examination, I passed with good marks. The result came in Wardha. Bhaiya started jumping and rolling on the *gadda* (a thick mattress), hollering and shouting, "How can she get good marks when she is a fool!" I was very pleased. This is how we grew up together. I have lovely memories of our childhood. I cannot vouch for my brother.'

Emotions flowed deep in December 1960 when Suman neé Bajaj and Naresh Chandra walked the parikrama for their wedding in New Delhi. 'Nehru attended the marriage and blessed the couple,' remembers Savitri. 'And Kamalnayan took Nehruji around the decorated pandal over which he had taken great pains.'

---

[13] *Dear Rahul* is a personal tribute prepared by Rupa Bajaj.
[14] Brother-in-law, Kamalnayan.

3

From Bombay and Back: 1945–62

Bajaj at St. Stephen's College, Delhi.

Kamalnayan and Ramkrishna grew up in Gandhi's Sevagram and Vinoba Bhave's Paunar ashram. As a toddler, Bajaj played in the heat and dust of central India along with the other ashram children. Gandhi had a sweet spot for each of them. Bajaj remembers sitting in Gandhi's lap. Towards the middle of World War II,[1] with freedom from the British raj in sight, the Bajaj family trickled out of Wardha. The joint family grew up on Bombay's posh Carmichael Road with the scent of mogras and splashes of bright colour from convolvulus bushes. On 14 August 1947, over the radio airwaves, the nine-year-old Bajaj was allowed to stay up in order to listen to Nehru's midnight freedom speech.

'I was extremely happy in Bombay,' wrote Savitri in her diary. 'I am basically a city girl. I love the city environment and its entertainment possibilities . . . when we arrived in Bombay, we stayed at Juhu. We had a large piece of land there. We built several shacks on the land, which were given out on rent. We stayed in one of them in the front, facing the sea. The surroundings and settings were lovely—very quiet and peaceful. Commuting to the city every day was anathema to me—very tiring and time-consuming. Kamalnayan did not mind. He preferred to stay in Juhu. He loved his early morning swim in the sea, walks on the beach and even sleeping outside in the veranda.'

'Growing up, my home was Bombay and not Akurdi, Pune,' says Bajaj. In early 1946 uncle Ramkrishna moved into a flat in the same building as Viren Shah—Shanti Bhavan on Walkeshwar Road. A few months later, most of the family moved to Bhagwati Bhavan on Carmichael Road. 'In my early childhood, my father was scarcely at home, and a somewhat distant figure,' recalls Bajaj, and his mother Savitri influenced him the most. 'She shaped my frame of mind,' he says.

'In the 1950s, Rahul and I grew up in the same building, playing gully cricket in Bhagwati Bhavan's compound,' reminisced Narotam Sekhsaria. 'He was Superman, smashing glass panes with his mighty hits of the cricket ball. For all of us, Shishir, Shekhar, Madhur, Niraj and myself, Rahul bhaiya was our leader.' In time, Sekhsaria would become one of India's biggest players in cement through Gujarat Ambuja.

Till Bajaj passed his Senior Cambridge examination, it was Ramkrishna who kept watch on him. 'My first impression of

---

[1] 1 September 1939–2 September 1945.

Chachaji must have been when I was about twelve or thirteen years old, and as a boy I would often listen to the elders talking,' enthuses Bajaj. It was not always light talk. Bajaj remembers Ramkrishna as a 'stern man, systematic man and a no-nonsense man'.

Bajaj was good at both studies and games. He was house captain, prefect, 'but Chachaji liked my sister more! I thought he was prejudiced against me. Of course, my sister was docile, unlike me. Then I learnt to handle him and after that, things were all right!' Bajaj adds. The overriding thought of his association with his uncle in his younger days was that Ramkrishna was a 'martinet'. Everything, whether it was time or money, had to be accounted for.

The Bajaj family's next relocation was a stunning building appropriately named Mount Unique, hidden from sight, protected from the roar of busy Peddar Road even in 2021. The topmost floors of the high-rise are two spacious duplex penthouse apartments, one each for the Ramkrishna branch and the Kamalnayan branch. They share a common terrace. The apartments were acquired through the intervention of Rameshwardas Birla, wrote Savitri in her autobiography. 'Without Mr Birla's pressure, I doubt if Kamalnayan would have taken a place in the city,' she added.

The Cathedral Boys' School

It was time for young Bajaj to study in a proper Bombay school. 'After we came to Bombay, I went to St. Xavier's High School,' reminisces Bajaj. It would be two years before Savitri could get a place for him in the elite Cathedral Boy's School.[2]

Founded in 1860, Cathedral is undoubtedly one of Mumbai's two most sought-after schools (the other being the Dhirubhai Ambani International School, founded in 2003). Even in the late 1940s, getting admission into Cathedral was challenging—but not if you were fortunate enough to be European or a child of the Indian business elite. As one of its early principals put it, 'We are an Indian school where foreigners are at home.' The statement remains an integral part of the admissions policy.

Among Bajaj's pedigreed contemporaries at Cathedral, for example, was Zulfikar Ali Bhutto, who would become the president

---

[2] Later renamed The Cathedral & John Connon School.

of Pakistan, and later its prime minister. The Tata presence was strong across generations. Ratan Tata, whose letter is quoted below, was in Bajaj's class for one year. Earlier, J.R.D. Tata studied for a few years at Cathedral, as did Cyrus Pallonji Mistry much later. Most members of the Godrej family contributed, and continue to contribute, a child or so at any given time. Adi Godrej, a few years younger than Bajaj, was a couple of classes junior. Yusuf Khwaja Hamied, the future founder of pharma giant Cipla, was another contemporary.

The irrepressible Bajaj swiftly commandeered the driver's seat. 'I was a school prefect in Standard Ten, house captain in Standard Eleven, school captain in table tennis, captain of the boxing team, enjoyed debating and what not . . .' he says as modestly as he can. Typically, he stood first in his class, graduating in 1954 from the Senior Cambridge Examination Board with a distinction securing him the ninth rank in Bombay state. 'I learnt a great deal at Cathedral. The teaching methods were very good and there was a lot of personal touch.'

St. Stephen's College

'I wanted to study economics and chose St. Stephen's in Delhi. In Mumbai it would take four years to graduate after Senior Cambridge, while in Delhi it took three,' says Bajaj. His admission application for the economics honours degree was approved. Delhi beckoned.

'The first three months or so I spent with my aunt Uma Agarwal because I could not get hostel accommodation,' remembers Bajaj, 'and I spent the last three to four weeks, just before the exams, with my aunt to study. The rest of my three-year stay was in St. Stephen's hostel room number L-6 in Rudra North.'

'The hostel experience was an attraction,' he continues. 'The gates closed at midnight. Sometimes we used to go to Connaught Place—there used to be a place called Palace Heights, it was like a nightclub. By the time we came back, it would be one o'clock in the morning. The gates closed at midnight. We would jump over the gate. It was great fun.' Inured to hi-kicks, St. Stephen's offered a large palette of attractions.

The Vespa in India was as loved as the Vespa in Europe, the first wheels alike of the rich and the middle-class. A young Sir Terence Conran, the British designer, scooted round London on his.

'My father gifted me a Vespa,' recalls Bajaj. 'It definitely boosted my popularity, mine being one of only two in the St. Stephen's complex when I was studying for my economics honours degree in 1955–58!' The thrill of a ride with a girl is like the first kiss in India.

His scooter saw heavy duty as its popularity spread. Arvind Dave, who would become the governor of Arunachal Pradesh, fondly recalls those days. 'Rahul and I spent two years together at St. Stephen's, checking out the best bars in Connaught Place and an occasional peep into Palace Heights.'

'But then my father made it a condition that I would not carry a pillion rider. It did detract from the fun, but I managed to enjoy myself thoroughly. My father told me, "Do what you want to do but once you decide what to do, try to be the best in the world in that . . .",' says Bajaj. He did his best to live up to Kamalnayan's guidance.

'My teachers included Professor Nag, Professor Ghosh, Professor Balbir Singh and others,' reminisces Bajaj. 'One night, a few friends and I lobbed a firework into a professor's bedroom. Obviously, the professor got angry, but he also pointed to me. "Only Rahul Bajaj can do this!" he thundered.'

'St. Stephen's was three years of *masti*,' Bajaj grins. 'A couple of American girls were visiting Delhi. We became friends.' 'We were jealous,' admits Lalit Mohan, 'while we were at St. Stephen's, it was not a co-ed. We were jealous of the *oohs* and *aahs* his wit and charm elicited from female students of Miranda House whenever we met them in the coffee shop.' In the years to come, Mohan would become an income tax commissioner.

'If you are in a hostel, you have to study,' says Bajaj impishly, 'but who was studying? I got a "royal" class, i.e., third class. To get a second class you had to have 50 per cent. I never thought it would happen, but I got 48 per cent. I lost that two per cent. I deserved it. Bajaj graduated from Delhi's St. Stephen's College with a BA (Hons) in Economics in 1958. He was twenty years old.

Then, it was back to Bombay and enrolment in the Government Law College. 'I didn't study in the law college either but managed to save myself with three weeks of cramming and got a second class in 1960.'

The Summer of 1956

'Very often when Kakaji[3] went abroad, he took a member of the younger generation with him,' remarks Bajaj. 'During the St. Stephen's summer vacation of 1956, he took me to Europe for a month. It was Suman for over two months in the summer of 1960 in Europe, just before her marriage, and it was Madhur in the summer of 1971, which turned out to be Kakaji's last trip abroad. For me, our 1956 trip was a vacation whereas Kakaji had work in some countries including the Netherlands, France, and Italy. He also had to meet some people in London from where he returned to India by air.'

The 1956 trip had a seminal business outcome. In the Netherlands, Kamalnayan met Frederik Jacques 'Frits' Philips which led to a joint venture in India for lighting. In Italy, Kamalnayan would introduce Bajaj to the Piaggios. The powerful Turin-based family ran an industrial empire which, according to David Lomax, author of *The Money Makers*, is 'so big and influential that no Italian government would dare either to ignore it or to adopt policies which would damage its overall interests'.

'We were importing vehicles from Piaggio,' recalls Bajaj. 'Piaggio's head office in those days was in Genoa and their plant in Pontedera. We were invited to the celebration of the production of their 100,00th Vespa scooter. I was told that they could achieve this figure because so many Americans bought the scooter after seeing the movie *Roman Holiday* starring Gregory Peck and Audrey Hepburn.'

'To wind up my holiday, I sailed on the SS *Victoria* from Genoa, Italy, to Mumbai.' On board the steamer and sharing a cabin with Bajaj was Kantilal Shah. 'Rahul was barely eighteen years old,' recalled Shah, 'and he was shocked by the amount of baggage I had. The cabin got blocked, but we became friends. In Bombay, Rahul often used to visit us at our home on Nepean Sea Road. My wife was one of Rupa's bridesmaids.'

The Induction Roundabout

Marwaris have a tried and tested induction formula developed over centuries to foster and develop entrepreneurship. No boy is exempt. No girl used to get a chance.

---
[3] Bajaj refers to his father, Kamalnayan, as Kakaji.

Rule number one: formal education gives one confidence and can help reduce inferiority complexes, but it is insufficient. Rule number two: observe and learn from others such as friends, family and customers. Rule number three: integrate the experiences of others and one's own in order to formulate effective action.

Any new step in a Marwari family begins with an aarti. In 1958, Savitri daubed the traditional tikka on Bajaj's forehead. Smiling, he left Bhagwati Bhavan on Carmichael Road for Radio Lamp Works (the forerunner of Bajaj Electricals). His entry coincided with a major turning point in the company's history. A few months prior to Bajaj's internship, in 1954, Kamalnayan, an early investor in the firm and a director on its board, bought out its ageing founder, Kishenchand Kaycee.

Kamalnayan inherited Manmohan Lal Gauba, the firm's talented general manager and future director. Gauba had studied engineering in pre-WW II Germany, salvaged Lahore-based Radio Lamp Works during Partition, and by the mid-1950s had built a profitable business in India for the Bajaj group. The burly manager would be Bajaj's first professional mentor with overall oversight by uncle Ramkrishna.

Bajaj started his apprenticeship not in manufacturing bulbs and tube lights at the main plant in Shikohabad in Uttar Pradesh. Nor in the small unit outside Bombay's city limits producing electrical transformers. He started in a sales and marketing office in swish South Bombay.

'The office in Churchgate was almost next door to the Government Law College,' recalls Bajaj. 'Office started at 9.30 a.m. The law classes were in the morning from 7.30 a.m. to 10 a.m. I signed up for the LLB degree, but don't ask me about my attendance. It was very good in the coffee shop.'

Or watching cricket matches. 'Rahul and I regularly watched cricket matches at the Brabourne Stadium,' remembers Shashi Chand Jain, who would go on to head DCW, a diversified manufacturer of basic chemicals. 'Many were the times we jokingly talked about how strict our fathers were and wished they could go out of Bombay for a few days so that we could have some respite from their watchful eyes.'

'I often think, if Rahul were to take up cricket, he would been an attacking batsman,' chips in Apte Group's Madhav Apte. 'However, given his good looks and charm, he would have been a most successful bowler, "bowling over maidens after maidens!".'

'I got a second class, not first class as I had always done in school,' squirms Bajaj. No matter. He completed his internship at Radio Lamp Works in time to be a useful, if young, family working member.

The Marwari rotation theory rolled on. Most of Bajaj's time in 1961 and the first half of 1962 was as a junior purchase officer at Mukand Iron and Steel. 'I would go to Kurla from my home on Carmichael Road every day,' says Bajaj. 'I had to leave at 8 a.m., reach there at 8.30, come back at 7 or 8 p.m., six days a week. I thought, I should have a car.'

> My father said, 'No, it is a training programme, I will not give you a car.'
> 'How should I go?' 'Scooter.'
> Mom said, 'Scooter is risky, no scooter.'
> 'How do I go?' 'Take the car.'
> 'Father doesn't allow.' 'So go by bus.'
> Father says no car, mother says no scooter, I said no to bus and turned to the scooter.
> My mother had to give in. For two years I went to Kurla on a scooter.

Or did he? According to the Mukand managers' grapevine, the trainee occasionally could be seen travelling to and fro by bus.

How about Bajaj Auto?

Unusual for a Marwari father, Kamalnayan offered Bajaj a choice. 'Even though we were in business, nobody told me I had to be in business,' recalls Bajaj. 'And later on, also, my father said, "Are you thinking of what you want to do, et cetera? You know we are in business. There is no need at all for you to go into business. You have to do what you want to do".'

'I went all over India, wherever we had our plants and offices, to decide where I would work. My father said, "Think, decide, you should decide." After the rounds, I asked my father, "What do you feel?" He said, "It's your decision, but what I would say is, it's good to go to Bajaj Auto and Bajaj Tempo." And I said, "I also was thinking of the same thing". I joined Bajaj Auto and Bajaj Tempo in November 1964. The official date we gave was January 1965.'

Real Training Begins at the Dining Table

'After I joined the business full time in 1965, whenever my father and I were together in Bombay, or more often in Poona, we would sit for a discussion after dinner, starting around 9 p.m. which often went on till 2 a.m. in the morning,' says Bajaj nostalgically. 'I would disagree with him quite often and at times vehemently. But he did not mind at all.'

'If any family member had any problems, he was always there to help. Of course, he also expected a great deal from each of us in the younger generation. He was a strict taskmaster in whose presence it was difficult to remain casual or careless—every action and word was observed. He had his own way of teaching and guiding us and at the same time he ensured that we also enjoyed ourselves.'

Bajaj's first job was as a deputy general manager. 'I had to see the commercial side which included purchasing, marketing, sales, accounts, finance, audit, everything but the production.' His boss was Navalmal Kundanmal Firodia, then chief executive of Bajaj Auto and managing director of Bajaj Tempo.

Chachaji was as strict as Kakaji. When about twenty-four years old, Bajaj took Rs 3000 from the family account for a legitimate purpose but on the clear understanding that he would give a full account of how the money was spent. Bajaj spent the money, but like any other youngster, he forgot to submit the account as had been agreed and in the stipulated time. 'I was summoned to the Presence[4] and questioned about the money and how it was spent. I truthfully answered that the money was spent properly and not wastefully.'

'But where is the account?' Chachaji asked.
'I forgot,' I told him.
'Let this be the last occasion. Where money is concerned, I expect you to be responsible. And no more excuses about forgetfulness!'

'Lord, he was a disciplinarian,' says Bajaj.

It was a lesson Bajaj says he has never forgotten.

'Kakaji never involved himself or spent time in the minutiae of day-to-day activities,' recalls Bajaj. 'I felt his absence most when I remember his grasp of business matters. If the need arose, he could give such insightful ideas and solutions that none of us could have ever thought of. He did not only act by his instincts. He had great faith in his analytical skills. He would apply his intelligence rationally and

---

[4] Rahul Bajaj's paternal uncle, Ramakrishna.

objectively to every issue, and yet with a humane touch. He believed in God, but he was not one who kept complaining about his fate. He used to say that those who rely on fate achieve little; whatever one acquires is possible only through a scientific and objective approach.'

'He had his own way of explaining work efficiency. Assume that we have two light bulbs—one has a rating of 100 watts, while the other is rated 10 W. A 100 W bulb that gives light equivalent to that of a 65 W bulb, will have to be called an inefficient one. On the other hand, a 10 W bulb giving off 11 W is not only efficient in itself, but it is also more efficient than the 100 W one. This was his favourite example.'

'Kakaji gave all of us the freedom to learn and grow by making mistakes,' continues Bajaj. 'He was never bothered about success or failure. He believed only in action. He believed that a person ought to try his best to complete a task that has been taken up, irrespective of how difficult it might be. He felt that the line dividing success and failure is a very thin one. Through these discussions, I learnt a great deal about business and about life.'

> Whoever would have thought
> that the quiet, well-behaved
> boy who sat in the corner of the
> classroom in Cathedral School
> would become such a flamboya
> and successful scooter king!
> Rahul's success has made
> all of us who know him proud
> to be his friend – even if you
> have to be the butt of his jokes
> The empire which he has built
> will not only be his legacy to his
> future generations, but a legacy
> to the nation.
> Well done Rahul. All the bes
> and good health to you.
> Yours

Ratan Tata to Bajaj in 2017.

4

From Pontedera to Goregaon: 1945–58

The Vespa 98, built in Italy, April 1946.

6339 km from Mumbai. Enrico Piaggio, his family and company were reeling in Italy. Piaggio and his brother Armando had moved into aircraft production at the outbreak of World War II. On 21 January 1944, an American fighter aircraft bombed the Pontedera factory. Unable to continue aircraft production after the war ended, Enrico settled on the scooter. He recruited and encouraged a talented

Italian aeronautical engineer, Corradino D'Ascanio, to come up with a great design. D'Ascanio delivered.

6339 km from Pontedera. Kamalnayan Bajaj, his family and businesses were reeling in India. For the British, India had become the place to scavenge for war materials. The end of WW II saw the British hastily flee India. Partition saw Kamalnayan lose a steel plant to Pakistan and just about managed to safely extract all his Hindu managers to India. His optimism never failed him.

The Latest Beauty in Town

Badged as the Vespa, no one at the time could imagine the scooter's global success. It was an absolute novelty because of its innovative framework: an enclosed engine to avoid damaging clothes, a comfortable driver position, easily replaceable tires, simple to park, and easy to step in and out of.

Production began on 23 April 1946. The Vespa made its debut at the spring Milan Fair. The first fifty sold slowly. The price of the standard model was 55,000 lire, the deluxe version 66,000 lire. With the introduction of payment by instalments, sales took off. Enrico started building a local dealer network. To boost low volumes and margins, Enrico began producing CKD[1] kits for the international market, including India. Piaggio would rapidly become the biggest manufacturer of scooters in the world. For a while. Until its competitors caught up.

Goregaon

'From World War II, the Korean and Vietnam wars, periods of growth and recession, the Cold war, etc., my father kept changing with the world,' shares Bajaj. 'He kept advising the managers in our companies to keep up with the latest technological developments globally. He invited the best partners, whether it was Piaggio of Italy, Philips of Holland, David Brown of UK for Mukand, and many others.'

---

[1] CKD packs, Completely Knock Down packs.

Rebuilding his battered infrastructure, Enrico Piaggio appreciated Kamalnayan's request for Vespa CKD packs. In Delhi, Kamalnayan angled for a licence to import Vespa CKD kits. The Jawaharlal Nehru administration granted his wish in 1948. The future scooter king started as an assembler for Italy's Piaggio in a tin-roofed shed in Goregaon, a Bombay outskirt.

Once the Goregaon plant was activated, Kamalnayan started offering dealerships. A national network gradually emerged. An early applicant for a Bajaj dealership was an athletic, tall, slim, good-looking youngster with a ready smile.

Muthiah Annamalai Chidambaram Chettiar saw the potential in the Vespa scooter as soon as he saw it. 'Mac, we used to call him,' recalls Bajaj, junior to Mac by twenty years. Mac connected with the Bajaj family through Jeewanlal Motichand Shah. In the early 1940s, both were directors of a Canadian venture, Indian Aluminium. Kamalnayan willingly granted Mac the Madras dealership. The third-generation member of a wealthy royal family turned out to be quite a businessman. The budding friendship between the Marwari and the wealthy Chettiar would receive a jolt in 1958.

Tiruvellore Thattai Krishnamachari

'When we applied for a manufacturing licence, the secretariat put it up to T.T. Krishnamachari, the then finance minister,' says Bajaj. 'Mr Krishnamachari rang up his friend Mr M.A. Chidambaram in Chennai and said Bajaj has applied to make scooters in collaboration with Piaggio. "Why don't you apply to make scooters in collaboration with Lambretta?" Mr Chidambaram mentioned that he was the Vespa dealer in Chennai to which, I am given to understand, Mr Krishnamachari retorted, "So what?".'

'Mr Chidambaram arranged a technical collaboration agreement with Italy's Innocenti,' Bajaj continues. Mac arrived in Milan to formalize the partnership with the firm's founder. Ferdinando Innocenti was delighted to meet the Indian and explore growth possibilities outside Italy.

During World War II, Italy's Ministry of War had awarded large tenders to Innocenti. Between 1938 and 1943, the number of employees at his Milan factory increased from 800 to over 7000. Innocenti contributed 17 per cent to Italy's total wartime production, especially artillery shells and ammunition cases. Postwar, Ferdinando needed new business.

Like Piaggio, Innocenti quickly rebuilt his war-damaged factory and converted the plant for peacetime purposes. The Lambretta scooter came on the market in 1947, offering strong competition to the Vespa. The Italian rivals began aggressively licensing manufacture in Spain, Argentina, Germany, France and Brazil. Mac's appearance in Milan was timely. Innocenti added India to his growing list.

'As soon as Mac applied for the industrial licence to the Government of India, he got it,' says Bajaj, his angst still raw. 'In 1955, Bachhraj Trading had applied to the central government for permission to manufacture scooters. Wait, my father was told,' recalls Bajaj, 'it's too early. Eventually, Bachhraj Trading was informed that the scooter quota was fully utilized, that adequate capacity to meet the likely demand has been sanctioned and hence our application could not be considered.' Optically, the government's decisions were completely kosher. Mac pipped the Bajajs to the post. Bajaj's application was filed. Quietly. On a shelf where it would gather dust.

Next on Mac's to-do list: find or build a scooter factory. He had discovered his manufacturing penchant while making industrial screws. The Tamilian located what he wanted in a 31.5-acre plot in Bhandup, on the Bombay Agra Road (today's Lal Bahadur Shastri Marg). The plant was a part of the Rootes Group, a storied British automobile-manufacturing family firm which wanted to uproot itself from India. Mac snapped it up. It was a lucky find, already filled with pretty much all the machinery Mac would need. And the machinery was fairly new.

As co-members of Madras' close-knit Tamilian high society, Mac believed T.T. Krishnamachari to be the cabinet minister Nehru could not do without. By February 1958, Krishnamachari was no longer the finance minister and a level playing field materialized. The Bajajs were awarded a manufacturing licence for scooters in April 1959 during Nehru's term as finance minister-cum-prime minister.

'In those days, we used to have something called the Director General of Technical Development (DGTD) in the Industry Ministry,' says Bajaj. 'They would say, "there is no demand for more than this". They used to control production and say, "you can't have excess capacity, we have scarce resources". We were told to make 6,000 scooters a year when we first received our industrial licence to make two- and three-wheelers. We were two years behind. When you have socialism and a closed economy, for anything you produce you need a licence,' says Bajaj.

Reflecting on that period, Bajaj bursts out with, 'My blood used to boil. The country needed two-wheelers. There was a ten-year delivery period for Bajaj scooters. And I was not allowed to expand. What kind of socialism is that?'

The End of the End

From 1972, Mac's luck began to run out. In Italy, Ferdinando Innocenti too was under pressure. A small group of civil servants from Lucknow on behalf of the Government of India played the white knight. They formed Scooters India (SIL), bought Innocenti's entire factory tooling and machinery equipment as well as the world rights of the Lambretta and Lambro brands, and shifted the plant from chic Milan to Lucknow's Amausi Industrial Area. The Vijai Super brand was offered in the domestic market and the Lambretta in the overseas market, including, ironically, Italy.

Bajaj was, and still is, sore. 'My anger was directed against the Government of India for allowing them to enter again. This was a wrong policy. I was not afraid of competing with foreign companies, and time has shown (this). They should have been told to withdraw their cases against an Indian exporter and then come to India.'

With its first-mover advantage, the Lambretta became a rage in the 1960s, but the Vespa quickly picked up speed and offered stiff competition. This decade saw Bajaj Auto concentrate on indigenising components and establishing a dealer network. 'Local content was only 26 per cent but climbed gradually due to the Indian government's emphasis on import substitution,' writes Nathalie Laidler of Harvard Business School (HBS).

By 1966 Bajaj Auto was India's largest scooter producer. Demand continued to exceed supply. 'Akurdi could not be planned properly for mass production. The capacities were added in piecemeal as and when the Government of India permitted increase in licenced capacity,' points out Gokhale Institute's Shakeel Ahmed.

In his odyssey, Mac expanded to three manufacturing centres: Bombay and Aurangabad in Maharashtra, and Ambattur outside Madras. In 1984, workers in the Bombay and Aurangabad units went on a go-slow. The Aurangabad unit manufactured components as original equipment for Maruti Udyog, Hindustan Motors, Premier Automobiles and Firodia's Bajaj Temp. There were complaints. Tension continued to simmer. Suspension of work in the Aurangabad factory, followed by a lockout from November 1986, intensified the situation.

As Bajaj's market share grew, a desperate Mac turned to a Japanese design company, Miyazu, to spruce things up a bit and the Lamby Polo was born in 1986. The Polo's styling looked sleeker than earlier models, but it had sharp corners and edges. The scooter never sold well. The Vikram range of rickshaws, derived from the Innocenti Lambro three-wheeler, means Automobile Products of India (API) kept trudging—barely. Anxiety in the boardroom seeped through the entire organization.

With the erosion of its net worth by 1987, API was placed under the Board for Industrial and Financial Reconstruction (BIFR). Efforts to improve three-wheeler sales and a licence to manufacture mopeds in Tamil Nadu never materialized. Mac died at age eighty-two, two years before API ceased production in 2002.

'By the early 1970s, we had already overtaken Mr Chidambaram just by better management,' smiles Bajaj. Over the next twenty years, they disappeared as a company. Bajaj Auto would enjoy a high share of a sellers' market for twenty-two continuous years.

5

Dad and the Election Manager: 1951–71

Left to right: Kamalnayan, Ramkrishna and Jawaharlal Nehru in Wardha.

'I remember campaigning for two weeks or so, in three Parliamentary elections for Kakaji in his Wardha rural constituency in 1957, 1962 and 1967, all three of which he won,' shares Bajaj. 'Of course, in 1957 I was only nineteen years old. It was a great learning experience for me.' Politics is an acquired taste and Bajaj never lost its charm.

'Campaigning in 1957 was nowhere like what it is nowadays,' continues Bajaj. 'The money spent was insignificant compared to the crores spent on a single Parliament seat today. Kakaji asked two to three close associates who campaigned for him, to let me accompany one of them during the campaigning. In each election I campaigned for about two weeks. The person I was accompanying knew a few persons in most towns and in some places we had to spend a few minutes and have a cup of "sugary tea" which, frankly, I found tasty! Sometimes Kakaji would discuss with me what happened that day—this was his way of teaching me.'

'People from Kakaji's constituency sometimes came home to meet him when he was in Wardha and asked for something to be done with the government. I remember an occasion when Kakaji found that the request was wrong, and instead of saying something to the effect that "I will see what can be done," he straightaway told the persons concerned that their request was not justified, and he would not be able to help them. Plain speaking!' adds Bajaj.

First Lok Sabha: 25 October 1951–21 February 1952

India gained Independence in August 1947, but it would take four years to organize a Lok Sabha election. The first General Elections were held in sixty-eight phases from 25 October 1951 to 21 February 1952 where 85 per cent of people entitled to vote could not read and write. Nehru travelled over 25,000 miles and addressed about 35 million people or a tenth of India's population. Fifty-three parties and 533 independents contested 489 seats across seventeen states and union territories.

Among them were Kamalnayan and his two brothers-in-law, Shriman Narayan (married to Madalsa) and Rameshwarprasad Nevatia (married to Kamla). Shriman picked Wardha in Maharashtra, Rameshwarprasad settled for Shahabad in Uttar Pradesh, and Kamalnayan for Sikar in Rajasthan. Obtaining tickets was a cinch, winning an election was another matter. Rameshwarprasad and Shriman won their seats. Kamalnayan was defeated by a candidate from the Ram Rajya Parishad. Ramkrishna, at a loose end after Acharya Kriplani's defeat, resigned from the Congress Party.

The INC (Indian National Congress) won a landslide victory, winning 45 per cent of the total votes polled with 364 seats out of a total of 498. The second largest, the Socialist Party, won twelve seats. Jawaharlal Nehru became the first democratically elected prime minister. Dr Rajendra Prasad became the first President of independent India.

Kamalnayan's eight-page post-election assessment for internal circulation within the party, recently fished out by historian Ramchandra Guha, is stark. 'Money was freely distributed particularly amongst Brahmins so that they may vote for the Ram Rajya Parishad,' Kamalnayan described. 'Sweets were also distributed amongst children for crying Ram Rajya slogans. Ram Rajya workers had offered money even to Harijans but at some places the latter spurned the offer and said that their votes would go to the Congress.'

'At many booths,' he continued, 'Ram Rajya workers with lathis and naked swords in their hands went round openly telling the people to proceed to the booths only if they wanted to vote for the Ram Rajya Parishad, otherwise they asked them to go back . . . Ram Rajya workers threatened the poor and ignorant voters to make it impossible for them to live their normal life. In spite of this, however, the general feeling that Congress was likely to eventually come to power prevailed and this was to some extent responsible for the Congress securing some votes even in areas dominated by the jagirdars . . . I have strong suspicion that ballot boxes have been tampered with and votes from the Congress and the Kisan Sabha boxes have been manipulated.'

For thirteen-year-old Bajaj, reading the news, listening to the radio, the mayhem generated over the four months of India's first election would likely to have been as much an eye-opener as the Partition.

Second Lok Sabha: 24 February–9 June 1957

The 1952 experience made it evident that election planning needed refurbishment. Several state boundaries were shuffled prior to the 1957 elections. For example, Wardha and Nagpur were transferred to Bombay State, alongside the Marathi-speaking districts of Buldhana, Akola, Amravati, Yavatmal, Bhandara and Chanda. Overall, the outcome was an increase in assembly constituencies from 184 with 232 seats in 1952, to 218 constituencies with 288 seats in the 1957 elections.[1]

Spread over three-and-a-half months, from 24 February to 9 June 1957, just forty-five women candidates contested. Half of them, twenty-two, won. Atal Bihari Vajpayee won his first election. Feroze Gandhi was re-elected from Rae Bareli in what was to be his last election. Kamalnayan won the Wardha seat handily.

Nehru's second term captured 371 of the 494 seats. The INC's vote share grew from 45 per cent to 47.8 per cent, nearly five times more votes than the Communist Party, still the second largest party. Yet it was a tough election, with Nehru fighting the right wing within his party, and the communists and the socialists outside it. The polls came in the backdrop of the Hindu Personal Law reforms and the 1955 Bandung Conference.

As Nehru and Kamalnayan grew into their roles, cracks began to appear in their relationship. While criss-crossing India inaugurating one industrial complex after another constructed by 'industrialists', the Fabian socialist laid the foundation for the licence raj. And there were pinpricks. Such as V.K. Krishna Menon. A member of Parliament (MP) and diplomat holding the external affairs portfolio, Menon was one of Nehru's most trusted advisers. Nehru received coldly Ramakrishna's complaints about Menon. The communists launched a campaign linking businessmen to the CIA.[2] Eye-popping and headline-grabbing, the campaign petered out for lack of credibility. Nonetheless, the Bajajs were dragged into controversy. Nehru depended on Menon. And Menon on Nehru.

Third Lok Sabha: 19–25 February 1962

Unlike the previous elections, the Third Lok Sabha elections restricted each constituency to elect a single member. The INC took 44.7 per cent of the vote and won 361 of the 494 seats. This was only slightly lower than in the previous two elections. In Wardha, with

---

[1] Akhil Bhartiya Hindu Mahasabha, Akhil Bhartiya Ram Rajya Parishad, All India Bhartiya Jana Sangh, All India Scheduled Caste Federation, Communist Party of India, Forward Block (Marxist), Ganatantra Parishad, Janata Party, Jharkhand Party, Peasants and Workers Party, Peoples Democratic Front, Praja Party, Praja Socialist Party and Revolutionary Socialist Party.

[2] CIA—The US Central Intelligence Agency.

a 69 per cent turnout, Kamalnayan won 3,40,328 votes, with a 11.2 per cent margin.

In early January 1964, Nehru suffered a stroke and Lal Bahadur Shastri took over the prime minister's work. Nehru's death on 27 May 1964 left a vacuum. Gulzarilal Nanda held the fort as acting prime minister in a vigorous thirteen-day no-holds-barred leadership tussle within the INC. Shastri won. His unexplained death in Tashkent, Uzbekistan, on 11 January 1966 paved the way for Indira Gandhi, patronizingly dubbed the 'gungi gudia' (dumb doll), to succeed Shastri.

Kamalnayan was convinced that Gandhi's leadership was not in the country's interest and would lead to authoritarianism. 'After the 1969 Congress Party split into the Congress (I) and the Congress (O),' Bajaj explains the background, 'Kakaji stayed with Morarji Desai's Congress (O) even though Congress (I) was with Mrs Gandhi as its leader and by far the larger faction of the Congress. Kakaji did not agree with many of Indiraji's policies such as bank nationalization. An annoyed Indiraji questioned how Jamnalalji's son could go against Jawaharlalji's daughter? After all, Jawaharlalji and Jamnalalji were like brothers. Incidentally, both were born in 1889.'

India's first female prime minister would hang on to her seat for eleven years and fifty-nine days, serving as prime minister from January 1966 to March 1977 and again from January 1980 until her assassination in October 1984, making Indira Gandhi the second-longest serving Indian prime minister after her father.

Fourth Lok Sabha: 17–21 February 1967

As the 1967 elections grew closer, the business elite stepped up to the plate. 'The two biggest houses—Tata and Birla—accounted for 34 per cent of the total contributed by 126 major companies,' noted historian Stanley A. Kochanek. 'Both gave money to the Congress. Tata was much less generous to Congress than Birla, but Tata was conspicuous for its large contributions to the Swatantra Party.' Other major Swatantra Party supporters were Martin Burn, Khatau, Scindia, Walchand and Thackersey. Congress received Rs 7.37 million, Swatantra Rs 2.52 million.

Of the total 521 Lok Sabha seats and nineteen players, the Congress won 283 seats, which meant the party lost more than 100 seats, and its vote share came down to 40.8 per cent. It bore significant losses in Gujarat, Madras, Orissa, Rajasthan, West Bengal and Delhi. Of the other key players, Swatantra won forty-four seats, the Bharatiya Jana Sangh thirty-five and the Dravida Munnetra Kazhagam (DMK) twenty-five. Gandhi was sworn in as prime minister on 4 March 1967.

In Wardha, on a Congress ticket, Kamalnayan received 1,44,756 votes, winning with a 40.39 per cent turnout. In Junagarh, Swatantra Party's Viren Shah won 1,08,303 votes and a 46.3 per cent margin. In Bombay, George Fernandes defeated S.K. Patil, the 'uncrowned king of Bombay', to win the Bombay South seat with 3,13,388 votes, a turnout of 67.4 per cent and 9.4 per cent margin.

Two years later, politics plunged. On 12 November 1969, the Congress party expelled Gandhi for violating party discipline. She retaliated by setting up a rival organization, Congress (I). As many as 220 Lok Sabha members stayed with Gandhi but Kamalnayan was not one of them, she noted. 'After the Congress split into Congress (I) and Congress (O) in 1969,' says Bajaj, 'Kakaji stayed with Congress (O) even though Congress (I) was the larger faction.'

'Kakaji spoke to me frankly after the Congress split,' Bajaj continues. 'Because of his decision to stay with Congress (O), he explained, it was possible that Congress (I) may not cooperate with the companies in the Bajaj Group. We may not get expansions, etc. He asked me whether he should resign as the chairman and director of our companies in order to insulate the group from the possible wrath of the government. I remember straightaway telling him that was out of the question, and we were not going to succumb to such pressure tactics.'

When other members of the family asked, 'Could an upcoming industrial house afford to antagonize the government?' Kamalnayan's response was short and simple. If members of his family did not agree with his views and felt that his stand was not in the family's interest, he was prepared to sever all connections with the business and go his own way. 'Everyone knew this was not an idle threat,' said Bajaj. He chose to remain with old friends in Congress (O). Among them was Morarji Desai.

An adamant Gandhi stripped Desai of the finance portfolio on 16 July 1969. Three days later, on 19 July, Gandhi's decision to nationalize banks and the way she went about it was perhaps the turning point that firmed Kamalnayan's thought processes. He did not have to oversee a bank under his charge being nationalized. He was the fifteenth chairman of the Punjab National Bank, one of the fourteen nationalized banks, and his three-year tenure had ended in 1967.

A Midterm Surprise: February 1971

The next election had a bite to it. On the evening of 27 December 1970, Indira Gandhi addressed the nation on radio and TV to announce that the Lok Sabha had been dissolved, and fresh elections would take place in the middle of February 1971. 'When *Newsweek* asked her what the main issues in the election were, she replied gleefully, "I am the issue",' noted Inder Malhotra, a prominent Delhi journalist, editor and author.

'Because of the partition of Bangladesh, Indiraji was the empress of the country,' says Bajaj. 'At the previous three elections, in my briefing notes to a couple of relatives in Mumbai, I had indicated that we were likely to win. However, I remember indicating that we are likely to lose the fourth election in March 1971. When my father shifted from Congress-I to Congress-O, headed by Morarji Desai, the Congress-O lost badly and so did Kamalnayanji. Obviously, I had realized the pulse of the voters.'

The Bajaj family's bête noir was on a roll. Indira Gandhi's decisive victory in the fifth Lok Sabha elections with a campaign focused on reducing poverty, overcame a split in the party, and regained many of the seats lost in the previous election.[3] She raised Indian self-esteem by triumphing in the India–Pakistan–Bangladesh war.[4] To cap it all, under project Smiling Buddha, India successfully detonated its first nuclear weapon in the Thar Desert on 18 May 1974, becoming the sixth nation in the world to do so.

When her main political foes, headed by the Congress (O), declared their single-point objective 'Indira Hatao (Remove Indira)', Gandhi's prompt battle cry was 'Garibi Hatao (Remove Poverty)'. The impact on the country was instant and electric. The poor, a vast

---

[3] Fifth Lok Sabha (15 March 1971–18 January 1977).
[4] Bangladesh War (26 March 1971–16 December 1971).

majority of the population, were overwhelmed with emotion. They felt that they had at last found their redeemer.

'It was a wave no one noticed,' wrote Inder Malhotra, but it was merciless. The Congress (O) fought on 238 seats and won just sixteen seats. The Bharatiya Jana Sangh contested 157 seats but won twenty-two. The Swatantra Party, the single-largest opposition party with forty-four seats, dropped to eight seats. The Samyukta Socialist Party which won twenty-three seats in the 1967 election, managed to bag just three of the ninety-three seats it contested. The Praja Socialist Party lost a major chunk of its seats and managed to win just two seats versus the thirteen seats it had won in 1969. The high hopes of a 'Grand Alliance' with the Congress (O), the Bharatiya Jana Sangh, the Swatantra party and the Samyukta Socialist Party turned to ashes.

The placebo was high voter abstentions compared to previous general elections. The electorate increased by more than 23 million between 1967 and 1971, but there were 3 million fewer voters in 1971 than in 1967, bringing the total vote percentage down from 61.32 per cent to 55.25 per cent.

The Congress (I) captured 352 seats, giving Gandhi the two-thirds majority needed to amend the Constitution. In March 1971, Gandhi formed a government with thirty-six members. A populist ten-point programme, the 'Garibi Hatao' slogan, and mastery over the Congress party machinery ensured the rout of Congress (O). Uttar Pradesh stood energized, winning seventy-three of eighty seats. Gandhi secured 352 of the 518 Lok Sabha seats—more than two-thirds of the House.

'Much later,' remembers Bajaj, 'in the early 1970s, I met Mr Narayan Dutt Tiwari, when he was the industry minister in the union government. We wanted permissions for an expansion of Bajaj Auto's two- and three-wheeler capacity. I remember his telling me, "Rahul, your father is in the opposition and so I am unable to help you".'

Swept up in the whirlpool of nationalist politics with its unending uncertainties, tensions and heartache, Kamalnayan died young, passing away in May 1972. 2006 would see his son enter the Rajya Sabha.

6

The Red Convertible: 1958–61

Rupa and Rahul at Ritz Hotel, Marine Drive, Mumbai, on 31 December 1960.

'The Taj Mahal at Colaba? Or the Ritz on Marine Drive?' Bajaj asked Rupa as he dropped her at her parents' place on Carmichael Road. 'We had better book soon before both places are blocked!' Only a few days remained before the 1960 decade would be over.

'We first met Rahul on New Year's Eve on the terrace of the Ritz Hotel,' recalls Arun Sanghi, a co-founder of the Sah and Sanghi Group. 'He was dancing away with his charming fiancée Rupa. In a dinner jacket and bow tie, Rahul looked smashing.'

'In those days, it was not easy for two people of dissimilar castes to marry,' says Bajaj. 'I am a Marwari Bania with a family business. Rupa was a Maharashtrian Brahmin and her father an ICS[1] officer. She used to tease me, saying, "I am marrying two levels below me, Rahul".'

The Brahmin and the Bania

'In my mother's circle of friends were the Kashyaps,' shares Bajaj. 'She was invited for dinner and took me along. Aside from the Kashyaps, there were only three guests: my mother, me—and Rupa Gholap. I'm still not sure if this was a set-up or pure chance. I don't believe in love at first sight, but that evening I did ask Rupa for a date. She showed the normal hesitation. Seeing that, I said I would call her. She agreed to meet for dinner on Saturday.'

Rupa: 'On a sultry June evening in Mumbai, Rahul and I met at a common friend's place. Our friend definitely had an ulterior motive in introducing me to this tall, handsome man with a twinkle in his eyes. Within ten minutes he asked me out to a movie for the very next day. What persistence and how aggressive a personality, I thought.'

'Both the Gholaps and we lived on Carmichael Road,' says Bajaj. Saturday arrived. As did Bajaj to pick up Rupa. 'We used to see the red convertible,' recalls Rupa's sister Chitra, 'but we didn't know Rahul.' 'Rupa and I continued to date each other,' smiles Bajaj. 'This went on for a few months.'

One morning, when I was about to leave for the office, my mother asked me, 'Are you serious about Rupa?' I was genuinely surprised, remembers Bajaj.

'Why are you asking me this?' I asked.

'Before you met Rupa, you used to tell me about whoever you went out for a date,' she replied, 'and there would be usually two or three different girls. But during the last few months, you have been meeting only Rupa. You haven't taken any other girl out on a date.'

---

[1] Indian Civil Service, post-Independence renamed Indian Administrative Service (IAS).

I mumbled something in response.

'Soon we realized we were seeing only each other!' recounted Rupa. 'After three or four months, we each knew how deep our affection was for the other. Though we were both only twenty-one years old, we wanted to be together always.'

'But Rahul, like any typical male, could not get the right words out of his mouth, so difficult it is for a male to make a commitment!' wrote Rupa. 'So, one romantic evening I proposed to him! He was red in the face and his eyes were popping out. He said, "You know that is exactly what I have been wanting to say!" I don't think I have told anyone about this. How could I puncture a hole in his male ego?'

'I went back home and told my mother that I did want to marry Rupa,' said Bajaj.

And Rupa told her family.

The Gholaps

In their own ways, the Bajajs and the Gholaps are both extraordinary families. Pre-Independence, they were on opposite sides of a wall. The Bajajs fought for India's Independence alongside Mahatma Gandhi. Lakshman Trimbak Gholap, Rupa's father, was a senior officer in the Imperial Civil Service, the elite arm of the British raj, and an erudite member of the Royal Economic Society. In 1946, King George VI acknowledged Gholap's contribution to the empire in the 'King's Birthday Honours' list as a Companion of the Order of the Indian Empire (CIE). Post-Independence, the Imperial Civil Service would be rebadged as the Indian Administrative Service (IAS).

To prevent one Partition tragedy in the making, Sardar Patel turned to Gholap, then controller of shipping and chairman of the Bombay Port Trust. By negotiating boarding facilities in Karachi, and disembarking spots along the Maharashtra and Gujarat shorelines, Gholap diverted all available ships to Karachi and managed to safely evacuate a quarter million Hindu, Sindhi and Sikh refugees.

In mid-October 1955, Verghese Kurien, founder of Operation Flood, the world's largest agricultural dairy development programme, was in trouble. Imported boilers were blocked in Bombay's congested harbour and the port was on strike. Gholap called an

emergency meeting of the Bombay Port Trust board. It decided
to grant Gholap's request. The ship jumped queue, offloaded only
the two boilers, and returned to its former place. Western Railway
transported the boilers to Anand.

As development finance kicked in, Gholap was appointed
ex officio joint secretary in the Department of Commerce as the
government nominee on the boards of publicly listed companies.
Among them was the Great Eastern Shipping Company, formed in
1948 by A.H. Bhiwandiwalla. For Bhiwandiwalla, getting Gholap
on board was a coup. In 1960, Gholap would request and obtain
permission to retire from the IAS and to accept employment.

The Test

'When Rupa and I decided we want to get married, I made it
clear that she didn't need to get the approval of her parents, but I
definitely would ask my parents for their approval. My mother said,
"Yes. Okay. But better to tell this to your father." He was travelling.
On his return, I described to him her family and her. He asked me
to invite Rupa over for dinner. She came. It was a very pleasant
evening. After the dinner, my father asked me to drop her home.'

'When I got back, he said, "She is a nice girl with very good skin.
Give me a couple of weeks to find out more about the family, and
I will let you know." He called me after a couple of weeks.'

'She is from Maharashtra, and we are Marwaris. There is no issue
at all, we are a family of Gandhians. But my father also said, "She
comes from a very different background. Our family was involved
in the freedom struggle, we went to jail, and are a business family.
In her family, her father was a civil servant in the ICS. During the
freedom struggle, he was on the opposite side until India achieved
Independence. Our cultures are very different. While you two may like
each other, you are very young. Where is love and where is infatuation?
If you are both prepared for no letters, no meetings, no phone calls for
a year, I will give you both my blessings and good wishes". "What is
the difference between blessings and good wishes?" I asked, upset.'

'I had no choice. I went to Rupa's house. She and her parents
were aghast and did not appreciate this condition. Rupa decided to
wait and not break off. While we maintained the condition of not

meeting, what happened was that two or three of my friends had also become her friends. They kept both of us informed.'

'In due course Rupa and I got engaged. It was official. We were to get married in six months' time. Chachaji and Mausi (Vimla, Ramkrishna's wife) took Rupa and me out for dinner to a restaurant. After dinner, I promised to take Rupa back to her home. Chachaji went back on his own. I was not supposed to take more than ten minutes to return. But well, what with this and that, I took an hour. When I finally reached home, Chachaji was waiting for me. I knew I was in trouble. He said: "Look, your father has left you in my charge. And I want you to behave. You did not need one hour to see Rupa home and return . . ." And this went on. I got a real firing!'

'We got married on Saturday, 16 December 1961,' says Bajaj. 'In my family, it was probably the first love and inter-caste marriage, and it was a shock to everybody—not of course to my immediate family—but the wider and conservative Marwari family. My brother and three cousins married at younger ages, and all to Marwari girls from Calcutta.' Shishir got married to Minakshi (née Jalan), Shekhar to Kiran (née Dhanuka), Madhur to Kumud (née Bagla), and Niraj to Minal (née Agarwal).

The Long Wait

Time slowed down for the energetic Bajaj as he impatiently waited for the letter of acceptance from HBS.

'Kamalnayanji was very good to Rupa,' recalls Chitra Pamnani, Rupa's sister. 'She was the first and only non-Marwari daughter-in-law in the Bajaj family. Rahul went for his MBA to Harvard soon after the wedding. It was Kamalnayanji who showed Rupa how a Marwari family works.'

'So, our roller coaster marriage started,' wrote Rupa in *Dear Rahul...*, 'in spite of knowing each other for two years, things are so different when you live together—*Khabhi Khushi, Khabhi Gham!*[2] I was given my first lesson the day after the wedding—how to place your toothbrush, how to use the toothpaste to the maximum, no wastage! I soon got used to these mini capsules of instructions. I don't seem to hear them so clearly now!'

---

[2] Reference to the title of a popular Hindi movie, *Kabhi Khushi Kabhie Gham*.

7

Akurdi: 1959

Bajaj Auto bhoomi pujan by Jankidevi Bajaj in Akurdi on 9 March 1961.

In her scratchy, sparkling white khadi saree, the frail sixty-eight-year-old grandmother seized the pickaxe, swung it high over her head and with one swing crashed it down on the square of dry earth prepared for the *bhoomi pujan*. Using a small bowl, Jankidevi gently poured water on the centre of the square. According to the Hindu calendar, Thursday, 9 March 1961 was an auspicious day to launch a new project. This one had been in the making since 1945. There had been many touch-and-go moments. The licence finally arrived in 1959.

Within weeks, Bachhraj Trading had in hand the critical technical collaboration agreement with Piaggio granting the Indian company the right to manufacture and market Piaggio's Vespas. Projects requiring more than Rs 1 million in foreign exchange had to be cleared by the minister for industrial development, internal trade and company affairs. Dozens of businessmen applied to build scooter factories. The ministry did not approve even one. Why? Was the government protecting the existing manufacturers? The Bajajs felt hamstrung. 'You couldn't make anything until you got an industrial licence, and you couldn't make more than 25 per cent of the licenced capacity. We were told to make 6000 scooters a year when we first got our licence,' Bajaj recalls.

The IPO[3]

To get started, capital was needed to buy the land, build a factory, and fill it with equipment and employees. 'At the time Kamalnayanji launched Bajaj Auto, the original company, Bachhraj Trading, had lost almost its entire capital in the export business,' remembered Rameshwar Prasad Nevatia, 'and his companions were not in a position to think of any new venture; but at his own risk Kamalnayan took the help of people who could be helpful in investment and management. His brain was really very sharp when it came to financial issues and the gainful use of capital. And he proved his mettle by making Bajaj Auto a success.'

The stock market began humming with anticipation as gossip spread of an imminent IPO: Bajaj Auto was about to go public. Bajaj was still working out his apprenticeship at Radio Lamp Works[4] but

---

[3] IPO, Initial Public Offering.
[4] Renamed Bajaj Electricals on 1 October 1960.

Kamalnayan needed more hands. He upgraded Bajaj, at age twenty-two, to the board of directors of Bachhraj Trading. The youngest board member asked a lot of questions, read every word of the prospectus, and edited the paperwork with the accuracy of an expert proofreader. 'I would never be a lawyer, but some background does help in business,' he admits.

The managing agency firm had to undergo a few name changes. It was initially incorporated on 29 November 1945 as Bachhraj Trading Corporation Ltd. The name was changed to Bajaj Auto Pvt Ltd on 21 June 1960 and to the present one—Bajaj Auto Ltd—on 24 August 1960 on its conversion into a public limited company.

An EGM (extraordinary general meeting) of the shareholders was held on Saturday, 15 October 1960 at 4 p.m. at Bajaj Auto's registered office at 134, Dr Annie Besant Road, Worli, Bombay. It was a private affair. The shareholders present were Bajaj (at age twenty-two, the youngest and latest addition to the board of directors), Vinod Kumar Nevatia, Purshottam Jhunjhunwala representing Bachhraj and Co, L.N. Panpalia representing Jamnalal and Sons, Navalmal Kundanmal Firodia and Balmukund Khanna. The Special Resolution No. 4 authorizing the directors to obtain the consent of the Controller of Capital Issues and issue 60,100 equity shares of Rs 100 each was quickly passed. Kamalnayan was not present, but he had already vetted all details.

Out of habit, Bajaj kept checking and rechecking the nine-page prospectus. His eyes paused over point number five on page one: 'The subscription list will open at the commencement of Banking hours on the 14th day of November, 1960 and will close at the close of Banking hours on the 19th day of November, 1960, or earlier at the discretion of the Directors but not before the close of banking hours on the 16th day of November, 1960.'

Prior to its IPO, Bajaj Auto's paid-up capital was Rs 9,90,000 divided into 9900 shares of Rs 100 each. In the IPO 34,360 shares of Rs 100 each were offered at par for public subscription and 25,740 shares of Rs 100 each at par for existing shareholders.

The Controller of Capital Issues gave his consent on 21 October 1960. As D-day approached, the directors—Kamalnayan, Bajaj, Rameshwar Prasad Nevatia, Viren Shah, Madanmohan R. Ruia,

Ramnath Poddar, Shantanu L. Kirloskar and Navalmal Firodia—
tuned in to the gossip on the Bombay Stock Exchange. Bajaj Auto
had ten brokers selling the issue, six in Bombay, two in Delhi and
one each in Madras and Calcutta. The Rs 6.01 million issue was one
of the biggest to hit the market. Relief! The issue was oversubscribed.
Bajaj Auto shares were first listed on the Bombay Stock Exchange
(BSE) in April 1961.

Now real work could begin.

M.I.D.C., The Game Changer

'We bought 300 acres of land in Akurdi,' says Bajaj, 'far in excess
of our immediate requirements, but with a view to the future. Back
then, Akurdi was designated as a "backward area". We got financial
benefits.' As usual, the Bajaj sense of timing was perfect.

The state of Maharashtra was formed on 1 May 1960 with
Yashwantrao Balwantrao Chavan as its first chief minister.
Four months later, Chavan constituted a Board of Industrial
Development (BID) with Sadashiv Govind Barve as the chair.
The BID framed the legislation, the state legislature passed it in
the form of the Maharashtra Industrial Act, which in turn gave
birth to the Maharashtra Industrial Development Corporation on
1 August 1962 (aka M.I.D.C.). Barve's efficiency would land him
the industries ministership, the department that he loved the most.

Barve promptly went on a buying spree, purchasing vast tracts
of land for manufacturing hubs, developing roads, railway links and
water supply infrastructure. Gossip in the nearby villages however
whirred around just one topic: what is M.I.D.C., what is a special
economic zone, and what would these strange events mean for the
villagers? Over time, hundreds of thousands of people would migrate
to the new hubs M.I.D.C. created to fill jobs and benefit from the
rapid economic development. In the 1967 general election, Barve
contested and won a Congress ticket but within months of winning
the seat, he suffered a heart attack and died.

Among Barve's early faithfuls was Kamalnayan who shifted
his scooter assembly production from Goregaon to Akurdi. The
IPO money was promptly spent on machinery for manufacturing

scooters at the Akurdi plant. Bajaj Auto had some catching up to do. More expensive than anticipated, a top-up was needed in 1964. Bajaj Auto's capital increased from Rs 1 million to Rs 7 million. The licence permitted the manufacture of 6000 scooters per year, but the plant was generously geared for 24,000.

Construction of the scooter factory began on 9 March 1961. The construction cost per square foot was Rs 12. Shantanurao Laxmanrao Kirloskar, then a director of the company, commented on the frugality of the cost and the high quality of construction. Technology transfer from assembly to manufacturing was a far more challenging undertaking than the promoters anticipated.

Localizing the production of castings, forgings, gears and engine components in small volumes turned out to be more expensive than estimated. Unlike the easy availability of Bombay's teeming industrial workers, the need to cajole and train farmers straight off the field was a tougher task than expected.

'Akurdi could not be planned properly for mass production. The capacities were added in piecemeal as and when the Government of India permitted increase in licenced capacity,' discovered Gokhale Institute's Shakeel Ahmed. However, 'local content climbed gradually to 26 per cent due to the government's emphasis on import substitution,' described HBS's Nathalie Laidler. By 1966, Bajaj Auto was India's largest scooter producer. Demand continued to exceed supply.

The First Homemade Vespa

On 9 March 1962, an excited young Bajaj saw the first scooter roll off the assembly line. It was exactly twelve months after the ground-breaking ceremony. As many as 3994 Indian Vespas followed. The licence was for the annual manufacture of 6000 scooters but the plant was geared for 24,000. For Bajaj, just a few months remained before he would head for the US and HBS with Rupa.

8

Harvard Business School: 1962–64

Savitri and Bajaj, leaving for HBS in the US, at Bombay Airport.

There is always purpose with a bit of bravado thrown in, in the way Bajaj organizes himself. At age twenty, having set his sights on HBS, 'I thought I must get training which will help me get admission,' Bajaj confessed to Datar fifty-six years later. The strategy was effective. The work experiences on his curriculum vitae, and particularly the IPO, were sufficient for the famous B-school to accept the twenty-four-year-old. 'Rahul became one of our very early students from India,' remembers HBS Dean Srikant M. Datar.

Word got around that Bajaj had been accepted to HBS. Bajaj played it cool. 'What's the big deal?' Bajaj asked Vinay Bharat Ram, two years his senior at St. Stephen's, who wrote to congratulate him. 'I am not getting a fistful of diamonds!'

Getting to America involved a holiday. Kamalnayan invited Bajaj to join him on a business trip to Tokyo. 'We stayed with Lalji Mehrotra, India's ambassador to Japan. Japan and India were close to concluding a peace treaty in which Japan would pay ¥ 9 million to India towards World War II reparations,' Bajaj elaborates. In 1973, Bajaj would invite Mehrotra to join the Bajaj Auto board.

'From Japan, my father and I then split up. He had some work in Europe, and I headed for Los Angeles via Hawaii. At the time, there were no direct flights from Tokyo to Los Angeles. Hawaii was an experience. A couple of Marwaris had arranged hostel accommodation for me. We visited Waikiki beach and retreated to Honolulu.'

Bajaj arrived at the Soldiers Field campus alone—a visa issue held Rupa back, and she would reach Cambridge six months later. 'I landed on the West Coast, took a red-eye flight to Boston, reaching the campus on 1 September. I needed a place to sleep—the hostel would open only on the second—I found a place in Cambridge for the night. My dormitory was in McCulloch Hall. Those days there were no married quarters, and I moved out of the dormitory to move into a rented apartment at Cambridge with Rupa once she arrived.'

The HBS MBA is a two-year programme. Bajaj joined the institution at a historic moment. HBS faculty in December 1962 voted to allow women to apply for the full two years of the MBA programme. In August 1963, eight women were accepted.

The First Day

But there was once a mischance.

'I missed my first lecture at HBS,' admits Bajaj ruefully. 'I made it to the second one. The professor looked sternly at me. "You are coming at this time, Mr Bajaj!" I needed a driving licence, and a friend had volunteered to take me in his car to the licencing authority. I got the licence and rushed back. But yes, I was late. After that, I rarely missed a class,' recalls Bajaj.

Harvard has a unique and specific formula, distilled over decades, of blending raw freshers. Bajaj was slotted in Section F, Class of 1964. As was John M. Trask. 'We were told,' recalled Trask, 'that ours was a very specially selected group, put together by Dean J. Leslie Rollins who had a good sense about human dynamics. I believe he understood the chemistry and culture of students who came from family-oriented business backgrounds—young people with a sense of where they come from and where they were going.'

'In those days, there were hardly any Indians studying at HBS. I met two friends I would make for life, Tom Beach and Michael Alpert,' recalls Bajaj nostalgically. 'I was in section F. They were in other sections, both unmarried at the time. We met for the first time at lunch in the dining room. Forget teen patti, in the US, it's poker all the way. I learnt and adapted.'

Beach has a very different version of their first meeting. 'My long friendship with Rahul began in a manner that I consider inappropriate but which he regarded as highly satisfactory,' Beach penned in a long letter to Bajaj. 'We met on our first day at HBS and somehow it came out that I had played a tournament of ping-pong. Rahul suggested that as a poor Indian he had no time or money to indulge in foolish games, but that since we had nothing better to do at the moment, he would play me for $10 if I would sport him 15 points (of the 21 needed to win a game). Naively, I accepted, feeling secure that I could easily dispatch this poor fellow. Of course, he beat me badly. When I produced the $10, he revealed that he had been ping-pong champion at his high school, and that I was a stupid American! With this disarming comment a friendship began that has gone on now for nearly forty-five years. I learnt a business lesson as valuable as any received in the classroom.'

Paul and Eula Hoff were another HBS couple with whom Rupa and Rahul chilled. 'We shared the same quarters, did we not, when Rupa and you, Paul and I moved into an apartment at High Rock Way for a while?' recalls Eula.

The Goings-on in Line Street

'I knew Rupa would arrive in December. I started looking for a place for us in Cambridge, just across the river and close to the school,' recounts Bajaj. 'Luckily, I found a recently renovated flat owned by a Polish landlady on the first floor.[1] Line Street was more of a lane than a street. It was a small flat but perfect for Rupa and me. There was even a supermarket nearby.'

'I needed a car to get to Soldiers Field in the morning and back to Line Street in the evening,' he continues. 'The Boston winter is sharp, dropping to minus 15° centigrade and below between December to March. A car rental those days was $120 per month—completely out of my budget. An HBS grad, Karl Herman, a German, wanted to dispose of his almost brand-new light blue 57 model Studebaker with a 1962 registration. It was a manual shift; his wife Alex preferred an automatic. I bought it off him for $350.'

At HBS, then and now, classes start sharp at 8.40 a.m., end sharp at 3.30 p.m., five days a week, three classes daily. 'Before Rupa arrived, I was in an after-class study group. After she came, I would head home, reaching our flat by 4 p.m. Then it was study, study, study. Three cases, two hours each on average. Rupa made roti and sabzi. We ate. Then back to work until midnight,' describes Bajaj. 'The next morning, get up at 7 a.m., leave for class at 8 a.m. to arrive by 8.30 a.m. before class opens. The drive was just fifteen minutes, but school parking was difficult. Winter was a problem—there were no tunnels in those days.'

HBS expects its students to reserve the sixth day, Saturday, for WAC aka written analysis of cases. 'We received our cases every Friday evening. The length of cases differed, sometimes just two pages, others between twenty to fifty pages. The HR papers were the longest. Our written analysis had to go down the chutes of either

---

[1] In American parlance, the ground floor is the first floor. Here, Bajaj uses the Indian nomenclature.

Baker Library or Morgan Hall sharp by 5 p.m. on Saturday. If one didn't, one was in trouble,' remembers Bajaj. 'Of course, I was never in trouble!'

But there was a problem. 'I could not prepare the finance cases,' says Bajaj, 'I could not understand them. Everyone else could. My calculations would go haywire.'

Neatly typed homework was a must. 'Before Rupa arrived, I would write everything by hand and give it to Mary Smith to type. There was a small pool of these ladies. One day, a 300-page book arrived. I asked Rupa if she would like a go at it. I handed over the writing to Rupa. She enjoyed the case, wrote the WAC and delivered the pages to me. I took it to the typist and put in the chute,' chuckles Bajaj. 'Rupa got a B+. After Rupa joined me, everything became easier.'

'HBS sharpened Rahul's analytical approach and ability to take quick decisions without losing his objective,' Rupa shared years later. Bajaj agrees, adding, 'HBS opened up my horizon. I learnt the rudiments of business, finance, accounts, marketing, and production in a very cosmopolitan environment. I learnt that in the case study method, the stress is on the ability to think and analyse, unlike the lecture method where the stress is on memory. In one case study, a question offered was on the buying or selling of a company. I opted to buy and my friend to sell. Both of us got a distinction.'

Summertime Hops

Come summer, the drill of prepping case studies gave way to exploring America. 'In the summer of 1963, Rupa and I travelled all over the US in our Studebaker. My father travelled in the car with us for half the time. We stayed in motels for $10 per night. He expected us to live like students . . . and he also lived like us! Mexico, Texas, Fort Worth, Austin, San Francisco, Yellowstone National Park, the Grand Canyon, Las Vegas—for three months we went everywhere.'

'Every week or ten days, I stopped at a garage or service centre. There was never a flat tyre or puncture. This jalopy was in good hands,' says Bajaj triumphantly. 'When it was time to leave HBS, I had to sell the car. I bought the Studebaker for $350. I sold it for

$700. It was the right price for a car that had seen 25,000 miles. That $700 was the first money I made.'

January 1963 saw Bajaj and Rupa back in India. Kamalnayan invited HBS professors Milton P. Brown (an expert in retailing and marketing) and James R. Bright (an engineer with a flair for technological innovation and automation) to visit India, vet the blueprints for Bajaj factories under construction, and discuss the group's plans for growth. The Mukand Iron and Steel plant was coming up at Kalwe. The machinery for the Akurdi complex was streaming in. Kamalnayan was quietly delighted.

Where's My Hat?

The month of May saw Bajaj graduate from the class of 1964, collect his MBA degree from Dean George E. Baker, and throw his hat up in the air. Back in India, Kamalnayan was thrilled when he got the news that Bajaj had received his degree. As an undergraduate in 1938, Kamalnayan had been forced to drop out of Fitzwilliam House, his Cambridge University's college, because of Jamnalal's passing away and a downturn in the family businesses. Bajaj's MBA from one of the most prestigious institutions in the world salved his father's past.

But before that: Europe! 'After leaving HBS, Rupa and I and another Indian couple, friends of ours, went to Europe for a month's holiday,' remembers Bajaj nostalgically.

'It was our stay in Boston where we really bonded well,' wrote Rupa. 'Our marriage was of two friends, two equal partners, two companions, a successful joint venture indeed! We learnt to complement each other rather than confront each other. Then it was off to India to settle in Akurdi.'

Forty Years Later

In 2005, Dean Kim B. Clark invited Bajaj to revisit HBS to pick up his Alumni Achievement Award. 'By the 1990s, Bajaj Auto faced problems worthy of an HBS case study,' the school declared. Sitting in the audience was Rupa, unwell but determined to enjoy this special moment with her husband. An MBA student living on the campus provided Rupa some rest and recreation.

Invited to the dais and asked to disclose a lifelong lesson, Bajaj responded with, 'The case method teaches you how to gather and understand the facts of a situation, and then how to analyse and make a decision. But even more important, this process requires you to think really hard. In my career, nothing has been more important than that.'

HBS

Government Law College,
Mumbai

St. Stephen's College,
Delhi

Cathedral Boy's High
School, Mumbai

9

The House of Orchids: 1964–2013

Rahul, Rupa, Rajiv, Sanjiv and Sunaina.

'It was decided in America with my father-in-law, who insisted that we stay in Akurdi, Poona,' confirmed Rupa, that 'we should not be staying in Poona in a big bungalow while our employees and other workers were in Akurdi.' Bajaj's upbringing and values were more upper middle class than aristocratic.

It felt good to be back at Mount Unique, surrounded by family members of all ages. The US and Harvard, Europe and its architectural beauty—both Bajaj and Rupa felt grateful for the freedoms they had tested and tasted during their sabbatical from India. In a few days, it would be time to head out.

Kamalnayan beckoned, Bajaj nodded, and they both moved quietly to the terrace. 'What would you like to do now?' he asked his son. 'Go to Akurdi, no question,' pat came the reply.

Leaving Mount Unique behind them, Bajaj and Rupa headed for the Bajaj guest house at Ganeshkhind, 15.6 km south of Akurdi. 'When we arrived in the Ganeshkhind colony, the family of Manmohan Lal Gaba, the general manager of Bajaj Electricals,[1] were already living in the Bajaj guest house,' wrote Rupa. 'Rahul and I were allotted a 10-foot by 12-foot room.' In the 1960s, the title 'general manager' had the same clout as today's 'managing director'. And Bajaj Electricals then was a bigger company than Bajaj Auto with sales in 1965–1966, double that of Bajaj Auto.

'I made Akurdi my home base in 1964, after I joined Bajaj Auto. For years we lived like a middle-class family,' remembers Bajaj. 'We even had snakes coming into our house, but Rupa loved it here,' Dussehra 1965 saw the couple finally in a house of their own. It was an unpretentious bungalow, a ground plus one. Rupa pottered around converting a house into a home. She turned to horticulture. The most luxurious objects in the spartan residence were the exotic orchids which Rupa started to grow.

With time on her hands, Rupa corralled wives in the colony to set up a charity, Vanita Mandal. Baby smocks and dresses began making their way to the Pune Club Sale. 'She was like a mother figure, always there for everyone,' describes a worker's wife. 'Many of the women from the colony would come to her for advice. She loved gardening and took an active interest in seasonal flowers and the

---

[1] Radio Lamp Works became Bajaj Electricals in October 1960.

vegetable patch in the backyard. Most of the vegetables consumed in their kitchen came from the garden.'

'With her vast medical knowledge, Rupaji was almost half a doctor herself,' an employee's wife remarked. 'Along with allopathic medical knowledge, she knew a lot about using natural common household herbs and ingredients to cure ailments such as colds. She would also make a nourishing hair oil using hibiscus flowers, aloe vera and fenugreek seeds with a coconut base.' 'Don't forget she was also fond of movies and theatre,' chipped in another.

In 1996, the couple would build a palatial annexe which completely dominates the original bungalow.

The Scent of a Woman

'I really got to know Rupa in Akurdi,' continues Bajaj. 'That's when I began to realize what a beautiful person she is, what a strength she was to me, and her transparent character. We had the usual husband-wife disagreements, she never raised her voice but did not give in to any demand. In the book *Dear Rahul* she compiled for me, Rupa wrote, "He says I speak too little, I say he speaks too much!".'

'When we married, buas, aunts, etc., asked me how a tall, educated Maharashtrian girl would fit into a Marwari household?' reminiscences Bajaj. 'The aunts were well-meaning but not used to this situation. But having known Marwari wives of relatives and friends, Rupa melted into the Bajaj family and won them over by her sobriety, integrity and intellect. She was very conscious of family traditions, conscious of our Gandhian traditions—though many of us don't live those nowadays,' says Bajaj. 'We mellowed with time,' added Rupa, 'but Rahul's energy did not diminish at all! Our family members had to help me keep up with him.'

'My father did whatever she said,' Bajaj shared with Datar. 'If we had a disagreement, my father would support the daughter-in-law. That he did for the rest of his life. After my father and my mother passed away, Rupa was the eldest in the family. She kept the extended family together.'

'She brought up our three children. That is my regret, that I didn't bring up our children. It seems so wrong today—I had the standard excuse of being busy and that I was travelling. And I think they are what they are today because of her. They are outstanding and I am proud of them. And I think she brought us great sobriety, maturity in our lives, which has helped us in our business also. I don't believe in superstitions. In fact, we don't do anything in our family which is a superstition, but I think she brought us a tremendous amount of good luck. We were married for fifty-two years when she died.'

Where Do the Children Play?[2]

What were the chances of a school, started by a Swiss nun in a boondocks, opening its doors in the same year as Rupa's and Rahul's arrival in Akurdi? Slim would probably be the normal response. Mother Nicholas Buhlman was made of stern resolve. St Ursula High School (Akurdi), managed by the Society of St Ursula, was founded in 1965, and has not looked back since.

Rajiv was born in 1966, Sanjiv in 1969, and Sunaina in 1971. One by one, Rupa enrolled them at St Ursula, and sent them off, not by car, not on a scooter, but in the school bus. Adds Bajaj, 'My children went to a school where my managers' children did not go because they lived in Poona. My workers' children and mine attended the local school and I am proud of that.' Holidays were often spent playing with the workers' children in the factory's open spaces.

'When they were about fourteen and eleven, Rajiv and Sanjiv asked Rupa for an increase in their pocket money,' recalls Bajaj. 'They didn't say it is not enough. They said, all our classmates get more than us. Rupa countered with, "So what? Let them get more." They said, some of them tell us that their father is an employee in your father's company, your father is the owner of the company, you have to get more than us. What did Rupa then tell the boys? "Tell them what they are saying is right. You are getting less because you are a Bajaj." This again was Rupa's upbringing of our children.'

Bajaj is not one who wears his heart on his sleeve, and it takes a friend to talk to a friend on family matters. 'When Rajiv got 93 per cent in the twelfth standard, Rahul's pride was very visible,' remembers family friend, Gul Mansukhani, 'although all he said was, "*Woh toh apne baap se bhi aage nikal gaya!*".'

---

[2] From the lyrics of '(Remember The Days Of The) Old Schoolyard' by Cat Stevens.

'Being the youngest of three and the only girl,' shares Sunaina, 'I was the cynosure of my mum's eye. I remember my early years with great fondness and joy. She was a towering personality with a reserved and strict demeanour on the outward and a lot of love, caring, knowledge and wisdom on the inside. She was not physically demonstrative in her affection, but she gave us so much emotional stability, security and care that we never lacked for anything.

'Our dad was always travelling and working late, so we didn't see much of him, but mummy was always there like a rock—our rock. Growing up in her care, life was simple and wholesome. In all three of us, she inculcated values like humility, honesty, kindness, respect and awareness of our responsibilities and duty to others.

'She came from a nuclear and liberal Maharashtrian family and adapted to the traditional joint Marwari family into which she married. She was quite a disciplinarian and authoritarian in her parenting as we were growing up, but she seamlessly eased into a friend mode as we transitioned into adulthood and marriage. She let go beautifully.

'Mummy had a wicked sense of humour and though quiet by nature she often threw the best punchlines at dinner parties! She had a way with words and wrote beautifully, something which I believe my older brother Rajiv has imbibed from her. She toyed with the idea of writing a column for a newspaper, but never got around to doing it.

'We had an unspoken and unwritten ritual of speaking with each other every evening between 5.30 p.m. to 6 p.m. If there was something troubling me, I didn't have to tell her. She just knew and would address it in such a way that I felt soothed, and felt I had a solution by the time the conversation ended. Family members used to joke that my umbilical cord never got cut! She left us with beautiful memories and lived a life with quiet strength and eternal grace like a steel magnolia. Even till today, sometimes, my hand reaches for the telephone at 5.30 p.m. . . .'

10

I'm Back! 1963–2013

Gear room under construction at Bajaj Auto Plant in Akurdi in 1963.

The Bajaj Auto plant sprang into life while Bajaj and Rupa were still at HBS. The scooter assembly lines were up and running by 1963, the heat treatment shop by 1964, and the two- and three-stage boring machines for the Vespa's crankcase by 1965. Some machinery was specifically imported to bring indigenous content up to 90 per cent. Planning, efficiency, perfect timing or just plain good luck, the bulk of Bajaj Auto's machinery import was completed by mid-1965. Had machinery imports been delayed, costs would have soared, and Bajaj Auto's balance sheet would have been a mess.

As all right-minded fathers do, Kamalnayan planned his firstborn's induction to a nicety. Some practical experience was in order, he figured, turning to his partner, Firodia, for advice. 'Bajaj Auto is growing rapidly,' pointed out Firodia, 'leaving all of us little time to look after our other companies. Bajaj could start out at Bajaj Tempo Motors and see to the commercial side, including purchase, marketing, sales, accounts, finance, audit, everything but production.' Kamalnayan agreed.

Bajaj joined Bajaj Tempo as Deputy General Manager, and became Managing Director of Bajaj Auto on 1 April 1970. His move came with an upgrade: the best view of the scooter plant. Factories in the 1960s and 1970s were designed for manufacturing activities on the ground floor, and a smallish office on the first floor with a huge window for the manager-in-charge, in this case, Bajaj. 'I could see each and every key activity,' he beams.

6/6/66

The year 1966 stands out not only because it saw three prime ministers (Lal Bahadur Shastri, Gulzarilal Nanda, Indira Gandhi, one after the other, of course), but also for the rough climate for manufacturing. The miserable failure of the Third Five-Year Plan led to three sequential 'plan holidays' (1966–67, 1967–68, 1968–69) and India's monetary situation remained precarious.

A war with China in 1962 and another with Pakistan in 1965, as well as droughts in 1965 and 1966 left India 'pathetically dependent on US food aid,' as Swaminathan Aiyar, economist, journalist, and columnist, reminds us. Faced with a ballooning deficit and a foreign exchange crisis, on 6 June 1966, Indira Gandhi switched the rupee from Rs 4.76 to Rs 7.57 to a dollar. When India won its independence in 1947, the rupee's value was on a par with the American dollar. Thankfully, the 1967 monsoon was normal.

Surveying the situation at the Bajaj Auto plant, the June-born Bajaj was in no mood to celebrate his twenty-eighth birthday. The company held permissions to make 12,000 scooters and autorickshaws. A major order for machinery luckily arrived just before the devaluation—but not all its parts. What could be installed was installed. With several pieces of the engineering puzzle missing, the work was unfulfilling.

The biggest challenge the father and son faced was forex to buy Piaggio components that they could not make in India. The only import option was via export earnings, a Herculean task for a fledgling Bajaj Auto facing a slew of babus who assumed that no significant increase in export earnings was possible. Policy turned with Morarji Desai as finance minister and exports became an important plank in economic policy.

Babudom works at its own pace. As the days went by, Bajaj Auto's stock of imported components whittled down. 'The import licence for the year ahead is likely to be meagre,' Bajaj discussed with Kamalnayan. Production gradually more or less stopped. The factory idled for almost four months. Toting up the disaster, Bajaj reckoned that sales in 1965–66 would decrease by 21 per cent. Profit was not worth talking about. 'We are trying to devise other means to maintain production,' wrote Bajaj to his father. A chat with the Piaggios, and Kamalnayan negotiated a deferred payment loan for $2,97,000. Imports against this loan kept the factory running. But for how long?

The best hope was the Industrial Credit and Investment Corporation of India (ICICI), headed by its then chairman, Gaganvihari L. Mehta. As India's ambassador to the US for six years between 1952 to 1958, Mehta was a familiar face in Washington. ICICI had earlier secured Bajaj Auto a $1.05 million loan to import machinery. In August 1967, Mehta was back in the US to pitch to the president of the World Bank, George David Woods, for a second round of top dollar financing for Indian industries. Mehta returned to India with $25 million.

In Akurdi, to keep morale high, Bajaj kept his team busy. A branch office came up near the busy Shivajinagar station on the Bombay-Poona Road. Its frontage was a sparkling showroom for its Vespa range of scooters and autorickshaws. On the side was a service station, and deep inside, a spare-parts department. The branch also served as an in-house training centre for service mechanics on its staff, and for those deputed by Bajaj Auto's distributors from all parts of the country.

Internally, staring Bajaj and Kamalnayan in the face was a real clanger. Bajaj Auto had imported machinery worth $4,26,850 in 1964–65 and spent another $4,27,058 in 1965–66. According to the terms of the ICICI agreement, Bajaj Auto had to repay a loan of $1.05 million in nineteen instalments. The first instalment of $37,000 was paid on the due date.

The cost of the remaining eighteen instalments jumped sky high. On 15 August 1947 the rupee and the dollar were equal. Post 6/6/66, Bajaj Auto's foreign exchange loans soared by 57.5 per cent in rupee terms. The situation in 1966 was so tough that 'in order to continue uninterrupted production, the government asked us to negotiate with Piaggio to defer our payments to the Italians,' remembers Bajaj, 'and fortunately they agreed'. But of course, there is always a price to pay.

Goodbye

The Indira Gandhi administration abolished the managing agency system on 30 March 1970. A relic of the British raj, it was a handy structure for British entrepreneurship. India needed a more relevant and up-to-date model. The death of the managing agency system would birth the role of the managing director.

'The managing agency was a peculiar corporate structure,' explains Omkar Goswami, 'that allowed a few partners to control a number of public limited and joint stock companies, despite a very small shareholding in the latter. It allowed men with great entrepreneurial drive and organizational abilities to be involved in a number of businesses and promote others, but it was also a system prone to abuse. The managing agency essentially managed these firms through long-term management contracts that gave them total control and big returns while investors got short shrift.'

The termination of the Bajaj group's numerous managing agencies would save the Bajaj group at least Rs 7 lakh, if not more, Kamalnayan calculated. The roles of family members in the businesses became more transparent. For decades Ramkrishna had run Bajaj Electricals, established in 1938, under varied nomenclatures. With the abolition of the managing agency system, Ramkrishna could upgrade to managing director of Bajaj Electricals. Bajaj ran Bajaj Auto for five years between 1965 to 1970 as 'Director—Managing Agents' under the umbrella of the managing agency firm of Jamnalal & Sons. To become a managing director, all that was now needed was to hold an Extraordinary General Meeting of Bajaj Auto shareholders.

A Special Resolution

Father and son looked at each other. It wasn't going to be easy.

'I admit I ruffled a few feathers,' says Bajaj when asked about the Firodias, 'but they started it!' Firodia's initial purchase of 1,04,250 shares worth Rs 450,000 representing 13 per cent of Bajaj Auto's issued share capital was completely kosher. Naval Firodia's contribution in roping in dealers as Bajaj Auto shareholders was equally cogent. In the 1960s, it was common practice as a means to tie dealers to a specific brand. Even in 1993, of Bajaj Auto's Rs 370 million share capital, about 51 per cent was controlled by the Bajaj family, roughly 10 per cent by company dealers, and around 20 per cent by the Firodias.

Returning to end-February 1968, the Firodias held 23 per cent. The shares had to be registered. Firodia himself had earlier suggested that young Bajaj look after the commercial side of the business. The shares came to Bajaj for transfer. He refused, naturally. Kamalnayan's shareholding when he launched Bajaj Auto was 28 per cent. Once he cottoned on to Firodia's intentions, skirmishes triggered several events during Bajaj Auto's silver jubilee year.[1] The 100,000th scooter was showcased. Kamalnayan gifted Bajaj Auto's first managing directorship to thirty-two-year-old Bajaj. The EGM[2] was scheduled for 13 February 1970 to obtain shareholder approval.

When Kamalnayan and Bajaj arrived at the hall, it was packed.

---

[1] Bajaj Auto was established on 29 November 1945 as M/s Bachhraj Trading Corporation Private Limited.

[2] Extraordinary General Meeting.

The special resolution sought shareholders' approval for Bajaj's appointment for five years at a monthly salary of Rs 7,500 plus commission at 1 per cent of the net profits for each financial year, with a ceiling of Rs 45,000 per year—in addition to other perquisites and benefits.

Stepping up to the podium, Kamalnayan sketched the role Bajaj had played in building Bajaj Auto. For a number of years, Bajaj was ex officio director of Bajaj Auto representing the company's managing agents, Jamnalal & Sons. 'He has been looking after Bajaj Auto's work since 1964, the period when much of the progress and improvement in profitability of the company took place,' Kamalnayan summed up.

'Bajaj's appointment came in for stiff opposition, and the fight at the EGM became particularly ugly. Prior to the EGM, the main body of dissenters had organised a campaign to collect proxies to oppose Bajaj's appointment,' recorded the reporter for the *Economic and Political Weekly*. Management brought a busload of shareholders from Bombay to the meeting at Poona in the company's vehicle!' whispered the dissenters, '*and* management transferred one share each to about thirty company employees to swell the number of its supporters!'[3]

Another group of challengers to the resolution described Bajaj as an 'immature and inexperienced' young person who had been working in a junior capacity of deputy general manager in Bajaj Tempo Motors from 1965 till September 1968 on a salary of Rs 2200 per month. This was an attempt to 'foist' the appointment of a Bajaj family member on 'fabulous terms in order to get back-door benefits lost on termination of the managing agency'.[4]

The proposal was put to vote: 200 shareholders with their 51,853 shares voted decisively for the resolution; 636 with 27,761 shares voted against.

The battle for shares continued. 'My father was a bold man,' Bajaj remembers with pride. 'Two financial institutions, Life Insurance Corporation (LIC) and Unit Trust of India (UTI), together had a 4 per cent block of Bajaj Auto shares which they were willing to sell. An auction was arranged. Basing their calculations on the share's

---

[3] The *EPW* and personal conversation with Rahul Bajaj.
[4] *Economic and Political Weekly*, 28 February 1970, pp. 431–2, 'For Whose Benefit', Hansavivek.

market price of Rs 260, the Firodias offered Rs 262.50 per share for the block. My father aggressively submitted an offer of Rs 411. He had an audacious streak in him.' Outdone, the Firodias walked out of the auction aloofly, saying 'they didn't have money to throw'.

Both parties went to the courts. Every time one party won a judgment, a reprise negated the other, i.e., Point Non Plus.

These skirmishes continued for years. The battle of 2005 erupted over the Bajaj Tempo Motors brand. The second generation under Abhay Firodia wanted to drop it and switch to Force Motors. Doing his homework, Abhay found the clause he wanted: under Section 22 of the Companies Act, 1956, a change in name could be carried out by an ordinary resolution. Bajaj was quick to the draw. 'Any proposition or resolution that drops the word Bajaj from the name will be opposed by us,' he warned, adding that a name change requires a special resolution under Section 21 of the Companies Act.

The Peace Pipe

After more than five decades of squabbling over cross holdings, the Bajajs and Firodias finally called it a day. The reconciliation's timing and venue turned out to be quite a surprise. In September 2013, at the annual convention of the Society of the Indian Automobile Manufacturers, Rajiv Bajaj and Abhay Firodia shared the dais. Both recalled memories of the ties between the families. 'I heard it from the grapevine,' Rajiv asked Abhay, 'but is it true that you said that as long as Rajiv is there as managing director, I will not sell my shares in Bajaj Auto?'

The ice melted. Over three months in the autumn of 2014, Bajaj Holdings (BHIL) sold 16.56 lakh Force Motors shares in the open market for between Rs 436 and Rs 592, fetching the Bajajs about Rs 91 crore. To a media agog at the action, Niraj played down the sale. 'We received a good price. There was no particular reason to sell the shares. We may still have some shares,' he responded to Sabarinath M. of the *Economic Times*. A significant 24 per cent stake in Force Motors actually, but relatively non-threatening. The Firodias owned less than 10 per cent of Bajaj Auto, valued at Rs 6177 crore at the time.

'The Firodias are free to sell their shares in Bajaj Auto to anyone,' Niraj Bajaj continued, 'there is no commitment or understanding between us.'

11

The Difficulty of Being Good: 1964–2002

Bajaj and Kamalnayan.

Bajaj returned from the US to an India brimming with paranoia. Indira Gandhi was convinced she would get no mileage from big business. Their influence had to be checked. She would turn to the people. Gandhi plucked Rabindra Kishen Hazari, initially spotted by her father, to help her create the populist agenda. Excited by the opportunity, the young idealist became her key architect to design controls on big business, a matter of some importance as she sought to steady her position as India's first woman prime minister.

Hazari got to work, only to become disillusioned. 'What are we seeking to control and for what purpose? Where have we gone wrong and why?' wrote an anguished economist Hazari shortly before he died. Hazari's substantial role in data collection on the growth of big business after Independence had become Gandhi's *astra*.

Another useful addition to Indira Gandhi's efforts was Srinivasan Chakravarthy who helped shape the Monopolies and Restrictive Trade Practices (MRTP) Act, 1969 and would become a member of the MRTP Commission. Like Hazari, Chakravarthy too would become disillusioned.

'Instead of relying significantly on market forces, ensuring competition and keeping the market functioning efficiently, the command-and-control approach triggered government intervention in almost all areas of economic activity,' wrote Chakravarthy. 'For instance, there was no contestable market. This meant that there was neither an easy entry nor an easy exit for enterprises. The government determined the plant sizes, location of plants, prices in a number of important sectors, and allocation of scarce financial resources.'

Gandhi's group of advisers cherry-picked legislation from around the globe. India's MRTP Act drew heavily on the US's Sherman Antitrust Act of 1890 and the Clayton Antitrust Act of 1914, the UK's Monopolies and Restrictive Trade Practices (Inquiry and Control) Act of 1948 and the Resale Prices Act of 1964, and stray ideas picked up from Japan, Canada and Germany, recalled Chakravarthy.

Without fuss, Parliament passed the MRTP Act on 18 December 1969. President Varahagiri Venkata Giri gave his assent on 27 December 1969. And the Act gently segued into the MRTP Commission. It came into force from 1 June 1970. The MRTP Commission would stymie big business and industrial growth for decades.

Scams were inevitable in this policy atmosphere, and there was at least one that made some noise for a few years.

Among the dozens of businessmen who applied for a scooter manufacturing licence in 1965–66 was P.N. Singh. Gandhi reportedly noted on his application that his request be considered sympathetically as eastern Uttar Pradesh (India's most populous state) where Singh proposed to set up his plant, was economically backward. Yet his licence did not come through. Singh alleged that the secretary of a senior politician had visited him to demand a bribe of Rs 3,00,000 for the licence. He had secretly recorded the conversation on tape and the opposition used it to attack the government. The tape was laid before Vice President V.V. Giri in the Parliament. Nothing happened. The case went to the Central Bureau of Investigation, and there it rested.

At the Bajaj Group, with a baker's dozen of talented, ambitious young men working in numerous parts of the extended family businesses, the Bajajs jumped from nowhere to India's nineteenth biggest business group in twelve short years. In 1964, the group had assets of Rs 29.25 crore, according to Hazari's estimates.

The Call

Bajaj Auto was initially licenced to produce 1,000 scooters and 50 autorickshaws per month. No problem—it was still at the teething stage. In 1962, Bajaj Auto applied to increase manufacturing capacity to 30,000 scooters and 6,000 autorickshaws per year. No response. In 1963, it applied to increase capacity from 24,000 scooters to 48,000. No response. In 1970, it asked for 1,00,000. No response. Eventually, in 1971, the government approved annual production of 48,000 scooters. But the permission was meaningless because the application remained pending with the Ministry of Company Affairs for clearance. 'It was just another ploy to further delay us,' recalls Dhirajlal S. Mehta, a senior manager, 'and we did increase production beyond the licenced limit, and we were liable to prosecution.'

Bajaj Auto had the capacity, manufacturing capability, financial resources, sales and distribution network. The government had the remote control. 'At the time, the Directorate General of Technical Development regulated production (DGTD),' Bajaj described to Datar. 'It would say, "there is no demand for more than this" or "you can't have excess capacity, we have scarce resources". Any manufacturer violating the conditions of his licence by producing more than 25 per cent of the licenced capacity, even if by improving productivity and utilization of existing equipment, was in trouble. I was quoted often enough for saying that I was ready to go to jail for excess production just as both my parents had for the freedom struggle.'

'One evening Kamalnayanji came to my cabin,' recalled Mehta. 'It was 9 p.m. He asked me, "What are you doing at this time?" I replied, "Preparing a note for the MRTP Commission." He remarked, "You may take all the trouble, but you are not going to get expansion." I responded, "Because of your politics we may not get what we want".'

This view was shared by the majority of Bajaj Auto's board of seven directors. Kamalnayan and Bajaj were taken aback when three of the four external directors—Ramnath Poddar, Shriyans Prasad Jain and Tanubhai D. Desai—hastily bailed out, leaving only one external member, Madanmohan Ruia, to hold fort alongside Viren Shah. Deep friendships held the Shah family and the Bajajs together, not only their joint ownership of Mukand Iron forged in 1939.

A new board of seven members was hastily cobbled with external directors: the reliable Ruia and the Gandhian Rishabdas Ranka with Shah as the consistent insider-outsider. The remaining four positions were manned by internal officers: Kamalnayan as chairman, Manmohan Lal Gauba of Bajaj Electricals, D. S. Mulla and Bajaj.

Who Should It Be?

Debating within himself as to who should represent the company at the MRTP hearing, Kamalnayan settled on Bajaj. The father was confident his son would somehow manage the situation. In April 1968, the thirty-three-year-old became the de facto CEO of the managing agency of Bajaj Auto, supported by majority shareholder approval.

'My father suggested I represent the company in the upcoming MRTP hearing,' recalls Bajaj. Technically, Bajaj Auto had increased production by 25 per cent beyond the licenced limit and was thus liable to prosecution. Mehta managed to obtain an opinion from a prominent lawyer that 'increasing production is not a crime, increased installed capacity is against the law.' An angry Bajaj was ready with his defence. The hearings started.

'I went to Delhi to face the three-member commission in New Delhi without a lawyer,' recalls Bajaj. 'M.A. Chidambaram, chairman of API, which manufactured Lambretta scooters, had been invited as a competitor. He tried to show that his scooter was superior by saying it weighed 100 kg and that the Vespa scooter weighed only 94 kg. I replied, "Yes, the Lambretta scooter is 100 kg of silver, the Bajaj scooter is 94 kg of gold!".'

'The MRTP Commission's bench of three, M.V. Paranjape, Justice Subramaniam and its chairman, A. Alagiriswami, a retired judge of the High Court, asked for a plethora of details, most of them irrelevant. I alone answered everything.'

As the hearings petered, one of the commissioners told Mehta, 'You gave all the information we wanted, even if we asked for irrelevant data. The Bajajs are completely transparent.' The hearing finally wound down in 1975—in favour of Bajaj.

'Not only did the members allow Bajaj Auto its expansion but their report also complimented me for my knowledge and command of the facts and figures of the case,' remembers Bajaj. 'The commission report also acknowledged that though there was a premium on Bajaj scooters in the open market and demand exceeded supply, our scooter was the cheapest.' But the Commission still refused to relax production restrictions. 'Political equations took precedence over merit,' remembers Bajaj. Lobbying by competitors like UP Scooters and API continued to fan anxiety about the power of big business.

'I used to spend my time in the corridors of Udyog Bhavan instead of the factory and became friends with many in the Directorate General of Technical Development, including even the section officer, H.C. Sharma. It was not easy to get an industrial licence either, because political equations mattered.'

Any positive learnings whiling away wasted time in the corridors of Udyog Bhavan instead of the factory? 'I learnt how difficult it can get to chase someone in Delhi for a licence,' says Bajaj, 'then some fool delays the whole project by procrastinating because he wants something for himself . . . but thank goodness I was never actually penalized. Even if giving money could have bought a licence, I can categorically say we did not give any ministers or any bureaucrat a single rupee to get a licence.'

You Can't Beat a Bajaj

Politicians wanted Bajaj scooters as badly as the ordinary man in the street. Every once in a while, the Bajaj scooter would become political fodder. On 13 August 1976, a member of Parliament alleged in the Lok Sabha that in the 1971 general election, Bajaj Auto gave Rs 1,20,000 and some scooters to the opposition candidate in Rae Bareli, Uttar Pradesh.

This was a loaded gun. Jumping to his deceased father's defence, Bajaj wrote to Pranab Mukherjee, the then union minister of state for finance, denying the allegation. As the company's chairman in 1971, Kamalnayan had certainly made priority releases of scooters from the manufacturer's discretionary quota to political friends both in the ruling and opposition parties, but only against payment of the full price, clarified Bajaj. 'As Kamalnayan belonged to the opposition,' Bajaj added guardedly, 'some scooters naturally were released to persons belonging to the opposition, some of whom could have had connection with the opposition candidate in Rae Bareilly.'

The Rae Bareli constituency in Uttar Pradesh was the litmus test of the Gandhi family's popularity since India's first general election, starting with Feroze Gandhi, Indira's husband, who twice won his seat from there. The opposition candidate this time was Raj Narain. His five-year term in the Rajya Sabha ended in 1971. His sights were on the forthcoming Lok Sabha election. He challenged Indira Gandhi on her home ground but failed to dislodge her. Accusing Gandhi of corrupt electoral practices, Narain filed a petition against her.

Five years passed. On 12 June 1975, the Allahabad High Court upheld Raj Narain's accusations and found Indira Gandhi guilty of violating electoral laws, triggering her call for the Emergency. This was a twenty-one-month period between 25 June 1975 to 25 March 1977. The Indira Gandhi administration fell, and the Janata Party took over.

Under Indira Gandhi's second administration, the MRTP Act 1969 was enacted and came into effect from 1 June 1970. It was repealed in 2002. Parliament passed the Competition Act, 2002, and established the Competition Commission of India on 14 October 2003. The MRTP Commission continued dealing with cases until 1 September 2009 when it stopped accepting filings. Nothing much changed.

Some observations from the report of the M.R.T.P. Commission

The Commission has complimented the Company for its efficient working and performance. The Commission states that "It is really creditable that Bajaj Auto has been able to keep the sale price of the scooter at Rs. 2,280/- for the last five years and absorb the increase in cost of raw material and labour." The report states "The NCAER study gives adequate proof to indicate that there is a definite preference for bajaj scooters in the market". The Commission has also appreciated the Research & Development efforts of the Company and the training facilities being provided by the Company to ensure the availability of a good and skilled labour force. The Commission was impressed by the high level of skill of the workmen and also the standards of quality control and formed a favourable impression of the Company as a result of their visit to its plant. The Commission notes that the Company has followed a prudent financial policy of declaring reasonable dividends and ploughing back large part of its profits in the business for the development of the industry.

The Commission observes that the comparative working has shown that Bajaj Auto has been able to manage more efficiently and generate more funds on its own.

The Commission has complimented the Company's Management and its Managing Director in particular. It states "we are later referring to the fact that the Management of the factory for the last five years has been very efficient. That is the

period during which Shri Rahulkumar has been Managing Director. Furthermore, during the course of the public hearing we were very much impressed by Mr. Rahulkumar Bajaj's command over the facts and figures of the case and his extensive knowledge of business matters."

The Commission states that the Company can expand its manufacturing capacity in the least possible time. It also notes that the price of the scooter to be produced by the new units, if any, which may come up, would be more by at least Rs. 300/- as compared to the price of the Company's scooter.

Expansion would not only eliminate the current shortage of scooters but would also enable the Company to spend substantially on Research & Development and enable it to be in a better position to exploit the export markets. The report goes on to state that if any durable goods in the present context need encouragement surely the scooter can be counted as one among them.

The Commission states that its recommendation to increase the manufacturing capacity of Bajaj Auto to 60,000 scooters per year has been made keeping in mind "the crying demand from the public for more scooters". According to the Commission, "the question has to be dealt with the utmost expedition and our recommendation must be such as can be implemented without any further enquiries or negotiations with the parties and the attendant delay."

Bajaj Auto annual report, 1971–1972.

12

God Is in the Detail: 1968–90

Akurdi, 1970s.

With over four years of experience under Kamalnayan's leadership, the new managing director's three-pronged strategy for Bajaj Auto's future was fully fleshed out by 1968.

The first called for a standardized product for the consumer at a price that allowed a healthy margin. The second recognized that the Bajaj scooter's popularity allowed the company to create capacity based on assured demand and long production runs which, along with a constant focus on costs, would earn high profits for the company. The third was detail. Despite the frustrations of managing in the 'licence-permit raj', Bajaj Auto did well. Adds Bajaj, 'a leader without a team can't do much, but howsoever good a team, if it doesn't have a good leader, it won't have a direction. So, you need both. I was lucky to have a very good team. This translated into a committed, dedicated management. Most of my competitors didn't have this.'

On Kamalnayan's turf, Bajaj Auto hit production and sales of 1,00,000 vehicles in a single financial year. The son matched the 1970 landmark in 1977. In reality, Bajaj had been running the company since 1968, even before he was officially appointed its managing director in 1970 and chairman in 1972 at age thirty-four. 'We did not advertise. I would get letters saying, give me a scooter. I had to write back a long letter saying why I could not give a scooter, a letter that ended with, "you should book now, you will get it after ten years".'

A slim ray of satisfaction wriggled its way in when a team of senior World Bank officials visited the Bajaj Auto factory from 23 January 1972 for four days. 'It is learnt that they rated this company as one of the most efficient units in the Automobile Industry,' a smiling Bajaj reported to shareholders at the 7 October 1972 annual general meeting (AGM).

With the fall of the Indira Gandhi administration in 1977, the Janata Party's new industries minister, George Fernandes, allowed Bajaj Auto to double its licenced capacity to 1,60,000 two-wheelers and three-wheelers. Licencing and price controls however loosened only marginally and pretty much remained in place as it had in the 1960s.

One of Bajaj's Many, Many, Many Rules of Three

The Chetak replaced the Vespa and became a blockbuster and waiting lists for Bajaj scooters stretched to ten years. 'We faced competition head-on, and I concentrated on three things. I said, I must have volume, the lowest cost, and the best quality. It is very simple,' explains Bajaj. 'There is nothing intelligent in that. You don't need to go to Harvard to learn that. If you don't have these three things, you are in trouble. Others failed to do so, and they could not compete with us on quality or price. Best quality would include the latest cutting-edge technology. And that is what I constantly did. I needed scale for both, so I kept going to Delhi to get approvals for expansions.'

Some readers may quibble here, but it's worth keeping in mind that the outcome of Bajaj's strategy can be gauged from the fact that barring Bajaj Auto, not a single scooter brand of the 1960s and 1970s survived the onslaught of the Indo-Japanese ventures in the 1980s.

Naresh Patni elaborated with an example. 'In the Raj of protected economy and licencing when Rahul bhaiya enjoyed absolute monopoly and the customer was not a king, I remember an incident which spoke volumes about his vision and concern about customer care and returning value for money. In 1975, Rahul bhaiya was crossing Nagpur Railway Station. I went to the station to greet him. The moment he got down from the train, he fired a question at me. "Naresh, what happened to the customer complaint that was received by us?" This was an eye-opener for me. In those times, it was a seller-driven economy. It created a permanent impression on me and changed my orientation completely!'

'Ensuring that the consumer obtains the best possible product at the lowest possible price, and the employee gets a fair wage for a day's work, is the criterion of ethics in business,' insisted Bajaj. The government fêted Bajaj and Bajaj Auto for not taking 'any undue advantage of its dominant position'. But it still refused to relax production restrictions.

To some extent, Finance Minister Vishwanath Pratap Singh's 1985 New Economic Policy unclogged avenues of growth. Broadbanding meant that a firm could manufacture products related to the ones they were currently making without the need to obtain a separate licence. Delicencing translated into firms being allowed to expand their plants. 'Who needs a marketing department when

there is a mile-long waiting list?' remarked Bajaj rhetorically. 'The
distribution department held sway—until 1988.' Two-wheeler
models sprouted across the country. Competition arrived with
predictable aggravations.

The New R&D Centre

After Piaggio's formal departure on 1 April 1971, the Vespa was
simply re-badged as 'Bajaj'. They had the machinery Piaggio left
behind, but no longer could Bajaj depend on a partner for technology.

'By the early 1970s, the black chapter for Indian industry had
begun,' explains Bajaj, 'and according to me, was the worst in the
history of independent India. Where did an Escort scooter go?
Nowhere. The two-wheeler division got sold to Yamaha. Jawa, I don't
even know where the company is now. During that decade, hardly
any new technology agreements were signed in the private sector,
especially in the auto industry and the engineering industry. That's
why we started a research and development (R&D) department in
the early 1970s.' A small but enthusiastic workshop emerged. The
Bajaj Chetak scooter appeared on roads in 1972.

A three-wheeler goods carrier had been in the making under
the Piaggio oversight. The energized R&D team reshaped the
design such that it could be marketed as an autorickshaw, a pickup
or a delivery van. 'This model was aimed for exports as well as the
home market,' evokes Bajaj. 'I wanted to smother competition, and
I had three key priorities—improve the fuel efficiency of existing
products, develop new products for niche markets, and come up
with a fundamentally new three-wheeler design.'

In mid-1973, the team showed Bajaj autorickshaw prototypes
with seating capacities of three and four passengers. Test marketing
went well. Now it was up to the management to secure approvals for
plying them as taxi-cabs from road transport authorities in the states.

The next year, the building, now officially dubbed the
'Engineering Centre', saw the team develop a three-wheeler with a
trailer and payload capacity of 715 kg. An earlier version of a pick-up
van got a rear flap and a stronger chassis. The three-wheelers now
came garnished with trafficator lights and an electric windscreen

wiper. Fuel economy, substituting imported parts in favour of local materials, redesigning the braking system, suspension plates, brake drums, reverse gear systems, satellite gear housing for maximum efficiency and economy were the names of the game.

With pretty much the same Akurdi team running Maharashtra Scooters, Priya, a motorized and geared scooter assembled at the Maharashtra Scooters Satara plant from Akurdi CKD packs popped up in showrooms in 1976. In the same year, Akurdi introduced the Bajaj Super, a two-stroke 150 cc scooter, which looked remarkably like the Vespa Super. Both had 8-inch wheels and a powerful headlight. The Bajaj Auto models continued to have a Vespa-like air.

The core problem of scooter parts remained until the late 1970s: Bajaj Auto didn't have the know-why and the know-how to make critical components and remained dependent on Piaggio imports. A two-pronged strategy developed: royalties and imports of components from Piaggio to be set off by funding from the World Bank. Though this strategy played out for some years, Bajaj recognized that this approach could not be more than a temporary relief. A strong export thrust to raise funds for imports became the mantra.

The R&D unit began to show promise when a rear engine autorickshaw, the RE, appeared in 1977, but the team's biggest achievement in 1979 was probably the successful modification of the Bajaj-Chetak scooter to conform to US Federal Motor Vehicle Safety standards during the legal court case battle with Piaggio in the US. The kudos began flowing in.

Skills improved in the 1980s as the R&D team learnt the ropes. 'Internally, in the mid-1980s, many changes were taking place inside Bajaj Auto,' describes Bajaj. The promise he sensed in the R&D team led Bajaj to make an unusual gesture: he situated an engineering research centre in a separate building of its own, including independent paint and assembly facilities.

Bajaj congregated a small ecosystem of knowledge providers. There were three from Italy—Vigel SpA for technical know-how and assistance for the manufacture of special purpose machine tools for captive consumption; IdeA for restyling of the rear engine three-wheeler body; and Industria Prototipi and Serie to create a body design for a new Bajaj scooter. From Spain, Bajaj invited Moto Piatt S.A. for electronic components like magnetos and electronic ignition system; from Australia, the Sarich Orbital Engine Company to develop a fuel injection system for 150 cc scooters to reduce fuel consumption and emissions; and AVL of Austria for engine development.

The pool of specialists expanded in the 1990s and extended to include the Japanese. A technical agreement was struck with Japan's Kubota Corporation in 1995 to source technology for a 417 cc four-stroke diesel engine for three-wheelers. Tokyo Research and Development Centre, a team of former Honda Motor specialists, worked on a scooter prototype from external design and styling to the engine. Americans and Italians continued to work alongside. The mandate to US's Unique Mobility, Inc. was to develop an electric power autorickshaw, as also a prototype electric and hybrid-electric system, and Cagiva, an Italian firm, for the high-end Cagiva CRX, a 150 cc four-stroke scooter.

The in-house R&D team slogged to develop a 100-cc scooter marketed under the brand name Bajaj Cub. A limited-edition release with an electronic ignition system, the Bajaj Cub was released in 1984 and was rather quickly discontinued. Local R&D had some way to go.

Expectations ran high also for the M50. A moped at heart, the M50 was not a regular motorcycle with a petrol tank in the middle. Mirroring Japanese technology in its packaging, the M50 differed only in its scooter-type handlebar-mounted gear shifter. As many as 1.1 million bookings poured in. The orders vanished into thin air just as quickly. Mismatched components affected driveability, fuel efficiency and reliability. Bajaj immediately set up a special task force. R&D suggested a bigger 80 cc engine. The M50 was converted to the acceptable M-80. 'The first day of booking for the Bajaj M-80 was memorable,' remembers Bajaj, 'in the city of Udaipur, there were such lines, with mounted police to keep order.'

A motorcycle, the Kawasaki Bajaj (KB) 100, was born in Waluj in the same year as the Bajaj M-80 was born in Akurdi. The modest success with in-house developed products led to higher confidence in core R&D capabilities. Nevertheless, Bajaj continued to allocate a relatively low amount on R&D as percentage of sales as compared to the amount spent by the global automobile majors stalking his territory.

Marching across India

'As a two-wheeler manufacturer, I saw India change from being a scooter country to a motorcycle country,' recalls Bajaj. 'To a large scooter manufacturer like Bajaj Auto, it naturally created some problems. I did not believe, however, that the scooter as a concept was out. Incidentally, neither did Honda. What was unlikely is that any company can sell hundreds of thousands of an essentially undifferentiated product, year after year, to an increasingly image conscious and relatively price insensitive customer.'

'By the late 1980s, our dealership was changing so marketing had to change,' reminiscences Bajaj. 'What I worried about in that period was competition which geared up faster than Bajaj Auto. We started looking for more dynamic dealers who would actively compete in the market. Our market share dropped from a high of 95 per cent in 1984 to about 64 per cent in 1992. On the other hand, the smaller three-wheeler segment saw a market share of about 70 per cent in 1985–86 surge to 91 per cent in 1992.'

'An automobile dealer naturally looks at the profits from his business and his status in the society and rightly so,' continues Bajaj. 'A dealer is known in his town by the brand he represents. When the market changed from seller to buyer, some dealers had designed for large-scale distribution, and not for individual customer management. In those days, an "invoice" generated by a dealer for a customer could be regarded as either the last point of contact or as the first point of a new relationship. Normally, the second approach would lead to success. No longer did a dealership sell a commodity or a product: it sold a brand. The dealer could create or destroy the value of a brand by the way he sold and serviced the product.'

'Due to our mindsets, we were unable to fully comprehend the implications of fierce competition, continually changing technology, and production capacities being much higher than demand,' recaps Bajaj. 'A big gap developed between customer expectations and the capabilities of some dealers. When the price and quality of all competing vehicles are the same, from which dealer will the customer buy his vehicle? This would depend on the customer's aspirations.'

'The manufacturer can raise the aspirations of a potential customer by the price and quality of his products and by advertising,' continues Bajaj. 'However, was the dealer in a position to honour and satisfy these aspirations by way of sales and service? Dealerships had to change from trading, to selling to marketing. Vehicle dealers began to see the face of the customer. They began to realize that they were selling transportation, a conveyance, and not just a product; that they had to provide quality service for the life of the product and not just redemption of a few service coupons.'

'Most dealers developed the skills and capabilities to achieve better sales volumes and better market share in their territories, but when it came to after sales service, our performance left a great deal to be desired,' said Bajaj. 'Our comparison with good dealerships in the developed world put us in a poor light. An automobile dealership should be in a position to cover its total expenses from the revenue of its workshop and spare parts.'

'A dealer needs to build a long-standing relationship with his customers. The customer has to feel "at home" at the dealership. The customer should be the dealer's permanent prospect for a repeat sale, cross sale and to continuously offer vehicles to him, to his family and to his friends. Customer retention is the best measure of a dealer's performance. Do we know how many customers willingly come back to us even though they have other choices? Do we understand those who do not? Why not? The end of a sale is, or at least should be, the beginning of a relationship between the customer and the dealer. Any successful long-term relationship has these characteristics: communication, understanding and transparency.'

'It is the responsibility of the manufacturer to manufacture the product at the desired price and performance levels and create a brand value or brand equity. However, the dealership is ultimately the place where the customer encounters what may be called the "brand experience". In other words, the manufacturer "builds" the dreams and the dealership "paints" the reality.'

A more robust and committed dealer network gradually emerged. Dealer conferences in Akurdi were initiated to further gain the trust of distributors and dealers. Once the VAX 8800 mainframe computer was up and running in Akurdi, more than a hundred dealers across the country began to interface with it through dial-up telephone links.

Faster, Better, Newer, Cheaper

From end-to-end, the change process took longer than Bajaj anticipated. Over the next eight years, Bajaj completely radically overhauled manufacturing, increased investments in R&D, entered all available two-wheeler segments, restructured its organizational set-up, and built a pan-India computer network. 'No functional area and possibly no one in its more than 18,000 work force, remained untouched by the upheavals,' described Sandipan Deb.

'Political compulsions drove policy, but policy did not only not deliver, it thwarted enterprise,' reprises Bajaj. 'Once, we had to import CRCA[1] deep draw steel sheets. We had to submit details of each component that would be made from it. It was a tough calculation since we needed varying thickness and their use depended on a varying product mix. Then, we needed to keep six months of inventory to cope with the vicissitudes of babudom.[2] Non-value-added activities consumed most of the organization's energies. We would never give a bribe, so our growth was slow. But because the owner was sitting in the company, and everybody was working hard, we did well.'

'Work gravitates to Bajaj like pins to a magnet,' says CII's Tarun Das, half-jokingly. 'He *always* knows the financials inside out, and daily monitors production figures. Low cost is his mantra and cost control his passion. Even though Bajaj Auto was highly professional, one could not spend Rs 5 without Rahul's permission!'

Where there is exciting growth, hierarchies inevitably emerge and multiply. In a dramatic sweep in the mid-1980s, Bajaj slashed management levels from eleven to six. 'Earlier, if a decision had to be implemented on the shop floor, it would be processed through three or four levels of management,' recalls Bajaj. 'We reduced the channel to one or two managers.' A perestroika in computerization enabled

---

[1] CRCA (cold rolled close annealed) is conducted after hot rolling and pickling processes to reduce the thickness of steel and harden the material.
[2] A colloquial reference to the Indian Administrative Service.

the company's four divisions—scooters, motorcycles, three-wheelers and engines—to work in a virtually autonomous fashion.

A global survey of automation and the use of robots in 1987 by *Robotica*, a prominent Cambridge University Press journal, singled out outliers ahead of the curve. A paint robot in the US. An aluminium casting robot in Japan. Machine vision in the UK. A Ford assembly plant in Belgium. And Bajaj Auto Ltd of Akurdi in India.

'It seems computerisation of the manufacturing processes will be a prolonged exercise, but Bajaj Auto has made a start,' wrote *Robotica*'s editors. 'The company plans to install high-speed machinery and some electronic equipment over the next three years. At Bajaj Auto, engineers are currently testing a limited online production control system and the tool room does have some computerised equipment. The manager for special projects believes it will be a long process to change the culture of the plant. The company has, however, shortlisted IBM, DEC and Burroughs to provide main frames with eighty terminals for use in production control and other applications. It also plans to have experimental robots for assembly. Bajaj Auto is probably the second largest scooter manufacturer in the world with sales of \$232 million in its most recent year of trading and with earnings at \$14 million. For the future, the effect of automation in India is difficult to foresee,' added *Robotica*'s editors.

'We wanted to be as good as anyone else in the world in technology, in reaction time, in customer satisfaction,' says Bajaj, 'then and now!'

The Patient Listener

Physically, Bajaj can never stay still. Arms wheel and fly. Toes tap. Mentally, he can be as calm as a pond without ripples when required, and his advice rarely what recipients expect to hear. A couple of examples are included below:

'One of the Bajaj companies had an ongoing dispute with mine,' wrote Shyam Ruia. 'Needless to say, no solution was in sight, and we felt that the staff of the Bajaj company was being quite unreasonable. I'm sure they felt the same about us. As a legal dispute between our families was quite out of the question, the only option was arbitration. It was then that I thought of Rahul as the arbitrator. His decision was overwhelmingly in our favour.'

Staring at a face-off with Datta Samant, Mumbai's feisty trade union leader in the 1980s, a harried Hariprasad Anandkishore Nevatia, managing director of Hercules Hoists, a Bajaj group firm, reached out to Bajaj for advice and solace.

'The trade union leader workers of Hercules Hoists had become very unruly,' recalls Nevatia. 'In 1981/82 while negotiating a settlement, I agreed for a burden of Rs 10 lakh per annum (p.a.) to avoid closure. However, I had to step-by-step increase it to Rs 13 lakh per annum. Finally, when the agreement was to be signed, the workmen insisted the figure be raised to Rs 13.50 lakh. The atmosphere in the factory had grown very tense. As suggested by Shri Ramkrishnaji, I along with Purshottam ji Jhunjhunwala met Rahul bhai to seek his advice. After listening to all the details patiently, Rahul bhai said that it was not a question of 50,000, but if you now agree, the workmen may ask more and even if they do not, it will become difficult for you to run the factory. Closure of the factory for ten months followed. It was reopened on our terms. Though it was a very painful experience, our relationship with workmen radically changed and we could handle the situation with greater confidence. It also helped in all future negotiations. Rahul bhai is a very attentive listener.'

'I find two things most striking about Rahul,' concludes Anami N. Roy, Director General of Police, Maharashtra, India and the former Police Commissioner of Mumbai. 'One is his belief that "God is in the detail". Whatever he undertakes, he must go into its roots, acquire thorough knowledge, and partly inflict that information on his family and at least a few friends. And the other is his capacity to say "NO". He can singularly say "no" to the highest and mightiest for anything and everything. Many of us public servants have been told about the abominable "No, man!" in our training academies, who find ourselves in situations required to say "no", and thereby face a lot of flak and "consequences". But Rahul, the lucky one, has none of it all.'

13

The Chairman: 1972–2021

The third chairman.

'Looking back, the 1970s was probably my toughest decade,' says Bajaj. His father's passing away on 1 May 1972 hit hard. Kamalnayan was en route from Delhi to Baroda with a stopover in Ahmedabad to see his sister Madalsa and brother-in-law, Shriman Narayan, then governor of Gujarat. Over dinner, plans were made to visit the Sabarmati Ashram the next day.

A diabetic, Kamalnayan had suffered a heart attack in 1969. He seemed perfectly happy and rested when they broke up for the night on Sunday, 30 April 1972, and Kamalnayan retired to his room. In the early morning of Monday, 1 May, he had a heart attack. 'Indications are that when he felt his last moment had arrived, he got up—by tradition, a Hindu should not die in bed—and lay down on the carpet, taking care to lay his head outside the carpet so as to pass away on the lap of Mother Earth. He was found the next morning in that posture with a serene expression on his face,' recounts Kamalaksha Vittal Kamath, Kamalnayan's long-time secretary. Hindus cremate as quickly as possible.

'My father did not only act by his instincts,' Bajaj recalls those moments stoically. 'He would apply his intelligence rationally and objectivity to every issue, and yet with a touch of humanism. He had great faith in his analytical skills. He did believe in God, but his logical way of thinking ensured that he never sought the refuge of fate. He used to say that those who rely on fate achieve little; whatever one acquires is possible only through a scientific and objective approach.'

'Kakaji founded and built upon the edifice of our business almost from ground up,' Bajaj recounts. 'He never involved himself or spent time in the minutiae of day-to-day activities, but he had a great grasp of business matters. If the need arose, he could give such insightful ideas and solutions that none of us could have ever thought of. It is because of such inputs that the Bajaj Group could rise to such heights within such a short span of time.'

'True to his nature, he was never bothered about success or failure,' continues Bajaj. 'He believed only in action. He believed that a person ought to try his best to complete a task that has been taken up, irrespective of how difficult it might be. He felt that the line dividing success and failure is a very thin one.' Bajaj adopted his father's credo.

The Bajaj Auto board composed of Madanmohan Ruia, Viren Shah, Manmohan Lal Gauba, D.S. Mulla, Rishabdas Ranka and Ramkrishna Bajaj, appointed Bajaj as chairman. He was thirty-four.

And he had a tough journey ahead of him: the Indian economy was tanking, the managing agency system was headed for its demise, business would have to be conducted differently.

Facing the Future

'Catch-up industrialization began in the early 1970s,' Deepak Nayyar, economist and academician, reminds us, but it didn't get far. Restrictive policies claimed they were there to protect and grow the market, but Bajaj felt stymied from all sides.

'I met Rahul bhai for the first time at my home,' Bakul Patel remarked at the time. 'He had come to see my husband, Rajni Patel, who was a close associate and adviser to Indira Gandhi, then prime minister of India. This was around 1974–75. Rajni was president of the Bombay Pradesh Congress Committee. Rahul bhai came in a "delegation" along with a young Sharad Pawar, then a promising politician, and Ajit Gulabchand, a scion of a prominent industrial family in Maharashtra and a budding industrialist.'

'They had come to discuss an issue concerning an industrial policy matter in Maharashtra,' continued Patel. 'Those were the days of the licence raj, and perhaps they sought Rajni's help and advocacy in presenting their case to the then union minister of industry for redressal of their problems. As I sat listening to their presentation, I was struck by Rahul bhai's powers of persuasion in driving home their point of view. Clearly, with his good looks, self-assured persona and facility with words, Rahul bhai emerged as the most articulate and poised spokesperson of the "delegation". This display of leadership qualities and power of advocacy stayed etched in my memory.'

For Bajaj and Bajaj Auto, the oil crisis triggered by a war in the Middle East[1] from 6–24 October 1973 by a coalition of Arab states led by Egypt and Syria against Israel was a thwack. Bajaj's scooters ran on petrol. He listened to the radio as oil prices quadrupled from $3 to $12. In the evenings, he watched Air Doordarshan's grainy black and white television signals, relayed from the Bombay TV station to Poona,[2] and launched on Gandhi Jayanti on 2 October 1973.

---

[1] Referred to variously as the Yom Kippur War, Ramadan War, or October War.
[2] Poona became Pune in 1978.

The oil crisis led to double digit inflation in India as well as a global recession. 'The mid- to late-1970s is when India got left behind China,' Bajaj shared with Datar. 'China's GDP, in the 1970s I believe, was about the same as India's. But under Deng Xiaoping, China de-collectivized agriculture, opened to foreign investment, and permitted entrepreneurs to start businesses.' India's economic growth rate averaged around 3.5 per cent per annum. The year 1980 was an eye-opener: according to World Bank data, 1980 saw India's real GDP growth drop to minus 5 per cent.

Corruption was rampant. The State Trading Corporation, a public sector company, for example, in the 1970s made money in quite bizarre ways. 'Foreign diplomats stationed in New Delhi could import cars through the corporation,' describes Tirthankar Roy, economic historian, 'cars which would be sold second-hand to Indians. The business was highly profitable for all concerned. The diplomats got the cars they wanted, the state earned tariffs of 200–300 per cent and given the famously dull design and inefficiency of Indian cars, second-hand cars sold at a premium on the original price, the benefits of which the Corporation pocketed.'

Ciao! Ciao!

'Both Piaggio and we wanted to renew the agreement for at least another five years,' remembers Bajaj, but *arrivederci*[3] was not an option. 'In the 1970s the Indira Gandhi government did not renew a single collaboration agreement in the automobile industry, as also in many other industries. We saw a period of extreme socialism.'

The licence-permit raj did not mean there was no competition. In the 1970s, there were half-a-dozen motorcycle manufacturers with Ideal Java, Enfield and Rajdoot leading the field. The Lambretta continued to hang around in the scooter category. Technologically self-sufficient scooter and moped segments enabled two new entrants in the scooter segment and three in the moped segment.

The Foreign Exchange Regulation Act (FERA), introduced on 1 January 1974, had a more far-reaching effect. The Act was

---

[3] Hello and see you soon!

formulated to regulate foreign exchange and imposed stringent regulations on certain kind of payments, the dealings in foreign exchange and securities, and transactions that had an indirect impact on the foreign exchange and the import and export of currency. The restrictions caused technological stagnation, as a consequence of which few new products or firms entered the market since this segment depended almost entirely on foreign collaborations for technology.

In the scramble for foreign exchange in the mid-1970s, the Indira Gandhi administration introduced a scheme of priority allotment of scooters against foreign exchange remittance equivalent to Rs 5000 per scooter. Under this scheme 18,200 'bajaj 150' scooters were released up to 31 March 1975, 'thus enabling the country to earn foreign exchange of over Rs 9 crore,' Bajaj wrote to shareholders with some satisfaction. The following year, the government earmarked 24,000 'bajaj 150' scooters to be released under this scheme. 'This will result in the Company's further contribution to the foreign exchange earnings of Rs 12 crore,' he added. And so on . . .

The Czars of Development Finance

'I first met Rahul bhai at the Akurdi plant in the late 1970s, where I had gone for appraising a loan proposal. He may not remember it,' described Kundapur Vaman Kamath. 'I saw a smart, young business leader, sharp, quick and easy to engage with. As a young officer in ICICI in the 1970s, I admired Bajaj Auto as a symbol of the new India. I was impressed by the can-do attitude of the company which produced a scooter so desirable to the Indian public that it had a waiting list of a few years.'

The concept of development finance and planning as an ideology arrived in India.[4] As K.V. Kamath's direct boss and ICICI's chairman,

---

[4] Financial institutions established in the early phase of planned economic development include: Industrial Credit and Investment Corporation of India (ICICI, 1955), Life Insurance Corporation (LIC, 1956), Refinance Corporation for Industries (RFI, 1958, later taken over by IDBI), Agriculture Refinance Corporation (1963, precursor of ARDC and NABARD), Unit Trust of India (UTI, 1964), Industrial Development Bank of India (IDBI, 1964), Rural Electrification Corporation (REC, 1969), Housing

Hasmukh T. Parekh, explained, 'Although an entrepreneur plans a project, it is a development bank which, in the process of financing it, vets the project and provides for a second independent assessment of its viability. Development banks do not seek to reject projects but endeavour to remove their shortcomings to improve their viability. Moreover, once a project is approved, development banks try to follow it till the execution stage thereby providing a constant check on the progress of the project.'

'Financing is a function independent and outside of project planning and implementation,' continued Parekh. 'The use of development banks in financing public and joint sector units is a recognition of this independent service.' And as Deepak Nayyar points out, 'Lower rates of return are justifiable for development banks in the short run or medium term, because these rates of return are much higher in the long term for patient capital with the benefit of inside information.'

In the 1940s, the Industrial Finance Corporation of India (IFCI) came up in 1948. In the 1950s, it was the Industrial Credit and Investment Corporation of India (ICICI, 1955), and the Life Insurance Corporation of India (LIC, 1956). In the 1960s, it was the Industrial Development Bank of India (IDBI) and the Unit Trust of India (UTI), both created in 1964 as apex lending institutions through a legislative act of Parliament and as subsidiaries of the Reserve Bank of India. The 1970s saw the emergence of the Industrial Investment Bank of India (IIBI, 1971); the National Bank for Agriculture and Rural Development (NBARD 1982) in 1982, and the Export-Import Bank of India (EXIM, 1982). Development finance kept increasing in vigorous milieus.

IDBI, under Serajul Haq Khan, grew to be a bigger financier than ICICI. IDBI's role soon extended to refinancing loans, technology development, and banking services, with an advisory role on projects, management and restructuring. On 16 February 1976, the Reserve Bank of India (RBI) transferred IDBI to the Government of India.

---

and Urban Development Corporation (HUDCO, 1970), Industrial Reconstruction Corporation of India (IRCI, 1971, precursor of IIBI) and General Insurance Corporation of India (GIC, 1972).

IDBI became the principal financial institution engaged in financing promoting and developing industry.

Access to state funding meant that DFIs could mobilize resources at interest costs lower than market sources, and made DFIs the first port of call for finance for Indian business, such as Bajaj Auto. Naturally, strings were attached. The terms included stringent conditions not only with regard to security, repayment of the principal and timely payment of interest but also 'dos' and 'don'ts' for the managements in running projects funded by them. There was a system of lead institution and participating institution in line with a consortium arrangement of banks. In many cases, the terms included a right to convert part of the loan to equity capital during the life of the loan at a predetermined price.

Disbursements in 1970–1971 were modest, amounting to a mere 2.2 per cent of India's gross capital formation but grew steadily, to reach 10.3 per cent in 1990–1991 and 15.2 per cent in 1993–1994. Gradually, several DFIs progressed from bodies created by various acts of Parliament to companies incorporated under the provisions of the Companies Act.

... and Their Nominee Directors

With a loan comes the financier's right to nominate one or more directors to represent its DFI on the board of an assisted company. 'Nominee Directors' enjoyed certain privileges such as being not liable to retire by rotation, nor were they required to hold qualification shares. Their primary role was to safeguard not only the interest of the nominating institutions but also public interest by acting as watchdogs against undesirable activities of promoter management.

To monitor companies, the DFIs determined the number of nominee directors on a board in consultation with either ICICI or IDBI. An elite corps of well-trained full-time directors representing the shareholder emerged. Representing DFIs at both the all-India level and state level, their appointments were institutionalized after government guidelines for conversion of loan into equity were issued in June 1971.

Once the novelty and the dust settled, guidelines blossomed riotously. The fiduciary duties of nominee directors expanded. The right to nominate one-third of the total strength of the board. One director less for the private sector promoter. The equity ratio of the private promoter, general public and DFI to be 26:25:49. The right to appoint the sensitive whole-time finance director position. And, critically, the DFIs had the right to nominate the chairman while the private promoter could nominate the managing director. The bundle of DFI rights was capacious and kept growing.

Overall, the chairmanship was the sole promoter victory. Or was it? Did the bureaucracy really back off?

'Appointing senior personnel such as Chairman and Managing Directors of the institutions as nominees on the boards of assisted companies was an undesirable practice,' suggested the Committee on Public Undertakings austerely, 'since the reports of Nominee Directors are reviewed by financial institutions and in case chairmen were appointed as nominee directors, the review of their reports would not be possible.'

Towards the end of the decade, *India Today's* sleuths discovered that between 1970 to 1979:

- The number of bureaucrats swelled from 10.5 million to over 15 million.
- The central government's expenditure grew from Rs 1661 crore to Rs 6000 crore.
- Government revenue from income tax spiralled 1100 per cent from Rs 106 crore to Rs 1365 crore.
- Total income from taxes leapt from Rs 2200 crore to Rs 8100 crore.
- Petrol prices jumped from Rs 1.11 per litre to Rs 4.43 per litre.
- A cooking gas cylinder cost Rs 23 in 1970 compared to Rs 40 in 1979.
- The Ambassador car, available in 1970 for Rs 20,000, set a buyer back by Rs 50,000.

No wonder Bajaj felt straitjacketed.

The Call of the Siren

'Maybe there is less fire in the belly,' Bajaj muses as he loosens the reins, allowing senior executives some say in policy and execution.

'I am totally with Lee Iacocca in one thing—I don't believe in consensus-based decision-making. I ask for other people's opinions in key matters, and I give a fair hearing, but I don't take a vote. I make the decisions.'

Smoking and a heart attack are the best of friends, but not yours. Somehow Bajaj managed to overlook the wisecrack, despite constant badgering by Murli Deora. Bajaj gave up smoking only after suffering a heart attack.

Every doctor Bajaj has met has a story to tell about him. 'I was in Breach Candy Hospital with Rahul,' recalls Purvez Grant, cardiologist and director of Pune's Ruby Hall Cardiac Centre. 'He suddenly saw a friend he knew. This man had just had an angiogram for a heart valve problem. Rahul strolled over, met the relatives and it was not long before Rahul started talking to the relatives on heart valve surgery. He talked non-stop, and I must say, he spoke very well and managed to impress the relatives. Finally, one relative put up his hand and asked, "Sir, are you a doctor?" Fortunately for the patient, Rahul said no.'

'I'm an orthopaedic surgeon,' adds Rajan Kothari, 'but when I met Rahul sir, I don't know if he was meeting one, or I was meeting one. He interviewed me with very incisive questions. What struck me most is his childlike thirst for knowledge, and ability to make complex things very simple.' Dr Appaji Krishnan pretty much underwent the same treatment at Bajaj's hand: 'Every time I have met him, he never ceases to surprise me with the perfectness with which he has prepared for the encounter.'

On 2 November 2001, after years of fighting, Deora won a landmark Supreme Court case directing all states and centrally ruled territories to immediately prohibit smoking in public places such as auditoriums, hospital buildings, health institutions, educational institutions, libraries, court buildings, public offices, and public conveyance, including the railways. But the legislation fell short of accepting the bidi challenge.

14

Foreign Affairs: 1972–2021

Indonesia. Time magazine.

In March 2015, the city of Hawassa in Ethiopia came to a standstill: the drivers of three-wheeler motorcycle taxis went on strike. With a population of 2,50,000, and only four state-owned buses, Hawassa relied on the taxis known as *bajaj*. As one passenger shared with research sociologists Daniel Mains and Eshetayehu Kinfu, 'If the *bajaj* is lost, then everything is lost. Without the *bajaj* we cannot move, and there is no city.'

1983: a quintessential chase scene in the James Bond thriller, *Octopussy*. The villain's henchman Gobinda (Kabir Bedi) pursues Bond (Roger Moore) through the streets of Udaipur, the British super spy clinging on for dear life to an autorickshaw driven with infectious glee by Vijay (Vijay Amritraj).

Spicy tales of Bajaj Auto's three-wheeler are legendary across the world. It's a tuk-tuk or rick in the Philippines, South Africa and Cambodia; a bajay in Jakarta, Indonesia; a chand gari in Pakistan; a posy in Madagascar; a raksha in Sudan; a bajaji in the city of Dar es Salaam in Tanzania; a baby taxi in Bangladesh; an autorickshaw in India; a keke napep or keke maruwa in Nigeria; and the tok-tok displaced the donkeys in Gaza. And this is just the short list.[1]

India has never been a stranger to three-wheelers—two wheels at the back and a skinny man on foot in front pulling the chariot forward. The motorized tuk-tuk originated from the design of rickshaws prevalent on the streets of Bangkok during World War II. A small engine was fitted inside a traditional rickshaw, and the tuk-tuk was born.

With the near destruction of European factories, a few Italian family firms like Piaggio were quick to rebuild from ground zero. They went all over the world, looking for local entrepreneurs with whom they could profitably share their technical expertise. Several versions of mechanical three-wheelers began popping up across the world, including Akurdi. Here 3,00,000 acres of barren land was about to sprout into an industrial enclave.

As Bajaj Auto's young plant grew, so did requirements for Piaggio's components. The only way to pay for imports in the early 1970s was to export. The catch-22 lay in the guidelines on joint

---

[1] Lapa, tukxi, pigeon, samosa, tempo, moto-taxi or simply auto.

ventures overseas promulgated by the Ministry of Foreign Trade in December 1969.

'On one hand, the Indian government sought to maximize foreign trade and net foreign exchange earnings through foreign investment,' analysed historian Dennis J. Encarnation. 'On the other hand, the ministry insisted on exporting original Indian-made equipment in lieu of equity; and preferred minority equity participation unless otherwise demanded by the hosts. These objectives were endorsed repeatedly by various parliamentary committees in the 1960s and early 1970s as the Indira Gandhi administration faced an evergrowing foreign exchange crisis and periodic recessions, particularly in the engineering and capital goods industries.'

Tally-ho!

In Akurdi towards early 1970, thirty-two-year-old Bajaj recruited a small group of managers dedicated to the new outreach: Jayant Shah as executive director, Ajay Bhargava as export manager and D.V. Borgaonkar as works manager. The group began scouting for foreign dealers interested in promoting and selling scooters and three-wheelers. Daringly, there were even hopes of assembly plants supplied by CKD packs from India. The Bajaj Auto team won a hit in Nigeria in its first attempt in 1972 when it secured a Rs 2.5 million order for 1000 scooters and three-wheelers and spare parts. Experiences in building scooter franchises in India would segue to discovering and developing a global franchise for Bajaj Auto's entire portfolio.

After gaining independence from Pakistan with a fair bit of help from India (including trucking petrol across borders by volunteer academics like Sumantra Ghoshal at the wheel), the newly created People's Republic of Bangladesh was in deep recovery mode. On a roll, the next year, the team secured an export order of Rs 6.2 million in 'free foreign exchange' for 1500 Bajaj three-wheeler chassis from the Trading Corporation of Bangladesh. The order was meticulously executed within four months.

With her treasury low in funds, the Indira Gandhi administration introduced a priority allotment scheme for the much-desired Bajaj

150 scooters. Towards the end of the 1974 financial year,[2] 18,200 scooters were released at Rs 5000 per scooter, earning Rs 9 crore of foreign exchange. Next year's permissions were a notch higher: 24,000 scooters bringing in Rs 12 crore of forex. Orders for scooters and three-wheelers began to trickle in from Australia, Sudan, Bahrain, Hong Kong and Yemen. The bajaj-Chetak would become so popular in the overseas market that there was nothing left over for the local market for quite some time.

Also in 1974, a meeting with Dhaka's Mukhlesur Rahman was an early turning point for the Bajaj export team. In short order, Bajaj and Rahman agreed on terms. Rahman founded Menoka Motors in Chittagong, and Bangladesh's first assembly plant for three-wheeler autorickshaws and two-wheeler scooters came up in 1978 under a technical know-how collaboration agreement with Bajaj Auto. A man of many parts, Rahman created a flourishing business empire stretching over a dozen sectors.

The team powered on. The first half of February 1975 saw Bajaj welcome two collaborators to Akurdi, keen to enter technical collaborations for his two- and three-wheelers: Indonesia's P.T. Tunas Bekasi Motor Company on 2 February; and a week later with Taiwan's Paijifa Industrial Company on 9 February.

A country of islands, Indonesia[3] was in fervent growth mode when the Bajaj Auto team recced Jakarta. Under the Suharto regime, oil production increased after the introduction of production-sharing contracts ended a period of uncertainty about the position of foreign petroleum companies in Indonesia. As economic historian Pierre van der Eng explains, real GDP accelerated to an annual average of 7.1 per cent in a country where the population was growing at 2.1 per cent.

The Uttara Group's biggest firm, Indonesia Motors, was not only an importer of new and used cars of Fiat, Holden, and

---

[2] India's current fiscal year was adopted by the colonial British government in 1867 to align India's financial year with that of the British Empire.

[3] Indonesia's island capitals: Bali, Biak, Borneo, Celebes, Ceram, Halmahera, Java, Lombok, New Guinea, Sumatra, Timor.

Mercedes-Benz, it also had several petrol pumps, and more than one finger in the oil deals awash in Indonesia.

Shades of Akurdi began flowing into Indonesia Motors' cavernous sheds where Bajaj's three-wheeler CKD kits were unpacked and assembled, ready to be rolled out for the local market. The news spread by word of mouth. The delta island of Banjarmasin started importing Bajaj three-wheelers for both locals and tourists. In a post-Suharto era, oil-rich Indonesia opened up further under President Abdurrahman Wahid, and a brisk rivalry bloomed between Bajaj Auto, Honda, Suzuki, Yamaha, Kawasaki, Vespa, Mahator and Jialing.

In the next near future, towards 2005, Bajaj began planning Bajaj Auto's first full-fledged three-wheeler plant for Indonesia. Having one's own plant would save on high import duties and effectively take on competition from the Japanese, Chinese and Taiwanese. A financial consultancy group, Boentaro, chipped in with 5 per cent equity. With K.S. Grihapathy as its new head, P.T. Bajaj Indonesia opened its doors.

Sufficiently happy with the Bangladesh and Indonesia outcomes, the Bajaj team's next foot forward was Taiwan. 'We signed a deal with Paijifa Industrial Company Ltd on 9 February 1975 in Akurdi,' recalls Bajaj, 'just a few days after the Indonesians left.' Over the next decade, the Paijifa collaboration headed by Eddy Tansil, worked well for both parties—until China's sudden cancellation of a US $2 million motorcycle order plunged Taiwan's largest scooter exporter into a financial crisis in July 1985.

There was history. Under Deng Xiaoping in 1978, 'Beijing put great store on growing economic interaction with Taipei,' explains Kuala Lumpur's Professor Muthiah Alagappa, 'believing that growing economic interaction with mutual benefits would reduce cross-Strait political tension, buy time for Beijing and eventually pave the way for Taiwan to unify with the mainland.' The PRC[4] waived tariffs on Taiwanese goods, gave them priority treatment and discounted sales to Taiwan by 20 per cent. Towards 1981 however, 'with a growing trade deficit and an overheating economy, the

---

[4] People's Republic of China (PRC).

PRC withdrew these preferential treatments,' continues Alagappa, 'causing Taiwanese exports to decline in 1982 and 1983.' China formally opened its domestic market to Taiwanese investment, shipping and trade in 1985, but the news on the street was tough. 'Taiwan's China traders turn cautious after an initial rush to trade with China,' blared the Business Times on 31 July 1985. 'Taiwanese businessmen are treading more cautiously after the cancellation of orders that have landed several companies in serious trouble.' 'A favourite example is the experience of Paijifa Industrial Co., a motorcycle maker,' reported Fortune's Louis Kraar and Patricia A. Langan, 'which suspended operations after several Hong Kong companies cancelled orders for 6400 motorcycles destined for China, leaving the company more than $2 million in debt.'

From the sidelines, the Akurdi group read and watched the news, flabbergasted at the unveiling of Tansil's real avatar and the unravelling of Paijifa Industrial Co. In a news statement, Jakarta's Movement of Citizens Concerned About State Assets revealed that Tansil, a former chief executive of the Jakarta-based Golden Key Group, was earlier sentenced to twenty years in prison for his role in a corruption scandal, and escaped from his Jakarta jail in May 1996 with help from prison guards. According to the Wall Street Journal, an Indonesian watchdog group claimed that Tansil was 'the country's best-known escaped convict, lives in China and was active in its beer industry'.

For the Bajaj team, looking eastwards didn't prevent looking westwards, upwards and downwards. Nigeria entered Akurdi's lexicon. With the end of the civil war with Biafra in January 1970, rehabilitation and road works started in major cities under General Yakubu Gowon's administration. The Organization of the Petroleum Exporting Countries (OPEC) flung open its doors in 1971.

By the mid-1970s, Nigeria, with its 6 million population, emerged as the dominant economy in sub-Saharan Africa. Oil prices increased Nigeria's terms of trade by more than 300 per cent in 1974, resulting in a significant transfer of wealth to the country. With coins jingling in their pockets, a ban on motorcycles hurt for some time, but was a gain for Bajaj's three-wheeler keke napep and keke maruwa.[5] Nigeria started shaping up as Bajaj Auto's largest market outside India for two- and three-wheelers, with TVS and Kinetic tagging behind Bajaj Auto.

A euphoric Bajaj ran an advertisement on the third cover page of the Asian edition of *Time* magazine, perhaps the first Indian advertiser to do so.

Changing of the Guard

'Rajiv took charge of exports from 2007 onwards, and he substantially expanded our overseas sales,' smiles Bajaj. 'I believe a company has to be a leader in its domestic market if it has to sustain the growth of its exports. Although I was very happy with Bajaj Auto's export performance, I was concerned that not only the Chinese but also the Japanese, may catch up in the markets where Bajaj Auto was a leader.'

'My decision to reposition Bajaj Auto from being a domestic player to becoming a global one was my toughest moment,' says Rajiv, 'this meant managing the new marketing, technological, and operational competencies that the company needed; and at the same time, managing old products, plants and people rendered obsolete by the new strategy. The width of an organization's product portfolio must be inversely proportional to the breadth of the markets that it is seeking to address. That for mature businesses to be successful, while good quality products are necessary, only sharply positioned brands are sufficient. In the words of Jack Trout, the American advertising guru, 'Solving the problem is easy, but selling the solution is difficult as one seeks to change mindset.'

---

[5] Named after Lagos' military Governor, Buba Marwa, in the late 1990s.

15

The Third Karta: 1972–94

Ramkrishna and Mohandas Karamchand Gandhi.

With Kamalnayan's passing in 1972, Bajaj became Bajaj Auto's second chairman and his uncle, Ramkrishna, the Bajaj Group's third Karta. 'To replace a legend is never easy. To replace a legend when times change, and the legacy needs an overhaul is even more difficult,' Sumantra Ghoshal once commented. And that was the challenge facing Ramkrishna.

As the elder, Ramkrishna automatically became custodian of the finances in the Hindu undivided family (HUF), responsible for the well-being of the group's businesses and every family member, besides maintaining strict discipline. On the cusp of turning fifty, he was shaky from his loss. Pulling himself together, Ramkrishna saw his new role as essentially being 'a bridge between Kamalnayan and the younger generation'.

Unlike his charismatic brother, Ramkrishna's was a quieter personality, and appropriate for the times. With the abolishment of the MRTP Act, the Bajaj business empire was ripe for growth. Plenty of talented family members, cousins and in-laws were available.

Ramkrishna's induction into the family business was at Hindustan Sugar Mills in 1947. October 1962 saw his portfolio expand to include Bajaj Electricals and its associates (Hind Lamps, Matchwell Electricals, Radio & Electricals, and Kaycee Industries). 'I am finding considerable interest in production work,' he admitted to Acharya Vinoba Bhave in a letter. After the abolition of the managing agency system, Ramkrishna took over as managing director of Bajaj Electricals in 1970, and of Radio Lamp Works between 1970 to 1980.

Every boy was expected to be bright. Failure wasn't in the lexicon. Each successfully enrolled either in the US's Ivy League or in Europe's. Each returned to base waving his MBA certificate. Bajaj graduated from HBS. Shishir from New York's Stern School of Business. Shekhar got his from New York University, Madhur from Switzerland's IMD and Niraj from HBS. The Bajaj group's third generation burgeoned under Ramkrishna's oversight.

On his return to India from Harvard, Bajaj chose Bajaj Auto. Shishir joined his uncle, Rameshwarprasad Nevatia (Jamnalal's eldest son-in-law), at Hindustan Sugar. Shekhar joined Bajaj Electricals and would become its managing director. Madhur made the Bajaj Auto's Aurangabad plant his berth. And Niraj settled down in Mukand Iron & Steel with oversight by Viren Shah and his sons

Rajesh and Suketu. Over time, each would climb his own corporate ladder to reach the chairmanship.

Below the promoter level were, and are, hundreds of exceptional managers, carefully selected, tested and retested for their backbone in the management of difficult situations, and to support the Bajaj ethos. Activities included scooters, three-wheelers, motorcycles, steel, alloy castings equipment, sugar, cement, engineering services, electricals (industrial and consumer), material handling equipment, switches and motor controls, trading, ayurvedic medicines, and consultancy. The group's myriad company annual reports are classic examples of the Bajaj group's ability and capacity to make every paisa work.

A journalist once asked Bajaj how he relates to Ramkrishna. 'My uncle is the head of the Bajaj family and is not to be lightly taken,' responded Bajaj. 'We accept his position unquestioningly. I don't have to consult him on every decision, but we talk over matters. There is no secrecy involved. He knows when to advise and what lines not to cross. His fairness and objectivity are legend. Not once in my lifetime have my brother or I felt that Chachaji was favouring his own sons as against my brother and me. Basically, it is his generosity, impartiality and his own acceptance of his limitations that keep us all together. He delegates power and that is no mean achievement.'

And how does Ramkrishna relate to Bajaj, asked M.V. Kamath. 'You see, in a way, we are all beneficiaries of the dynamism and success of Bajaj Auto as it has helped trigger what has been described as "the Bajaj Renaissance". Still, success has not gone to Rahul's head. He is humble, without much ego and is loved by everybody. His brother and my own children adore him. To them he is a hero. Even I have learnt a lot from him. Besides, he has had a major role to play in preserving the family unity. In spite of the success and achievement, he has never been overbearing. On the other hand, he has been considerate and fair in his attitude and, in his own as well as his family's lifestyle, has consistently endeavoured to conform to the common family standards. Because of the example set by him, there is harmony among all brothers and their wives.'

The Constant Gardener

Managing the political environment is central. Ramkrishna's relationship with the Nehru family was close but not particularly cordial. It reached its first nadir at the fag end of Jawaharlal Nehru's election campaign held between 19–25 February 1962 for the third Lok Sabha. A few weeks earlier, on 5 January, Ramkrishna wrote to Congress president N. Sanjiva Reddy, resigning from the Congress and Youth Congress. Nehru won with over 70 per cent of the seats in the Lok Sabha.

Fences needed mending. Nehru agreed to meet Ramkrishna on 1 May 1962 in New Delhi. Ramkrishna wanted to rejoin the Congress. 'Nehru was cagey,' wrote M.V. Kamath. 'He could not have easily forgotten that, only a few weeks earlier, Ramkrishna had challenged his moral authority. Nehru told Ramkrishna that it would not be proper for him to rejoin Congress so soon, in order not to cause an uproar in the party. Ramkrishna assured Nehru that he would work from outside the Congress until he received the green signal from the prime minister. Nehru remained unmoved. All Nehru would say was "Let's see what people think".'

Nehru died on 27 May 1964. Three prime ministers[1] later, the bane of Ramkrishna's life arrived. Where Indira was concerned, rules were different for different people. Nestled inside freshly generated legalese, a new clause had been quietly introduced. Buried in the hundreds of pages was a restriction on judicial scrutiny of the post of prime minister. Indira was India and India was Indira was the new slogan, free to do whatever she liked, and by association, so would her younger son, Sanjay.

The Emergency (25 June 1975–21 March 1977) is one of the most controversial periods in the history of independent India. Fakhruddin Ali Ahmed, the President of India, bestowed on Indira Gandhi the power to rule by decree, suspending elections and civil liberties. A historic amendment was introduced and rushed through the Lok Sabha on 7 August 1975. The next day the amendment was introduced and rushed through the Rajya Sabha. Seventeen state assemblies, summoned on Saturday, 9 August, ratified the amendment.

President Ahmad gave his assent on Sunday, 10 August. Civil servants issued the gazette notification in the afternoon. The Emergency arrived. It remained intact for twenty-one months

---

[1] Gulzarilal Nanda 1964. Lal Bahadur Shastri 1964–66. Gulzarilal Nanda 1966–66. Indira Gandhi 1966–77.

(25 June 1975–21 March 1977) and coloured the dynamics of the country's political system. The Bajaj family would become a pesky thorn for Indira for life.

What's Up at the Kendra?

The mood was grim at a meeting of the trustees of the Vishwa Yuvak Kendra, chaired by Naval Tata. Tata had surprising news. He recently had talks with Sanjay Gandhi and Yashpal Kapur, Indira Gandhi's close aide. Sanjay Gandhi told him that although at an earlier stage he had been interested in the Kendra building, he was now no longer interested in it. Sohrab P. Godrej chipped in: 'When he met Sanjay Gandhi, the latter gave the impression that he did not know the manner in which the building was acquired but was still interested in it.'

More alarming was Ramkrishna's update. A few days earlier, Ramkrishna had met Vidya Charan Shukla[2] and Mohammad Yunus,[3] separately. Shukla had urged all the trustees to resign and leave the matter in the hands of Sanjay Gandhi. Yunus went one step further. Accept Shukla's advice and don't antagonize the government, Yunus told Ramkrishna bluntly. 'If the Trustees offer any resistance, they could be put behind the bars.'

On hearing this, an upset Tata 'expressed himself against the highhanded way in which the Government had dealt with the Trust . . . and was of the view that all the Trustees should resign'. On this note, he excused himself before the meeting was concluded as he had another engagement elsewhere. As he was leaving, Tata said he was sending his resignation to the Trust.

The debate seriously ruffled Professor V.V. John. 'I told the Chairman, Mr Naval Tata that I was not prepared to resign. I further told the Trustees present in the meeting that I could not abdicate the trust reposed in me particularly in the circumstances in which we have been landed by the Government . . . I told the Trustees that

---

[2] Vidya Charan Shukla: minister of parliamentary affairs of India (1993–96) and member of the Lok Sabha (1991–96).

[3] Mohammad Yunus: joined the Indian Foreign Service in 1947 to become one of Indira Gandhi's most trusted advisers, particularly during the Emergency (1975–77).

I had no intention (of) making it easy for any outsider to step in. I further said that the threat of detention in jail could have no effect on me and that people much better than us had already been sent to jail,' John would depose to the Shah Commission.

Ramkrishna had sensed something was brewing when Shukla approached him that Saturday on 22 May 1973. The prime minister would like a change in the composition of the Board of Trustees managing the Vishwa Yuvak Kendra, requested Shukla innocuously. A few days later, Ramkrishna reverted to Shukla: the Board of Trustees of the Vishwa Yuvak Kendra had met and decided not to accept the suggestion.

Indira Gandhi was indignant. She was one of the six founders of The Indian Youth Centres Trust established on 10 August 1961, along with Morarji Desai, Naval Tata, Ravindra Varma, Viren Shah and Ramkrishna. Morarji Desai was founder chairman, and Ramkrishna the founder managing trustee.

What Ramkrishna didn't know was that Sanjay Gandhi's coterie of Shukla, Om Mehta[4] and Ambika Soni[5] had checked out the Vishwa Yuvak Kendra building in Delhi and wanted it to be the headquarters of the Youth Congress. The premises included a fully furnished hostel and was conveniently located in the lush environment of Diplomatic Enclave in tony Chanakyapuri. Sanjay's wedding to Maneka Anand on 23 September 1974 was a diversion but shortly afterwards Indira personally reminded Ramkrishna of his duty.

August 1975 saw a flurry of activity. The Vishwa Yuvak Kendra should be requisitioned, Indira Gandhi informed the Lieutenant Governor of Delhi Krishan Chand. She had been receiving complaints relating to undesirable activities of foreigners in the building. Government machinery moved swiftly.

The Vishwa Yuvak Kendra building was requisitioned on 30 August 1975 under Section 23 of the Defence and Internal Security of India Act. In his testimony to the Shah Commission, Ramkrishna would describe how 'the possession of the building was taken forthwith . . . all the inmates of the hostel numbering about

---

[4] Om Mehta: union minister in Indira Gandhi's government.
[5] Ambika Soni: President of the Indian Youth Congress and worked closely with Sanjay Gandhi.

eighty were forced to vacate the rooms. Every piece of furniture in the Kendra building was brought down to the Conference Hall on the ground floor and after sealing the Hall containing the furniture and the books, the inmates were ejected from the building on August 31, 1975 at 11 a.m.' The building and the main gate were immediately sealed.

The next few months saw an invisible tug of war as trustees, politicians, bureaucrats, administrators and undesirables pressurized each other to get their point of view accepted. The attempts were futile. 'A lengthy communication with the then Union home minister Brahmanand Reddy followed, but Ramkrishna's plea fell on deaf ears,' writes journalist, author and political analyst Rasheed Kidwai in 24 Akbar Road. India was Indira and Indira was India. And Indira wanted whatever Sanjay wanted.

The building lay mostly unutilized and kept changing hands from one government department to another. Nobody wanted this hot potato. Indignation continued to prickle Ramkrishna for years.

Ramkrishna took up the matter with Indira, who spent six hours with him while visiting Wardha to see the ailing Vinoba Bhave. Aboard the return flight to Delhi, Ramkrishna asked her in Hindi, 'Aapki mujhse koi naraazgi hai kya (Are you angry with me about something)?' To which she replied, 'Haan, shikayatein to hoti hi rehti hain (Yes, there are always some complaints).' Ramkrishna tried to draw Indira's attention towards the Kendra, but the prime minister chose not to respond.

This was a period of income tax searches by the government. The Bajaj group faced income tax raids and harassment for over forty-six months. The biggest one, spread over a week, started on 18 May 1976. Deploying about 1100 officials, Income Tax Department sleuths simultaneously swooped on the premises of 114 Bajaj establishments across the country. The establishments were searched and nine surveyed, including the Mukand group.

They questioned even Jankidevi, Bajaj's eighty-four-year-old grandmother, who had renounced all worldly possessions after Jamnalal's death in 1942. The officer who led the party sent to Wardha, reported that her house was surveyed 'without any results worth reporting'. Wrote Savitri in her memoir, 'Mataji did not wish to spend anything on herself. The old house was really in a ramshackle condition. The tax officers were taken aback at the sight and also a little ashamed for having bothered the old lady. They touched Mataji's feet when they left.'

The Shah Commission Report

If Era. Sezhiyan was Indira Gandhi's bête noire, for the Bajaj family, Sezhiyan was the upholder of truth. Their truth. Unvarnished. For Sezhiyan, a DMK parliamentarian, was seemingly the only person in the world who had a full three-volume set of The Shah Commission Report, 1977.[6] Indira had had every copy destroyed. Or so she thought. Sezhiyan found a brave printer and republished his copy of the report in book form titled *Shah Commission Report— Lost and Regained*. The book was an instant hit. Page after page after page, the report described the torture of thousands of people wrecked in the Emergency and named the abusers.

A coalition headed by Morarji Desai took office on 24 March 1977. The Janata Party government appointed Jayantilal Chhotalal Shah, a retired Supreme Court Chief Justice, to head a commission to look into the Emergency's excesses, malpractices, and misdeeds. The Shah Commission began its investigation on 28 May 1977. Among the multitude of entries was the Bajaj Group.

Memories flooded Ramkrishna as he read his copy of The Shah Commission Report. Indignation, even after so many years, continued to prickle him. He was on page sixty-six of Justice Jayantilal Chhotalal Shah's Interim Report II.

In his testimony at the hearing, in a written note read out to the Commission, Ramkrishna deposed that the family's relationship with the Gandhi dynasty started deteriorating with his brother Kamalnayan's opposition to Indira Gandhi in her bid for the prime ministership in 1966. He claimed the raid was 'an act of political vendetta'. 'Ever since then, the previous regime assumed that our family was against them especially as it was their stand that those who are not with them are against them.'

Under persistent grilling by Justice Shah, part of the truth emerged with the needle of suspicion pointing to S.R. Mehta, the chairman of the Central Board of Direct Taxes. Gradually, more

---

[6] Interim Report I, 11 March 1978; Interim Report II, 26 April 1978; Third Report, 6 August 1978.

sordid details tumbled out about procedural 'lapses' and a messy 'smirch' Bajaj campaign, but little came to light about who and what exactly triggered the raid.

Ramkrishna lost favour because he refused to allow Sanjay Gandhi to take over the Vishwa Yuvak Kendra in Delhi. Viren Shah's involvement in the Baroda Dynamite Case made him an enemy of the state. Several members of the Bajaj family were clustered around Jayaprakash Narayan's hospital bedside when the latter urged the public to protest against the Emergency. If further kindling was needed, it was provided by Shriman Narayan who organized a *sammelan*, partly funded by the Bajajs, for an agitated Acharya Vinoba Bhave. The Bajaj group faced forty-six months of constant harassment which ended only with the lifting of the Emergency.

On 23 January 1977 Indira Gandhi released all political prisoners and called elections. The Congress Party suffered a crushing defeat.

On 24 March 1977, a coalition headed by Morarji Desai took office. The Janata Party administration withdrew the case against Viren Shah. George Fernandes became industry minister.

In January 1980 Indira Gandhi returned to power. The Supreme Court found that as the special courts were not legally constituted, the courts were dismissed. No trials were conducted. Several officials indicted by the Shah Commission went on to successful careers.

On 23 June 1980 Sanjay Gandhi died in a plane crash.

And that was the end of that. At least for one decade.[7]

A Mini-liberalization of Sorts

By the opening of the 1980s' decade, Ramkrishna's role as head of the joint family and its businesses was on a sturdier footing and less ceremonial. Family trusts blossomed to ring-fence the group in this era, as did the attention required to administer them. Rahul in his forties, Shishir and Shekhar in their thirties, educated in the best universities of the West, held leadership roles. Madhur and Niraj were in their twenties and dreaming of universities.

Ramkrishna's grounding and experience enabled a strong focus on a burgeoning group, tectonic economic shifts, and a petulant Indira

---

[7] Refer to Chapter 21 for more.

Gandhi who as a child boarded in the same school as Kamalnayan and Ramkrishna and didn't much care for them. 'No major decision in any of the group's twenty-two operational companies was taken without Chachaji,' remembers Bajaj. 'His instinctive appreciation for hard work, efficiency and positive results gave us confidence.'

'Once India started to liberalize from the mid-1980s under Rajiv Gandhi,' Bajaj continued, 'new technologies were allowed, as were new entrants, though largely as joint ventures between Indian and foreign companies. During 1950–1980 we moved at what came to be known as the Hindu rate of GDP growth of about 3 p.a. This barely budged the per capita income growth as population was increasing at around 2 per cent p.a. In the 1980s we grew at around 5 per cent p.a.'

Import substitution rules demanded that companies demonstrate to bureaucrats why any import was essential. 'The doctrine of indigenous availability ensured the purchase of Indian inputs even when lower-quality products cost more than superior imports,' writes Omkar Goswami. 'Import substitution was sustained by quantitative restrictions, governed by various types of import licences, and high tariffs. By 1985, the mean tariff rate was 146 per cent for intermediate goods and 107 per cent for capital goods. While some of the policies certainly helped to establish industrial capacity, especially in engineering, drugs and pharmaceuticals, chemicals, fertilizers, and petrochemicals.'

The state monitored growth, group by group, case by case. The Bajaj Group began to feature prominently in India's business house rankings. According to the Monopolies and Restrictive Trade Practices Commission, the Bajaj group was fortieth in the hierarchy in 1964, the year the Commission began collating data. By 1990, the Bajaj group was India's seventh-largest business group. Tata as usual headed the list, the B.K.–A.V. Birla father-and-son duo stood second, Dhirubhai Ambani third, Lalit Mohan Thapar fourth, Gaur Hari Singhania fifth, and Rama Prasad Goenka sixth. In 2020, the Bajaj group was in third place.

The Last Farewell

Ramkrishna passed away on 21 September 1994, missing out on the weddings of Rajiv with Deepa, and Sanjiv with Shefali by a few short weeks.

16

Satara: 1975–2021

The Priya.

'Don't kill the goose that lays the golden egg,' Sanjiv Bajaj recommends to his audience. 'Thanks to Maharashtra Scooters' investment in group companies, your company's NAV[1] has zoomed. Your Rs 1 lakh invested in share capital has yielded Rs 2 crore in dividend and grown to nearly Rs 15 crore through share appreciation according to the current price.'

The minority investors did their best to maintain a stern front.

The forty-first annual general meeting of Maharashtra Scooters Ltd (MSL), held in July 2016 at Bajaj Auto's Akurdi premises, had none of the fireworks typical of minority investors clamouring to liquidate a sleepy company and unlock shareholder value. For form's sake, a few questions were raised. Now, time for tea, snacks and gossip.

Satara Forty Years Earlier

The Italians returned to Italy in 1971. Bajaj's modest R&D team cobbled the Chetak. In an ideal world, Bajaj would have expanded within Akurdi, bought more and better equipment, added workers, stepped up production and appointed more dealers. But permissions under the Indira Gandhi administration were hard to get. When the Satara option was offered to him, Bajaj took it.

The joint sector concept was fresh on the hob in 1971. Concept designers and bureaucrats expected it to be an effective instrument to 'control monopolies and reduce the concentration of economic power'. From the private sector point of view, it had the potential to sidetrack MRTP clearances. The central government issued letters of intent to the states and lobbed the ball in their courts. Competition developed among chief ministers to attract entrepreneurs and large 'industrial houses' to their states, irrespective of whether these were linked to the party in power at the Centre or not.

Original objectives diversified briskly. Well aware of API's struggles and Piaggio's imminent exit, state-owned Western Maharashtra Development Corporation (WMDC) focused on the breach in the market. In July 1972, WMDC quietly acquired an industrial licence to manufacture 24,000 scooters per annum. And approached Bajaj Auto.

---

[1] NAV: Net Asset Value.

'WMDC's joint venture proposal to us was for an assembly plant with an annual licenced capacity of 24,000 scooters,' recalls Bajaj. 'We began our talks in late 1972.' The core dos and don'ts for both parties were sorted out by 16 August 1975. Bajaj Auto's shareholding in Maharashtra Scooters was 24 per cent with operating control, while WMDC's was a plain vanilla 27 per cent. All dos and don'ts were captured in three core Maharashtra Scooters Limited documents: a Memorandum of Association, Articles of Association and a Protocol Agreement. The initial capital was Rs 5.1 million, again based on the 24:27 formula.

At birth, Maharashtra Scooters, Bajaj and Srinivasan Prabhakaran jointly held the chairman-cum-managing positions with Jayant H. Shah and Dhirajlal S. Mehta representing Bajaj Auto. Three directors, Madhav Govind Pawar, Jayavantrao Krishnarao Bhosale and Padmakar Mahadu Naik, represented WMDC. Maharashtra Scooters was incorporated on 11 June 1975, exactly a fortnight before Indira Gandhi declared the Emergency on 25 June.

For Bajaj, the Satara project was a first in several ways: partnering with the government and building a pure play assembly unit. Neither of the realities were what Bajaj deeply wanted. The early outcome turned out better than he had expected. As the saying goes, half a loaf is better than none.

The Welcome Mat

At the M.I.D.C. office located near National Highway 4 and Satara railway station, news of the imminent arrival of the Maharashtra Scooters plant was a lifesaver and game changer. Three older plants had recently downed their shutters. Early feelers scoped that the scooter assembly plant might employ as many as 770 workers and staff. Hopefully, Maharashtra Scooters would also provide indirect employment via work at local garages.

The teams worked to make infrastructural facilities like land, water, and electricity easily available. Its Environmental Engineering Department made provisions for a separate 24/7 water supply centre. The local Maharashtra State Electricity Board sanctioned 2000 kilovolt ampere (kVA) with a connected load set at 3455 kilowatts (kW). Land at cheaper rates was made conceivable. The office of the District Industrial Centre (D.I.C.) found a niche for itself in the area. A telephone exchange, police station and branches of various banks appeared.

The all-important certificate of commencement of business arrived on 17 July 1975. A couple of weeks later, so did a lease for 1,90,000 square metres from M.I.D.C. for ninety-five years, starting 26 August 1975. Factory construction began in October 1975. Paint, assembly and fabrication lines were completed in August 1976.

Maharashtra Scooters entered the capital market in November 1977. The issue was for Rs 49 lakh and oversubscribed ten times. Central Bank of India sanctioned a term loan of Rs 25 lakh and deferred payment-guarantee facilities of Rs 50 lakh against a mortgage of land and other assets, as well as a regular Rs 20 lakh loan.

Priya, Would You Like Some More?

The blueprint called for two-wheelers to be assembled at Satara M.I.D.C. from CKD packs offered by Bajaj Auto's Akurdi factory. Bajaj Auto would also market the scooter under the 'Priya' brand.

The first 'Priya' scooter, motorized and geared, was paraded out on 13 August 1976. It was an instant smash hit. Even better, towards the beginning of 1978, the central government withdrew the Scooter (Distribution and Sale) Control Order. Both the 'bajaj-Chetak' and the 'Priya' could now be sold to anyone and anywhere.

The challenge for Bajaj now was the huge backlog of pending orders with dealers. To ensure equitable distribution while manufacturing cranked up, Bajaj decided to continue the procedure for scooter distribution at both Akurdi and Satara until the backlog eased.

Those first two years of its existence were Maharashtra Scooters' golden age. Local farmers became industrial workers without any major hiccups, their learning skills honed by skilled technicians loaned temporarily by the Akurdi plant. Machinery and conveyer belts ran smoothly. Production numbers increased regularly. Sound marketing and a sound dealer network ensured strong customer interest. As the workload increased, Maharashtra Scooters started farming out work to local sheds, gaining even more local respect.

An exuberant Akurdi sent a record 54,735 CKD packs to Satara. Manufacturing activity, particularly in the upgraded chassis shop, got into full swing. As sales soared, minor tinkering kept the Priya model fresh. The only hitch Maharashtra Scooters' managers faced was the perennial hunger for more Priya CKD packs from Akurdi. Slightly over half a million customers proudly picked up a Priya in less than a decade.

As the CKD packs poured in from Akurdi, the number of direct employees at Satara grew from 239 in its first year of full production in 1978 to 527 by 1989. The turn of the decade saw a wonderful year. Maharashtra Scooters was the highest paymaster in the state. Bajaj Auto and Maharashtra Scooters' combined market share in this space was an unassailable 70.70 per cent.

The Troubles

When the problem started in June 1979, it was not at Satara but at the Akurdi plant. The usual CKD shipments failed to arrive. Maharashtra Scooters' management initially couldn't figure out what was happening, but a few calls later it was clear that a strike shot deliveries until the lockout was lifted in Akurdi.

The next year, it was the turn of Maharashtra Scooters' workers to go on strike. 'Daily rated workmen struck work on 24 April 1980,' Bajaj reported to the shareholders. 'After negotiations, the strike was called off on 5 June 1980. The closure of Bajaj Auto until 8 November 1979 and the strike at the Maharashtra Scooter plant led to a severe setback in the production of "Priya" scooters.' The forty-two-day strike in 1980 halted but didn't really resolve issues.

Eleven months later, the daily rated workmen were back to press their wage demands on 18 May 1981. They called off the strike on 27 June. A settlement was reached on 17 August 1981. 'As a result of labour trouble, production of Priya scooters dropped to 24,166 units,' remembers an aggrieved Bajaj.

A Change in the Air

Maharashtra Scooters staidly meandered into the 21st century. The normally dormant stock on the BSE woke up with a headache in 2006. Snippets from its annual reports show a slow and steady decline. Shareholders started asking questions, first from Bajaj, and after the 2007–2008 demerger, from both Bajaj and Sanjiv.

The Thirty-first AGM on 15 July 2006

'Maharashtra Scooters has ceased to be a manufacturing company,' announced Bajaj to shareholders at the company's thirty-first AGM on 15 July 2006. 'From 30 June, there are nil stocks of completely knocked down kits (CKDs) since Bajaj Auto no longer produces geared scooters. From July onwards, and for the rest of the year, there will be zero sales.'

' . . . Since it is no longer a production unit, the issue of its 640 employees also has to be settled,' he continued. 'A wage agreement with the 487 workmen is overdue by thirty-three months . . .'

And the final touch: '. . . in January 2006 WMDC declined the Rs 151.56 per share offer, and has approached the Bombay High Court. With the case in court, it is anyone's guess how long it could take to be resolved.'

Twelve months later, at the thirty-second AGM on 12 July 2007:

'We are not going to liquidate Maharashtra Scooters. The option is there but we don't want to.'

' . . . Why can't we restart operations at Satara?' asked a shareholder. 'With no fiscal benefits at Satara, products assembled there would be expensive compared to operations in other locations with fiscal benefits,' was the quick response.

' . . . WMDC has a right to have five directors on the company's board of directors,' points out an outraged shareholder, 'we seem to be missing some.' The WMDC nominee, V.H. Deshmukh, steps in to explain that with unfilled vacancies on the WMDC's own board, there aren't sufficient nominees for boards where it holds stakes.

Six months later, January 2008: WMDC directors R.N. Joshi, V.H. Deshmukh and S.S. Survase step down. Mary Neelima Kerkatta, P.R. Suravanshi, D.W. Patil and R.K. Nikharge sign in. Jayant H. Shah and D.W. Patil offer themselves for reappointment as does Sanjiv Bajaj.

Share Me Not

In drawing up their agreement in 1975, WMDC and Bajaj Auto had agreed that if either partner wanted to part with or transfer its shareholding, the other would have the first option to purchase Maharashtra Scooters' (MSLs') shares. WMDC informed Bajaj that it wanted to exit Maharashtra Scooters and cash out. It wasn't exactly a surprise. Joint-sector partnerships established in the heydays of the 1970s, lost their glamour and utility after the 1991 liberalization. WMDC offered to sell its 27 per cent shareholding in Maharashtra Scooters.

For Bajaj, the possibility of combining WMDC's 27 per cent shares with his 24 per cent was tempting. But at what price? He offered Rs 50 per share, later revising it to Rs 75. MSL's market cap had dropped from Rs 80 crore in 1995 to Rs 20 crore in 2000. Would it drop further? Or rise once the bulls, especially the egregious Calcutta ones, found out what was happening?

On the ground, Maharashtra Scooters' situation slid from poor to dire. Sales dropped drastically and losses started mounting. 'There is no plan to close down the undertaking,' Bajaj assured shareholders and workers at the 26 July 2002 AGM, 'but if Maharashtra Scooters is to stay afloat, Bajaj Auto needs to have the flexibility to rationalize and restructure Maharashtra Scooters' production facilities.' Adding heft to his words, the normally ebullient chairman added. 'The future of Maharashtra Scooters is bleak. The delay in selling the government's stake to Bajaj Auto is only eroding its market cap.'

Eight months before the AGM, a miffed Bajaj had given notice to Vilasrao Deshmukh, Maharashtra's then chief minister, that Bajaj Auto would be stopping the supply of CKD kits to Maharashtra Scooters. Bajaj explains the rationale: 'At the time, scooters assembled at Maharashtra Scooters attracted an additional sales tax of Rs 384 but the scooters had to be sold at identical prices as that of scooters from the Bajaj Auto plant.'

Inevitably, since neither Bajaj nor WMDC could agree on a sale price, both parties referred to a sole arbitrator. When this didn't work, there were a couple of rounds in various courts. The next level was Crisil, a credit rating agency then headed by R. Ravimohan. Its report, presented on 31 August 2002, valued Maharashtra Scooters at Rs 232 per share. Bajaj disagreed and demanded a new counter valuation by an agency of his choice.

The Vilasrao Deshmukh administration ended. It was now Sushil-kumar Shinde's turn to take on Bajaj. Shinde set up a nine-member

committee headed by Chief Secretary Ajit Nimbalkar. It too failed
to decide on a price. There wasn't even a creeping option. The rock-
solid WMDC-Bajaj Auto agreement permitted the offloading of no
more than a fraction of shares in market operations in the event of
either party's unwillingness to buy out or sell its stake. The government
decided to appoint a retired Supreme Court or Bombay High Court
judge to arbitrate. Uniquely, retired Justice Arvind Sawant found a
solution where others failed. Action speaks louder than words. WMDC
managing director R.N. Joshi was not available for comments.

Bajaj Holdings (BHIL) bought WMDC's 27 per cent stake
in Maharashtra Scooters for Rs 232 per share plus 18 per cent p.a.
interest from 14 January 2006. Assuming compounded interest, the
value per share came to circa Rs 2000 per share plus a dividend of
Rs 228 per share during the disputed period. In short, BHIL paid
WMDC Rs 670 crore to leave. BHIL's holding in MSL jumped
to 51 per cent, and MSL became a BHIL subsidiary. The moment
should have been momentous, but overall, the time and cost spent
on the litigation destroyed significant value for BHIL.

Bajaj Auto paid Rs 46.78 crore (Rs 51.63 per share) to buy out
WMDC's shareholding in Maharashtra Scooters. Confirming this
to reporters, Bajaj said, 'I am ready to buy it as early as tomorrow,
but I think the Maharashtra Scooters board may convene a meeting
before selling the stake to us. It is a win-win proposition for all.'

The Maharashtra Scooters' scrip was quoted at Rs 4640. Its
investments in various Bajaj group companies as well as in other
instruments stood at Rs 174.27 crore. MSL's investments in the
Bajaj group included 3.38 million shares in Bajaj Auto, 1.02 million
in Bajaj Auto Finance and 1.25 million in Bajaj Hindustan. MSL
owned 33,87,036 shares of Bajaj Auto as part of its Rs 154.30 crore
investment portfolio. MSL stocks moved up from Rs 18.80 in
August 2001 to about Rs 88.

MSL still had two businesses—manufacturing die casting dies,
fixtures, and die casting components primarily meant for the automobile
industry; and treasury operations involving management of surplus
funds invested by MSL. MSL held a significant investment in Bajaj
group companies. Wrapping up, Bajaj made it clear that Maharashtra
Scooters would not be merged with Bajaj Auto. The long battle ended on
17 June 2019 with WMDC transferring its 27 per cent stake to BHIL.

17

Mobility for the Middle Class—
the Chetak: 1975–2021

The Chetak and the Chetak Reborn.

With Piaggio's exit, Bajaj's scooter needed a new name. 'Once I realized that the government was not going to renew the agreement with Piaggio, I knew I had to drop the brand name Vespa for our scooters and APE for three-wheelers,' says Bajaj. 'It was equally clear to me that we should have the "Bajaj" brand name for our vehicles. I discussed it with Kakaji, perhaps mentioned it to the Board, and discussed it with our advertising agency, Lintas, headed by Alyque Padamsee.'

Bajaj finally chose a double-barrel—the bajaj-Chetak, after the fabled horse of Maharana Pratap Singh who saved his rider in the Battle of Haldighati on 21 June 1576. 'The name change was no problem at all because Bajaj scooters and three-wheelers had a ten-year delivery period. Our brand easily replaced the Vespa,' says Bajaj.

'Buying a scooter in the 1970s was complicated,' Abhilash Gaur, a scooter enthusiast blogger, reminds us. 'You had to write an application to a dealer to grant a scooter for personal use. Then you went to a post office, opened a savings account, and put in a security deposit of Rs 250. The post office gave you a passbook, and you pledged this to the scooter dealer as proof of intent to purchase. Then you waited for your turn. On the happy day, the dealer returned the passbook and "authorized" you to withdraw your Rs 250 to make the full payment. If you applied just before your wedding, you had school-going children by the time you got your scooter. This procedure was laid down in a rule called the "Scooters (Distribution and Sale) Control Order, 1960".'

India scuttled its own scooter bazaar. The middle class was growing and wanted wheels. The Planning Commission estimated that 210,000 scooters would be needed in 1973–74. A think tank, the National Council of Applied Economic Research (NCAER), calculated that annual demand would increase to 243,000 scooters by 1979–80. These numbers were far off the mark. The number of pending scooter bookings on 31 March 1970 was already 84,883 for the Lambretta and 1,76,933 for the Vespa, re-badged as the bajaj-Chetak.

A customer fortunate enough to be allotted one could sell it the next moment at double the price. A Bajaj scooter became a regular dowry demand among middle-class families. Dealers unofficially charged customers huge premiums to jump the queue. Of course, for those who couldn't wait, they had only to pay a premium and pick up a bajaj-Chetak from a flourishing black market.

Roundaboutation

'A few people could avoid the long queue,' reminds Bajaj. 'The government formulated a foreign exchange scheme under which if the customer paid for his bajaj-Chetak in foreign exchange, he would get early delivery.' The thought also went down well in the head office of Bajaj America, headed by David Jones at the time.

At best, the US response to the Chetak was lukewarm, however. 'Consequently, Bajaj introduced a scheme whereby Indians in the US could purchase the Chetak, pay in dollars and re-export them to India to their relatives,' shared Jones. 'The recipients of the scooters would avoid the long waiting periods and Bajaj would be able to procure foreign exchange.'

The scheme worked just fine with everyone happy. '400 scooters were re-exported to India,' said Jones. 'In spite of the fact that the scooters are manufactured in India and eventually used in India, they still have to make the trip to the United States and back to satisfy bureaucratic formalities. The scooters are unloaded at a Bajaj America warehouse in Columbia, South Carolina, and shipped back without even un-crating. Ship carriers have now accorded us the privilege of special round-robin freight rates.'

Under the Morarji Desai administration, life became breathable for scooter manufacturers when The Scooter (Distribution and Sale) Control Order 1960 was guillotined on 1 January 1978. 'However, in view of the huge backlog of pending orders for "Bajaj" scooters with our dealers and to ensure equitable distribution,' realized Bajaj, 'for some time, we had to continue the procedure for distribution of scooters similar to the existing prior to the withdrawal of the order.'

Adds Bajaj, 'I was always under pressure from workers, dealers and vendors to raise scooter prices and share the higher margins, but I refused. The shortage regime meant they were making money. The market premium of the quota regime, apart from customers, went to a few dealers and brokers who made a killing by first booking their orders and then selling scooters in the black when their turn came.' An exceptional case once crossed Bajaj's table: a personal request from Air Chief Marshal Idris H. Latif to grant a priority scooter.

'Very early in the 1970s,' remembers Latif, 'I was commanding our fighter and bomber base at Lohegaon, Poona, a base with about 10,000 personnel, including a number of civilians. One of them, Vincent, was a key member of my staff. The air force is always on call, twenty-four hours of the day. With the Bangladesh conflict round the corner, we were on high alert. Vincent lived far from the camp with his family of four, including a severely handicapped daughter. And clearly it was becoming very, very difficult for him to be available round the clock, at short notice. One morning, with great hesitation I could see, he asked me if I could help him purchase a Bajaj scooter on "priority". It was a prized possession in short supply. With great hesitation, with Vincent very much in mind, I agreed to write to Mr

Rahul Bajaj, a person I had only heard of, but never met. Explaining at some length the circumstances, I requested "if, as a special case . . ." Within a week, I had a personal response: of course!'

'Hamara Bajaj'

'The "Bajaj" logo was actually taken from Bajaj Electricals,' says Bajaj. 'To celebrate its twenty-fifth anniversary, Bajaj Electricals decided to change its name from Radio Lamp Works to Bajaj Electricals. For the name change, in 1962 it held an all-India contest. Kakaji selected the logo out of hundreds of entries. This prize-winning logo was designed by Heros Publicity and Bajaj Auto also adopted it in 1962 for its corporate use. We needed a monogram or symbol, and we got Vinayak Purohit, who used to work in Mukand, to design the "B" in a hexagonal form. During the 1970s and 1980s we developed three scooter models. We named the first one as Bajaj 150 and the second and the third as Bajaj Chetak and Bajaj Super.'

The name change was backed by full-bodied advertising. 'Hamara Bajaj' and 'You just can't beat a Bajaj' became famous base lines. Endowed with the persona of a 'work horse', its reasonable price and low maintenance cost made Bajaj's scooter a huge hit among middle-class Indians. There was nothing wrong with distribution, and the pricing was reasonable.

'The *Hamara Bajaj* campaign rung so true,' wrote social commentator Santosh Desai. 'If the Indian middle class man were to be reborn as a product, chances are it would be as the Bajaj scooter. Squat, a belly going to pot, wearing a grey safari suit, undistinguished but resourceful. With a wife perched uncomfortably at the back, Gudiya squeezed between the two and Cheeku standing up front . . . It had a stepney (a spare wheel), which provided a welcome safety net on independent-minded Indian roads. It had space to squeeze in a full family, a place to carry vegetables, a dickey to store sundry needs of the family . . . It needed to be kicked incessantly, first aggressively and then pleadingly, at times it needed to be tilted at an impossible angle for the fuel to start flowing and its spark plugs needed more cleaning, but it blended in perfectly with how we lived and what we believed in. Restrained, repressed, versatile in an unassuming way, the scooter spoke for us and our way of life like nothing else.' And perfect for movie directors shooting scooter chases.

The Unmaking of the Chetak

The early scooters on Akurdi conveyors were based on the Vespa Sprint, a 150 cc, two-stroke machine that Piaggio made globally from 1965 to 1976—but with a slightly smaller 145 cc engine.[1] The technical collaboration ended in 1971 after the Indira Gandhi administration refused permission to extend its term.

Bajaj continued to make more or less the same product rebadged as the Chetak. Given the heavy demand for the scooter, Bajaj Auto did not feel the need to introduce a completely new design, and merely tinkered with the old Vespa design. The Chetak's production was so fine-tuned over thirty years that forty workers on an assembly line didn't have more than two seconds free between one activity and the next.

Besides, with a ten-year waiting list, Bajaj didn't need to measure customer perception for the Bajaj Chetak. Bajaj stubbornly refused to upgrade. The Chetak—which provided 60 per cent of scooter sales countrywide in the 1970s and 1980s—didn't have an electric ignition but had to be kick-started. Its two-stroke engine had an emission performance that, while acceptable in the Indian context, was highly polluting according to international standards. (India began setting emission norms by the late 1990s.) R&D spend for a long time was a minuscule 1 per cent. The average cycle time for new product development was four–five years compared to two–three years of Japanese competitors.

'For forty years Chetak had the same look, same quality and style,' laments management professor Harish B. Nair. 'Even after the opening up of economy in the 1990s, the scooter segment initially did not witness much competition. While API's Lamby

---

[1] For the technically minded: pre-2002, the Chetak was powered by a 145 cc, two-stroke engine producing 7.5 bhp of maximum power at 5500 rpm and 10.8 Nm of peak torque at 3500 rpm, mated to a four-speed gearbox. Post-2002, with the introduction of stricter emission norms, Bajaj Auto introduced a four-stroke version of the 145-cc engine.

did not have much success, Kinetic Honda managed to carve a niche with its gearless scooters. Another growing segment was the scooterette dominated by TVS Scooty.'

Loyal friends like Jyoti Kainth and Tanmay Mathur stood fast. 'When Bajaj introduced its first indigenous scooter brand, its practicality and reasonable price made it a blockbuster product for the company. Bajaj's name became synonymous with scooters, just like Colgate stood for toothpaste,' they said.

The Day the Music Died[2]

And then came the Japanese with their motorcycles.

'I was in an engineering college during 1984–1988 in Pune,' recalls Rajiv. 'Joher, my best friend in school and college, wanted to buy a Chetak. There was a ten-year waiting list for it. But I had the power and he the begging bowl. I spoke to my father who suggested a "Bajaj Super" (another brand of scooters), saying it was the same thing. I insisted that Joher wants a Chetak. It was to be available in a few days. In 1984, TVS introduced a motorcycle. Joher went and bought an Ind Suzuki motorcycle . . . my best friend, who was so desperate for a Chetak, suddenly bought a motorcycle.'

'Retrospectively, we should have seen the switch within the two-wheeler market from scooters to motorcycles in 1999–2000,' admits Bajaj. 'Even so, though the waiting periods vanished, Bajaj scooters continued to sell well until about 2000. In 2001, I had no hesitation in saying that the year under review was a very bad year for Bajaj Auto even though the company's profit after tax, though lower than before, was higher than competitors. We discontinued Chetak production in 2005, and scooters in 2009.'

A national synchronized wistfulness swept India. Almost every Indian who rode a bajaj-Chetak had a Chetak moment to share when Bajaj Auto announced it was shutting down production. A medical student related how his faith in his father's scooter multiplied the day he travelled from Mathura to Delhi to appear for the CBSE medical

---

[2] 'American Pie', a 1972 hit track, referring to 3 February 1959 as 'the day the music died'.

entrance examination. 'There was a bus strike, but my father was confident that the scooter will see us through.' After his wedding, a bridegroom took his newly-wed bride all the way from Aligarh to Hisar on his Chetak with their luggage. 'I had a belief that it will not ditch me. After all my father rode his Bajaj Cub until he died at the age of seventy-five.'

Did Bajaj Auto make a mistake in discarding the scooter segment? Contrary to expectations, the scooter refused to die. Though it took a while for the Bajaj Auto team to get to where they wanted to be, the new-age Chetak segued into a battery-operated proud look and feel. Production at the Chakan plant started humming on 25 September 2019. 16 October 2019 saw the unveiling of the Chetak under the Urbanite EV sub-brand.

The Last Word

On Friday, 1 January 2021, in its seventy-fifth year of operations, Bajaj Auto's share price closed at Rs 3479 on the NSE, contributing to a market capitalization of Rs 1,00,670.76 crore (US $13.6 billion). Bajaj Auto became not only the most valuable two-wheeler company in the world, but it also stood as the world's third-largest two-wheeler maker and the largest three-wheeler maker.

Daytona Beach is a town on Florida's Atlantic coast where American bikers flock to race on its famous hard-sand beaches. On 8 September 1971, the *Daytona Beach Morning Journal* published a report with the headline 'Scooters Sold Out':

> Ten people were killed and four injured last week in Udaipur when thousands of people stormed a scooter showroom to register for vehicles. More than 600 policemen were marshalled to contain the crowd of scooter buyers, who gathered near the showroom the night before it was scheduled to open . . . A scooter costs about 3460 rupees or $460, half a year's wages for the average Indian worker . . . Two years ago, Bajaj applied to the government for permission to increase production. 'Every time we ask about the status of the application, we're told that it's being considered,' he said. 'You see, this matter is political as well as economic. Our board chairman, Kamalnayan Bajaj, is also a leader of the Congress opposition party.'

DAYTONA BEACH MORNING JOURNAL

DAYTONA BEACH, FLORIDA, WEDNESDAY, SEPTEMBER 8, 1971

Scooters Sold Out

NEW DELHI, (AP) — A sign in the window of a motor-scooter dealer advises prospective buyers: "Delivery period approximately 10 years."

G.C. Choadhry, the scooter dealer, smiled at the visitor and remarked," Yes, that's right; if you wanted to buy a scooter, you would have to wait 10 years for delivery."

The demand is so great that 10 people were killed and four injured last week in Udaipur, 300 miles southwest of here, when thousands of people stormed a scooter showroom to register for vehicles.

More than 600 policemen were marshaled to contain the crowd of scooter buyers, who gathered near the showroom the night before it was scheduled to open.

Those waiting to register had already paid a small charge to the government—a guarantee to the dealer of intent to buy and to the purchaser of delivery, even 10 years later.

A scooter costs about 3,460 rupees or $460, half a year's wages for the average Indian worker.

The government, noting the gap between demand and supply, has announced plans to produce scooters at the rate of 100,000 annually, but its production is not expected to start for another five years.

Choadhry's firm, Bajaj Auto, and Lambretta are the only two sanctioned scooter manufacturers in the country now. They produce a total of about 60,000 units a year, far below the current estimated demand of 230,000 annually.

"We have the capacity to produce more scooters and, of course, we want to, but the government prohibits us," Choadhry explained.

In general, the government's socialistic policy is to limit the expansion of prosperous private industries, preferring to fill consumer needs with public, or government-controlled manufacturing.

Scooters provide the only form of private transportation for millions of Indians—students, physicians, farmers, dentists and government workers. Cars are too costly.

In many villages scooters are a status symbol, but in sprawling cities such as New Delhi they become a necessity because of irregular and inadequate public transportation.

Two years ago Bajaj applied to the government for permission to increase production.

"Every time we ask about the status of the application, we're told that it's still being considered," he said.

"You see, this matter is political as well as economic. Our board chairman, Kamalnayan Bajaj, is also a leader of the Congress opposition party."

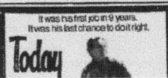

18

The Winds of Discontent: 17 June 1979

Bajaj Auto, Akurdi.

'In the second shift, past 12 o'clock midnight, hundreds of workers came to my house shouting and saying, "We will fight for our rights!" I came out from my bedroom and said, "Guys, you are talking to a Bajaj. The first eight years of my life and my father's first twenty years of his life were in Gandhi's ashram. You know how ashram life is; you are living much better lives. By fighting, you will get nothing. You can close the plant (for) as long as you want. Talk to us, negotiate, I will be fair, but I will be firm".'

'That would be my policy throughout in dealing with all my stakeholders, including workers and unions—firm but fair,' continues

Bajaj. 'If you are not fair, you can't run a company. If you are not firm—some of these multinationals who came, they didn't know what was happening, they used to give in to everything, and they spoiled the whole climate.'

The idea of living inside an industrial complex was not ludicrous to Bajaj as it would be to his peers in the Marwari aristocracy. 'Actions speak louder than words. I did not and do not believe in absentee landlordism,' Bajaj is fond of declaring.

Saturday

The labour agreement[1] was due to expire in March 1979. Negotiations between management and the workers' union on the renewal of a charter typically begin well in advance. In the early summer of 1978, talks began between the Kamgar Sanghatana and its leader, Rupamaya M. Chatterjee, a young Bengali socialist, and Bajaj. Bajaj's determination to improve the company's performance matched Chatterjee's zeal for his union. The company then had an authorized installed capacity of 2,00,000 scooters per year, besides the three-wheelers.

A forty-five-day strike from July to September 1978 was withdrawn after management agreed to discuss the new charter. Suspension notices, however, were served on three union leaders. The suspension of a fourth union member led to yet another protest, this time a tool-down strike for an hour every day. Irritated, management contacted Chatterjee, but he insisted that this was a spontaneous, individual gesture, and his union was not behind the protest.

Within activists, a jostling often led to the formation of two unions in the same factory. In Bajaj Auto, one worker group accepted the leadership of Sadashiv Bagaitkar of the Poona Labour Union, while another group preferred Chatterjee of the Poona Workers Federation. 'Both leaders are personally honest,' reported J.N. Pradhan in *Economic and Political Weekly*, 'but the two unions accuse each other of corruption and retain separate existences. For a working-class movement, the role of activists is to educate, mobilize, and organize workers in order to put up united struggles for their demands.'

---

[1] At this time, Bajaj Auto's total workforce was almost 5000 people. Contract workers were the largest group, then trainees. The smallest group were the elite 'permanent workers': unionized, powerful and feisty, cushioned by labour contracts and three-year labour agreements.

Stress shimmered throughout Poona's pleasant winter. Spring came and went. Neither party could agree on terms, and the March 1979 deadline evaporated. Bajaj announced that unless the union accepted the productivity norms fixed by the company, there would be no discussion on any of the union's demands. A meeting was scheduled for the morning of 16 June 1979 between the union and management. In a bid to avert trouble, behind the scenes, Chief Minister Sharad Pawar declared a five-day closure of all industries, ostensibly due to a power crisis. The ploy didn't work.

Chatterjee, a busy man who was also the vice-president of CITU's[2] Maharashtra unit, called to request a day's postponement as he was not feeling well. Management acceded to this request. The workers, unaware of the reason for the postponement, became agitated, particularly when management handed memos to two union members, warning them against indulging in 'unauthorized' actions. Interpreting this as a charge sheet, the two union members and their supporters walked out and squatted on the lawns in front of the factory building.

Possibly a security officer's provocative language was the trigger for violence. Nine hundred workers were soon in the grip of a mob mentality. A running battle ensued with the police lathicharging and tear-gassing, and the workers hurling the canisters straight back. 'Construction work was going on in the factory and the workers had ready access to stones which were freely used on the police, the company's security staff and the company's property, namely, the buildings and in particular on the glass-panes,' noted judge M.F. Saldanha austerely when dismissing the appeal of fifty-one protestors on 1 September 1993.

They threw acid and metal parts and rolled barrels across the road to prevent the police from following them. They made bonfires out of wooden cartons and scrap. A scooter belonging to a Bajaj Auto security officer was set on fire and the company's bus was seriously damaged. As more and more areas of the plant were torched, every fire engine and every fireman from Pimpri-Chinchwad, Dehu Road, Pune Municipal Corporation and Khadki Cantonment rushed to the Bajaj Auto plant. Flames extinguished, the situation gradually came under control around 11.30 p.m.

---

[2] Centre of Indian Trade Unions. Founded 1970, CITU is a national-level trade union politically affiliated to the Communist Party of India.

Some workers stormed the main office. The furniture and fixtures in the reception area were smashed and stones were freely hurled at everything inside. Bajaj was working on the first floor. 'Our chief security officer's head was gashed from the stone throwing,' he recalled. 'Four watchmen reached my office before the workers came charging up. Somehow, they contained them. There was some slogan mongering and *speechofying (sic)*. After the police came, they dispersed.'

According to police records, Inspector Maruti Sankoli of the local Pimpri police station directed his staff to remain on the campus throughout that night in order to prevent any further recurrence of violence.

Sunday

The next morning, 17 June, not only was the police action now headed by Deputy Commissioner Sarbdeep Singh Virk, but very visible also were the State Reserve Police Platoon, fire brigade squads, the local constabulary who were deputed to the Bajaj Auto plant, and Anami Roy, the deputy commissioner of Pune city.

On a normal day, the first shift at Bajaj Auto started at 6 a.m. Workers loyal to management lined up as usual to punch their cards. At a late-night strategy meeting, management had decided, as a precautionary measure, to allow workers only in groups of ten to enter the premises. The decision took time to trickle down and misfired.

The police contingent—now fully reinforced—initially refused to allow the workers in. Once they received their orders, the police began letting the workers in ten at a time. As the line and wait stretched, frustrated workers insisted on entering the factory in the normal manner. A restless crowd kept growing.

One worker group peeled off and blocked vehicular traffic on the Bombay-Pune Road by erecting various road blockades. Another took to pelting stones at the police. Finding themselves outnumbered, a message was transmitted from a wireless van, Fox Mobile, requesting Pimpri Static, a control room, to immediately rush additional reserve police force.

Sankoli responded immediately. He managed to bypass the workers' barricades, climbed into Fox Mobile and broadcast appeals to the workers to keep the peace and not commit any illegal acts. The workers eagerly responded—by attacking him and Fox Mobile.

The van was turned on its side, the petrol tank was broken open and with the assistance of pieces of gunny bags the inflammable liquid was taken out and the van was set on fire. The three inmates of the van jumped out and managed to save themselves.

To bring the situation under control, after due warning to the workers, a cane charge was resorted to and teargas was also used, but to no avail. The police personnel became targets of the violence, and several sustained injuries. Forty policemen were injured. 'Sankoli is a huge man,' recalls Roy, 'and he was badly hit on his stomach by a large boulder. He was in hospital for months.'

A fire engine arrived and extinguished the flames engulfing the wireless van. Unable to control the situation, the police fired twenty-nine rounds. Two workers and a shopkeeper were killed.

The injured were sent for medical aid. Statements of various witnesses were recorded, some on that day and the rest on succeeding days. The accused were placed under arrest and on completion of the investigations were chargesheeted and put on trial. Of all the mayhem, perhaps what most galled the authorities was the upturning and burning of a police wireless van.

As news of the firing spread, protests skyrocketed. Municipal workers, returning to work after their own eight-day strike, immediately struck work in support. As did workers in other factories, including even small ones like Silver Bright, a newbie who started making steel rods in 1974. More than 4000 workers attended the funerals. The next day shopkeepers observed a bandh.

Rupa

Rajiv perfectly recalls the weekend of 16–17 June 1979. A thick clump of trees on one side prevented them from seeing fully what was going on, but it didn't cut off the sounds of anger and violence. 'We were all gathered on the balcony outside our room,' he said, 'Mummy, Sanjiv, our maid Hirabai and me. Anxiously Mummy watched in the direction of Papa's office, set on fire by some workers. Hirabai too looked that way—her son was employed as a worker, she was worried for his safety. Perhaps she was conflicted. I certainly was. I asked Mummy, "Why is this happening? Who is right? Who is wrong?" As softly and surely as she always spoke, she said whenever you're in doubt, just listen to your conscience, it is that little voice inside you through which God speaks to you.'

'That night we hardly slept,' Rupa told this author. 'We received a couple of crank calls saying it would be better if the children and I go away to Bombay. Rahul and I thought about it. I said no. I wanted to be with Rahul, and I didn't want people in the colony to think that Rahul's wife and children could just take off for Bombay when things became difficult. I also thought that if I went away, it would be a long, long time before I could come back. Once you go away in such a situation, it is very difficult to feel secure enough to come back. Since there was firing, an inquiry would take place which would be a long-drawn-out thing. The workers were in a mood to fight the management for a long time. I wanted to stay here with him.'

Rupa's faith strengthened Rahul and their children.

Creating a Win-win

An agitated Mohan Dharia, a well-regarded local politician and Lok Sabha member, called for a judicial inquiry. As did Maharashtra's Home Minister Bhai Vaidya, a former trade union leader. But Sharad Pawar hesitated. The newly formed Police Mitra Mandal threatened that if a judicial inquiry were to be held, all eighty-five policemen of the Chinchwad police station would resign. Workers responded with a massive demonstration of 10,000 people. The state government was forced to order a judicial inquiry.

As the inquiry dragged on, Chatterjee and Bajaj quietly arrived at a settlement, and the factory reopened after five months. Fourteen years after the incident, the Bombay High Court fined thirty-one workers Rs 1,00,000 each. These were the highest-ever fines imposed on workers. A lower court had earlier sentenced them to three years of hard labour.

Bajaj attributes this remarkable peace to the fact that 'somehow, we managed to create a situation of win-win and relations became better and better, and that is how my relationship with Chatterjee became excellent. After that we signed another agreement. And after Chatterjee died, we signed another agreement with his main deputy, Gangadhar Ambedkar, when everything was beautiful.'

Bajaj, the only industrialist at Chatterjee's funeral, is all praise for his antagonist: 'He was a gentleman. I don't know the inside story of the man, but he lived simply. He used to ride a bicycle. Even in the 1970s, union leaders used to ride in cars, or on scooters at the very least. But not Chatterjee. He used to eat chana and dressed just like a worker.' Bajaj has fewer kind words for the workers. 'What is the point of staying away from work, losing production and wages?' he asks acerbically. 'Why didn't they work and donate part of their earnings to the families of the three men who died?'

Sunlight and Shadows

Support for Bajaj came from an unexpected quarter. 'Nobody could have been a bigger union leader and more anti-industry than George Fernandes,' recalls Bajaj. 'The day after the firing, I got a call that the minister of industry would like to talk to me. I was already very down. It was the day after three people died in front of my factory. It is not a nice thing, and it has never happened before or since then.'

An understanding of the past helps in making sense of the forces driving this crisis at Bajaj Auto. Across India, during the Emergency,[3] workload was arbitrarily increased. After its withdrawal, the Janata Party won the 1977 election, the Morarji Desai administration took over and workers demanded that workload revert to pre-Emergency levels. When this did not happen, workers fought for a better, fairer deal, and struggles erupted across India.

In Poona, at least twenty-four strikes, involving approximately 7000 workers, broke out in July 1977, starting at Phillips India, Traub, and Formica. Of these, eight were withdrawn after a settlement. The length of the strikes typically ranged from eight days to 130 days. Even the Reserve Bank of India was not immune. On 4 July 1979, a few days prior to its collapse, the Janata Party administration assumed powers to prohibit 'strikes or any conduct which is likely to result in cessation or substantial retardation of work in the Reserve Bank of India'.

Meanwhile, Sharad Pawar broke away from Vasantdada Patil's Congress (U) party to form a coalition government with the Janata

---

[3] 25 June 1975–21 March 1977.

Party. In the process, at the age of thirty-eight, he became the youngest chief minister of Maharashtra. Pawar instituted an inquiry. The judicial system creaked to life but not in the style and pace required to pacify worker angst against the police. Workers came forward to name policemen in the courts and demanded they be dismissed. Singled out was one particular police inspector connected with a number of incidents of police repression at David Brown, Greaves, SKF, Garware, Nav Nagar Palika and other companies.

Post negotiations, the Bajaj Auto factory reopened after five months. At the end of it all, summed up Bajaj: 'The workers' right to strike is recognized, so should be their right to work. A militant minority often prevents the silent majority from going to work. This is neither democratic nor fair.'

An Unusual VRS[4]

'India's big advantage in the 1990s lay not in cheap labour but in cheap design and engineering skills,' pointed out Swaminathan S. Anklesaria Aiyar. 'The Akurdi factory had 20 per cent daily wage earners, 80 per cent skilled workers, and no engineers at all on the shop floor.' Headcount was 17,000. Wages averaged Rs 11,500.

'It was a difficult year,' explains Bajaj in BAL's annual report for 2000–2001. 'Sales took a beating and the EBITDA (earnings before interest, taxes, depreciation, and amortization) margin dropped to 9.8 per cent of total operating income. Even in those tough times, I had reposed my unwavering faith in the company, when I shared with you Bajaj Auto's vision of the future and its path of transformation. I still recollect a sentence that I wrote: "A year's adversity does nothing to change my belief in this vision".'

Considering a Voluntary Retirement Scheme (VRS) for the first time in Bajaj Auto's history was a tough, emotional issue for Bajaj. Of the 3150 employees across management, supervisory and workmen levels eligible under the VRS scheme (open for employees of forty-five years and above), 1976 opted for early retirement. 'The VRS pay-out bill was approximately Rs 80 crore,' recalls Ranjit Gupta, the then vice-president, HRD, to *The Hindu BusinessLine*. The generous VRS payments enabled BAL to halve the workforce. But was the pruning

---

[4] Voluntary Retirement Scheme.

sufficient? Four years later, a second VRS was offered between 1–21 July 2004. As many as 638 workmen opted for it.

The third VRS, offered on 3 September 2007, led to a sit-in strike of about 1600 workers for sixty-five days in front of the plant. The Akurdi plant shut down its manufacturing operations. 'The conflict ended with the workers, most of them in their forties or fifties, being paid Rs 10,000 per month for the next ten years,' writes University of Nottingham's Jörg Nowak, in his work on mass strikes during depressions in India.

'Never say never' is engrained in the Bajaj lexicon. Seven years later, Kawasaki was back in Akurdi and 2014 saw Akurdi's lines rolling again—but for Kawasaki bikes, not Bajaj scooters.

'Kawasaki wanted to sell big bikes in India,' recalled Bajaj, 'and to get lower import duties, assembling big bikes in India was necessary. These high-value and small-number production they wanted to do under their control. We gave them space in Akurdi. Their 100 per cent Indian subsidiary (India Kawasaki Motors) set up assembly lines and also used this facility to assemble 250/300 cc bikes, which Bajaj was assembling for them in Chakan till then. That made sense—enhancing capacity utilization of the assembly lines in Akurdi and releasing space and capacity in our Chakan factory for Bajaj's capacity increases.'

'The interim arrangement made perfect sense since Kawasaki also needed time to get its India retail business plan in place,' Bajaj elaborates, 'Kawasaki, in their long-term plans considered India an important big bike market. They wanted to be in control of their destiny and manage this by themselves. This decision by Kawasaki necessitated a transition to the arrangements that they drew up, to manage the big bike customers in India. They set up their 100 per cent owned subsidiary India Kawasaki Motors (IKM), deputed staff from Japan to run the company.'

'They managed the production of Kawasaki bikes and the market,' Bajaj continues, 'and post-transition IKM successfully catered to this segment of big bikes and introduced many new models as well and is continuing to do so. Relations between Bajaj and Kawasaki continue to be good, and we partner well in the Philippines, where their subsidiary is our distributor, and in Malaysia, where their joint venture is our distributor.'

19

Bajaj US: 1980–87

Bajaj-America, 1237, Gadsden Street, Columbia, South Carolina, 29201.

On 1 April 1971, April Fools' Day, Umberto Agnelli wrote to Kamalnayan, thanking him for years of 'really friendly cooperation' and wishing Bajaj Auto 'the most successful future'. With this letter, Piaggio's eleven-year technical collaboration with Bajaj Auto to manufacture Vespa scooters under licence in India ended on 31 March 1971. A decade later, Piaggio would accuse Bajaj of pilfering

Piaggio designs in a California district court. A special business relationship ended in India and turned into a legal tangle in multiple law courts in the US, Europe and Asia.

Initially, both sides tried to find a middle path. 'I remember a whole week in Genoa with four of my colleagues in 1975,' recalls Bajaj. 'A deal was about to be finalized. Everything was done. Without charging any royalty and fees, without any equity in our company, Piaggio would give the plans of their scooters and three-wheelers. In return we would give them the worldwide right to export our vehicles. We fixed the minimum value they would export each year for the next ten years. It got stuck on one small point. We wanted R&D cooperation. They wouldn't agree to that. But we broke up amicably as we had done in 1971. Later our exports increased a little bit. They were still chicken feed. But Piaggio thought it was a threat.'

Between 1978 and 1980, Bajaj exports rose steadily from $9.21 million (Rs 63.5 million) to $14.8 million (Rs 133.2 million). The year 1980 saw Bajaj register Bajaj-America Inc. in Columbia, South Carolina with an equity capital of $15,000, representing 30 per cent of the new company's equity.

The export strategy was robust. The first batch of Indian scooters arrived in the US: 3244 scooters and 3005 three-wheelers (including 2518 CKD packs) sailed out of India, earning Bajaj Auto foreign exchange equivalent of Rs 6.29 crore as against Rs 2.23 crore previously. Plus, Bajaj sold 1,03,863 Bajaj Chetak scooters booked against remittance of foreign exchange. The foreign exchange received against these sales was equivalent to Rs 62.32 crore. To top it all, Bajaj Auto received another slice of foreign exchange equivalent to Rs 6,00,000 as the fee for technical know-how from its licensees abroad.

'Put a Bajaj in every garage' became Bajaj-America's 1983 slogan, used to aggressively market three-wheelers at suggested retail prices varying from $2695 for the Gopher, to $2895 for the Tristar pickup, to $3395 for the Autorickshaw people carrier. But he was still many steps away. Piaggio's production in 1981 was 9,05,000 vehicles, that of Bajaj Auto, 1,73,000. Piaggio's sales were lire 626 billion (about Rs 4.7 billion at the then current rates). Bajaj's were Rs 1.16 billion.

Within four months, Bajaj sold 250 three-wheelers and the response 'is very, very good,' David Jones, president of the American division, told

India-West. To the local reporter of *The Turf Vehicle Guide*, Jones was equally exuberant. 'At Bajaj-America, the favourite expression is "what recession?" Bajaj produces a low-priced, high-mileage turf vehicle, the Bajaj Gopher, that has been very successful since its introduction in mid-1982. Our car has done really well, and we expect an excellent year in 1983,' said Jones. 'It is premature to predict an upturn,' he admitted. 'Some businesses are expecting too much from the recent drop in rates.' The Chetak scooter, oddly enough, which Bajaj introduced at the same time, got a lukewarm response in the US.

Piaggio US

Piaggio had its own challenges in the US. Agnelli bonhomie suddenly evaporated. After all, it was the Americans who created the world's first scooter shortly before World War II broke out. In the 1950s, Piaggio under Umberto Agnelli started selling its scooters in the US, both under its own name and through the Sears, Roebuck brand, the Allstate Crusaire. Sales were never high but enough to keep Piaggio interested in the American market. Bajaj's US entry was a jolt.

Piaggio and C.S.p.A. Italy jointly with Vespa of America Corporation filed a suit in the Federal Court in the Northern District of California in San Francisco, seeking injunctive relief against the entry of 'Bajaj' scooters in the US. and $50 million in damages. The Italians claimed that the Indian firm had violated the terms of their collaboration and had not returned Piaggio's original drawings, and so had no right to manufacture scooters. Piaggio also filed suits in India, Britain, West Germany, and Hong Kong, asking that Bajaj be prevented from exporting its scooters to those countries.

Bajaj brushes aside the arguments, claiming he had Piaggio's tacit permission. 'How else could it have been? We couldn't be expected to invest crores of rupees in plant and equipment and then one fine day cease to manufacture and let our investment go to seed. And, if Piaggio had not acquiesced in our action, it should have taken legal action then, not ten years later.'

Bajaj approached the Indira Gandhi administration, back in power once again,[1] to bring 'gentle pressure' on the Italian company to withdraw its lawsuits. 'It is clearly not in the interest of the country

---

[1] 14 January 1980–31 October 1984.

to allow Piaggio to derive any further benefits from India until such time as it gives up its tactics designed to limit India's exports,' argued Bajaj. 'The Italian company should not be allowed to have its cake and eat it, too,' he grumbled to the *Times of India*. At the very least, would the government reconsider its decision to allow the Italians to enter into new collaborative agreements in India?

The request went unheeded. On the contrary, Piaggio India was permitted two new licencing agreements: with Andhra Pradesh Scooters, a public sector company; and with Lohia Machine Tools in the private sector. 'Piaggio's motives in providing technical expertise to the two new joint arrangements appeared to be questionable,' Bajaj pointed out to Ramesh and Bina Murarka, *India-West* reporters from San Leandro, California.

The US District Court for the Northern District of California

Piaggio's lawyers—Ream, Train, Horning, Ellison and Roskoph, fronted by Indians—took a dim view of the situation. 'It's a matter of national importance that Indian companies abide by the agreements that they enter into with foreign companies. We want a greater inflow of foreign technology. How can we inspire confidence if we violate agreements?' they chorused.

Bajaj hired Baker-McKenzie, one of the largest international law firms in the world, pouring in $1 million for Bajaj Auto's defence. It was an impressive figure for an Indian company in those days.

Court hearings for the jury trial began on 10 September 1984. Piaggio maintained that the Vespa design was so well-identified in the American mind that the similarity of the Bajaj scooter represented an infringement of an unregistered trademark. 'Bajaj had copied thirty-five to forty of its designs even after the agreement was terminated,' alleged the Italians. Bajaj riposted that his lawyers had asked Piaggio to give specific examples of designs that had been copied, and that Piaggio was unable to cite even one. Adding grist to the mill, Bajaj referred to Piaggio's monopolization of the US market.

The US District Court for the Northern District of California at San Francisco not only dismissed Piaggio's claims of breach of contract and conversion against Bajaj Auto Holdings Ltd, but it also refused Piaggio leave to appeal. All that Piaggio could ask for would be that sale of Bajaj scooters having particular technological features, which would have to be clearly defined by them, be forbidden.

With the win in his pocket, Bajaj cocked a snook at Piaggio. A few three-wheelers from the Bajaj Auto Akurdi plant arrived in the US. 'For marketing purposes only,' Bajaj told shareholders decorously, 'we are just exploring possibilities.'

Towards the end of the big fight, Piaggio simply gave up marketing and selling its scooters in America. Pollution norms changed. Piaggio did a hard stop of its exports. Pugnacious as always, even though they did not have a product to sell in the US, Piaggio continued to fight with Bajaj. Losing face is not a simple matter.

The fracas wasn't over. On the contrary, it was about to go global. Piaggio launched legal action against Bajaj distributors, filing patent infringement suits to block Bajaj scooter sales in the United States, the United Kingdom, West Germany and Hong Kong. 'I remember that Piaggio filed suits in US and Germany. Piaggio also filed suits against our distributor in Italy,' recalls Bajaj.

Zweirad Roth

The retaliation was not slow in coming. The target: West Germany.[2] Vespa GmbH, a Piaggio subsidiary, filed a suit against Zweirad Roth, a newly recruited Bajaj dealer, prohibiting Roth from selling the Indian scooters.

The first round went badly for Roth and Bajaj at the hearing in the Regional Court at Darmstadt on 15 June 1983. Zweirad Roth could not be forbidden from selling Bajaj scooters in West Germany, agreed the judges. And all that Vespa could ask for was that technological features specific to the Vespa be forbidden to the Bajaj scooter. The Indian scooter's external appearance was not distinct from the Vespa, said the judge. The Indian scooter technical design was too close to that of the Vespa in three characteristics: 'direct rear wheel drive', 'one-sided wheel suspensions on both wheels', and the 'self-supporting chassis'. Zweirad Roth was directed to abstain from offering, advertising, or selling the Bajaj motor scooter.

The feisty Zweirad Roth's owner refused to give up. He successfully filed an appeal against the decision of the Darmstadt's Regional Court

---

[2] Federal Republic of Germany.

at the Appeal Court in Frankfurt. Piaggio GmbH promptly filed its counter appeal against this decision in the Superior Court. The matter lingered and lingered. Documents were freshly dusted in June 1989 for a hearing, but it came and went unresolved. Both parties finally arrived at a settlement in 1990: Bajaj Chetak scooters sold in Germany had to carry the lettering 'Made in India' on its scooters.

But

The great scooter war ended on a whimper. 'We had only the Vespa collaboration—a technical collaboration, and we had good relations with them, until of course in 1971 the government said no more collaboration, and then there was some litigation. But I won't blame Piaggio for that. We won that case,' Bajaj shared with Datar.

In the US, Piaggio offered an out-of-court settlement. Piaggio's initial $50 million compensation demand was scaled down to $50,000. Bajaj refused to budge. 'The settlement agreement did not provide for any monetary payment by Bajaj Auto,' recalls a satisfied Bajaj. 'And in the final settlement the only promise we gave was not sell to Bajaj scooters of Piaggio design in the US.' By then demand for scooters in the US had dropped anyway. 'Our exports suffered during this period,' said Bajaj. 'Piaggio succeeded in their aim to that extent.'

But if Bajaj didn't lose, neither did he win. 'Piaggio came to India claiming they had better technology, a better vehicle and a better deal for the Indian customer. If they were so much better than us, they could have easily beaten us in America and Germany. Why did they take recourse to the courts? But then, they are in business. We are in business. Journalists like to dramatize but quite frankly there was no hate. It was a serious business fight. In their position, I might have done the same thing.'

But Bajaj won the argument that Piaggio had given the Indian company the right to manufacture the scooter for export; and that the Indian government had given Bajaj Auto the right to export scooters anywhere in the world after the expiration of the licencing agreement. An unhappy Piaggio reluctantly agreed to Bajaj's export access to fifteen countries.

The Italian firm returned to the US in 2001.

In Akurdi, winning the battle further kindled global ambitions.

20

The Waltz of the Bike Moghuls: 1982–2005

Sanjiv, Bajaj and Rajiv.

September 1989 finds Bajaj in San Francisco to attend the International Industrial Conference hosted by the Stanford Research Institute International and attended by business leaders from sixty-two countries. This year's theme was 'Managing in a Competitive Global Economy'.

Walking around the campus, listening to Sony's Akio Morita summit opening speech, chatting with buddies Viren Shah and Ashok Birla, Bajaj's mind kept returning to the question: could deregulation and import liberalization lead to quality products which can take on international competition. 'At present it looks beyond our reach to be global,' he figures despondently.

To the *India Abroad* reporter Batuk Vora, however, Bajaj is his usual gung-ho self: 'I must say this, and I told this to many delegates here, that what India needs is a few more years. I hope Rajiv Gandhi will come back to power after the elections and gradually open up our economy.'

'My major aim in attending that conference was to exchange views with some of the top business giants,' reminiscences Bajaj. 'When we were somewhere near a $300 million group, they were worth $300 billion. Bajaj Auto had begun exporting scooters and three-wheelers around the world, but we were nowhere near international standards. I even wondered if what we needed to raise the bedrock in India was 100 per cent ownership freedom for foreign investors.'

Namaste

'The entire environment changed from the mid-1980s. We were no longer a Robinson Crusoe island, isolated and backward,' he shared with *Fortune's* Louis Kraar in 1986. The relationship between India and Japan had diminished to near-nothing after the testing of the Smiling Buddha, India's first successful nuclear bomb on 18 May 1974.

The game changer turned out to be Indira Gandhi. She did her best to chip away at India's sequestration. Her third term as prime minister between 1980–1984 saw her make forty international state visits, including one to Tokyo on 5 August 1982.

Helpfully—and unusual for such conversations—Zenkō Suzuki and Indira Gandhi were able to meet thrice[1] in the course of Suzuki's two-year term as prime minister. India needed Japan to reduce its dependence on the Soviet Union. Japan's Prime Minister

---

[1] (1) North–South Summit in Cancun, Mexico, 22–23 October 1981, attended by representatives of twenty-two countries from five continents. (2) State visit to Tokyo, 5 August 1982. (3) Funeral of the Soviet Union leader, Leonid Ilyich Brezhnev, in Moscow, 15 November 1982. Twelve days later, Yasuhiro Nakasone would take over the prime ministership from Zenkō Suzuki.

Zenkō Suzuki was looking for new markets to whip up slackening economic growth and export stagnation in a global recession. The leadership of both countries began to reflect on the benefits of the 'politics of harmony'. Suzuki's term ended a few months later, on 26 November 1982. The policy approach towards India of the next Japanese prime minister, Yasuhiro Nakasone, remained consistent.

'A Japanese premier will be visiting India after twenty-three years, reaffirming that both countries are looking at each other afresh,' reported T.N. Ninan, sent by *India Today* to Japan to capture a historic turning point. 'Japan senses a new affinity in Indian foreign policy. India sees in Japanese technology and resources an ideal springboard for its own modernisation and industrial growth. Bilateral trade is growing, and likewise industrial collaborations have increased in both numbers and significance.'

Nakasone's two-day visit to India between 3–4 May 1984, along with his minister for foreign affairs, Shintaro Abe (Shinzo's father), was a revival of bonhomie between the two nations after a gap of twenty-three years. This was a much-needed salve by the Japanese. Still, in April, before arriving in India, Nakasone had dropped by in Pakistan to meet Zulfikar Ali Bhutto. Japan was the largest aid donor to Pakistan. He advanced funds for Afghan refugees and called for the immediate withdrawal of Soviet troops from Afghanistan.

'Aid was now described in Tokyo as strategic rather than developmental,' described Nathaniel B. Thayer. 'Japan has neither important economic interests in Pakistan nor close cultural ties with Afghanistan. The visit was totally political. In India, Nakasone's talks with Indira Gandhi simply reflected his long-held belief that Japan can play a special role in the third world.' To show he meant business, Nakasone brought with him senior executives from Japan's biggest auto manufacturers to suss out potential Indian partners.

Re-elected for a second term a few days before Indira Gandhi's assassination, Nakasone was back in India with Shintaro Abe for her funeral on 31 October 1984 and to introduce himself to Rajiv Gandhi. Once again, Nakasone came with a large delegation. This time with a 'high-level' economic team to consider areas of co-operation with India.

Sustaining the policy his mother had set, in 1985 Rajiv Gandhi would invite eighteen businessmen to a state visit to the Soviet Union.

India opened its doors to the world's biggest two-wheeler companies. But the question remained: who would dance with whom at this ball engineered by Rajiv Gandhi and Nakasone? And who would leave with whom after the ball was over? Indian auto majors smiled, but the swiftness of the Japanese encroachment was unnerving.

'Accustomed to dominant positions in protected markets, local companies suddenly faced foreign rivals wielding a daunting array of advantages: substantial financial resources, advanced technology, superior products, powerful brands, and seasoned marketing and management skills,' explain HBS professors Niraj Dawar and Tony Frost.

Four Japanese: Honda, Kawasaki, Suzuki, Yamaha. One Italian: Piaggio. 150 Indian applications whittled down to five: Bajaj, Firodia, Munjal, Nanda, TVS. The waltz began. Who would tie up with whom?

Escorts-Yamaha

The credit of being the first off the mark was neither Honda nor Kawasaki but Yamaha. The Escorts-Yamaha partnership with the Nanda family in 1983 badged the two-stroke Yamaha RD 350 in India as the Rajdoot 350 (RD stands for 'Race Derived'). 'The bike had already proven its mettle throughout the world,' recounts motorbike blogger Farhan Kashif. 'It succeeded in impressing Indian motorcycle enthusiasts but price limited sales.'

For Har Prasad and Yudi Nanda, the opening up of India's bike industry to the Japanese came at an awkward moment. In 1983, London-based Swaraj Paul launched a takeover attack on the Nanda family's biggest company, Escorts. The Nandas had only 7.3 per cent of Escort's equity. After months of serious lobbying, Paul retreated. Now back to real work.

Reverting to the 1960s for a moment, the brothers were on a spree. They acquired a licence from the US's Ford Tractor Company based in Minneapolis, Minnesota[2] to assemble tractors in India. The first one strode out in 1965 with decent quality. Multiple collaborations followed over the years: with Westinghouse for X-ray machines, heating elements with Elpro, Minneapolis-Moline (large tractor and farm and industrial machinery producer based in Hopkins,

---

[2] Distinct from Ford Motors.

Minnesota). In 1969, Ford Motors permitted them to produce tractors under licence for India. Massey Ferguson (again, agricultural equipment but based in Brantford, Ontario), pistons arrived in India from Germany, sourced from Goetze-Werke and Mahle.

The list goes on and on. The Nandas had an agreement with Poland for its Ursus SA tractors business, but it went bust during the Solidarity Movement just when the Nandas could have put the tractors to some good use. Hughes Communications, J.C. Bamford Excavators, Claas, Carraro, First Pacific Company, Jeumont Schneider, Dynapac—almost all the names mentioned, entered India. A quick scan reveals that even in 2020, most of the Indian subsidiaries of the foreign organizations are doing well—which is rather a nice compliment in itself to the Nanda family. And then came Yamaha.

The Rajdoot 350 bike, also known as the RD 350 was assembled from 1983 to 1989 at the Nandas' Surajpur plant in Noida's industrial estate in Uttar Pradesh. The Rajdoot 350 was a licenced copy of the outdated Yamaha RD 350B, modified to suit Indian conditions. Production of the air-cooled bike had ended in Japan in the mid-1970s due to stringent emission norms but arrived in the Indian market in 1983. Technically, it was an advanced motorcycle.

For bike aficionados: the RD 350 had a seven-port two-stroke parallel twin engine, Yamaha's patented Torque Induction System using reed valves, six-speed manual transmission, auto-lube system, mechanical tachometer, 12-volt electrics for a 0–60 kmph-start in less than four seconds. In the interest of costs, the front disc brake of the RD350B was substituted with a 7-inch twin leading shoe drum brake from the Yamaha RD250.

And it flopped.

Following the dismal sales of the Rajdoot 350, Yamaha needed to make a comeback product, and the success of Suzuki's AX 100 demonstrated the potential for small-capacity motorbikes in India.

This time round, Yamaha participated much more actively in developing the Surajpur plant. Yamaha sent a team of ten managers to train Indian employees in Japanese production practices. The plant followed a typical Japanese design, and work was organized on a cellular basis. Numerous Japanese management practices, such as just-in-time inventory, were adopted. In addition, the scope of the plant was expanded to include the full manufacture and assembly of motorcycles.

In November 1985, Yamaha-Escorts released the Yamaha RX 100. With its lightweight body and high-power output, the power to weight ratio of the bike made it a decent 100 cc bike for mass production. Almost simultaneously, Suzuki-TVS brought out its 100 cc two-stroke offering as the Ind-Suzuki AX100. Between them, Yamaha and Suzuki successfully established a brand-new segment in India and the beginning of a new era of 100 cc two-stroke motorcycles.

Honda: Opportunity or Threat?

Kawasaki, Yamaha and Suzuki had two-stroke engines on their motorcycles. Only Honda had four-stroke engines. Other things being equal, a four-stroke engine is more fuel-efficient than a two-stroke one and this was the advantage Honda enjoyed over the other three motorcycle manufacturers in India.

Honda had been eyeing India and its huge domestic market for some years. Under its new president, Tadashi Kume, who took charge in December 1983 from founder Soichiro Honda, Kume was quick to enter the investment door when the Indian government cracked it open. Once in, Kume immediately announced Honda's intention of coming to India with one or more joint venture partners.

Over 150 applications poured in, and with typical Japanese conscientiousness, the Honda team painstakingly narrowed down the list to twelve hopefuls. In order to further prune the list to the most suitable three, between 1983–84 Honda executives visited the manufacturing facilities of all twelve. It quickly became apparent that Bajaj Auto, the Firodias' Bajaj Tempo Motors, and Brijmohan Lall Munjal's Hero Motors, a Ludhiana-based cycle and moped manufacturer, led the pack by a wide margin. Back in Tokyo, the Honda directors decided to tie up with the two weakest. Munjal and Firodia were preferable to Bajaj. A partnership with the latter would not work because Bajaj 'wanted too much'.

In Akurdi, Bajaj and Rajiv were tinkering with motorcycle concepts in the summer of 1984 when troops stormed the Golden Temple at Amritsar as part of Operation Bluestar (1–8 June 1984) and northern India blew up. Despite this trauma, the Ludhiana-based Brijmohan Lall Munjal managed to ink their technical collaboration with Honda to begin motorcycle production in India through Hero Honda Motors. A few weeks later, on 9 August 1984 Hero Honda Motors made its first public offering.

The first 100 cc Hero Honda motorcycle came off an assembly line in Dharuhera, Haryana in April 1985. It was an instant hit, with its 'Fill it, shut it, forget it' slick advertising campaign asking Indian men to get off their scooters to ride its 100 cc CD100 bike, a bike which promised a mileage of 65–70 km per litre. 'Indian consumers could now enjoy the performance, refinement, technology and fuel efficiency of Japanese design and technology at very competitive prices,' was the message.

But there were a few hitches.

Honda was not confident of Indian quality and insisted on component imports from Japan. The Munjals also were steeped in component manufacture since Partition in 1947. A falling yen-rupee exchange rate left the Munjals on the losing end: each bike sold lost money. Behind these setbacks and other minor irritants also lay the question, who would make how much money—would it be Honda, or would it be the Munjals? The transfer pricing game is always a delicate balancing act.

Eventually, profits trickled in. A year later, the Japanese firm reaffirmed its partnership with Hero for the next ten years, and Hero and Honda together biked into a brand-new sunrise.

By the Way, a Scooter is Available Too

Honda simultaneously signed a joint equity venture with the Firodias to make scooters through Kinetic Honda. Sophisticated consumers in the Pune area loved Firodia's newly badged Kinetic Honda scooter, its sleek design, low fuel consumption, and hi-tech features. The rest of the country looked at its stiffer price tag. Bit by bit, Bajaj relaxed. In 1993, Kinetic Honda sold 85,000 scooters (11 per cent market share) compared to Bajaj Auto's 5,38,000 (76 per cent).

Honda, now firmly committed to a leadership position in India, viewed the Kinetic statistics through a contrasting lens. According to Koji Nakazone, their man in India, Kinetic Honda had done very well in reaching sales of 85,000 scooters at a time when the market shrank by 12 per cent. In 1993, Honda hiked its stake in Kinetic Honda to 51 per cent, beefed up its representation on the board, and enlarged its scooter capacity.

There came a time when Honda played Firodia vs Munjal. Honda finally allowed the Munjals to move into a domain that was, until then, the absolute monopoly of Firodia's scooters. Honda gave Hero the nod to manufacture them with Honda technology. For the Munjals the offer was late in coming. 'We were still focused on motorcycles,' remembers Pawan Munjal, Hero Honda Motors' CEO. 'It was decided that for the first couple of years, Honda would make scooters in a separate company, and we would make motorcycles. Thereafter, both of us would be free to make all kinds of two-wheelers.' The Munjals entered the scooter market with the launch of its 100-cc Pleasure in 2006.

Outwardly the partners presented an amicable front, but tension roiled under the surface. For instance, which model should be introduced in the second round? The impasse delayed the building of the Gurgaon plant, allowing Bajaj Auto to seize market share. Bajaj brought out a four-stroke engine scooter with the cheeky advertising line—'*Kyon Hero?*'.

Though the Munjals' motorcycle business grew larger than scooters, a disappointment lingered over the bar on scooter manufacture. The scab became raw when Honda decided to bring cars to India. The Japanese did not come to the Munjals, they went to the Shrirams. All this gave the Munjals food for thought. Pawan Munjal recognized that they could not for ever hang on to Honda's coat-tails. The twenty-six-year-old partnership ended in 2011.

As for the Firodias, they terminated their joint venture in 1998. Kinetic Engineering continued to sell scooters under the Kinetic brand until 2008, when the family sold the business to tractor maker Mahindra & Mahindra (M&M).

As Honda flexed its muscles in India, Bajaj faced a few anxious moments. 'A closer look at the situation however convinced Bajaj's managers that Honda's advantages were not as formidable as they first appeared,' explain Niraj Dawar and Tony Frost. 'Instead of forming a partnership with Honda, Bajaj's owners decided to stay independent and fortify their existing competitive assets. While Honda would enjoy some advantages in product development, Bajaj would not have to spend heavily to keep up. The makeup of the Indian scooter market, moreover, differed in many ways from Honda's established customer base. Consumers looked for low-cost, durable machines, and they wanted easy access to maintenance facilities in the countryside.'

Bajaj sold rugged scooters through an extensive distribution system and its ubiquitous service network of stalls run by roadside mechanic fitted the Indian market well. Honda, which offered sleekly designed scooters sold mostly through outlets in major cities, did not. The latter beefed up its distribution and invested more in R&D. Its strategy paid off. Honda managed to grab 11 per cent of the Indian scooter market, but its share stabilized at just under that level. Bajaj's share, meanwhile, slipped only a few points from its earlier mark of 77 per cent. In the third quarter of financial year (FY) 1998, Honda threw down the gloves, and announced it was pulling out of its scooter-manufacturing equity joint venture in India.

Bajaj Auto and Kawasaki Heavy Industries now sized each other up properly for the first time. 'Our problem with Honda was that they wanted equity,' recalls Bajaj, 'and we only wanted a technical collaboration agreement. That is why we went with Kawasaki, who, like us, wanted only a technical collaboration agreement.' This approach suited Kawasaki Heavy Motors perfectly then and would suit both perfectly over the next three decades. On 6 August 1984, Bajaj and the president of Kawasaki Heavy Industries, K. Hasegawa, along with Dr Hiroshi Ohba, managing director of the Kawasaki Motorcycle Group, signed their agreement.

'Bajaj Auto chalked out a strategy for co-existence with Kawasaki,' write Arthur A. Thompson Jr, A.J. Strickland III, John E. Gamble and Arun K. Jain in *Crafting and Executing Strategy: The Quest for Competitive Advantage.* 'Bajaj would concentrate on developing products in the price range of Rs 30,000–60,000 and Kawasaki would offer a wider choice of products priced from Rs 35,000 up to Rs 2,50,000. Bajaj Auto became a key manufacturing base for Kawasaki and accounted for 60 per cent of the latter's global sales.' Even though the market was changing, and the waiting periods vanished, Bajaj scooters continued to sell well till about 2000.

TVS-Suzuki

When the Suzuki Motor Company came calling, like Bajaj, the TVS group preferred a technical know-how and assistance agreement, not a joint venture. TVS already had a moped division and was in the process of setting up a plant for engines and transmission parts. The two organizations could not be more dissimilar: a rather dictatorial Japanese loner vis-à-vis a large multigenerational Indian clan, both parties with deep roots in engineering for decades. Osamu Suzuki's primary focus for his Asia trip in 1982 was the opening of two assembly car plants (Maruti Udyog in India), two-wheelers (TVS), and the Pakistan market. October saw him win over the Indian government to take him as a joint-venture partner in Maruti Udyog. For the bikes, TVS and Suzuki signed up for an initial one-year relationship aimed at technology transfer specifically for the Indian market.

The next five years saw a bout of activity. Rechristened from Indo Suzuki Motorcycles to TVS Suzuki, the partners brought out several models, all of them beginning with the same name: Suzuki Supra, Suzuki Samurai, Suzuki Shogun and Suzuki Shaolin. TVS group and Suzuki Motor Corporation parted ways from their fifteen-year-old joint venture on 27 September 2001.

Piaggio Circles Back

Piaggio re-entered India in 1983—but not with Bajaj. Instead, the Italians signed collaborations with Deepak Singhania of Lohia Machines (LML) for Vespa's P-series scooters, and with Andhra Pradesh Scooters for the supply of CKD packs and technical know-how.

October 1989 brought signs of an accord between Piaggio and Bajaj. Piaggio's home base was under attack from the Japanese and in India, LML was doing badly. The Italians began to wonder whether the LML investment had been such a good idea after all. Giovanni Umberto Agnelli, heir to the Fiat empire, and Piaggio's vice-president, brokered a secret visit by Bajaj and his team to Piaggio headquarters in Pisa to work out a strategic alliance. A key element was a 10 per cent cross-holding in each other's companies. Also on the negotiating table was a collaboration for spare parts and the ending of a few remaining bits of the long-running court battle in West Germany. As before, this attempt too fizzled out.

The Italians went back to LML, which by now had slipped deeper in the red. To rev up its image in India, Piaggio picked up 23.6 per cent of LML's equity for Rs 80 million in 1990. The fuel injection soon got used up. By 1993, LML's losses hit Rs 360 million.

The September of 1993 also saw Agnelli attempt a third futile attempt at reconciliation. Agnelli flew from Turin to Akurdi. Piaggio wanted to replace the Singhanias with a new Indian partner. Would Bajaj consider this? Bajaj chose instead to revive the idea of a 10 per cent cross-holding between their companies. The talks came close to success but broke down when Piaggio apparently started talking of raising the cross-holding. Suddenly LML's asking price began to look too high. If Bajaj gave in to Piaggio's demand for more equity, he would expose his soft underbelly. Were Bajaj to give away more than 10 per cent, his former partner could use it as a dangerous lever if things didn't work out with Piaggio later.

Scenting an opportunity, other Indian industrialists immediately made a beeline to Italy. Among them were the Nandas of Escorts and the Munjals of Hero Motors. At one point it looked as if Rajan Nanda, Escort's' vice-chairman, had clinched the deal. Piaggio decided not to separate from the Singhanias until and unless someone more interesting turned up.

After a protracted dispute with Piaggio, LML bought out the Italians in 1999. LML continued to produce and export the P-Series rebadged as the Stella in the US market, and by other names in their markets for half a decade. At the 2012 Auto Expo held in New Delhi, the Vespa re-entered the Indian market alongside Piaggio's latest range of scooters—without a local partner. And why not? Shortly before the Expo, Piaggio inaugurated its own plant in Baramati (Maharashtra) for the local market. From the sidelines, *Business India* smirked: 'Piaggio tried to dent Bajaj's growing market share but only got its nose bloodied.'

LML issued a notice of insolvency on 2 June 2017 and closed down permanently in 2018.

The Desolation of the JVs

Coming back to the two questions posed at the beginning of this chapter, 'who would dance with whom?' and 'who would leave with whom?', the short answer is that the dances mostly ended in divorces—and a few rare win-wins.

Under the Atal Bihari Vajpayee administration, the government tried to contain the dancers through Press Note 18 of 14 December

1998. At the CII Partnership Summit in Kolkata in January 2005, however, Prime Minister Manmohan Singh announced the withdrawal of Press Note 18 of 1998 and issued Press Note 1 (2005 series) on 12 January. Meant to make life easier, national and international auto majors instead jostled even harder to make their needs heard.

Taking up their case, FICCI's general secretary, Amit Mitra was scathing of PN1 (2005):

'Press Note 18 issued on 14 December 1998 was a landmark notification that saved the demise of many of today's celebrated Indian companies,' wrote Mitra in the *Economic Times*. 'PN1 has anomalies: it benefits foreign investors after 12 January 2005, whereas those who entered into JVs earlier investors need prior approval. It ignores cases where separate tie-ups in parts of India that do not necessarily prejudice existing tie-ups in sectors such as hotels, hospitality, and hospitals. It is redundant in sectors already dominated by foreign players, e.g., advertising. It applies also to changes in shareholding patterns caused by events like global mergers and acquisitions . . . Scrapping PN1 could be another trigger in making India one of the most attractive FDI (foreign direct investment) destinations.'

Divorces started piling up: Yamaha-Escorts, Honda-Hero, Honda-Kinetic, Suzuki-TVS, Piaggio-LML, BMW-Hero. The Bajaj-Kawasaki alliance held, but Bajaj lost its number-one position to Honda in this churn. Overall, while Indians gained confidence in developing products on their own, the Japanese made themselves capable of studying and understanding the Indian market in a comprehensive manner. The market expanded. Technology improved. Customers had wider and better choices.

A new, long line appeared of global auto manufacturers wanting to join hands with Bajaj, including those from Europe such as KTM and BMW Motorrad. The next couple of decades increasingly saw visitors drop in for a chat at Akurdi. Barring a few exceptions, the newcomers blended in.

21

Waluj: 1985

President Giani Zail Singh and Bajaj at the inauguration in 1985.

Tuesday, 5 November 1985. Overwhelmed officials pinned smiles on their faces and soldiered on. The tiny airport of Aurangabad had never seen aircraft land and take off in such tightly compressed time frames. Thousands of chattering men and women kept pouring into the airport. From the guest of honour who would inaugurate the plant, President Giani Zail Singh, with his gun-toting entourage, his press secretary Tarlochan Singh, to humble technicians and support staff, eye candy film stars and business barons, each individual needed to be processed—quickly. Guided by Bajaj managers, the officials did their best.

The guests came from all over India and globally to celebrate Bajaj's spanking new plant at Waluj built at a cost of Rs 2 billion in a record sixteen months. Bajaj had waited twenty-two years for this moment. The curious peeked into the plant's cavernous innards. Others enjoyed the balmy weather outside, the elegant greenery curated by Kumud marking the footpaths, and floral creations on the several podiums dotted inside various sheds.

The only celebrity missing was Indira Gandhi, assassinated by her security guards on 31 October 1984. The collaboration between Bajaj Auto and Kawasaki Heavy Industries had begun under her aegis. Bajaj's specific interest lay in motorcycles, and his eye was on a partnership with Kawasaki, the maker of the fastest motorcycle in the world, the Ninja. But for the moment, he would have to content himself with the KB 100.

Permissions for Bajaj Auto was a somewhat erratic flow in the 1980s. Under the short-lived Charan Singh administration, babudom permitted Bajaj Auto to double its two-wheeler capacity from 80,000 to 1,60,000 vehicles. A few months later, a prime minister with a long memory, Indira Gandhi, less generously granted Bajaj a rise in three-wheeler capacity from 15,000 to 20,000 vehicles plus a micro increase in scooter CKD packs from 30,000 to 32,000 for the Maharashtra Scooters joint sector plant at Satara.

Rajiv Gandhi's top-up was more genuine and generous. Industries Minister Narayan Dutt Tiwari cleared the proposal to build a plant at Waluj on 7 October 1982. Bajaj was stunned. The permission came in a mere sixty-three days. The Indian government machinery worked overtime to please the new prime minister. Rajiv Gandhi also kept adding to the pot. Licenced capacity climbed from 3,00,000 vehicles per annum to 1 million to 1.5 million in 1990. Bajaj Auto's share of the two-wheeler market grew from 30 per cent to 43 per cent.

That Top-of-the-World Feeling

'It's true that Rajiv Gandhi could not dismantle the industrial
licencing system but under the "broad banding" umbrella,' says Bajaj,
'he gave us as many licences as we desired.' Nor was it a problem
to tap funding outside India. International Finance Corporation,
Washington topped up Waluj's requirements by sanctioning a \$22
million loan (Rs 242 million) to import capital equipment.

In a serious ease-of-business attitude, installed machinery was
permitted flexibility. Production licences were issued for a broader
product group as opposed to single-product licences issued earlier.
Clearances to diversify within product groups no longer required
permissions as long as the diversification did not necessitate new
investment in machinery. 'The scheme freed manufacturers to select
the right product mix for their products and thereby make optimal
use of their capital investments,' describe professors Mahipat
Ranawat and Rajnish Tiwari.

The initial permission for the Waluj plant was for 3,00,000
scooters, motorcycles and three-wheelers. In 1987, Waluj was asked
if it wanted to additionally supply 87,000 CKD packs annually to
Maharashtra Scooters to top up the 2,00,000 already being supplied
by Akurdi. Yes, of course, and why not? The permissions came
handy. Local and international competition was hotting-up. Bajaj
Auto's world-size plant, well-laid out to take care of the mass
production, gave it a vital edge. As the plant would become older,
fixed costs would reduce and so also the cost per vehicle.

Best of all, scooter production at Waluj started in mid-May 1985
as planned and on time. The automated plant was then amongst
the most modern in India's auto industry. Scooter number 1,00,000
marched off the assembly line on 16 August 1986. Waluj's CKD
packs for Maharashtra Scooters jumped from 69,700 to 87,000, i.e.,
from 30 per cent to 50 per cent. The next year, Maharashtra Scooters
upped its order of CKD packs from 87,000 to 2,00,000.

On the Waluj drawing board appeared a three-wheeler division
to produce up to 50,000 units per annum. Maybe this line could be
ready as early as March 1988, Bajaj mused. Another thought drifted
through his mind. Could the licence stretch to an assembly unit for

a 1,00,000-two-wheeler plant in Surajpur in the Ghaziabad district of Uttar Pradesh? Yes, of course it could, came the response from the Rajiv Gandhi administration.

The Making of the KB 100

As these exciting events were taking place, behind Bajaj's back, fiddling with motorbike concepts was a fun hobby among Bajaj Auto's Akurdi designers even though they knew it was highly unlikely for anything to materialize with a scooter-obsessed chairman. With the opening of the modern Waluj plant and the alliance with Kawasaki, a world champion in motorcycle racing, dreams were born. When they heard that the first output of the collaboration would be a staid commuter bike and not a Ninja-like racing monster, they were more than a tad disappointed.

With three Japanese giants throwing down their gauntlet into the ring, it was up to Bajaj, with no JV and only a technology agreement with Kawasaki, to create a space in the market for his bike. Bajaj's mastery of economies of scale and his cookie-cutter approach, fine-tuned in the Akurdi plant, making for an extremely profitable operation, spilled over to the Waluj plant. The downside was inadequate attention to R&D and technology, and limited tolerance for ingenuity or experimentation.

Bajaj loosened the purse strings a bit and R&D spend began to trickle in at both Akurdi and Waluj with Maharashtra Scooters getting regular benefits. Scooters were still the priority. Bajaj assembled a separate R&D team for the Sunny scooter. The motorbike team began to accustom itself to playing second fiddle.

'We had XLO machine tools and HMTs, not the same piece of equipment but the same family, same platform, same generation. Waluj would try to implement the instructions—not on finely calibrated modern machines such as the Japanese used, but outdated XLO Machine Tools and HMTs,' recalls Rajiv.[1]

'Kawasaki were not joint-venture partners,' Rajiv continues, 'so they didn't put their people here to teach our people. Drawings

---

[1] Hindustan Machine Tools Ltd.

were transferred to our engineers. The engineers sat in Akurdi, and the motorcycle plant was in Waluj. Akurdi would specify tolerances recommended by the Japanese.'

The bike team had to get on with a task that was rapidly turning into a Herculean effort. Was something wrong with Kawasaki or with Bajaj Auto, questioned the cynics.

Both Bajaj's sons pitched for change. 'At the HBS, my reading of great companies such as Honda, Toyota and Apple taught me one thing: a successful company needs a good product,' remembers Sanjiv. 'But most of our workers did not believe that we could bring in Japanese management practices into India. There was stiff resistance to the move.'

Adds Rajiv, 'The problem was one of attitude: Bajaj Auto was a scooter company and therefore the motorcycle department was given second-class treatment (it was only 10 per cent of their business in 1996). The product quality was poor, and they did not offer fuel efficiency the way the Japanese bikes did. Simply put, Bajaj Auto did not know how to make motorcycles and the people at Bajaj Auto were not willing to change at that time.'

'There was no strategy to fix it,' Rajiv continues. 'In the five years from 1995 to 2000, we started working on technology and product development. We said we will put together our strategy over three steps: First, we would do what is doable. So, I took a four-stroke motorcycle, put a whole bunch of young guys on it. Then told my father that I want to run the motorcycle business.'

Quality and cost effectiveness depend heavily on ancillaries. The brothers discovered that they had over a thousand vendors supplying components many of which were plain bad in quality. They decided to prune them down to under 200. Bajaj accepted his sons' decision with deep heartburn.

'This was supposed to be a four-stroke motorcycle to take on Honda, Yamaha and Suzuki. Kawasaki was always in big bikes; they never had a small bike. They were designing a small 100 cc motorcycle for the first time,' reminds Rajiv. 'It had no relevance to their market so they never manufactured it themselves.' When Kawasaki managers visited the Waluj plant, they politely refrained from comments, but the local shop floor could sense the condescension.

'Each time the Kawasaki guys came and went, our general manager, Vasant Mohan Rao, a fantastic engineer, would be sad,' said Rajiv. 'He would say, every time they come, we teach them what to do. That's why we never learnt from Kawasaki. You know how the Japanese are. They are anyway not willing to tell you anything. And if you are happy to talk, they are happy to keep shut. They are getting their royalty—they are not here to teach you.'

'Once, when I was in Tokyo,' recalled Rajiv, 'I asked a senior Kawasaki manager why other Japanese JVs are doing well but not our arrangement? He said, "Who is at fault, the teacher or the student?" That sparked off a lot of change internally.'

When the Kawasaki Bajaj KB100 finally arrived in 1986, it was late for the party.

As the first KB100 bikes rolled off the Waluj conveyors, the local design team had mixed feelings. The initial Bajaj-Kawasaki offering was passable, but it needed work. The Japanese agreed. A couple of years later, an improved KB100 RTZ was offered. Its maintenance cost was higher than for a scooter and comparatively poorer fuel efficiency than scooters.

'We slashed the price drastically. That's how the Boxer came about—the redone 4S Champion. We sold it at a loss initially. Naturally, it got a big response. We worked hard on quality because we knew that if we compromise on quality and sell half a million vehicles, we will never get a second chance,' said Rajiv and Sanjiv Bajaj.

KB100 aficionados were kinder. 'It revolutionized the industry in terms of features and technology,' they argued in their blogs. The bike was first-in-class in featuring a tachometer, later seen in the Yamaha RD 350. The fuel gauge and a central lock with inbuilt ignition were also industry firsts. The double cradle steel frame of the KB100 was sourced directly from its international sibling—the Kawasaki KH125.

For better safety, it came equipped with a concealed carburettor. The bike also had bigger 130 mm drum brakes at both the wheels, another first-in-class feature. The wider rear tyre on bigger rear wheel complemented the largest wheelbase and mass centralized design of KB100. 'All these features came as standard with the KB100,' they chorused.

'The KB100's performance was not too far behind the lord of the street, the Yamaha RX 100 but the low-end torque difference between the two bikes made a difference of two worlds,' was the bloggers' consensus. There were more naysayers than bloggers. 'Putting it bluntly, it bombed and had to be expensively relaunched three years later. Bajaj had a tough task placing the sophisticated Kawasaki KB100 somewhere in between the now almost saturated 100 cc market,' continues Kashif. 'Another reason for its difficulties was that Bajaj did not advertise efficiently.'

'Hero Honda's motorcycle had a Rs 80 a year warranty and the Bajaj motorcycle had a Rs 800 a year warranty. It was as simple as that. Obviously, nobody would buy our motorcycle. We didn't realize then that we were still a me-too in the space already occupied by Hero Honda,' remembers Rajiv. 'The only 100 cc motorcycle that made money in India was Hero Honda.'

Learning from mistakes, Bajaj Auto introduced a sleeker variant of the KB 100, the KB 100 RTZ, and backed it with a television ad campaign dubbed 'Own a Cheetah', which plugged the 'Delta super-tuned engine'. 'People started considering the Kawasaki Bajaj KB100 RTZ as an alternate to the Yamaha RX 100 and Ind-Suzuki AX 100. Those who bought the KB 100 RTZ appreciated its stability and control. Ergonomically, it was undoubtedly a better motorcycle than the competition,' shared the team.

A third version appeared in 1996, the KB 125, equipped with a re-bored 125 cc engine capable of producing 12.7 PS of power and 11 Nm of peak torque. The motorcycle was identical in looks to the earlier iterations, distinguished only by the KB 125 logo and its graphics. Bajaj upped its game but continued to look less than formidable. Production ended in 2000. After the introduction of stricter emission laws, the golden era of the two-stroke engine disappeared over the western horizon. A new engine would rise on the eastern horizon.

22

Raiders of the Lost Tax: 1985

*Jankidevi Bajaj after her Padma Vibhushan investiture ceremony with
President Rajendra Prasad, Prime Minister Jawaharlal Nehru,
Ramkrishna Bajaj (second from left), Rahul Bajaj (fourth from left) and others in 1959.*

In the 1980s, for all its fame as India's hottest company, Reliance was not India's fastest-growing company. Reliance grew 1110 per cent with sales surging from Rs 200 crore to Rs 1840 crore. Bajaj Auto's growth shot up 1852 per cent, from Rs 51.9 crore to Rs 1850 crore. Despite the escalation, Bajaj Auto carried practically no debt in its balance sheet. By maintaining an iron-fisted control on costs and continually improving productivity to lower costs per vehicle, Bajaj funded this growth almost wholly out of internal earnings.

Bajaj Auto's market share saw significant fluctuations in this period. The Japanese had arrived. 1985 was particularly rough with a steep 33 per cent dip. Nonetheless, the combination of manufacturing efficiencies, sharper focus on marketing and distribution, and the rapid introduction of three new products—the 100 cc Bajaj Cub scooter designed by the in-house R&D team; a step-thru, the Bajaj M-80, aided by Italian design engineers; and focus on a motorcycle, the Bajaj KB100, backed by Japanese technology—ensured that Bajaj Auto made and sold half a million vehicles.

Déjà Vu

The mid-1980s saw the dawn of the 'raid raj'. Behind the scene, Vishwanath Pratap (V.P.) Singh, the then Finance Minister, ordered investigation of Bajaj Auto, for income tax infringements.

Singh picked up Gandhi's 'clean' mission with alacrity. Singh invited D.N. Pathak to be Bombay's new director of investigation. Both men were from Singh's home state, Uttar Pradesh. For five months, Pathak and his team studied the market, gathering information piecemeal. Gandhi approved Singh's request to investigate Bajaj Auto.

On 17 December 1985, at precisely 7.45 a.m., 285 income tax officials arrived at sixty-five locations across India, clutching 101 search warrants. The welter of warrants included Bajaj Auto.

Nothing was found. Including the chairman. Bajaj had left the previous night for Bombay. Caught off guard by this elementary gap in their information, the party recovered enough to call Bombay and request a local team to be dispatched immediately to Mount Unique. The Bombay-Pune lines hummed with anxious inquiries until the tax sleuths finally caught sight of the tycoon engaged in this favourite activity—chatting on the telephone. After Bajaj had satisfied himself as to the correctness of their identity, he agreed to their 'request' to accompany them to his office at Bajaj Bhawan at Nariman Point. There he was interrogated for six hours.

The officers repeatedly confronted Bajaj with the Patna dealer's books and the listed payment of Rs 12 lakh. Bajaj said that there were heavy premiums in the sale of the three-wheelers but added that he or his company had no responsibility other than ensuring that the machines were supplied according to priority. He also said that they had no control on what his customers did with the vehicles after buying them.

Word spread of the nationwide income tax raid on Bajaj Auto. The reaction was one of disbelief. Wasn't it the same company the government had declared that 'despite its dominant position, the company did not take undue advantage'?

With their backs to the wall, Pathak and his team produced a Bajaj Auto distributor of three-wheelers in Patna. A Rs 12 lakh payment appeared twice in the distributor's accounts. Pathak and his excited unit seized both the actual and the fudged books. A hit finally.

The raid report was sent to the Finance Ministry which authorized further research and a more detailed report on the 33,000 three-wheelers that Bajaj Auto produced annually. 'A substantial premium is being charged on the three-wheelers,' offered department officials to H.O., 'and a portion of the premium collected was being pocketed by the dealers. In fact, through the searches, we recovered more evidence which showed that certain vehicles had been booked by the *benamidars* of the dealers.'

On an official price tag of Rs 27,000, the premium ranged between Rs 10,000 and Rs 20,000. Pathak's team relaxed: here was considerable scope for under-reported income.

In the next round, the sleuths seized over Rs 1 crore from four Bajaj dealers in cash, jewellery and fixed deposit receipts. The dealers included Automotive Manufacturers in Bombay and its branch offices in Gujarat and Andhra Pradesh; Ranjit Automobiles, Ahmedabad; Amin Automobiles, Ahmedabad; Project Automobiles in Malad, on the outskirts of Bombay; and Sah and Sanghi.

Sah and Sanghi's Ranjan Sanghi promptly denied that his companies were involved in any premium racket. 'They could not be in the premium racket even if they wanted to, as all the lists are computerized and open for public inspection. We go strictly by the rules. There is no question of hanky-panky anywhere,' said Sanghi.

The raiders went away empty-handed. Instead of the Bajaj family being feathered and tarred, it was the government which came under flak for using its muscle to harass businessmen for their political convictions.

A Life of Their Own

In those days, 'tax raids rarely led to convictions and action seldom taken against the guilty,' wrote Rasheed Kidwai in the *Telegraph*, 'but they took a life of their own, triggering speculation that often caused more damage to the person at the receiving end than the outcome of the raids themselves. The raids served as handy tools to harass opponents or settle scores with adversaries, especially when the targets were powerful personalities. Instead of unearthing black money or evidence of fraud or financial wrongdoing, many raids turned into a witch-hunt, serving to "discipline" the targeted individuals or companies.'

'The 82-year-old giant of the engineering export industry, Shantanu Laxman Kirloskar, was interrogated by seven Directorate of Revenue Intelligence officials,' collectively reported indignant *India Today's* newsroom stars, Inderjit Badhwar, Prabhu Chawla, Jagannath Dubashi and Ramesh Menon. 'The questioning started at 6 p.m. on 6 December and ended at 3 a.m. the next morning. His wife was grilled for several hours as well.'

Asked what happened, Kirloskar was forthright: 'We export Rs 200 crore worth of engineering goods every year. The Rs 2.5 crore that we are said to have not repatriated are bad debts that occur in any business. There is no under-invoicing involved here. We hammered the price down. It is a legitimate business deal. When the Government of India hammers down the price of its imports, is that under-invoicing?' In court, the company was charged for not paying customs duty on air compressors and violating foreign exchange regulations by investing in Germany. The authorities lost the case in court.

During the Singh campaign, 6000 raids were conducted about which the Finance Ministry authorized further research, 1,00,000 residences searched, and almost half a million people subjected to interrogation. On 24 January 1987, Singh was transferred from the Finance Ministry to Defence.

Are You Mr Clean?

Ten days later, in Mumbai for a three-day 100th anniversary celebration of the Congress party, Gandhi declaimed that 'corruption is not only tolerated but even regarded as the hallmark of leadership'. He promised to reform the system and was promptly dubbed Mr Clean.

'Unfortunately, Rajiv Gandhi's "clean" image did not last long. The externalization of corruption began,' noted Kochanek. 'In early 1987 his Congress (I) led government, was rocked by a series of major scandals involving alleged favouritism to Congress business allies, illegal secret overseas bank accounts held by Congress supporters and huge kickbacks on government defence contracts involving a Rs 4.5 billion submarine deal with the west German company Howaldt Deutsche Werke (HDW) and the Rs 17.05 billion Bofors scandal involving the purchase of Swedish artillery pieces. For the first time in post-Independence Indian history, a prime minister had to assure Parliament publicly that neither he nor his family were involved in any illegal activity.'[1]

The Last Word

'For every businessman who welcomes a move to liberalize, there is at least one to lobby against it,' Rajiv Gandhi said ruefully. Vishwanath Pratap ('V.P.') Singh would become India's eighth prime minister in 1989 for 343 days.

---

[1] Stanley A. Kochanek (1996), 'Liberalisation and business lobbying in India', *Journal of Commonwealth and Comparative Politics*, 34:3, 155-173, DOI: 10.1080/14662049608447729.

23

Plane Truths: 1986–2011

Sharad Pawar and Bajaj.

The first half of the 1980s stands out for hijackings. But luckily during Bajaj's term as its chairman, no Indian Airlines aircraft was hijacked. That's the good news. The bad news was the Ahmedabad air crash.[1]

---

[1] Two aircraft crashed that morning within an hour of each other. A Fokker Friendship plane operated by the smaller domestic airline Vayudoot, crashed in north-east Assam,

Indian Airlines Flight IC 113

Dalaya to
Nagpal: I am not well *aur zyada lagta hai. Raat ko* I was sweating
and suddenly cold.
*Neend aa rahee thee, jaa rahee thee. Hota hai na? Theek hai,
badh gaya to kuch kar loonga.*
Dalaya: *Neeche nazar aa jaye to bata dena.* (Tell me if you see
the ground.)
Dalaya: *Kya hai? (What do you see?)*
Nagpal: *Solid bad, sir.*
Dalaya: *Bada hi bekaar weather hai.* (It's really bad weather.)

The above conversation is the situation in the cockpit on 19 October
1988, recorded by the aircraft's black box which was extracted after
the crash.

The flight was scheduled to depart at 5.45 a.m. but was delayed
by twenty minutes due to one no-show passenger. Indian Airlines
flight IC 113 from Bombay to Ahmedabad was operating a twin-
engine American-made Boeing 737-2A8. The missing no-show had
a lucky day.

In technical terms, at 6.41 a.m., while the aircraft was descending,
the flight deck was instructed to report to the Ahmedabad VOR
(VHF omnidirectional range). The flight crew duly reported the
VOR[2] overhead and prepared for a localizer-DME to runway 23.
Visibility was reported as 2000 metres in haze with calm winds and
a QNH of 1010 mb (a barometric measure in millimetres). In short,
Ahmedabad airport was shrouded in early morning haze.

In layman words, the last radio contact with the flight was at
6.50 a.m. The aircraft hit a high-tension pylon in poor visibility.
ploughed through some trees, slammed into the ground and broke
up, with much of the wreckage catching fire. All six crew members,
and 124 of 129 passengers were killed. The five survivors, including

---

killing all thirty-four passengers and crew. As in Ahmedabad, bad weather was once
again believed responsible for the disaster.

[2] In VOR/DME radio navigation, the VOR is a radio beacon that allows the receiver to
measure its bearing to or from a beacon, while the DME provided the slant distance
between the receiver and the station.

a thirteen-year-old boy, were rushed to a city hospital, but only two lived to tell the tale.

Like many others, Bajaj too has painful memories of that morning. In addition to stress as the Indian Airlines chairman, was a personal loss. 'I had a meeting with Indian Institute of Management Ahmedabad Professor Labdhi Pat Raj Bhandari (LRB),' recalls Bajaj. 'LRB arrived in Pune on Monday, the 17th, met the Kirloskar management at their offices, and also stopped by at the Bajaj Auto headquarters. He was advising us on marketing and corporate strategies. He was on that flight.'

Rajiv Gandhi's Invitation

Ratan Tata was in his Bombay office when Jagdish Tytler, the union minister of state for civil aviation, came on the line from New Delhi. Would Tata consider the chairmanship of Air-India?[3] 'I was taken aback, but thrilled,' Tata told Ninan. 'I fly myself and I have always been interested in aviation.'

Bajaj, on the same day, was at a seminar in Italy when his assistant Hariharan called from Pune: Tytler wanted to invite Bajaj as chairman of Indian Airlines. 'I didn't know what to make of this offer,' recalls Bajaj. 'When I asked Hariharan whether I can give my reply soon after I return to India, he said that Mr Ratan Tata has accepted to be the chairman of Air India and they would like to make both announcements together that evening. Hence, I spoke to Rupa, and called my uncle Ramkrishnaji in Bombay to find out what it meant and was advised to accept. In any case, how could I refuse? I then confirmed to Hariharan to inform the government that I accept the appointment as chairman of Indian Airlines.'

'A few months after I joined as the chairman of the Indian Airlines board, by chance I met Prime Minister Rajiv Gandhi and he

---

[3] Air-India dropped the hyphen in 2005 after the global adoption of the Computer Reservation System (CRS).

asked me how I was doing at IAC.[4] I mentioned to him that it may not be appropriate for me to speak to him alone and that he may, at his convenience, call a meeting in which Mr Jagdish Tytler, Ratan Tata and myself will be present and I will brief him. He immediately asked his secretary, Vincent George, to fix up the meeting.

'In the meeting, the PM asked me about IAC, and, in brief, I mentioned that there are, occasionally, instructions which come from the Ministry of Civil Aviation to the Managing Director of IAC which naturally he has to follow. I also mentioned to him that naturally I know something more about the management of a company whereas Mr Tytler would definitely know much more than me about how an election can be won in Delhi. The PM did not comment on this but mentioned (all three of us were present) that I can report directly to him/Prime Minister's Office (PMO) and not to the Ministry of Civil Aviation.

'I, on my own said, sir, this will not be appropriate in our system of government as the Ministry of Civil Aviation has to answer questions in Parliament about the working of IAC as well and hence the Ministry will have to be in touch with the management of IAC. Incidentally, the Ministry, including Mr Tytler as the minister and the civil aviation secretary, never asked me to do anything. After some general comments, the meeting ended. If I remember correctly, I do not think Mr Tata mentioned anything about Air India.

'It was a major acknowledgement,' Bajaj shares with Datar. 'I was Indian Airlines chairman for three years. In 1986, when there was still socialism, every Congressman was full of socialism in his mind. It should not be a free market; it can't be capitalism—that kind of thinking. And you make a capitalist a public sector company chairman?' Bajaj's appointment was significant in other ways also. Barely nine months earlier, Rajiv Gandhi's Finance Ministry headed by Vishwanath Pratap Singh had conducted a tax raid on Bajaj Auto and its dealers.

---

[4] IAC: Indian Airlines Corporation.

Rajiv Gandhi's strategy was to replace embedded senior civil servants with two youngish, savvy industrialists as chairmen of the two airlines, and about ten talented and experienced managers. Bajaj and Tata filled the bill, but Gandhi had to settle on a smaller mix for the rest.

In the promoter group were Prathap C. Reddy (chairman, Apollo Hospitals), Vivek Bharat Ram (executive director, DCM Toyota), and Ritu Nanda (managing director of Niky Tasha). In the professionals' group were two Tata heads: Russi Mody (chairman of Tata Steel) along with Francis Menezes (director of The Tata Institute of Management). Others were Yogi Deveshwar (president of the Welcomgroup chain of hotels), Z.R. Rangoonwala (chairman, Bombay Mercantile Co-Operative Bank), and Arun Nanda (head of advertising agency Rediffusion).

This was an audacious experiment in public sector management. Indian Airlines was the world's third-largest domestic carrier at the time, according to encyclopedia.com. The appointments were announced—over a weekend, a sure sign of bureaucratic anxiety. The new appointees replaced permanent secretaries from the Ministries of Finance, Civil Aviation, External Affairs, and included the Chief of Air Staff.

Chairmen of large corporations get to be chairmen because shareholders appoint them. A union minister gets to head his or her ministry because of neat political footwork. 'Initially, the boards seemed to be under the impression that they would be the decision-makers,' wrote Ninan. 'Indeed, both Bajaj and Tata suggested to Tytler that he and the ministry should restrict themselves to broad policy issues and leave the rest to the board. Tytler apparently agreed in principle, but (and this is the way the boards saw it) continued to do what he wanted. He would send letters to both airlines with suggestions on the minutest detail, down to in-flight menu.'

Tension between the boards and the ministry roiled under the surface. Superficially, Tytler made an attempt to calm troubled waters. 'There has been a lot of duplication on the boards, and bureaucrats do not understand international commercial businesses,' the politician tried to explain to Khozem Merchant, a journalist with the UK's *Financial Times*. 'How can you,' continued Tytler, 'for example, expect them to react on fare structure changes after sharp falls in oil prices? We need professionals who have excelled in their own business, can handle large turnovers, and can improve the management of the airlines.'

As chairman of Indian Airlines, Bajaj expected to have some say in selecting its managing director. Gerry Pais, Vayudoot's chairman, was not Bajaj's first choice and a Rajiv Gandhi appointee. Pais would continue as Vayudoot's part-time chairman in addition to his responsibilities at Indian Airlines. At Air-India, Tata had suggested two possible choices—one in-house and the other a man brought in from outside. Rajan Jetley, however, was the new managing director.

One particularly depressed member of the Indian Airlines board vented, 'We achieved hardly anything. There is no money, there is too much ministerial interference. The managing director is threatened with transfer unless he does something the ministry wants, and the board is nowhere in the picture. I keep wondering, should we complain, or just resign?'

'We tried to bring a lot of changes in attitudes,' wrote Prathap C. Reddy, 'especially on courtesy, as well as in the working of the organization and punctuality of flight schedules. It was Rahul's diplomacy and power of influence with the Ministry and the Planning Commission that tilted the scales in India possessing the first fleet of the modern Airbus aircraft. I believe there was far greater interaction between the government, the core team, as well as several non-government members of the board when Rahul was chairman. The way he managed the board is a great example of public-private partnership.'

Reddy continues, 'Very few may believe this, but though Rahul was a smoker, he actually encouraged a smoking ban on all Indian Airlines aircraft!'

Work began on drafting the Act of Parliament required to reconstitute the boards. 'The Indian Airlines chairmanship will be for less than eight months,' Bajaj had been told initially. 'The two airlines will definitely be merged by May 1987. In any case, it's a non-executive chairman position.' The months seemed to drag on and on and on.

The next tripwire was the plan to merge the two airlines via a three-phased merger programme. Common utilization of the two airlines' fifty to sixty jet aircraft and their crews would be introduced first. For example, Indian Airlines' airbuses were not used at night. Air-India could use the aircraft for international night-time long hauls. This would be followed by a merger of engineering facilities, then administration and sales.

A merger must, in theory, result in savings. Both airlines were profitable. Indian Airlines' passenger traffic was growing by 10 per cent a year. A 90 per cent passenger load was common. The boffins estimated that their joint profit of Rs 123 crore would provide savings of Rs 80 crore a year.

Collectively the two airlines had a staff of about 40,000 and ferried nearly 12 million passengers a year. 'There is some management and trade union opposition to the merger plans,' Tytler admitted, 'especially in Air-India, but we hope to overcome this with consultation. The combined airline would probably be called Air-India.'

'Casualness and indifference are recognized hallmarks of Indian Airlines, air travellers assert,' reported *India Today*'s Raminder Singh. 'Even Chairman Rahul Bajaj says, "Without competition we cannot improve. The airline has almost no power to reward and punish. We treat horses and asses alike".' Nobody wanted to hear this.

Forget Me Not

At the post-mortem inquiries of flight IC 113, Boeing was quick to point out that the crash was due to 'probable' error by the pilot-in-command and co-pilot due to non-adherence of procedures under poor visibility conditions. The seventeen years and eleven months' aircraft was a registered VT-EAH and delivered in December 1970. It had flown for a total of 42,831 hours with 47,647 landings.

The commission inquiring into the crash also piled the blame as pilot error. Subsequently, it was proved in the Ahmedabad Civil Court that navigational aids at Ahmedabad airport were not functioning accurately and that the Air Traffic Control (ATC) failed to ensure that the latest weather information was communicated to the aircraft before the accident occurred.

'What scares passengers is the cavalier way some pilots treat their planes and their jobs, exhibiting a callous disregard for their own and passengers' lives: landing without wheels, hitting buffaloes on runways and flying into flocks of birds,' reported *India Today*. On 8 February 1985, an Indian Airlines Boeing 737 crash-landed at Calcutta airport because the two pilots, Captains Nangia and Chandok had 'forgotten' to lower the undercarriage before landing. The plane was destroyed and over 100 passengers narrowly escaped death.

The crash came amid mounting complaints over Indian Airlines poor on-time performance and safety record. On 18 June 1988, the near-tragedy described above was replicated at New Delhi airport. Here too, the two pilots forgot to lower the landing gear and the Boeing 737-2A8 with 134 occupants skidded the length of the runway, sparking a minor fire. There were no casualties, but it was the second such incident in under four years. Luck and quick action by the firefighting staff at the airport prevented casualties.

'Mandatory safety related procedures are often reduced to a paper exercise by airline employees,' scolded *India Today*. 'Doctors who are supposed to conduct pre-flight alcohol tests of pilots routinely signed clearances without doing the examinations.'

Technical experts expressed concern over maintenance. The high use of equipment due to a shortage of aircraft meant that the Indian Airlines fleet of Boeing 737s was overused by up to 3000 flight-hours per year.

The root of Indian Airlines' problem was a severe shortage of aircraft. Aircraft spent so little time on the ground that maintenance inevitably was often sketchy. Prior to the Ahmedabad crash, the airline flew 28,000 passengers a day, with 90 per cent flight occupancy, and a total of forty-seven aircraft. Expansion was impossible as the government did not allow airlines to grow at more than 8 per cent a year. 'Air travel was considered a luxury item by India's socialistic standards,' political reporter Tavleen Singh pointed out.

India needed better aircraft and better regulation. Rajiv Gandhi took steps. Among them was the establishment of two major institutions: The National Airports Authority in 1986 and The Bureau of Civil Aviation Security in 1987.

Fly-by-wire

Fifteen years after the Ahmedabad crash, in 2003, a judge ordered Indian Airlines and the Airports Authority of India (AAI) to compensate families of the Ahmedabad victims with higher amounts than the Rs 2 lakh offered by the carrier. Punitive damages were awarded against the Airport Authority of India for wilful misconduct, and against Indian Airlines for acts of omission. This was upheld by the Supreme Court.

The Ahmedabad crash was the perfect opportunity for Airbus, a European consortium, to enter India. As the world's first digital fly-by-wire (FBW) aircraft, Airbus Industrie's A320 was positioned as bringing commercial flying and flight management into the twenty-first century.

The A320 saga dates back to August 1983 when directors of the Indian Airlines board set up a committee under the chairmanship of Air Chief Marshal Dilbagh Singh and three other experts to formulate a fleet development plan for the period 1984–91.

The committee recommended the purchase of twelve Boeing 757s with a seating capacity of 206 against the Boeing 737 with 126 seats, and Airbus 300 with 273 seats. In June 1984, the IA board accepted Boeing 757 as the most suitable aircraft for the national air network and a letter of intent was placed for Boeing the following month. A refundable advance of $900 million was paid, reported *UNI*.

Four months later, the Civil Aviation Ministry asked Indian Airlines to evaluate in just three days a proposal sent by Airbus Industrie. R. Prasad, the financial adviser to the Indian Airlines managing director, said that no such proposal had been submitted to the airline. The ministry persisted.

In June 1985, Rajiv Gandhi, along with his cabinet colleague and childhood friend Satish Sharma, visited the Airbus headquarters near Toulouse in France. On his return to India on 2 August 1985, Gandhi chaired a meeting where the decision was taken for Indian Airlines to go ahead with Airbus 320 aircraft with the V 2500 engines. Among those present in the meeting were Tytler, Cabinet Secretary P.K. Kaul, and Special Secretary in the PMO Gopi Arora.

Neither the A320 nor the engine V2500 had been manufactured, tried or tested. A newbie in the business, Airbus badly wanted the deal and snatched the order from Boeing with the offer of attractive financing arrangements. Monetary sweeteners included 'free' leasing of interim 737s and A-300s until the delivery of new aircraft.

On 15 March 1986, Indian Airlines and Airbus Industrie signed a $1.4 billion contract for nineteen A-320s, with an option for twelve more of the technologically advanced 'fly-by-wire' passenger jets. The airline exercised the option in June 1989.

A miffed Boeing, supported by the Ronald Reagan administration, took the matter to the European Commission, alleging that the support to Airbus Industrie represented an export subsidy. It charged Airbus of selling the A-320s at less than cost and put political pressure on the Indian government for violations of Articles 4 and 6 of the General Agreement on Tariffs and Trade (GATT). The complaint was examined by the GATT Committee in Trade in Civil Aircraft in 1986 but did not result in a ruling.

A year later, Tytler discussed delivery of six Airbus A310 aircraft so that Indian Airlines would have nineteen new Airbus A-320s in 1989. 'We are in talks with The Boeing Company and Airbus Industrie about replacements needed in 1992-4 for Air-India's fleet of nine Boeing 747s,' Tytler disclosed to the *Financial Times*.

'The government finalized nineteen new Airbus A-320s during my time between 1986–89,' recalls Bajaj. 'We had an option for another twelve, making a total of thirty-one A320s. I remember asking for permission from the Finance Ministry for ordering twelve aircraft but the Finance Ministry replied saying India does not have the foreign exchange. I went to the PM, Mr Rajiv Gandhi, to make this request and he asked me to speak to the finance secretary (I believe it was Mr Venkatraman). However, Mr Venkatraman also expressed his helplessness.'

The two boards' second term, starting on 30 June 1988, saw old faces and new at Indian Airlines and Air India. Bajaj was requested to continue as Indian Airlines chairman, and additionally join the Air India board as director with Ratan Tata as chair. At Indian

Airlines, the positions switched with Bajaj as chair and Ratan Tata as director. Significantly, the managing director of Indian Airlines joined the Air India board, and Air India's managing director came on the Indian Airlines board. Was integration of the two airlines on the cards? Or simply better coordination?

At Air-India were pals and business peers Vivek Bharat Ram, Gautam Khanna, Cyrus Gazder, J.K. Mehra, Bilkees Latif and Tarun Das; and at Indian Airlines, hotelier Ajit Kerkar, businessman Suresh Krishna, media owner Shobhana Bhartia and actor Sharmila Tagore. Rajiv Gandhi, Ratan Tata, Bajaj and the two airlines' management appear to have tried hard to broaden the board with the induction of scientists, technologists, senior and reputed industrialists and professionals from areas related to both airlines' activities.

Interestingly, the Lok Sabha entry put forward the specious thesis that 'workers and employees of Indian Airlines participate in the management of the airlines through the Works Committee and the Labour Relations Committee; and in Air India, it is through a scheme of employees' participation of the workers in management of the airlines, workers have not been represented on the Boards. Their representation on the Boards of the airlines will be considered at the appropriate time in an appropriate manner.'

'Towards the end of 1989 and before the elections which Rajiv Gandhi lost and V.P. Singh won, Sheila Dikshit whom I knew well and who of course was very well known to the Gandhi family, asked me to come over to her Delhi home for a discussion. She mentioned to me that Prime Minister Rajiv Gandhi was happy with the work I was doing as chairman of Indian Airlines (I used to keep him informed once in a while), and desired to bring me to the Rajya Sabha, but for that I would have to resign as chairman of Indian Airlines,' recalls Bajaj. 'As I had done a reasonable job and was frankly getting a bit bored, I mentioned that I will be happy to consider being elected to the Rajya Sabha if the prime minister so wanted. Soon after that however the dates for parliamentary elections were announced where Rajiv Gandhi lost and V.P. Singh won. Hence, the question of the Rajya Sabha became defunct. I immediately sent my resignation letter as chairman of Indian Airlines.'

The airlines' headaches transferred to the new prime minister. The Bangalore crash of an Indian Airlines A320 on 14 February 1990, killing ninety-two passengers and fifty-four casualties, brought back the original deal to the forefront. Four days later, the then civil aviation minister, Arif Mohammed Khan, ordered the grounding of the entire A320 fleet.

'India has lost out in aviation,' wrote Naresh Chandra in 'The Report of the Committee on a Road Map for the Civil Aviation Sector', 2003. 'It has missed the travel boom of the nineties, ceded its natural geographic and economic advantages as a cargo and courier hub to other countries and air travel still remains confined to a tiny section of the domestic population.'

A Proud Private-sector Man

Looking back at Bajaj's chairmanship between 22 September 1986 and 2 December 1989, Rupa said simply: 'The chairmanship meant a lot to Rahul.' And the chairmanship came with deep learnings. 'The airline had almost no power to reward and punish. Without competition how could we improve?' evokes Bajaj.

Bajaj's response to the media on the failure of Vijay Mallya's Kingfisher Airlines revealed a new maturity. In 2011, Kingfisher's loss was Rs 1027 crore, debt of Rs 7057.08 crore and climbing. Civil Aviation Minister Vayalar Ravi offered to talk to the Finance Ministry to see if banks and oil firms could provide some relief to the cash-strapped airline. Bajaj's views differed and came out in plain sight at the India Summit of the World Economic Forum on 13 November 2011. In his speech, Prime Minister Manmohan Singh said that steps would have to be taken to help private sector entities if they get into difficulties.

Bajaj, on the other hand, was at his blunt best. 'I am a proud private sector man, and I don't see any logic in bailing out any private sector company either for the sake of employees or customers,' Bajaj told news channels. 'I am not even in favour of what's being done for Air India . . . Air India should be privatized, sold off or closed. It is taxpayers' money going down the drain, but we need to re-look at taxation. If all airlines are in losses, everyone can't be inefficient.

If Bajaj Auto gets into a mess, would you bail me out?' he asked, adding. 'In a free market economy, those who die, must die.'

Statement

Boards of Directors of Air India and Indian Airlines with effect from 30th June, 1988

Air-India	*Indian Airlines*
1. Shri Ratan Tata, Chairman.	1. Shri Rahul Bajaj, Chairman.
2. Chairman, Indian Airlines	2. Chairman, Air India.
3. Managing Director, Air India.	3. Managing Director, Indian Airlines.
4. Managing Director, Indian Airlines.	4. Managing Director, Air India.
5. Director General, Tourism.	5. Director General, Tourism.
6. Financial Adviser, Ministry of Civil Aviation and Tourism.	6. Financial Adviser, Ministry of Civil Aviation and Tourism.
7. Joint Secretary, Ministry of Civil Aviation and Tourism.	7. Joint Secretary, Ministry of Civil Aviation and Tourism.
8. Shri C.L. Sharma, Dy. Managing Director, Air India.	8. Shri C.L. Sharma, Dy. Managing Director, Air India.
9. Shri R. Prasad, Dy. Managing Director Indian Airlines.	9. Shri R. Prasad, Dy. Managing Director. Indian Airlines.
10. Shri Vivek Bharat Ram.	10. Shri Harsh Vardhan, Managing Director, Vayudoot.
11. Shri Gautam Khanna, Hotelier.	11. Shri Ajit Kerkar, Managing Director, Indian Hotels Limited.
12. Shri Cyrus Gazder, Ex-Chairman, IAAI. (Travel Trade).	12. Shri Suresh Krishna, Industrialist, Madras.
13. Shri J.K. Mehra, Chairman, NPCC.	13. Shri Krishan Amla, Hony. Secretary, PATA.
14. Mrs. Bilkhis Latif.	14. Smt. Shobhna Bhartia, Managing Director. Hindustan Times.
15. Shri Tarun Das, DG, Confederation of Engineering Industry.	15. Smt. Sharmila Tagore.

(c) The Boards of Directors of Indian Airlines and Air India are constituted under Section 4 of the Air Corporations Act, 1983 (No. 27 of 1953). While constituting the Boards, efforts were made to broad-base the Board of Directors by induction of scientists, technologists, senior and reputed industrialists and professionals from areas related to activity of the Airlines.

(d) and (e) The workers/employees of Indian Airlines participate in the management of the airlines through Works Com-

24

Where's My Truck? 1987

Bajaj and Margaret Thatcher.

Margaret 'Maggie' Thatcher was never one to mince her words, and she didn't hold back on 2 May 1975. The UK's future prime minister was in stumping mode. She was in Derby to speak to the workers of British Leyland, a company teetering on the brink of survival.

'British Leyland is of great significance to the economy as an employer, and exporter,' she said, 'so, we accept, of course, that the government has a duty to help British Leyland to find remedies for its own failures and to find a way out of its critical position . . . The next step should be for British Leyland's new management, and the unions, together with financial and industrial advisers, to work out alternative plans to restore the firm to a profitable basis . . . and reorganize in the light of realistic assessments of what can be sold and at what price . . . we must build a prosperous and profitable motor industry in Britain which offers security and a good standard of living to those who work in it, and those who depend upon it.'

In India, a few days later, on 25 June 1975, Prime Minister Indira Gandhi announced the Emergency. In this interregnum, she recruited bureaucrat Mantosh Sondhi to not only head the Department of Heavy Industry but also chair Ashok Leyland, a British subsidiary in India. Two years later, in 1977, George Fernandes as the Janata Party's industry minister introduced a 40 per cent limit to foreign shareholding. British interest in Ashok Leyland, already stretched, declined further.

As a troubled public sector corporation with a large employee base, debates on British Leyland's future erupted in the British Parliament. Margaret Thatcher was appointed prime minister on 4 May 1979. Her administration pumped £300 million into British Leyland in December 1979. Less than six months later, the firm needed an even richer dose. More debates. The fact that strikes were down 52 per cent in 1979 over 1978 didn't cut much ice among the MPs.

British Leyland did have several profitable marques in its portfolio such as Jaguar, Rover and Land Rover, as well as the bestselling Mini. After much restructuring and divestment of subsidiary companies, British Leyland was renamed as the Rover Group in 1986 with a new chairman, Graham Day, a Canadian. Its 39 per cent shareholding in Ashok Leyland was put on the auctioneer's block. Hill Samuel, a British merchant bank and financial services firm, won the mandate.

In Akurdi, Bajaj quietly bought just under 1 per cent of Ashok Leyland's equity on the Indian stock market and made a private offer to Rover management in mid-1986. 'Nothing much came out of these talks,' admits Bajaj. Hill Samuel had barely settled into sorting out the paperwork before Hill Samuel itself was swallowed by TSB Group Plc in 1987.

The Line Up

Before that happened, Hill Samuel managed to attract twenty offers from countries, including India. At least eight had potential: General Motors and Cummins (US), Fiat Iveco (Italy), Hino Motors (Japan, who already had a technical collaboration agreement with Ashok Leyland), MAN (West Germany), DAF (Holland), Hinduja (UK) and of course Bajaj Auto from India.

'Five Indian-owned companies are believed to be interested in buying Ashok Leyland,' reported John Elliott and Kenneth Gooding of the *Financial Times*. 'It is India's second biggest truck and bus producer with an output of about 6000 vehicles a year, larger than Leyland's UK factories. The sale will raise capital (for the UK firm) but lose dividends of £8,00,000 annually. Ashok Leyland has close to 30 per cent of the Indian bus and truck market. Sales are currently about £12 million. However, it has been facing sales problems in recent years. Indian government-owned financial institutions hold about 35 per cent of the equity and the remaining 25 per cent is widely held.' The remaining 40 per cent, of course, was held by its parent, the Rover Group.

'The sale is attracting international attention because of the expansion potential of Ashok Leyland,' explained Elliott, 'which has 30 per cent of the Indian truck and bus market and had started a recovery after several years of decline.' Ashok Leyland's sole competitor in the two-legged race was the well-entrenched leader, Tata Motors, chaired by J.R.D. Tata and run by Sumant Moolgaokar. Curiously, in the auction year, Ashok Leyland's profits rose to Rs 64.1 million after more than three years of consistent losses.

Climbing Walls

Everyone knew that Bajaj Auto was the world's second largest scooter producer. They also knew Bajaj strengths and weaknesses.

'He lacked a partner from the international truck industry, which meant his bid did not strictly conform to the requirement that the winner should have expertise to develop the company's products,' continued Elliott. 'Mr Bajaj had hoped to tie-up with Fiat Iveco, but now says he will find a technological partner immediately if he wins.'

The Finance Ministry had a ban on foreign exchange to buy foreign-held stakes in Indian companies. Bajaj Auto had a significant Rs 1.2 billion war chest (at a time when $1 was equal to Rs 20) but no dollars or pounds. Unlike many Indian business houses, the Bajaj Group had no offshore funds.

'Brijesh Mathur used to work in ANZ Bank. By nature, he was a very straightforward and helpful person and very much wanted to help me in trying to buy Ashok Leyland,' said Bajaj, 'but the person who helped me the most regarding my offer to the Rover group was Andrew Korner, who was with Merrill Lynch in New York at the time. Andrew tried his best to make up for my inability to provide foreign exchange for this transaction as the government, in spite of Rajiv Gandhi's desire, was not able to help me. Andrew persuaded a very senior Merrill Lynch person in New York to agree to provide the guarantee for Bajaj Auto's bid saying that if we win the bid, Merrill Lynch will pay the foreign exchange amount (and recover it from Bajaj Auto in rupees).'

The night of Wednesday, 30 September, was the original deadline for the bids. It had to be extended for ten days at the request, it was believed, of General Motors and Hino Motors. After several days of negotiations between the bidders, offers were submitted secretly in London. Rover wanted to choose the winner and conclude the deal by 20 November. In reality, there were only three contestants left standing, each of Indian origin. Manu Chabbria, an Indian businessman based in Dubai, and owner of a $2.5 billion transnational conglomerate, the Jumbo Group, dropped out. And then there were two.

Shortly before the Rover board met on 16 November for the final round, Bajaj upped his bid by 10 per cent to £27.45 million. The Hindujas came in at £26 million. 'Ours was the higher bid, but we lost primarily because they had the foreign exchange and I didn't,' he says. Bajaj left the UK even before the bids were opened. The decision was eventually announced on the 26 November. Arriving in India, journalists swamped Bajaj. 'Naturally, I was disappointed. But I hadn't lost anything that I already had, and I will get on with my business,' was all he was ready to say.

That didn't stop the gossip:

'The big surprise was that Bajaj lost and the Hindujas won because of non-financial considerations,' reported T.N. Ninan and Ramesh Chandran of *India Today*. 'Hill Samuel told Bajaj that Ashok Leyland's management preferred the Hindujas,' an oblique reference to managing director R.J. Shahaney.

An Ashok Leyland manager offered that the real reason for the rejection of Bajaj's bid was the absence of a partner with truck technology: 'Had Bajaj gone with Fiat Iveco, he would have got the company.'

Iveco was not happy with the international financial institutions Bajaj had brought together. It also disapproved of Bajaj's plan to acquire a direct stake in Leyland in a manner that would reduce Leyland's foreign shareholding.

ANZ Bank, Bajaj's representative in London, said his deal with Iveco fell through as it insisted on bringing its own technology into Leyland, whereas Bajaj wanted to keep his options open.

Bajaj called the Hindujas in London to congratulate them on their success. Some years later, Srichand Hinduja wrote back, 'We recall the time when we competed strongly to acquire Hinduja Ashok Leyland in 1987. Even though we were successful, we find no change in Rahul's warmth and friendship towards us.'

25

The Morphing of BAFL[1]: 1987–2010

Sonia Gandhi and Bajaj.

Indira Gandhi opened the door to the world's biggest two-wheeler companies. Rajiv Gandhi ushered them in. For the foreigners who swarmed into India in the mid-1980s, the hire-purchase bait was old wine in new bottles. For Indian consumers, the concept felt radical.

---

[1] Bajaj Auto Finance Limited (BAFL).

In a hire-purchase agreement, the seller retains ownership until the final instalment is made. The hirer is duty-bound to take care of the goods and cannot dispose of the goods until the term is completed. As the trend got going, hire-purchase developed shades of expertise and ethos. At Bajaj Auto, everyone knew the facts. Every word in black and white. A rock-solid company with a start-up capital of Rs 55 crore.

In the 1980s, Bajaj, J.R.D. Tata, Dhirubhai Ambani, Basant Kumar Birla and 335 others easily adopted the hire-purchase version that evolved in the 1980s. In Mumbai, Tata Finance opened shop on 26 April 1984. In Calcutta, Birla Capital & Financial Services on 7 May 1985. In Ahmedabad, Reliance Capital & Finance Trust on 5 March 1986. In Akurdi, Bajaj Auto Finance on 25 March 1987. There was a short hiatus before the latter could replace the 'private' tag and embellish its surname with 'Limited' on 20 October 1987. An early bird, Sundaram Finance had opened in its doors on 11 August 1954 and listed in 1961. In 1997, Reliance Capital would shelve its plans to enter auto finance business.

The Carpet Bombers

Bajaj Auto Finance's first managing director was Dipak Poddar, Bajaj's cousin from Calcutta and a science graduate from Massachusetts Institute of Technology (MIT) in the US. Town-by-town, they meticulously planned a sales and distribution package. The first step: put together funds for an all-out carpet-bombing approach. On 25 March 1987, they launched with hire-purchase products covering all Bajaj two-wheelers and three-wheelers.

To execute his strategy, Bajaj planned Bajaj Auto's sales and distribution meticulously, town-by-town, gaining the trust of distributors and dealers. A robust and committed network emerged. Holding the price line became an ethical issue. 'Ensuring that the consumer obtains the best possible product at the lowest possible price, and the employee gets a fair wage for a day's work, is the criterion of ethics in business,' insisted Bajaj. The government fêted Bajaj, admitting that Bajaj Auto had not taken 'any undue advantage of its dominant position', but it still refused to relax production restrictions.

Between 1987 and 1993, BAFL distributed over Rs 100 crore and created a franchise of about 89,000 customers holding a BAFL hire-purchase financing scheme. 'In the late 1980s, our dealership was changing so marketing had to change,' recalls Bajaj. 'Recessions come and go. What I worried about during that period was competition. We were now looking for more dynamic dealers who would actively compete in the market.' Fortunately, the smaller three-wheeler segment saw a market share of about 70 per cent in 1985–86 surge to 91 per cent in 1992.

By the turn of the century, Bajaj Auto Finance's branch network had sixty outlets. In those days, BAFL's cost of funds ranged in the 11–14 per cent bracket, and its offered average rates of interest between 18–21 per cent. With Bajaj looking over his shoulder, Poddar piloted a tight ship. Non-performing assets stood at 2 per cent and other administrative costs around 4 per cent.

'We are targeting a Rs 150 crore rise in loan disbursements to Rs 650 crore in the current fiscal to attain critical mass,' Poddar proudly shared with *Business Standard* in 2001. 'We are aiming at smaller cities and towns. The high competition in urban markets has led to wafer thin margins.'

Poddar's oblique reference was to ICICI. ICICI has always been an aggressive institution and continued to be so under Kundapur Vaman 'K.V.' Kamath, who took over as its managing director and CEO in 1997. Kamath engineered a string of acquisitions including SCICI (Shipping Credit and Investment Corporation of India), and ITC Classic Finance which had a strong retail base in Eastern India and a strong base in the West.

But the auto financing industry was commoditized, competition was intense and collections a problem. Nine years later, in the face of mounting defaults and uncertain interest rates, ICICI simply shut down its auto finance business.

The BAFL IPO

For effective functioning of an IPO market, the offering process has to be efficient. The Indian IPO market in the 1990s was plagued by fly-by-night operators pushing issues and then disappearing, leaving investors in the lurch. Investors had to wait for weeks to get their allotments and refunds. Prior to the introduction of book-building in 2000, in the event of oversubscription, the allotment mechanism in the Indian market was based on a formula decided by the company on the advice of the investor banker, but strictly based on the guidelines issued by the regulator and supervised by the stock exchanges, i.e., a rationing mechanism.

Bajaj Auto and Bajaj Auto Holdings together launched Bajaj Auto Finance on 25 March 1987 with ten shares as the subscription to the issue's memorandum. A stash of 9,99,990 shares was added to the kitty on 10 June 1987, followed by rights issue of 4 million shares on 20 October 1987. A second round of 5 million shares on 15 May 1990, and with over 10 million shares in hand, BAFL could now comfortably go public. Or could it? An unexpected fiesta of 2713 IPO offerings turned up between 1990 and 2004.

Given the slew of local IPOs, BAFL's timing had to be meticulously planned. There was also a ding ringer: Nimesh Kampani, Bajaj and his core team were due to make Bajaj Auto's GDR London debut in October 1994.

Bajaj announced BAFL's debut on 28 May 1994. In India, BAFL ceased to be a Bajaj Auto subsidiary, and listed on the BSE and NSE in Bombay, Ahmedabad, and Pune. By 1995, BAFL had completed the planned allocation of 4,15,000 equity shares of Rs 10 at a premium of Rs 80. Its paid-up share capital was Rs 16,48,84,500 on 31 March 1995.

American Crusaders Ahoy

By 2006, the news flew like lightning: the triumvirate was considering raising Rs 900 crore. The first tranche of preferential shares and convertible warrants was set at Rs 324.5 crore. And intriguingly, BAFL was about to taste globalization at home.

Crisil reaffirmed BAFL's 'P1+' rating assigned to a Rs 3 billion commercial paper programme (enhanced from Rs 2 billion). 'The rating continues to reflect the strong managerial, operational and financial support derived by BAFL from its parent, Bajaj Auto Limited, rated "AAA/FAAA/Stable/P1+" by Crisil,' agreed the major financial dailies and accordingly informed their wide readership.

'We are bringing in New York-based hedge funds as investors in the preferential allotment round in January,' Poddar shared with the *Economic Times*. 'Copacabana will pick up 10,35,000 fully paid equity shares, El Dorado Holdings II 10,35,000 shares, Tiger Global Management and affiliated funds 7,15,000 shares and Blue Ridge Limited Partnership and/or Blue Ridge Offshore Master Limited Partnership 7,15,000.'

The four who turned up in India were an interesting mélange of idiosyncratic promoters who launched their businesses in the 1980s. The promoters of Blue Ridge and Copacabana evaporated into the ether but two stayed the course: Mike Ingram and Julian Hart Robertson.

Mike Ingram founded El Dorado Holdings in 1987 with a staff of one and a single escrow property south of Phoenix. That property, John Wayne's El Dorado Ranch, was the catalyst for growing a network of investors and landholdings strong enough to weather the real estate cycles and economic swings of the next few decades. His India investment was his second fund, El Dorado Holdings II.

Julian Hart Robertson Jr founded Tiger Global Management in 1980. He did a stint as an officer in the US Navy; joined the Massachusetts-based securities firm, Kidder, Peabody & Co and headed its asset management division before moving with his family to New Zealand for a year to write a novel. On his return in 1980, Robertson launched Tiger Management and discovered in himself an interest in India.

A big picture started looking even bigger.

'Later, in the next fiscal,' Poddar shared with the Indian business media, 'we will raise the balance of our requirements (over Rs 550 crore) through a rights issue. Existing and new shareholders will be able to participate in the rights issue. While there can be a slight change in the medium term, over the long term, this is expected to remain stable. If BAL has to pick up any unsubscribed portion of the rights issue, its equity stake could rise. In the current preferential share allotment round, BAL will bring in Rs 167 crore and the outside investors Rs 157.5 crore.'

'Under this preferential allotment BAFL will issue 10,03,260 fully paid equity shares of face value of Rs 10 each. BAL will also be issued 30,06,540 warrants, each warrant convertible into one equity share on payment of an aggregate price of Rs 410 per share (including premium of Rs 400 per share). The option to convert warrants into equity shares would be exercised no later than 18 months from the date of their allotment. All investors will be offered fully paid equity shares of face value Rs 10 each at Rs 450 each. The preferential allotment is subject to the approval of shareholders at the extraordinary general meeting to be held on 12 January 2006,' Poddar announced.

Also on the table was a non-convertible debentures issue. 'The board of directors have not finalized either the quantum of shares to be issued or the rate,' he added. 'That will be done closer to the time of issue. Following the preferential allotment and the rights issue, the promoter stake in the NBFC (Non-Banking Financial Company) is expected to remain at the current level of about 47 per cent.'

Then came the demerger. Pamnani stepped on to the BAFL's board as its vice-chairman, and Bajaj Auto Finance segued into Bajaj Finance.

A few rare days stand out in a company's history. Wednesday, 16 May 2007 was one of those turning points:

Dipak Poddar resigned as the Managing Director with effect from 1 April 2008. Rajeev Jain was appointed Chief Executive Officer.

On 5 July 2010, BAFL became a subsidiary of Bajaj Finserv.

The change in the company's name from Bajaj Auto Finance to Bajaj Finance took place on 6 September 2010.

The final morphing—Bajaj Finance becoming Bajaj Finance Limited (BFL)—was witnessed on 10 September 2010.

The future beckoned.

26

The Bombay Club and All That Jazz: 1991–93

Bajaj and Manmohan Singh.

'The whole idea got completely *ultafied*,' Bajaj recounts to Datar, 'I was shouting away in the 1980s for liberalization but then in 1993, I became infamous. When I asked for a level playing field, everybody thought this was a euphemism for protection. All we were saying was that the government should enable us to face foreign competition. Nobody listened to me, not from the media or anybody else.'

On 24 July 1991, without much fanfare, not even a ministerial press conference, Prime Minister P.V. Narasimha Rao announced the abolition of the Industries (Development and Regulation) Act (IDRA), 1951. All licencing of new industries, barring a few sectors placed in a negative list, was removed. The 'licence-permit raj' of nearly forty years ended, marking the beginning of massive economic reforms and the movement of ease of doing business.

'What we wanted was for Indian companies to become multinational corporations and for Indian firms to grow,' says Bajaj. 'The simple economics of Adam Smith teaches us that everyone cannot make everything, so we must decide what we want to manufacture and adjust import duties accordingly. Economic liberalization was good for India, and I said so in speeches at various industry associations. But somehow, I was labelled the chief spokesman of the so-called "Bombay Club" in the nineties. And the Bombay Club was synonymous with protectionists and nothing else.'

Let's Meet at the Belvedere?

The first meeting was arranged by Hari Shankar Singhania from the J.K. Group, and Ashok Jain of Bennett Coleman. 'We met at the Belvedere Club in the Oberoi in Bombay, about sixteen of us. Jamshyd Godrej was there, Keshub Mahindra was there, I was there,' remembers Bajaj. Most were members of one or more of the three biggest business lobbies—Associated Chambers of Commerce and Industry of India (Assocham), CII and FICCI.

The Belvedere is a private space in the Oberoi in tony Nariman Point. The group anointed Bajaj as its leader. Reporter Sucheta Dalal broke the story and dubbed them the Bombay Club. The moniker stuck.

'Ashok and Hari Shankar finalized a representation to the finance minister for a level playing field after import duties were satisfactorily reduced,' emphasizes Bajaj. 'Our point was simple: most consumer goods came from the developed world that did not have our handicaps like rigid labour laws, high interest rates, poor infrastructure and so on. We were being made non-competitive.

So, when in 1993 I asked for a level playing field, what I only said was, we have a labour policy problem. I can't get rid of people. We have a high rate of interest, high transaction costs, and I have to compete with imports which don't have those limitations. And that got misconstrued as protectionism. All the others kept quiet after the Finance Ministry asked them not to go public after they made their representation—except me.'

When asked to join the new forum, a few, like Calcutta's Rama Prasad Goenka and Bombay's Essar Group's Shashi and Ravi Ruia flatly refused. Other abstainers included Dhirubhai Ambani, Aditya Birla and Ratan Tata.

The Thirteen-point Charter

After detailed deliberations, a thirteen-point charter was prepared. 'The industrialists who met finance minister, Dr Manmohan Singh, in New Delhi on 10 November 1993, consisted of Bharat Ram, Lalit Mohan Thapar, M.V. Arunachalam, Rahul Bajaj, Bhupendra Kumar Modi, Chandrakant K. Birla, Jamshyd Godrej and myself,' wrote Hari Shankar Singhania in his memoir twenty years later. 'This note was released to the press immediately.' Special adviser Montek Singh Ahluwalia was also present. The message from the Bombay Club was clear. 'Domestic liberalization today, and external liberalization later,' remembers Ahluwalia.

The Bombay Club took the view that greater openness to imports and FDI should follow and not precede domestic reforms. The apprehension was that in the absence of domestic reforms, the Indian private sector would be overrun by foreign competition, with adverse consequences for local entrepreneurship and employment.

Kochanek summed up the Bombay Club's five areas of concern:

First, the Bombay Club demanded that government focus upon a comprehensive series of internal reforms which would enable domestic producers to become more competitive and provide for an extended period of adjustment for domestic industry prior to any attempt to open the Indian economy to external competition.

Second, the Bombay Club objected to government liberal policies towards private foreign investment. They especially expressed anxiety over the government's decision to raise foreign investment equity levels from 40 per cent to a controlling 51 per cent, the takeover of Indian local companies by foreign multinationals and attempts by non-resident Indians (NRIs) to gain control of Indian companies by buying large blocks of shares and replacing the original promoters of the enterprise. The Indian business elite also charged that government was providing benefits to private foreign investors that were not being provided to domestic industry, especially in the case of infrastructure projects.

Third, they opposed the planned reductions in protective tariffs on Indian industry and the opening up of the Indian economy to foreign goods. Since the tariff on finished goods would decline while local excise and sales taxes on industrial inputs remained high, the cost of Indian-made goods would become uncompetitive. This would result in unfair competition and would lead to plant closures and increased unemployment.

Fourth, the Bombay Club charged that tight credit policies and high interest rates placed domestic industry at a competitive disadvantage compared to foreign capital.

Finally, they charged that the failure to reform India's complex labour laws, the failure to enact an exit policy that would enable unprofitable industries to close and the failure to reform or privatize the public sector limited the impact and effectiveness of the reforms.

The Invisible Level Playing Field

If that was all that the Bombay Club wanted, no rationalist could object. Manmohan Singh, the then finance minister, promised sympathy. Pranab Mukherjee, then commerce minister and a former finance minister, added that the government would not allow Indian companies to be 'wiped out'. Of rather more significance was a warning by Serajul Haq Khan. 'Hasty steps towards globalization without ensuring a level playing field will lead to the eclipsing of Indian industry,' he cautioned.

There were diverse issues.

'Before 1991, India by and large followed the policy of a mixed economy,' Bajaj looks back. 'In the 1960s, 1970s and 1980s we had a protected economy. None of India's industries were internationally competitive. Costs were high, quality low and technology obsolete. There was however a positive side to this situation. Owing to the policy of import substitution, India could develop a manufacturing base unlike the screwdriver technology-driven South Asian countries.'

'When liberalization started in 1991, the government had foreign exchange troubles,' describes Bajaj. 'Foreign exchange was not even a couple of weeks' worth of imports. The government did the external liberalization very fast. "We want free trade" meant quick imports. We didn't want import licence raj. That is correct. And ultimately, it helped us, I am not saying it did not.'

'The developed world is protectionist when it suits them— for example, when it protects its farmers—but we need foreign technology and capital,' said Bajaj. 'Certain technologies are in the hands of only a few corporates in the world and they will not part with them unless they have a majority stake in the company in India. We should readily offer them this equity, otherwise we will not get the required technology.'

The government took the Bombay Club seriously, at least outwardly. In the mid-1990s, a decade after the 1985 New Economic Policy,[1] the government permitted Indian companies to raise preference shares of up to 25 per cent of their issued capital. As these shares did not carry any voting power, it eased the way for businessmen to raise money without giving up control. In addition to private lobbying, the Bombay Club organized seminars to publicize the effects of opening up the Indian economy.

The P.V. Narasimha Rao administration admitted that it had received numerous representations from the industry justifying the protectionist move on the grounds that it provided a level playing field to Indian entrepreneurs. 'Post the representation, the Finance Ministry asked us not to go public. All the others kept quiet—except me,' says Bajaj with more than a touch of smiling cynicism.

---

[1] India faced an economic crisis in 1990 and was 'on the brink of default' on its debts. The New Economic Policy of 1991 was a neoliberal Structural Adjustment Program that allowed India to qualify for aid from the World Bank and the International Monetary Fund (IMF).

'At the time, I asked the question, "Should we not have at least a hundred Indian-owned companies in the top two hundred companies in the country?" I was not saying that the Indian industrialist should be protected, but countries have to support not only its industries, but also its nationals,' said Bajaj, wryly. 'Every country in the world, including the developed countries, supports its domestic industries. I continue to believe that the big Indian companies of the future should not be foreign-controlled.'

Is Industry Important or the Industrialist?

'Some industrialists did not initially realize the full implications of liberalization,' says Bajaj. 'Between 1991 and 1994, the pace of liberalization was so fast that industry was pleasantly surprised.' As trade and investment policies changed drastically, open economy process started.'

'In industry there is only one guru who teaches you to be efficient and that is not a business school, but a buzzword called competition,' asserts Bajaj. 'Without competition, industry will perish. There is clearly no alternative to this if we have to become internationally competitive. This also implies survival of the fittest and hence we need to change our industrial relations legislation and devise an exit policy. This would also help prevent fragmentation of manufacturing capacity amongst more than the required number of companies in any one sector. We have to also ensure that foreign companies do not start dumping their goods in the Indian market as import licencing disappear. The government would have to keep a close watch on each industry sector and support the champions in each sector. The laggards will have to face the consequences.'

'In infrastructure projects where large capital is required and Indian companies may not be able to raise the required resources, we should welcome the multinationals,' Bajaj continues. 'However, in sectors such as cement, sugar, textiles and steel, there is no reason why we should offer multinationals above 26 or 40 per cent equity.'

'Lest I should be misunderstood, let me clarify that we still need a lot more liberalisation,' Bajaj recapped to *Frontline*. 'Let the government not privatise defence-related sectors and the railways, as in some countries. But there are over a hundred companies in the

public sector that can be privatised and disinvestment can take place
so that the government's holding drops to less than 50 per cent.
But there is no consensus. If the government maintains its more
than 50 per cent ownership, the Comptroller and Auditor-General
comes into the picture, which means that bureaucrats and ministers
can interfere, claiming that they are answerable to the Parliament.
If the government holding comes down to below 50 per cent, we
could eliminate this problem, but political expediency rules this out,
at least for the moment.'

The Other Side

'There were those who were very uncomfortable with the pace of
economic reforms,' describes Das. The so-called Bombay Club with
the likes of Rahul Bajaj, Lalit Thapar, Hari Shankar Singhania said,
"Slow down, slow down . . . we are not ready". We at CII (supported
by Ratan Tata and others) countered that by "you are overestimating
the threat and underestimating yourself". Rahul and I had some
heated exchanges on this, but it never got personal.'

'The opponents of open-economy policies included not just small
firms but also conglomerates like Godrej, a consumer goods giant,'
describes Jalal Alamgir. 'Krishna Kumar Birla, FICCI president at
the time, let it be known publicly, which did not endear him to the
authorities, that the reforms "were not in the best interests of the country
or industry". Freddie Mehta, a prominent Tata director, commented,
"Indian industry in the coming months will see a few dramatic winners
and a large number of losers. The staying power of Indian industry is not
comparable to that of global players".' Ratan Tata, on the other hand,
began a major consolidation move to integrate eighty of its companies
and 2,72,000 employees into thirty large entities.

After 1994, the liberalization process slowed down considerably
owing to political reasons. A weak coalition government was up
against a fractious industry exposed to serious internal and external
competition. 'This group found a willing audience in the BJP and
other opposition parties,' continues Alamgir. 'There were some
weaknesses in the policies pursued by both the P.V. Narasimha Rao
and the Deve Gowda governments,' agrees Bajaj, adding placatingly
'although the 1997 Budget was outstanding.'

The Bombay Club's Unremarked Demise

As Montek Singh Ahluwalia once remarked, 'in government, it is very easy to persuade yourself that you are rewriting the future.' India's powerful businessmen were similarly disposed. The Bombay Club appeared out of nowhere as an expression of widespread insecurity. And, not surprisingly, it shot itself in a rather short period of time.

One of the major tasks of formal business organizations like Assocham, FICCI and CII is to clingfilm consensus on contentious issues among its members. The members of the Bombay Club held divergent views and vested interests, and didn't see why one's view was better or worse than another's. They bickered. When it came down to brass tacks, the club crumbled.

Towards the end of 1993, the club's membership shrunk to Arunachalam, Bharat Ram, Modi, Singhania, Thapar—and Bajaj. By the end of 1994, 'it was a club of one,' accepts Bajaj ruefully. 'Nobody wanted to be a member as the government was angry'. The sore was salved on Bajaj's seventieth birthday. 'In the book the family brought out on my seventieth birthday, both Manmohan Singh, the then prime minister, and P. Chidambaram, the then finance minister, wrote very nice letters about that time.'

'We were not saying anything new,' Bajaj continues, 'we were saying, choose items to make in India, and give us flexibility. For the rest, the government can reduce import duty. Only an open but independent economy or nation can prosper in the long run. The problems of developing countries are more, at least as much, internal than external. The globalization process, from this perspective, can help developing countries by demanding better skills and products to survive in the international market. It is this demand of the market, resulting from competition, that is responsible for a focus on productivity and quality, which is the long-term basis for prosperity. Moreover, insulation is not feasible and it historically has led to only inefficiency, which in the long run leads to economic decline.'

'The cards are stacked against developing countries but the only way to face them is by playing the game with a desire to win,' continues Bajaj. 'In fact, Prime Minister Narendra Modi is saying the same thing with "Make in India".'

A Quarter Century Later

With business continuously demanding protection from multinationals and imports, the opaque shadows of the Bombay Club remained active for over twenty-five years. Looking back at those days, in an interview to *Indian Express*'s Shaji Vikraman, Manmohan Singh is remarkably generous: 'I think in a crisis, we act constructively. The Bombay Club and traditional industrialists were opposed to the reforms we introduced. Certainly, Indian industry is much more confident now.' Nikhil Meswani of Reliance Industries endorsed this view. 'I particularly respect the stance you took in adhering to the values and principles in forming the Bombay Club.'

Three Quarters of a Century Earlier

Two years before India's Independence, in January 1945, eight Indian businessmen—J.R.D. Tata, G.D. Birla, Sir Ardeshir Rustomjee Dalal, Ardeshir Darabshaw Shroff, Sir Sri Ram, Kasturbhai Lalbhai, Sir Purshottamdas Thakurdas and Dr John Mathai—submitted a 'plan of economic development for India', better known as the Bombay Plan. Nothing came of it. The Bombay Club wasn't the first to be binned.

The Learnings

'If we want to make our companies world-class, we also need rules and regulations that are in line with global corporate and financial norms,' commented Swaminathan S. Anklesaria Aiyar, the then editor of the *Economic Times*. 'We should not need the Bombay Club to tell us this.'

In none of these three time bands did businessmen succeed in shaking the political system. And as Ninan pointed out, 'the world of Indian business is changing, and it's not just old Indian business family vs the multinational. It's also old family vs new entrepreneur.'

27

The Waltz of the Insurance Moghuls: 1998–2001

P.V. Narasimha Rao and Bajaj.

Bajaj watched the television screen and listened to newsreaders with increasing awe at Operation Shakti. India conducted a set of five nuclear tests, Pokhran-II, between 11–13 May 1998. Attempting to calm down the uproar, Rakesh Sood, a former diplomat involved in the post-nuclear test diplomacy, said India had three objectives. 'First was to validate new designs to ensure the credibility of the nuclear deterrent as the data set from the 1974 test was limited. Second was to declare that India was now a nuclear weapon state and modify the terms of our engagement with other states accordingly. Third was to generate an acceptance of India as a responsible state with an impeccable non-proliferation record.'

And there will never be a right answer to the question why the world's biggest insurance companies called on India just after the Pokhran-II tests.

Among cognoscenti with a wide world view, India was a ridiculously late entrant into insurance. The first edge of the wedge appeared in 1993 under the P.V. Narasimha Rao administration. 'With reforms underway in the banking sector and in the capital markets, it is necessary to address the need for similar reforms in the insurance industry aimed at introducing a more competitive environment subject to suitable regulation and supervision,' intoned Finance Minister Manmohan Singh in his 27 February 1993 budget speech to the Parliament.

The budget passed. P.V. Narasimha Rao, Manmohan Singh and Chakravarthi Rangarajan, the RBI governor, quickly got to work. Seasoned by time and experience, there's little that the prime minister, the finance minister and the RBI governor did not know about the machinations of politicians, the bureaucracy, the media— and incumbents, i.e., LIC (Life Insurance Corporation of India, founded in 1956) and GIC (General Insurance Corporation of India, founded in 1972). The trio knew they were skating on very thin ice where the privatization of insurance was concerned.

If Manmohan Singh's 1993 budget speech was the beginning of the end of two monopolies, the finale seemed forever elusive, puttering over seven years of policy making, lobbying, politicking and trade union unrest. The Insurance Regulatory and Development Authority Bill had to be withdrawn twice from Parliament. It would take five prime ministers, four Lok Sabhas, three parties (Congress, Janata Dal, the BJP-led National Democratic Alliance) and five finance ministers to end the monopolies of the state-owned LIC and GIC along with the latter's four subsidiaries.[1] Few bills have had such a chequered history.

Eventually, both houses of Parliament passed the Insurance, Regulatory and Development Authority (IRDA) Act, 1999 in April 2000, which in turn permitted the birth of the key regulatory authority, the Insurance Regulatory and Development Authority of India (IRDAI) with N. Rangachary as its first chair. 'The symbolic value of the IRDA Act, 1999 is as significant as its real worth,' noted journalist Rohit Saran in *India Today*. 'No more does India enjoy the dubious distinction of being one of the only four countries along with North Korea, Cuba and Myanmar in the world to have a closed insurance market.'

It's a 'No'

A human is extraordinarily lucky if they are alive at the turn of a century, whatever be their age. Bajaj is one such individual. Only he wasn't exactly feeling lucky as midnight struck. 'By December 1999, I was already looking at a potential drop in operating profit in Bajaj Auto,' he explains. 'No doubt profit after tax increased to Rs 6137 million by March 2000, but operating profit dropped 9 per cent and was less by Rs 610 million.' With Rajiv pushing the new motorcycle line, how quickly could Bajaj Auto recover ground, he mused. Insurance wasn't on Bajaj's horizon. This was about to change.

Bajaj's stand in 1999 was that he would be happy to consider a foreign partner interested in investing in the two-wheeler business to beef up his balance sheet with a hefty capital dose, rather than jeopardize family capital in the unfamiliar field of insurance.

'My father wasn't convinced about a future in insurance,' agrees Sanjiv. 'We had no interest in insurance when the government opened it up. I had just come back from Harvard and was not involved in

---

[1] GIC's subsidiaries: National Insurance Company, Kolkata; The New India Assurance Company, Mumbai; The Oriental Insurance Company, New Delhi; United India Insurance Company, Chennai.

any of the serious discussions. Nothing had changed in his mind about focus. But then Niraj uncle mentioned to my father that this is a good opportunity to look at.' Under pressure from Niraj, with great reluctance, Bajaj finally agreed to explore the general insurance business. Life insurance was completely ruled out.

Now it was Deora's turn to try and convince his friend. Having swayed many a recalcitrant politician to accept his views, surely Bajaj would at least hear him out before it was too late. As a former board member of India's biggest insurance monopoly, the Life Insurance Corporation, Deora knew which balls to pitch at Bajaj. And as chair of the Parliament's standing committee on finance to which the Insurance Bill had been referred, he had all the numbers at his fingertips.

The Marriage Market Whirligig

The stipulation that Indians had to have a foreign partner combined with India's sheer potential drew insurance companies from across the world. At the beginning of the twenty-first century, India was virtually a virgin market. An indicator accepted globally is life insurance premium as a percentage of gross domestic savings. In 1999, this in the US was 24 per cent, the UK was 41 per cent, Japan at 31 per cent and South Korea at 32 per cent. India was about 6 per cent. The premium income from all schemes was Rs 3,40,000 crore ($8 billion at 1999 rates). Over the next ten years, the size of the Indian market was estimated to treble to over Rs 10,00,000 crore ($25 billion).

Every time the IRDA Bill came up for discussion in the Parliament, representatives of global insurance majors promptly declared that they were ready to enter the market with innovative products at the shortest notice. By 1995, they were actively scouting for Indian partners. It was Waluj all over again—on steroids. Air traffic controllers at Mumbai and Delhi airports grew used to guiding corporate jets from the US, Europe, Japan, and Australia as CEOs arrived clutching cheque books and agreement papers.

Seduced by suitors, the list of Indian entrepreneurs keen to enter insurance grew longer by the day. A fertilizer co-operative, a chemical and engineering firm, an armaments trader—the Indian firms eager to enter the insurance business came in all shapes and sizes. The foreigners were slightly more strategic. Indian companies that typically attracted them broadly fell into three categories: the big multi-product business dynasties, the financial sector and pharmaceutical firms.

Among early partnerships in the multi-product category was the American International Group (better known as AIG) of the US with the Tatas; Rothschild with the Adi Godrej group; and CGNU (non-life) with the Wadias. In the financial sector, the UK's Royal & SunAlliance tied up with Sundaram Finance.

Pharmaceutical firms were attractive because the IRDAI, while issuing licences, said it would give preference to companies offering health insurance. Early birds included New York Life with Max India, Allstate with Dabur, and Cigna with Ranbaxy. Germany's Allianz was attracted to Alpic Finance, a tiny cog in the Cipla group.

The heavy jousting intensified after the RBI clarified in April 2000 that it had no objection to the entry of banks in the insurance business. Several foreign insurance companies stopped chasing business dynasties, preferring to wait for this particular door to open. They were rewarded when the government issued a much-awaited notification under the Banking Regulation (Amendment) Act, 1994. The RBI began giving clearances to individual banks to enter insurance on a case-by-case basis. Eight Indian banks were eagerly waiting in the wings.

Naturally, all eyes were focused on State Bank of India's (SBI's) choice as its mate. The general feeling was that it was the only organization with the capacity to take on LIC. And it was equally powerfully connected: through some savvy footwork, SBI managed to obtain permission to invest 74 per cent shareholding in its proposed insurance venture. Other banks had to be content with 50 per cent. Hopefuls such as Zurich Insurance Group, Switzerland's largest insurer, Belgium's Fortis and GE Capital from the US finally conceded ground to Cardif, France's third-largest life insurer and a subsidiary of BNP Paribas.

One possible reason why Cardif won the race is that it did not insist on building its own brand and downplayed any possibility of posing a future threat to SBI. On its part, SBI favoured Cardif because it was owned by a bank, one moreover that was a leading player in bancassurance in France where 60 per cent of life insurance is sold through banks. 'We are the wholesaler, we develop the product, the pricing, systems and training and if necessary also bring in telemarketing and direct marketing skills while our partner brings in the distribution network. SBI is a strong brand and we propose to make the most of it,' remarked Cardif's Gerard Binet, announcing the tie-up.

The Losers' Ball

Once the SBI deal was sealed, several partnerships had to be modified.

The jilted searched among the jilted. Zurich Insurance finalized its partnerships with Punjab National Bank and the Munjal Group after long months of negotiation with the Bank of India proved futile. Dutch Insurer, ING Insurance roped in Mumbai's Damani group after Vysya Bank could not raise its net worth to the minimum cut-off level for banks entering insurance. CGNU, which started life as Commercial Union before ending up as Aviva Life, left K.K. Birla for Mohit Burman.

The US-based Metropolitan Life Insurance Company (aka MetLife) tie-up with the M.A. Chidambaram group collapsed. MetLife then crafted a unique holding pattern that made it the only foreign insurer to become the single largest shareholder with management control with only a 26 per cent stake. Jammu & Kashmir Bank and Mumbai-based construction magnate Pallonji Mistry held 25 per cent each and the remaining 24 per cent was distributed.

The key Indian players—Ratan Tata, Mukesh Ambani, Kumar Mangalam Birla—watched, listened and waited for the best suitors to come to them. By the time the music stopped, Tata had matched with AIG, Birla with Sun Life. The Ambanis kept to themselves by launching an indigenous organization.

But Where is Bajaj?

'Ranjit Gupta worked in Bajaj Auto in many senior positions from the 1990s,' says Sanjiv. 'He and a few senior people talked to some companies and came back with an encouraging report. He then became fully involved with my father in choosing partners. I was in some of the meetings, but he had the full background.'

'We held preliminary talks with US-based Chubb and France's AXA. However, neither was interested in making significant investment in the business while holding a 26 per cent stake,' recalls Gupta. 'Allianz were also looking for partners. Their talks with Cipla's Alpic Finance had broken down. Allianz then signed a JV agreement with Jet Airways but could not get a licence because of Jet Airways' weak financial position.'

The Allianz go-to man in India was Soumen (Sam) Ghosh, an Indian of Australian nationality, heading its Mumbai representative office. By recruiting Kamesh Goyal, Ghosh achieved a coup de force. Goyal had worked for a major public sector insurance firm and came armed with deep KPMG experience. Rangachary engaged KPMG to support the framing of insurance regulation. KPMG deputed Goyal to help the regulator, Goyal became close to Rangachary.

After twice failing in getting a licence because of partner unacceptability, Ghosh and Goyal met Rangachary for advice and suggestions on a suitable local partner. Murli Deora stepped in, and both he and Rangachary recommended the Bajaj Group to Allianz.

The JV

Swinging into action, Ghosh and Goyal contacted Bajaj. The first formal meeting was held in Mumbai in September 2000 with Uwe Michel, then executive assistant to Michael Diekmann, the Allianz board member responsible for Africa, Asia and Australia. Bajaj showed interest, but only in the general insurance business. A few weeks later, Heinz Dollberg, vice president for Asia, dropped by in Akurdi to meet Bajaj.

The meeting outlined the joint venture's structure. Allianz would initially have a 26 per cent stake with a call option to raise its stake to 50 per cent as and when permitted by Indian regulations. It would pay Rs 45 crore to Bajaj Auto for the use of the Bajaj name in the JV.

Both parties agreed to the CEO being an Allianz nominee, and the non-executive chairman a Bajaj nominee. Both also agreed that the partners could each nominate the CFO and the COO. The new company would be board-run with Bajaj majority directors according to regulations but in spirit it would be a 50:50 company. Both shareholders had some veto rights. Bajaj and Allianz signed the JV agreement on 13 March 2001.

A seasoned Allianz hand, Dollberg was a pragmatic business leader. 'He always tried to understand the viewpoint of the partner, or potential partner, and would look for a solution fair to both sides and good for business,' described Gupta.

In a subsequent meeting, Dollberg proposed to Bajaj the entry of Allianz in the life insurance market. Bajaj came on board.

A potential red flag appeared. Their JV agreement provided for payment of goodwill of Rs 45 crore to the general insurance company and Rs 72 crore to the life company, amounting to Rs 117 crore. The transaction required the regulator's approval.

Rangachary was initially unwilling to give the approval. Bajaj met the regulator in the latter's New Delhi office. 'There are only two options,' Bajaj pointed out. 'Would Rangachary prefer this amount be off-shored illegally or paid to Allianz in India?' Taken aback by Bajaj's bluntness, Rangachary approved the payout.

'With Allianz, we ended up finding a meeting of minds,' adds Sanjiv. 'Both of us are old groups, traditional, conservative. We were in the first lot, but towards the end of the first lot Gupta began drawing up the agreements. I became involved in the agreements and joined the board of Bajaj Allianz from day one.' It was a good call.

Ready, Get Set, Go—Finally

The Insurance Regulatory and Development Authority of India (IRDA) opened the window for a two-stage registration process on 16 August 2000. 'Once you clear R1 stage, you can be fairly sure of going through R2. If you can cross the sea, we do not expect you to be consumed by a puddle,' said N. Rangachary, adding that IRDA would issue the first certificates of registration before the Hindu festival on Diwali, falling on 26 October 2000. An applicant granted a certificate of registration was expected to commence business within twelve months. The IRDA could grant an extension of another twelve months.

On 22 October 2000, IRDA announced that three private insurance companies could begin business. A few days before the public broadcast, Rangachary personally made a call to Deepak Parekh and Deepak Satwalekar. HDFC Standard Life Insurance, HDFC's joint venture with Scottish insurer Standard Life, would be the sole private sector company in life insurance to challenge state-run LIC. 'I couldn't believe it. We thought we would be one among several applicants whose proposals would be accepted,' Satwalekar was quoted on rediff.com.

Anything less would have been unusual for HDFC. Five years earlier, on 5 January 1995, HDFC's Deepak Parekh had got a call from RBI governor C. Rangarajan's office. The banking licence was through. Once the RBI had released the licences, Sharad Marathe, the first chairman of the IDBI and a noted economist-bureaucrat who had been charged by the government to review the 113 applications for a banking licence, discreetly told Deepak Parekh that HDFC's application was the best. This time round also, HDFC was given to understand that its proposal that was put up to the IRDAI was the best.

Waiting for his turn was ICICI's K.V. Kamath. Prudential ICICI Life Insurance Company, promoted by the UK's Prudential with Industrial Credit & Investment Corporation of India (ICICI), India's second largest development financial institution. The second was Dabur Allstate Life Insurance, a healthcare joint venture between Delhi's politically savvy Burman family, and Allstate from the US. Subsequent days saw a burst of activity as executives of other joint ventures in both life and general insurance appeared at IRDA's ground floor office in the multi-storied Jeevan Bharati building in the heart of New Delhi. That week, IRDA received eight applications for life insurance and four for non-life.

In the initial round IRDAI accepted ten applications for life insurance and six for non-life. Bajaj Allianz General Insurance opened its door on 8 May 2001. Allianz Bajaj Life Insurance followed on 1 October 2001.

The Last Word

With the minutiae in collaboration agreements sorted, the incorporations of Bajaj Allianz General Insurance and Allianz Bajaj Life Insurance Company quickly followed. As the majority shareholder, Bajaj Auto invested 74 per cent of the initial share capital in both: Rs 110 crore in general and Rs 150 crore in life. Allianz AG gave Bajaj Rs 117 crore as goodwill. The Indo-German partnership launched its operations in October 2001.

28

The Irrepressible Mr Viren Shah: 1946–2012

Rahul Bajaj and Viren Shah.

'Every time Viren bhai landed in jail, I had to take up the reins of Mukand though I was the younger one,' remarks Bajaj. 'After some time, I got used to it.' Mahatma Gandhi launched the Quit

India Movement in 1942. Bajaj was four years old when sixteen-year-old Viren was at the forefront of student agitations in Wardha. In 1946 Viren was arrested in Bombay for participating in a banned procession. A few months later, he was in Lahore defying curfews and saving lives during Partition.

The Mukand plant was in Lahore, the head office in Karachi. As Partition became a certainty, one of the younger partners of the managing agency, Rameshwar Prasad Nevatia, suggested dismantling the Lahore factory and relocating it near Delhi. A promising idea fell through. The partners lost at least Rs 60 lakh worth of assets to Pakistan. On the positive side of the human ledger, almost everyone who wanted to leave Pakistan returned safely to India.

Kamalnayan got the permissions, Rameshwar the funding and Viren a second-hand bulldozer. Work on a foundry in Kurla started in 1948. The lost Lahore plant was far larger than the more affordable Kurla foundry, but the plot size decent enough. Viren rolled up his sleeves, built a thatched hut, and levelled the uneven land. Sheds budded. Machinery arrived. As business expanded, a larger plant at Kalwe would come up in 1967 to manufacture EOT[1] cranes.

By the mid-1970s, Mukand was a significant metal basher in the private sector. With both plants commissioned, Viren worked in sales and accounts for four years and became Mukand's CEO in 1956. By virtue of the Shah family's shareholding and Viren's obvious talent, inevitably Viren came to dominate and shape Mukand's future. He was Mukand's chairman and managing director for twenty-seven years, starting in 1972.

The Trainee

'I remember in 1961, Rahul bhai started coming to Kurla,' describes Mukand's general manager, Pratap Ashar. 'He used to come by bus from town, and sometimes on a scooter. He was not allowed to go to the executive canteen, so at lunch time, he used to come to the general store where Mathurbhai Nandola, Kanu Goradia, Ashok Mehta and I used to bring our tiffins, and we all lunched together.

[1] Electric Overhead Traveling Crane.

Rahul bhai was not permitted to go out, so sometimes he used to ask me to bring cigarettes for him from outside. Those were the days!' Those were the days indeed. Both Rupa and Bajaj strictly adhered to Kamalnayan's dictum for a twelve-month isolation period before the young couple could marry. Rupa, a beauty queen of many interests and talents, had her days full. Bajaj's days would have felt longer were it not for the excitement of being part of a growing business. The isolation period ended in December 1961, and as a married man, he was permitted a personal vehicle.

'Rahul was working in Mukand's purchase department,' recalls Sajjan Gupta. 'My father and I had gone there for some work. He had a table in the outside common area. My father wanted a glass of water, and since there was no peon at the time, Rahul got up and got the water. My father and I were very moved by his humility!'

'Again in 1975, during the Emergency,' Ashar continues, 'I worked with Rahul bhai very closely because he was looking after Mukand in the absence of Viren bhai. Two-and-a-half days in a week, Rahul bhai would come from Poona and clear all the work. If anything was pending, he would take me to Poona in his car, and on the way, he would finish all matters with quick and specific instructions. Rahul bhai always kept in mind that if Viren bhai had to take the decision, what would he have decided? Rahul bhai and I used to go to Arthur Road Jail to meet Viren bhai. As soon as Viren bhai came out of jail, Rahul bhai immediately gave the charge of Mukand back to Viren bhai.'

The Baroda Dynamite Case

The authorities claimed they had seized 836 dynamite sticks and eighty rolls of fuse wire along with three suitcases and forty-two detonators from a consignment meant for operations in Bihar. In Patna, the police claimed they had recovered fifty dynamite sticks and seventy-six pieces of fuse wire. In Bombay, the authorities recovered thirty-three sticks of dynamite, sixteen detonators and ten rolls of fuse wire. The prosecution also charged the accused with causing explosions at Bombay Central railway station, the Express

Highway overbridge at King's Circle, the Bombay office of the mass circulation Left-wing weekly tabloid *Blitz*, and also railway bridges and tracks in Bihar and Karnataka. With 575 witnesses listed for the prosecution, it was obvious that the Indira Gandhi administration was not taking any chances.

Among the accused stood Viren, a sitting member of the Rajya Sabha as an Independent from Gujarat, and former member of the Fourth Lok Sabha. The ringleader was his friend George Fernandes, chairman of the Socialist Party. Twenty-five people were chargesheeted on Friday, 6 September 1976. It was a mixed group of the powerful and the modest.

The arrest marked a defining moment in Viren's relationship with Indira Gandhi. She was nine years older than him. They had shared memories through M.K. Gandhi and the Wardha days, and their paths crossed often in Delhi. The cordial relationship underwent a change as her politics turned statist. The rapport further unravelled as Viren's friendship with Fernandes grew.

Fernandes, as president of the All India Railwaymen's Federation, organized a twenty-day strike starting on 8 May 1974. According to Wikipedia, the 1.7 million workers' strike was the largest recorded industrial action in the world at the time. In Mumbai, taxi drivers, electricity and transport workers joined the protests. In Chennai more than 10,000 workers of the Integral Coach Factory marched to the Southern Railway headquarters to express their solidarity with the strike. Similar protests erupted across the country. The strike was called off unilaterally on 27 May 1974 by the Action Committee.

The Indira Gandhi administration reacted by issuing an arrest warrant for Fernandes. He promptly went underground. Failing to capture Fernandes, the police arrested his brothers, Michael and Lawrence, as also Snehalatha Reddy, a chronic asthmatic. 'Lawrence, an apolitical printer, was tortured so brutally that he was broken for life,' wrote Ramchandra Guha. Many historians believe that this strike significantly contributed to Gandhi's insecurities, leading her to impose the Emergency.

An outraged Fernandes decided to take on the Gandhi administration. In July 1975, he arrived in Baroda. There he met

Kirit Bhatt, president of the Baroda Union of Journalists, and Vikram Rao, a staff correspondent of the *Times of India*, to discuss what could be done to topple Gandhi. They settled on a strategy of blowing up toilets in government offices and engineering explosions near the venue of public meetings to be addressed by Gandhi. The idea was not to injure anybody, but only create a scare. The explosions were to be carried out either late in the night or hours before the public meeting was to begin to avoid injury. The most ambitious was a plan to blow up the dais four hours before Gandhi was to address a meeting in Varanasi. [2]

Viren agreed to help Fernandes find contacts to source dynamite used extensively in quarries around Halol (near Baroda).[3] The conspiracy, later dubbed the Baroda Dynamite Case, was hatched.

A Pimpri angle appeared in the plan. Under the Raj, the British army had built a cantonment there, and Pimpri remains an important military base. Bajaj Auto's scooter plant is located a few kilometres away in Chinchwad. There was nothing to tie the military base and the scooter factory. But the 'Pimpri' name itself tweaked imaginations. As recounted later by Bhatt, Fernandes wanted to rob a train used to carry weapons from Pimpri to Mumbai. The weapons were to be used to blast government offices.[4]

The authorities nabbed Fernandes on 10 June 1976 in Calcutta. Viren was arrested sometime in July 1976. Under interrogation, Viren claimed he did not shelter Fernandes, admitted that he knew where Fernandes was hiding, and had organized interviews with the international media for Fernandes while he was underground. Viren was housed in Bombay's Arthur Road Jail with some excursions to Delhi's Tihar Jail. The case was tried in Delhi, as the CBI argued that even though the site of the incident was Baroda, the case had national ramifications.

---

[2] See www.indiafacts.org, 'Three Heroes of Emergency', http://indiafacts.org/three-heroes-of-emergency-40/.

[3] Ibid.

[4] Ibid.

Upset by the situation, Krishna Kumar Birla stepped in. In his autobiography, *Brushes with History*, Birla describes his failure to help Viren. In this situation, Birla reckoned, only two people could soften Indira Gandhi's attitude to Viren. And they were Rajni Patel and Sanjay Gandhi. Birla visited both. In Mumbai, Patel refused point-blank to intervene. 'Sanjay was furious when I told him that I had come to plead for Viren,' wrote Birla. 'He asked me how I could recommend the case of a man who was suspected of being involved in a criminal conspiracy against his mother.'

According to C.G.K. Reddy, business manager at *The Hindu*, had Viren 'been a little more cautious and less enthusiastic to be involved in many matters, he would have survived the mopping up following the Baroda arrests. Like me, he was arrested because of a single common contact, Bharat Patel, who became an approver in our case.' By the time the case came up for hearing in Delhi's Tis Hazari court, two approvers were pardoned, two absconded, and one was out on bail.

Fernandes and his fellow accused came handcuffed and in chains, accompanied by a dozen policemen armed with Sten guns. They pleaded guilty to the charge of attempting to overthrow Gandhi but did not accept the specific charges put forward by the government. The defence team was headed by V.M. Tarkunde with Acharya Kriplani as chairperson of the defence committee. The prosecution did not add the names of two women conspirators, Snehlata Reddy and Dr Girija Huilgol, probably because they felt it would attract sympathy for the movement.

'Although granted bail after the trial, all the accused were re-arrested and detained under MISA.[5] The trial became a cause célèbre,' writes Coomi Kapoor in *The Emergency: A Personal History*. Foreign correspondents from all over the world flew down to cover it. The Indian media was, however, prohibited from reporting details except for dispatches from the news agency Samachar.'

Indira Gandhi lost the general election. All imprisoned politicians, intellectuals and activists which by then included G.G. Parikh, Prabhudas Patwari and Devi Gujjar were released in January

---

[5] The Maintenance of Internal Security (MISA) Act, 2 July 1971–77.

1977. Snehalatha died within days of her release from prison. On 18 January 1977, Indira Gandhi called fresh elections for March though the Emergency officially ended on 21 March 1977. As an elected independent Rajya Sabha member from Gujarat (albeit with some help from the Jana Sangh), Viren Shah's first day in the Rajya Sabha was Thursday, 14 August 1975—and he was still in jail. After coming to power in 1977, the Janata government withdrew the case against Shah and, for additional punch, made George Fernandes a minister.

The Governor

In 1999, Viren did a number on Bajaj for the third time. On being appointed governor of West Bengal for a five-year term (4 December 1999–14 December 2004), Viren requested Bajaj to once again take over Mukund's chairmanship. And Bajaj once again agreed. In terms of personalities to handle, as chair, Bajaj had a larger flock to manage.

The third generation blossomed into three families. Viren's son Rajesh joined the firm armed with a master's degree in mathematics from Cambridge University in the UK and an MBA from the University of California, Berkeley, in the US. Rajesh's younger brother Suketu and Ramkrishna's son Niraj, are MBAs from HBS and BCom graduates from Sydenham College, Bombay University. The top-notch education their parents provided would no doubt come in handy, but their capabilities and shareholdings would shape their future and the future of Mukand.

The future came roaring at the youngsters in 2003.

In 1995, the young team had enthusiastically conceptualized a greenfield project to produce a world-class alloy steel in a 'green' plant in a 'Strategic Alliance' with Pune's Kalyani group.

In the early 1990s Mukand had a large cash surplus. The chairman was distracted, lobbying for the West Bengal governorship. He could have, but didn't, nip the Ginigera Integrated Steel Project. Or, given the easy funding options available at the time, Viren was content to ride the enthusiasm of the third generation. Either way, the project brought Mukand into the Reserve Bank of India's Corporate Debt

Restructuring (CDR) programme and the Financial Restructuring Scheme. It would take twelve years to pull the company back to a stable footing.

The most difficult years were 1999–2004 when Viren was in Kolkata. Bajaj mentored Rajesh, Suketu and Niraj as Mukand ploughed through its multiple challenges. A 'reduction of capital and rights' issue in January 2004 brought some relief. To prevent promoter stakes from weakening, Bajaj authorized Jamnalal & Sons, a private Bajaj family firm, to purchase 28 per cent of Mukand's total paid-up capital. Mukand returned to profitability in the financial year (FY) 2005. But there was no sign of seventy-nine-year-old Viren wanting to claim back his chairmanship.

Nor was Bajaj keen to hang around. He was ready to move on the next major event in his life—the Rajya Sabha. At the July 2007 Mukand board meeting, Bajaj stepped down as Mukand's chairman, Niraj was appointed chairman and Rajesh co-chairman.

Over the next five years, Mukand yo-yoed through bad times and less bad times. A global recession in FY 2008 led to losses in FY 2009. Niraj, Rajesh and Suketu managed a turnaround in FY 2010, only to spiral down in FY 2012 on high global iron prices and a rupee depreciation. But Mukand was not the only metals firm in trouble. At Bombay House, Ratan Tata was struggling with his acquisition of Corus Steel in Europe. Kumar Mangalam Birla had his fair share of frustration with Novelis in the US. In India, thirty-three steel companies were under tremendous pressure, including Jindal Vijaynagar Steel, Essar Steel, and Ispat Industries. Mukand did another rights issue in 2014, exited the CDR in May 2015, and settled down.

The fourth generation waits in the wings. Mukand's logo is 'infinite resolve'.

29

Stuck in the Slow Lane: 1979–2002

Wishing you a road with many more milestones.

'The Common Man' by R.K. Laxman in 1998.

Bajaj dreamt of cars for almost his entire life. Preferably high-speed ones of the James Bond archetype. 'My wife Pushpa, Rahul and Rupa and I were returning from Juhu,' recalls Mukul Upadhyaya, a senior Bajaj Auto manager. 'Rahul was driving rather fast. Rupa, sitting in the rear seat, asked him to slow down. "Those who are scared can get off the car," growled the driver. There was an awkward silence.'

As Bajaj Auto grew bigger, so did the number of cars in the garages of his various homes, but none built in his plants. The Bajaj Qute would be born in the high-tech workshops of Akurdi of Rajiv's making, not the father. But a man can always dream.

Pie in the Sky

The man dreaming of an automobile revolution in 1979, however, was not Bajaj but George Fernandes. 'George called me to Delhi, at my convenience,' recalls Bajaj. 'It was most probably in 1979 when I met him in the Industry Ministry. He said all automobile companies—Tata Motors, Hindustan Motors, Ashok Leyland, Premier Automobiles and Standard Motors—will be nationalized and merged to create the Automobile Corporation of India. He offered me its chairmanship. Bajaj Auto and other two-wheelers would be kept separate.'

'I told him that as my two sons are studying and as there is no one else from my family to look after Bajaj Auto, this will be a problem,' Bajaj continues. 'I also mentioned to him that as I am against nationalization, I will not be able to show my face to any of my peers. He said he wants me for only five years and I can go back to my company after a successor is found by me for the automobile corporation.'

'I also asked George whether Morarji bhai had agreed to the nationalization, and George said yes. I asked whether I could ask Morarji bhai, and to this also George said, "yes of course".'

'When I met Morarji bhai the next day and mentioned to him what George had told me, he said, "Over my dead body!" I said, "George has said so". Morarji bhai thought about it and said, "Yes, Atalji had come to him and mentioned something to this effect by George Fernandes, and I had just told Atalji that we will see. Maybe Atalji took this as okay and conveyed it to George".'

'I came back to George and told him this is what has happened. Luckily for me, George's project fizzled out.'

LPG's Flat Tyres

The nerd working in the back room of the Federal Research Bank of Philadelphia stretched and cracked his knuckles. His bosses weren't going to be happy with his report. The Big Three—General Motors, Ford and Chrysler—were losing market share to foreign competitors. 'Market share fell 1.7 percentage points in 1989 to 63.8 per cent in 1990,' calculated the American-Chinese. 'As each percentage point represents about $1.5 billion in sales, the decline is notable, especially since the Big Three had a commanding 80 per cent of the US market less than a decade ago.' His work done for the day, he left.

Overarching the data was the reality of the growing Japanese presence at the expense of the Big Three. Their plant capacity in 1989 rose to 2.2 million vehicles and rising. Two European majors, BMW and Mercedes-Benz, weren't far behind. Both groups were ready to export from the US or their home markets or wherever they could find a hotspot. A global replay of *Barbarians At The Gate* was about to twitch.[1]

India in 1989–90 faced none of these challenges and opportunities because it didn't have much of a passenger car industry. On the other hand, it did have decent two-wheeler options, and demand outstripped supply. LPG aka liberalization, privatization and globalization arrived under the Atal Behari Vajpayee administration.

Bajaj in 1990 was the world's fourth largest manufacturer of two-wheelers, one step behind Japan's Honda, Suzuki, and Kawasaki. Revolving in Bajaj's mind was a critical thought: could the same high-volume, low-cost strategy that had served him so well in the past for scooters, apply to cars as well?

'In the mid- to late-1990s, we thought about entering the passenger car market, negotiated with American, French and Japanese manufacturers, and almost finalized a joint venture with Chrysler,' says Bajaj.

Chrysler was already in talks with Keshub and Anand Mahindra to make the Cherokee in India. 'It was predictable given that Chrysler

---

[1] A 1989 novel based on the true story of R.J.R. Nabisco by Bryan Burrough and John Helyar.

had a marginal stake in M&M and had a long association with the company for the Willys brand,' describes Autocarpro. Just when it seemed that the two were set to make a formal announcement of their joint venture, M&M settled on Ford as partner. Chrysler had to make a beginning all over again.

At one point, it was widely perceived that Bajaj and Chrysler were close to signing a deal. Bajaj was categorical that India needed an affordable car. Chrysler began working on an Asia model of the Dodge Neon due to debut in the US and could potentially compete with the Maruti 800 based on Suzuki's 1979 Alto. 'Bajaj made no bones about the fact that he would not settle for an equal partnership, and would hold a majority stake in the joint venture,' reported Autocarpro. Equity stake resolution became more relevant than an American Neon.

'We did consider making a small car jointly with Renault, Ford, Chrysler and Fuji,' says Bajaj, 'but at the end of the day, our investigations and the performance of other car manufacturers in India made us realize that in terms of marketing and branding it was not the correct decision for Bajaj Auto, which was and is known as a two- and three-wheeler manufacturer.'

'JVs are learning platforms but doesn't mean walking hand-in-hand into the sunset forever,' Anand Mahindra shared with PTI. 'You must understand, JVs by nature are creatures of short duration. They are created because the two sides have some particular goals, and the goals are different. When goals are realized, the JV has a half-life.' M&M, for example, partnered with Ford between October 1995 to March 1998.

As Bajaj pointed out, 'What's the point in several manufacturers making 20,000 cars each? You've got to make at least 1,00,000 cars, preferably 2,00,000, in order to overtake Maruti. If I can't do that, I don't want to be in cars.' Bajaj decided that it made little sense to get into cars especially when it involved heavy investments with hardly any role for the Indian partner.

Selling Family Silver Can Be Complicated

At the cusp of the twenty-first century, with both Rajiv and Sanjiv hard at work in growth businesses, Bajaj, now in his early sixties, allows himself to dream of cars again. 'I am in the automobile business,' he announced to the media, 'and therefore interested in acquiring any automobile company up for sale in the country.' Implicit in the message was Maruti Udyog.

Windows curtained, Michael Jackson on one wall, a tiger on another—Bal Thackeray's living room in Bandra breathed energy. Bajaj and Balasaheb were tightly focused on Prime Minister Atal Bihari Vajpayee's disinvestment programme, and the strategies needed to bring Maruti Udyog successfully into the Bajaj fold.

As an organization, the Shiv Sena was at a peak. For three consecutive terms, it returned an MLA to Pimpri-Chinchwad. Second, with sixteen Lok Sabha MPs, Thackeray could call almost as many shots at the Centre as did Andhra Pradesh Chief Minister Chandrababu Naidu. Third, Thackeray was already piqued at Vajpayee for passing over Manohar Joshi, Maharashtra's chief minister from 1995–1999, and handing the disinvestment portfolio to the more junior Arun Shourie.

Thackeray didn't require explanations from Bajaj as to why Bajaj Auto would be the best suitor for Maruti Udyog's privatization. Instead, Thackeray straightaway demanded that Vajpayee call a halt to disinvestment activity in Maruti Udyog until he dispatched a Sena delegation of three ministers and three Lok Sabha MPs to 'discuss' threadbare the issue.

In Delhi at the 18 November 2000 Cabinet Committee on Disinvestment meeting, 'Shiv Sena's Manohar Joshi, who looks after heavy industry, objected to the sale of Maruti Udyog, the only minister to do so,' reported the *Telegraph*. 'When Shourie repeatedly tried to convince Joshi, arguing that there was nothing imprudent about the move, Joshi pleaded with Shourie to talk to Thackeray.'

Unnerved by the Shiv Sena's opposition, Shourie turned to Vajpayee for advice. It was short and sweet: visit Mumbai and root out Thackeray's objections. Shourie duly 'dashed to Mumbai to meet the Shiv Sena chief and persuade him to support the disinvestment decisions, and succeeded in making the Sena chief see reason,' the *Telegraph* bemusedly informed its readers the next day.

A few days later, *India Today*'s V. Shankar Aiyar buttonholed Joshi: What should have been done?

'Maruti should have been privatized two years ago'.
What went wrong?
'Nobody called the bluff of unions, bureaucrats and ministers—all entrenched interests.
Competition has ruined Maruti's market share and there's nothing it can do except privatize.'

Maruti Udyog declared its first loss. The union threatened a prolonged agitation. 'By this time, the disinvestment process was in the doldrums with politicians openly damaging Maruti,' rebuked Sucheta Dalal.

'The solution is a strong government with the strength to communicate the benefits of privatization to the unions and public at large,' urged Bajaj in July 2000, 'and then resolutely carry out disinvestment in an open and transparent manner without worrying about consequences.' A restless Bajaj accelerated the pace in November 2000 by offering to buy the government's 50 per cent stake in Maruti Udyog. Bajaj Auto had a cash pile of Rs 1700 crore and no debt. 'So long as it did not damage my bottom line, liquidity would not be a problem,' he figured.

Also watching, waiting and listening for the right moment to intervene was Osamu Suzuki. India's Pokhran-II nuclear tests conducted between 11–13 May 1998 had triggered an en masse exit of Japanese companies. Very few trickled back. But one never left: Suzuki Motors, Maruti Udyog's Japanese godfather.

A veteran empire-builder, Maruti Udyog was among Osamu Suzuki empire's more modest outposts. Osamu built assembly plants in Thailand (1967), Indonesia (1974), Pakistan (1975), Philippines (1975) and Australia (1980). In 1982, a couple of days before landing in India, Osamu was in Pakistan for the upgrade of the Pak Suzuki assembly plant near Karachi into a full-fledged manufacturing operation. He then hopped over the border to inaugurate the Maruti Udyog's Gurgaon assembly plant joint venture with the Indira Gandhi administration.

The Maruti 800 arrived on 14 December 1983. The midget was 'a huge improvement over the tank-like proportions of the Hindustan Motors' Ambassador and the unprepossessing appearance of Premier Automobiles' Fiat,' rejoiced the paparazzi.

'Maruti made believers out of cynics,' chorused the advertising community. The bottom line: it outperformed entrenched competitors, sold 1,00,000 cars within five years of its inception, turned in profits, a rarity among public sector undertakings. According to an early agreement between the Indian government and Suzuki, 'Suzuki was permitted to veto the choice of buyer and may do so if the buyer is a foreign party—other than General Motors of the US, which holds a minority stake in the Japanese company,' reminded the *Financial Times*' correspondents Khozem Merchant and Angus Donald.

In 1992 Osamu managed to raise Suzuki Motors' stake in Maruti Udyog to 50 per cent. A decade of tense negotiations later, satisfaction of sorts finally appeared all round between February and May 2002. Suzuki Motors paid Rs 1000 crore as control premium, made a Rs 400 crore rights issue, increasing its stake to 54.2 per cent, and introduced ten finance companies (8 + 2 JVs). The June 2003 IPO was subscribed thirteen times, attracting bids as high as Rs 360 per share despite the Rs 115 per share floor price. The first hour of trading on the BSE and NSE on 9 July 2002, saw the Maruti Suzuki stock climb 30 per cent. Relief all round.

The Last Word

That evening, with a Bloody Mary in his hand, Bajaj and Rupa watch the evening news with their children and grandchildren romping around them in Bajaj Vihar.

This time round, it would be Manohar Joshi who had the last word: 'One incidence is still fresh in my mind. As minister of heavy industry, we were instructed in disinvestment of Maruti Udyog Ltd. You approached me to buy the shares. You made it clear to me that you would like to purchase the shares, but the entire deal should be transparent, and you will not bribe anybody, any time. In my long political career, you were the only industrialist who was so honest and outspoken, Rahul ji, I am proud of you.'

30

The Banking Licence: 1993–2015

Planning sessions at Akurdi.

In the race for a banking licence, everyone expected a Volcker[1] but got a Yellen.[2]

---

[1] As the United States Federal Reserve chairman (1979–87), Paul Volcker introduced restrictions on US banks from making certain kinds of speculative investments that do not benefit their customers.

[2] As the United States Federal Reserve chairperson (2014–18), Janet Yellen was more concerned with unemployment than with inflation, and advocated monetary policy to stabilize economic activity over the business cycle.

In this tale, C. Rangarajan, Reserve Bank Governor between 1992 and 1997 is a Volcker. Under his watch, the RBI was a hive of unprecedented central bank activism. A comprehensive set of measures improved and strengthened the financial sector's competitive efficiency. New institutions and instruments were introduced. Exchange rate management culminated in the establishment of a unified exchange rate. In monetary policy, a historic memorandum was signed between the RBI and the government, which capped automatic access to treasury bills by the government.

Significantly, 22 January 1993 saw the P.V. Narasimha Rao administration open up banking to the private sector. The RBI promptly approved the Deepak Parekh-led HDFC Ltd, a non-banking financial institution focused on home mortgages, as one of the ten applicants selected to set up a bank. Four out of the ten carefully selected banks failed. The Times Bank faltered under the Atal Bihari Vajpayee administration on 26 February 2000. The Centurion Bank of Punjab went under on 23 May 2008 during the Manmohan Singh-Sonia Gandhi administration. Both were willy-nilly merged with HDFC Bank. The third, Global Trust Bank, was a scandal beyond redemption. YES Bank got one in 2004 and went under. Sixteen years later, as of 6 March 2020, the RBI was still trying to resuscitate YES Bank.

Outside the HDFC conglomerate and the systemically significant IDBI, and ICICI Bank, the survivors of the 1993 round were Unit Trust of India Bank (renamed Axis Bank in June 2007), Bank of Punjab, IndusInd Bank, and Development Credit Bank. Uday Kotak received a licence to start Kotak Mahindra in February 2003.

Raghuram Rajan who took over from Duvvuri Subbarao is our Yellen.

With the likelihood of the entry of private sector banks, in 2011 Subbarao unleashed a major clean-up of small banks across India. Between 21 January and 22 December, the RBI penalized eighty-four banks and cancelled six licences. A couple of years later, Subbarao announced the re-opening of doors for new private sector banks. 'Our effort will be to make a judgement as transparent, objective and contestable as possible,' said Subbarao as he stepped down. 'Not everybody who is fit and proper will be given a licence because we expect the number of eligible applicants will be much larger than a meaningful number of licences we can give,' he warned. The deadline was 1 July 2013. The date kept slipping. Subbarao's term got over. Raghuram Rajan took over on 4 September when Manmohan Singh was prime minister, and P. Chidambaram the finance minister.

By April 2014, the RBI's twenty-third governor had granted twenty-three banking licences to new players. Two were given universal banking licences (2 April 2014), eleven were issued payments bank licences (19 August 2015) and ten were given licences for small finance banks (16 September 2015). Nil to big business.

Supporting the government's decision, Deepak Parekh suggested that corporates stay out of the banking business. IMF's Christine Lagarde, Nobel laureate Joseph Stiglitz, the RBI's nineteenth governor C. Rangarajan, former Finance Minister Yashwant Sinha, economist Percy Mistry: support for Parekh had an impressive global and local elegance. Unmoved, the Aditya Birla Group, M&M, and the Tata Group lined up alongside Bajaj. All four had full-fledged non-banking financial companies taking deposits and lending funds.

Laying Out the Case

Bajaj had only two simple points to make: one, on probity and two, on Chinese walls. 'The RBI must ensure new banking licences aren't given to corporates or large houses whose track records don't suggest probity in public life and ethical behaviour,' he defined. The second call was to erect Chinese walls within a conglomerate in order to avoid lending funds between group companies and its bank.

More acerbically, Bajaj regretted that 'this argument of not granting licences to corporates is absolutely misconceived and not in the interest of inclusive growth in India. When people speak about global companies, they speak of banks in the US and the UK, such as Citibank, Morgan, Bank of America and many others, which were the cause of the financial meltdown of September 2008. These were publicly-owned banks but managed by professionals who were greedy for short-term profits.'

Bharat Doshi, chairman of Mahindra & Mahindra Financial Services, was equally vehement. 'It would be a folly if banking licences were denied to corporate houses in the belief some errant players might misuse the licence and divert funds to companies of that corporate house. More than the ownership, RBI needs to put greater emphasis on corporate governance, transparency, the business model and long-term commitment. This will ensure organisations, corporate or otherwise, engage in fair business practices and operate within the regulatory framework, as prescribed by the RBI,' he told *Business Standard's* Dev Chatterjee and Abhijit Lele.

'In its draft guidelines, the RBI has already stated the parameters for industrial and business houses to set up banks,' Doshi added. 'Safeguards such as the dilution of promoters' stake, limits on group exposure, and strict controlling and reporting guidelines are among the requirements to shield the bank from misuse by promoters. In any case, the RBI now has sweeping powers to penalize those who bypass safeguards.'

Picking up the thread, Aditya Birla Group's Santrupt Misra asked a moot question: 'Transfer pricing already happens today on an arm's-length basis. Lending is nothing but transfer pricing of an instrument called money. So, why can't it be done in banking?'

Bajaj Finserv

The RBI had indicated that NBFCs with an existing financial services network were likely to get priority in the award of banking licences. Rumours flew as analyst views blossomed.

Bajaj Finserv, incorporated on 7 April 2007, applied to the RBI for the banking licence on 27 June 2013. It was a zero-debt company with loose cash of Rs 800 crore and a subsidiary, Bajaj Finance, which could easily be converted into a bank according to the RBI guidelines.

The application created a mild flutter among the auto paparazzi. Sanjiv's finance company was one of the main providers of loans to customers who bought Rajiv's motorcycles. 'At a time when rivals like Hero MotoCorp and TVS are strengthening their finance arms, this could erode Bajaj Auto's competitive edge,' pointed out *Business Standard's* Clifford Alvares. 'We need clarity on the rules for new banks and we are looking to find a solution to these problems,' agreed Rajiv mildly. The regulator was particular that banks limit inter-group transactions.

Initially, Sanjiv was hopeful of starting the bank within eighteen months of the RBI's permission. 'We had a significant business that could be transferred into a bank,' he recalls. 'We had the right set of customers with us. We knew that cross-selling was the right thing to do if you want to increase your return on equity. We were already making provisions like a bank. Had we got the licence, converting into a bank would have been relatively easy for us,' he says.

'We were already a non-bank bank in the way we behaved. We did many things that banks do. We applied when the licencing process opened up but unfortunately only two bank licences were announced, which we clearly believe went against the whole initial preamble of opening up bank licences to spread banking services for greater competition and financial inclusion.'

The RBI

'Banking in India is a vast problem and a huge opportunity,' reminded *The Economist*, 'when new licences for private players are granted, fortunes are made. The last two permits, awarded in 2003–2004 when the industry was recovering from bad debts helped make $10 billion for their backers. Now the RBI plans to issue new licences. Applications are due by 1 July and a frenzy is building.'

'I don't think that the RBI Governor has any ceiling in mind,' said P. Chidambaram. 'The fact that somebody applies doesn't mean he is an eligible applicant. A large number of banks will mean more competition and a quicker reaching into the country and faster financial inclusion.'

Replying to questions on bank licences, P. Chidambaram said he had made no recommendations to the RBI. 'The Bimal Jalan Committee has been appointed to scrutinize the applications. It is before the RBI. I have not seen the Jalan Committee report. The RBI will take appropriate decisions. If at some stage the governor wishes to share its content with me, then I would be very happy to listen. But I don't intend to speak.'

In its clarification, the RBI said, 'Entities getting licences to open new banks will be given eighteen months to open branches, and promoters would have to transfer their holdings to the non-operative financial holding company (NOFHC) in a stipulated period.'

Several applicants roped in heavy artillery to get them through the RBI gate. JM Financial's Nimesh Kampani and his son Vishal tied up with ex-Citibank Vikram Pandit. Reliance Capital pulled in Japan's Sumitomo Mitsui Bank and Nippon Life as strategic partners with a 4–5 per cent stake each. Religare Enterprises offered to sell a 6 per cent stake to Customers Bancorp Inc for $51 million (about Rs 300 crore) if they got through.

Government or government-owned institutions, various shades of finance and investment firms, microfinance companies, and family business conglomerates made up the balance. Former PSU bank chiefs in particular were much in demand.

Two organizations that decided to give the opportunity a miss were Mukesh Ambani's Reliance Industries and the Mahindra & Mahindra group.

By Monday 1 July 2013, the RBI had received twenty-six applications for banking licences. It had already made it clear in June that there would be no predetermined number of approved licences. October 2013 saw a committee constituted under Bimal Jalan to examine the criteria, business plans and corporate governance practices of applicants. Its members were Usha Thorat, C.B. Bhave and the director of the RBI central board of directors, Nachiket M. Mor. They submitted their report to the RBI on 25 February 2014.

When the RBI did hand out the coveted banking licences, instead of dishing them out to India's top corporate names, the RBI granted only two permits: IDFC, an infrastructure finance firm, and Bandhan Financial Services, a micro-lender to the poor based in Calcutta.

Sanjiv

'Aiming for a banking licence was clearly a positive step for what we were doing. Giving out only two licences went against the whole initial preamble of opening up bank licences to spread banking services for greater competition and financial inclusion,' recalls Sanjiv.

'I believe the RBI should give out at least three–five bank licences a year for the next ten years—that's when we will see an increase in banking penetration and quality competition. We saw that happening in insurance, from four–five government insurance companies in 2001 to over forty now.'

'If banks can operate in different lending segments, so can we,' adds Rajeev Jain. 'We say to our investors we will deliver 18–20 per cent sustainable return on equity (RoE). Private banks generate RoE of 15–16 per cent; NBFCs in a single line of business generate 24 per cent RoE. With 18 per cent RoE, we provide the agility of the NBFCs and the risk management processes of the banks. We feel our diversified presence helps in mitigating risks while growing at a decent pace. Investors did not believe in our story then. Every company takes time to be discovered.'

Adds Sanjiv, 'When we started transforming Bajaj Auto Finance to Bajaj Finance, we decided to be multi-line. There are many mono-lines like Mahindra Finance focused on tractors or Muthoot Finance on gold. When we looked at private sector banks, we saw that if one does a mono-line, they could wipe you out in a down cycle.' The foresight proved prescient. SBI, for example, started aggressive lending to the farming community challenging Mahindra Finance, and HDFC Bank turned the heat on the market leader in gold loans, Muthoot Finance. 'The banking licence was important for us but not urgent,' Sanjiv continues. 'When the next set of regulations come about, we will be in a better position to again evaluate the licence.'

31

The GDR: 1994–2017

The UK's Prince Charles and Bajaj.

Invited to the dais, Bajaj strode to the lectern, pressed a key, and a roomful of hard-bitten international fund managers burst into appreciative chuckles. A Bajaj Auto three-wheeler converted into a school bus appeared on the screen, and the audio-visual showed one tot after another tumbling out of the vehicle in a seemingly endless disgorgement. Bajaj's ability to control his audience at its best.

The venue was Kleinwort Benson's elegant London office on 20 Fenchurch Street. The date, 20 October 1994. The raison d'être: the launch of Bajaj Auto's GDR[1] offering on the London Stock Exchange.

Bajaj didn't need the money. India did. Which is why Finance Minister Manmohan Singh and C. Rangarajan, governor of the Reserve Bank of India, permitted a select group of Indian businessmen to raise funds on the London Stock Exchange and the older Luxembourg Stock Exchange. These large capital markets with their lower costs of capital offered enhanced liquidity, cost efficiency and the elimination of investment barriers such as domestic accounting and tax practices. The GDR experience would turn out to be a profound learning experience for all parties.

The cross-listing of Indian companies on initially the European, and later the American stock exchanges, was a significant turning point in state-business relations. It symbolized the state's recognition of the importance of big business in an economy struggling with a severe balance-of-payments crisis. Here was another route to pull in some forex, however meagre, in the larger picture.

A tussle broke out among the three biggest business groups— Tata, Birla, Ambani—as to who would be permitted to issue the first GDR. Unsurprisingly, Mukesh Ambani's Reliance Industries won. Its GDR issue debuted successfully in May 1992, with each GDR having two Rs 10 underlying equity shares. The issue went viral, listing on the Luxembourg Stock Exchange, trading on the OTC market in London, and available on a private placement basis in the US. Ambani raised $150.42 million. RIL's equity increased by Rs 184 million as a result, and reserves by Rs 4,440.8 million. The achievement is all the more remarkable as the timing coincided with the Harshad Mehta scam which left Indian stock markets reeling. In 1999, Infosys Technologies would issue India's first ADR[2] in the US.

In Akurdi, the GDR idea became increasingly irresistible. Preparing for the challenge and legwork, Bajaj roped in Nimesh

---

[1] Global Depository Receipt (GDR), a financial instrument traded on the London and Luxembourg stock exchanges; American Depositary Receipts (ADRs) on the US stock exchanges.

[2] American depositary receipt. The US invented the instrument in 1927.

Kampani from Mumbai, alongside international firms Kleinwort Benson Securities, Asian Capital Markets, and CS Boston. The required permissions streamed in.

Question Time

Despite the great beginning of the Bajaj Auto London roadshow, the mood in the room was aggressive. The fund manager's code demands it. A sceptic fund manager asked, 'How can you expect to win this war with a twenty-five-year-old Vespa model?'

'What do people want from a scooter?' Bajaj responded promptly. 'Cost, shape, fuel economy and emissions. Shape, yes, customers want a new shape and in 1997 it will get more contemporary. Honda brought the latest and best technology to India, but customers want change, not necessarily technology. My engine is as good, if not better.'

A major grouse among investors was the lack of fungibility of Indian GDRs over which Bajaj of course had no control. Foreign institutional investors (FIIs) were keen to see slimmer differences between local and international shares of Indian corporates. Suggestions included giving GDRs voting rights and two-way conversions, i.e., permitting GDRs, which were converted into Indian shares to be reconverted.

The lack of commonality of economic interest between promoters and shareholders also came in for vociferous indictment. The knotty issue of preferential allotments and its abuse by Indian managements propelled a tide of hands to surge for the mic. Nobody wanted to hear Harsh Lodha, of the Bombay-based Lodha & Company, point out that multinationals such as Unilever and Colgate-Palmolive had started the trend. India-bashing is so much more fun than reading the guidelines issued by the Finance Ministry and SEBI.

Indian accounting standards—or rather the lack of them— provoked some heat, particularly when the attack was led by an Indian employee of a foreign firm. 'He is trying to be whiter than the white man. Look at the Guinness trials, at the Asil Nadir case. In the BCCI scandal, where was the Bank of England?' fumed a patriotic Indian. As speaker after speaker focused on deficiencies in

Indian issues, Indian companies and Indian legislation, Roy Rohatgi of Arthur Anderson summed up the mood when he said: 'There is considerable disenchantment with the malpractices in India.'

The extraordinary lack of information among London-based fund managers on the stream of guidelines and regulations issued by Indian authorities didn't help. Few doubted the Finance Ministry's sincerity in tackling complex issues, yet at the same time, the issues raised by the international community could not be swept aside as if they were unimportant or irrelevant. Bajaj's GDR debut meeting started to morph into a forum for debate and had to be nipped—which Bajaj did with his usual aplomb.

The grilling was worth it. At the end of the meeting, the analysts gave Bajaj the thumbs up. He pulled in $800 million worth of demand. Bajaj Auto's GDR issue was an overwhelming success with fund managers begging for allocations. 'It was great fun,' recalls Nimesh Kampani.

'The share premium from the GDR issue was Rs 3,410 million, which in 1994 was a pretty sizable amount. Normally, this would come at the cost of dilution in voting for the promoters. Bajaj, however, found a master stroke solution for such a dilution,' recalls Jayaraman Sridhar, Bajaj Auto's company secretary. 'The Bankers Trust Company, the Depository to the issue which later became Deutsche Bank, entered into an agreement whereby the voting rights on the GDRs were assigned to the promoters of Bajaj Auto. This was typical Bajaj out-of-the-box thinking style,' adds colleague Kevin D'sa. Bajaj Auto repatriated into India the full balance amount of the proceeds of the GDR US$36 million issue.

Reverberations

Call it chance or coincidence or simply pure luck, the timing of the Bajaj Auto GDR was impeccable. Between 1992 and 1998, Indian firms listed sixty-six GDRs with a total issue value of over $6.5 billion on European stock exchanges, primarily in London and Luxembourg. At the opening, all were priced at a premium over the underlying Indian stocks. The months between November 1993 and May 1994, however, saw most Indian GDRs making losses for their new owners. Before November 1993, with the exception of Bombay Dyeing, all scrips were making money. After May 1994, Indian GDRs were either static or slightly profitable. The Bajaj Auto GDR debuted on 27 October 1994. Bajaj somehow managed to sidestep the sandwich. But it was a profound learning experience.

Drilling into the undercurrents of this period, approximately 25 per cent of the issues changed hands in the first month of trading as international speculators moved in and out. About 5 per cent were converted into Indian shares in arbitrage activity. Some advisers were better than others in ensuring that its clients' GDRs were in the hands of quality investors. Mahindra & Mahindra, for example, issued its GDRs just as the market was surging forward towards the January 1994 peak. Speculators pushed in and almost 50 per cent of M&M stock changed hands. A few months later, the stock was in the hands of long-term investors who genuinely believed in India's economic progress and planned to hold on to their holdings.

Overseas fundraising became an intoxicating game. By June 2001 seventy-two companies successfully tapped the international capital markets, with hundreds of companies waiting in the wings. The wave subsided by 2016, displaced by newer instruments such as the QIP (qualified institutional placement). The Bajaj GDR journey ended with its delisting on 24 March 2017. In 2018, sixty-eight GDRs and sixteen ADRs continued to trade.

Curiously, China surged as India faded, entering the GDR market for the first time in June 2019 through Huatai Securities.

And the last word goes to S. Ravikumar, one of Bajaj's colleagues managing the GDR issue: 'I'll always cherish the gift of a bottle of wine Rahul sir gave me post the Bajaj GDR issue!'

32

The Pulsar: 1998–2014

Rajiv, Bajaj and Sanjiv.

1982. 'My marketing department? I don't require it. I have a dispatch department. I don't have to go from house-to-house to sell,' said Bajaj.

1997. 'Whatever product or service a company offers, it must meet the customer's wants in the most satisfactory manner. That should be the aim of the company,' said Bajaj.

The early 1990s opened with a recession that hit the entire automobile industry, including its poster child, Bajaj Auto. Sales plunged by almost 50 per cent, leaving unprecedented levels of unsold scooters. 'The reasons for the slump were macro economic in nature and had little to do with the auto industry itself,' Bajaj explained to shareholders.

The media snapped to attention. 'The uncertainty in the marketplace has forced the company's chairman Rahul Bajaj, to make a break from the past practice of setting targets for Bajaj Auto at the company's AGMs,' wrote various publications. 'Since 1 July 1991 the changing economic and industrial policies of the Government of India have made foreign companies sit up and take a fresh look at India's potential as far as their business is concerned.'

And for no fault of his, because of Bajaj Auto's large volumes, the smallest drop in its market share benefited other players lavishly. A 10 per cent drop in Bajaj Auto's scooter sales in FY 1992, for example, translated into a 14 per cent growth for Kinetic Honda and 8 per cent growth for TVS Suzuki in a year when the overall scooter segment grew by 0.8 per cent.

'Competition and openness can only help build rather than destroy,' Bajaj reassured shareholders. 'While there is a degree of unequal competition between foreign companies and Indian companies because the former has greater technological capabilities, Indian companies are closer to the Indian market and if they try, they can compete on Indian turf with the world's best.

'In the automotive sector, in trucks and two-wheelers, the world's best have entered the Indian market. However, strong Indian companies like Telco and Bajaj Auto have been able to further consolidate their leadership during this period,' Bajaj said. 'Many countries in the world, including Japan and Korea, built their international competitiveness by encouraging ruthless competition at home. The government should support the champions in each sector. Laggards will have to face the consequences.'

At the January 1998 annual Delhi Auto Fair, Rajiv announced that seventeen new models would hit the Indian market within the next twenty-four months.

Chakan

Monday, 9 March 1998 saw Savitri bless her grandsons and perform the bhumi pujan. Unlike Akurdi and Waluj, Chakan was built to produce just one bike, the Pulsar. The idea was to offer a performance motorcycle for bike enthusiasts, one that would be relevant at least for five years after its launch.

The turn of the twenty-first century saw new ways of doing business and of creating customer choice. 'Innovation was not central to Bajaj's value creation logic,' reminded Sumantra Ghoshal. 'Bajaj continued to focus on giving customers "the best value for money" with tight control over all costs and by building a high scale infrastructure for both production and distribution.' Used to its comfortable position, it took Bajaj a couple of years to recognize a shift. But as supply constraints relaxed, innovation became key, prices started coming down and a recession developed, leading to the erosion of the market position and share.

The brothers agreed they needed a new workforce and management ethos. They picked graduates fresh from college and open to new ideas. Working alongside the new recruits, Rajiv and Sanjiv aimed for fresh standards. The new team comprised mostly males who loved riding bikes and understood biking. Design and development were handled by a nineteen-member team with average age of twenty-nine. And in an unusually generous mood, Bajaj chipped in with a Rs 50 crore R&D budget spread over three years.

'It's easy to find faults in retrospect,' Bajaj shares with Datar, 'but when the scooter market changed to a motorcycle market, sometime between 1999 and 2001, could my team and I have anticipated that or seen it coming earlier? Where I disagreed with Rajiv was his decision to stop making scooters. My question to Rajiv at the time was, why stop? Yes, the geared scooter we are making is not viable if we sell only 50,000 scooters or so a year but we were making 70,000 to 80,000 scooters a month—that is a million scooters a year. Why completely stop making scooters? We even publicly disagreed on the same platform on TV. He thought that his was the right decision and I thought that it was a wrong decision. I could see his point, but it was a difficult call for me. You rightly ask,' Bajaj admitted to Datar, 'who told you to stop making scooters, when your son decided to stop making them? Why did you allow him? You are the chairman, you happen to be the Bajaj family head. Yes, I represent the promoters, I have that control.'

Clearly Bajaj Auto needed a reboot.

Designing Fresh Standards

The going was tough. 'Rajiv wanted to set up a plant in Chakan and I put my foot down on the proposal,' said Bajaj. 'I wanted Rajiv to use the 400 acres of land that were already available with us in Aurangabad for the project, but he argued about the need for a new mindset in a state-of-the-art facility. He persisted and eventually he won.'

'Our R&D team and R&D capabilities were much smaller in 2000,' says Bajaj, 'and Rajiv's thinking was, "I have to put 100 per cent of my attention on motorcycles, otherwise I may not succeed. If I don't put all the strength of my R&D team on to motorcycles, I won't succeed. And the scooter is dying anyway". That was a strong argument.'

Rajiv and his team began scoping the world's technology boutiques. Over a dozen agreements were signed over the next few years. Austria's AVL to improve vehicle emissions and fuel economy and to develop a direct fuel injection system for two-stroke engines. Australia's Orbital Engine Company for combustion systems. Italy's Cagiva Motor Company for scooters. US-based Unique Mobility for pollution-free electric-powered scooters. The existing Kawasaki Heavy Industries tie-up for motorcycles expanded in Japan to include specialists Tokyo R&D for scooterettes and mopeds, and Kubota for diesel engines for three-wheelers. Bajaj Auto's R&D expenditure in FY 1998 was more than the combined outlay of TVS Suzuki, Hero Honda, and Kinetic Honda.

'We needed to do something different,' says Rajiv. 'We were always looking from the outside in, we had to do something ourselves. We had this great passion—we wanted to build a sports motorcycle in India. And then, after doing the doable, we were going to do the unexpected. When people said that we have a Kawasaki bike, we would make our own bike. When they said we cannot make a 100-cc bike, we were actually making a 200-cc bike. When they said Bajaj can barely make a low-cost bike, we would make the most expensive bike. When they said we can barely make a reliable bike, we said will make the fastest bike. People did not expect us to make a sporty, sexy, fast, sturdy and an expensive bike. This is how the Pulsar started.'

Rajiv continues, 'We quickly developed a dislike for benchmarking. We knew we were so far behind that benchmarking did not make sense. We were on the shop floor in T-shirts and jeans—there were no uniforms then—and we literally built the bikes drawing by drawing, dimension by dimension, tolerance by tolerance, the value of being 10 microns off, which is just 1/100th of a millimetre.'

For the product development process, Rajiv borrowed Chrysler's platform concept. Bajaj Auto's six platforms were composed of engineers from product engineering, manufacturing engineering, component development, product management and quality assurance. Simultaneous and concurrent engineering concepts were extensively applied. The brainstorming sessions often included first tier suppliers before a concept was finalized.

The Japanese introduced cellular manufacturing alongside just-in-time process (JIT). With Kawasaki as its technology partner, Bajaj Auto adopted the mantra fairly easily. Workers and section managers were grouped into cells and guided by the principle of 'visual self-management of quality and productivity for continuous improvement'—an elaborate name for a simple but highly effective system for improving operational efficiency. Every aspect of each cell's performance—from man-machine balancing and material handling to preventive maintenance and process control—were monitored through ten charts.

Rajiv's design department came up not only with the frame and aesthetics, but also ten designs. This narrowed down to three or four. In-house market surveys sought feedback on the styling. Towards the end of 1998, the brothers made a mid-course correction and decided to offer the bike in two engine capacities—150 cc and 180 cc. Rajiv supervised the minutest nitty-gritty details, from the styling and paint to the design of the console to the right grip. Finally, two prototypes were made with at least two to three engine variations. What made the performance impressive was the fact that the Pulsar had completely new engines and chassis, a five-speed gear box, counterbalance, disc brakes, and a starter motor. All this took twenty-four to thirty months.

What really woke up engineers around the world was Rajiv's unique engine design: the DTS-i system (digital twin spark ignition). The Pulsar's 150 cc engine needed more power as well as better fuel economy. DTS-i gave 18 per cent more fuel economy and 12 per cent more power. The concept itself was not unique nor was it a discovery, but Rajiv and Abraham Joseph were the first inventors to take the concept forward into a two-wheeler.

The combustion chamber of an engine is packed with air-fuel mixture. The spark plug does the job of a match. The first plug gives the master spark. The second, the slave spark, follows it after a delay. There is a coil to control each spark plug, the two must not burn simultaneously. If the second charge is too quick, there may be a detonation. For better power and fuel efficiency, they must burn variably in relation to each other depending on the temperature outside, the speed of the vehicle, and the load on it. And at no point should the engine overdo anything. There ought to be balance among the various things going on. This balance was achieved through a new algorithm Rajiv developed, using Bajaj Auto's own software.

Rajiv's marketing team provided the inputs for the concept bike. They uncovered a market segment looking for something more than just a bike for commuting. It wanted rugged styling and more power. 'We are specialists in different areas. Sanjiv keeps the company's books and I make the bikes. I can't keep the books and he can't make bikes,' grins Rajiv.

The dramatic changes at Bajaj Auto combined with a touch of suave wooing began to attract top talent. The gearing up of production from twelve models in 1993 to twenty-nine by 1999 was led by Arvind Gupta who left Telco for Bajaj Auto in 1991. 'A company that did not have a marketing department worked hard to attract R.L. Ravichandran who helped raise TVS-Suzuki's market share by 11 per cent,' described Professor Christopher Bartlett. 'All employees, workmen and managers alike, began to recognize and glean cost efficiencies. Every task was evaluated on the basis of three parameters of time, quality and cost,' recalls S. Ravikumar, who left Enfield India for Bajaj Auto in June 1984.

To ensure all departments had access to the right information at the right time and at the required point, a Digital Equipment Alpha host computer linked 400 concurrent users at Bajaj Auto's three plants[1] and some key suppliers and distributors, to support the new way of working. Well-managed supply chains deliver expected, and sometimes unexpected, cost-cutting avenues. Supply chain rationalization increased outsourcing considerably. The greatest benefit was improved speed: what took 1.9 man-days dropped to 1.4 days.

'We knew we had to make money, but we had to fix the problem dimension by dimension. I remember we had a big meeting to review the situation,' Rajiv shared with Sucheta Dalal. 'The meeting went well, and McKinsey's Ranjit Pandit remarked, "You finally have a foot in the door", and then somebody said we are losing money on this. We were used to a ten-year waiting period. My father jumped, "What, we are losing money?" Ranjit said, "Do you know what you are doing, Rahul? You are putting Rs 1200 on the seat of that motorcycle and telling customers: Take this!" My father went red in the face. I said this is an investment we need to make now. You need to get visibility on the road. That's the only way to start because we didn't have anything on our side—we didn't have a product; we didn't have a brand.'

Rajiv captured the interaction between cost reduction and revenue growth with managing emotions and feelings in the organization: 'Cost has to be looked at in a different way. The wrong way is to tell people we are cutting costs. People want to come eager to work. But, in an internal meeting, if I say that today I want to talk about cost cutting, I am sure they will do their best, but they will not be motivated. I will be talking in isolation. This is especially true in an owner-managed company. Inevitably, there is a feeling among executives that the benefits of cost cutting will go into the owner's pocket. Managers and workers also see cost cutting as a way to rip them off, and to make them work harder. Outside the company, among vendors and customers, the moment you talk about cost cutting, people think that the product's quality has gone down. Here at Bajaj Auto, we feel that cost cutting is all about improving quality at lower cost. That's how profitability improves. That's how customers keep coming back. And that's how everyone in the company benefits.'

---

[1] Akurdi, Waluj, Chakan.

'We lost money, which was okay, because we had enough money from the three-wheeler and treasury portfolio. We started gaining scale, started absorbing the advertising cost with larger numbers, replacing local equipment,' said Rajiv.

Post-launch, new learnings became a daily feature. 'When we conceived the bike,' says Sanjiv, 'we thought the target audience would be the twenty-five to thirty-five. But when we saw the sales chart, it was being picked up by thirty-five- to forty-five-year-old customers.' The reason became obvious when the brothers saw the stance and body language the riders took while driving the bike. 'The Pulsar fulfils a desire for a youthful persona in the same way an executive in the US drives a top-of-the-tree SUV to create the image of a man seeking adventure,' wrote an unknown blogger. Within Bajaj Auto, the raising of the R&D bedrock boosted confidence and developed a taste for more.

Shortly after a November 2001 Pulsar pre-launch, *Business Today*'s Kushan Mitra buttonholed Pawan Kant Munjal for comments on Bajaj Auto's experiments. 'While Hero and Honda have managed to chip away at its lead, Bajaj is reaping the dividends of its R&D efforts. Can Hero match that?' asked Mitra. 'We have a large R&D team working mainly on the frame and looks of our products,' conceded Munjal, accepting that Hero was 'a bit thin on the engine side of things.'

The Board

'I kept the board involved,' says Bajaj. 'At the time we had a sixteen-member board. Naresh Chandra, six years our ambassador to the US, cabinet secretary which is the senior-most civil servant, and governor of the state of Gujarat, Serajul Haq Khan, former chairman of IDBI. Balaji Rao from ICICI. Pamnani, my relative who was at Citibank, who could have become a vice-chairman like Victor Menezes were he willing to shift to New York. Jamshyd Godrej, a top industrialist. My son-in-law, good in financial matters, a Harvard MBA and Baker Scholar, Manish Kejriwal. They were as much concerned about the stoppage of scooter production as I was.'

Says Rajiv, 'Each time I tried to push a radical idea, I always got the answer—directly or indirectly—that it's okay in Japan, it doesn't happen in India. I was desperate to prove that it can happen in India. I wanted a plant where we could start the right way from day one.'

Says Sanjiv, 'We realized that sometimes people have to be taught by example. That's what we did in Chakan.'

Bajaj Auto's reaction to declining sales was to introduce a revitalized Chetak with a geared four-stroke, four-speed engine with TRICS (Throttle Response Ignition Control System—an early version of their variable ignition system) in a largely metal-bodied scooter on 10-inch wheels. Named the Chetak Legend—a bit odd given that it was launched in 1999, just before the new millennium— the spirit of Vespa still clung to the latest Chetak.

The Last Word But One

In May 1998, after announcing the FY 1997–98 results for Bajaj Auto, Bajaj was at the receiving end of a number of questions from a panel of business journalists. Two sample responses:

> On the large cash reserves of the Company, 'I'll keep the money with the Company, in case of an emergency . . . I have given enough to my shareholders in the past. I am not in the business for charity . . . Can you name four companies who have gone in for acquisitions and are doing well. I can name many more who are down in the dumps . . . We are a focused Company.'
>
> On the loss of market share over the years: 'If the competition starts from a zero base, they are bound to get some market share . . . Live and let live, that's my philosophy . . . '

The Last Word

'My biggest satisfaction is the way I handed over the baton to Rajiv,' says Bajaj. 'It took him and me some time—I am talking of 2000. De facto he had already started making policy decisions, but still, the responsibility was mine as chairman and managing director. Maybe I could have seen the coming changes earlier, maybe we could have woken up a bit earlier and alerted my people because I was then the hands-on manager. And of course, there were justifications on our side and the reasons. I had started gradually delegating to Rajiv, but I was still there. I can't say I was not there.'

'When in 2005, Rajiv was appointed CEO, I told him, "What matters are results. The day I find in totality you are not good for the company, I will talk to you. The fact that you are a Bajaj will not save you." I could see the guy was so good in totality. Not because he is my son, but because he is a very strong person, fully confident of himself. I never asked him, but there was a good possibility, if I had said no to scooters, he would have said, "Papa, you run the company, you have done it for forty years, run it; when you want me to run it, get me back".

'What was also on my mind was, what if he leaves? His leaving would be bad for the company, I thought. I think we are two strong-minded individuals. So, it's not a question of fear, it's not a question of blackmail—that I would not tolerate. Rajiv was doing a very good job. Who would I have in his place? So, what I did was for the good of the company.

'Finally, I said to myself, for forty years, you listened to everybody and you ultimately did what you thought was right. The management committee is a debating society in which, I used to say, I never took a vote—the decision was mine.'

The New Last

The boys were ready, as was the Legend.[2] The competition to be the first to bring out a four-stroke scooter was global and hot. Rajiv and Sanjiv were determined it should be ready in time for Bajaj's sixtieth birthday—and yes, the Legend was a first in the world.

Six years later, in May 2014, Rajiv gave a two-hour presentation to the board on scooter production, the scooter market in India, the motorcycle market and his plans.

---

[2] For aficionados, the Legend was powered by a new 'environmentally friendly' designed 145 cc four-stroke, single cylinder engine, with 9 bhp @ 6000 rpm and torque of 11.3 Nm @ 4000 rpm. This was coupled to a four-speed transmission operated through a classic Vespa-style grip gear shifter. The front suspension utilized a 'leading link' and the rear suspension a 'coaxial hydraulic dampner'. The wheelbase was 1272 mm, weight 110 kg, ground clearance 145 mm and the petrol tank capacity, 5 litres (Wikipedia, retrieved on 22 August 2020).

33

The Finserv Gameplan: 2001–07

Bajaj, Sanjiv and Nanoo Pamnani.

Sanjiv wanted a simple, easy-to-remember name for his new organization. He came up with Finserv. His father came up with Nanoo Pamnani.

'Rahul called me. He knew I was coming back,' Pamnani recounted to *Business Today's* Nevin John. 'He was demerging Bajaj

Auto into auto and financial services businesses, and Sanjiv was going to handle financial services. He wanted me to help Sanjiv. I was planning to relax and travel around the world after retirement, but I agreed to help Sanjiv because they are from my wife's family.'

Sanjiv began crafting a detailed map of Finserv's future in consumer lending and insurance. Sanjiv started by designing Bajaj Finserv (BFS) to be his key holding company. BFS carved out a 55.13 per cent stake from Bajaj Finance. The two Allianz insurance companies with their 74 per cent stakes each were re-badged as Bajaj Allianz Life Insurance (BALIC) and Bajaj Allianz General Insurance (BAGIC). He took the blueprint to his father. The boss gave the go-ahead. Pamnani gave his thumbs up. Headhunting began. Building a diversified financial conglomerate would be a challenge, due both to missing in-house expertise and an evolving regulatory environment for insurance and NBFCs.

The Sea Lounge

'Since we had to build from scratch, we went out to hire,' recalls Sanjiv. Rajeev Jain and Pamnani met in the Sea Lounge of the Taj Mahal Palace hotel in Mumbai. They spent a couple of hours talking before Pamnani made the job offer. 'He is a smart businessperson with great execution skills. His ability to think broadly is outstanding,' Pamnani reported back to Sanjiv. 'We were lucky to get Rajeev. He turned out to be brilliant,' agreed Sanjiv.

'I like the start-up atmosphere and the enthusiasm associated with it to create a growth story,' says Jain. He was amongst the first ten employees to join GE Money in the mid-1990s. He was the first employee of AIG in India, joining as deputy CEO in 2006. He joined Bajaj Finance on 3 September 2007 as its first CEO and would become its managing director on 23 March 2015.

Sanjiv, Pamnani and Jain sat down to strategize. 'We started mainly with a few products which were commonly done like consumer durables financing. Which is why that segment became a central pillar for us,' recalled Pamnani.

Initially, the trio had diverse views on growth plans but over the years their ideas converged. 'We were so aligned that we didn't need to debate on anything, because the minute someone puts an idea on the table, the other two would be on the same page,' Sanjiv added. Later, Pamnani would take over as Bajaj Finserv chair when Bajaj moved into the chairman emeritus role.

'The next question was how can we be in financial services and pick the right businesses to be among the top-five players in terms of profit share,' Sanjiv shared with *ET*'s Harish Rao. 'I do not care what my top-line is as long as I am a part of the significant profit share. The minute we think like that, it helps us to focus on being innovative, to look at businesses which make money and are not just temporary market cap businesses. I also see us significantly leaning on the retail side because that is where our strength lies. I see us being mass India. I would rather do a few things and do them really well. We would not do any business which we are not passionate about.'

'While Finserv was formed in 2007, we did not rebrand it then,' Sanjiv shared with afaqs! at the brand launch. 'By 2008, we felt the timing was appropriate with the new logo displaying a uniform look and feel. We wanted to present a common identity across the independent businesses and unite them so that the consumer experiences the core values of the group.'

'It was a journey to understand the financial industry domain, its customers and aspirations,' described Indi Design's Sudhir Sharma, 'which led to the new positioning—"Your Confidence". It's simple, straightforward and reliable. The customer will always be with Bajaj Finserv as a brand and not with many different companies for different purposes.'

GE. Not!

Sanjiv had been watching US-based General Electric (GE) for years, admiring it for its culture and competencies. Events at GE would play a major role, if unintended, in the making of Bajaj Finserv. From the 2007 financial crisis through to early 2015, 7800 miles from the Finserv office, thoughts were swirling at Fairfield, Connecticut, GE's headquarters, about what GE should be.

In April 2015, its ninth chairman, Jeff Immelt, announced that GE would exit its financial arm, GE Capital. At the time, GE

Capital was bigger than its parent. In India, GE Capital began to slowly unwind itself. In February 2013, for example, India's Magma Corporation acquired a substantial mortgage business from GE Money Housing Finance after a year-long negotiation. In 2016, GE India's commercial lending business came on the block.

The Finserv trio was clear about where they wanted to be—and it didn't include GE. A takeover could have easily propelled the vertical. Instead, Sanjiv and Jain noticed the quiet early rumblings and began identifying local talent. In September 2015, Sanjiv and Jain took a group of ninety managers to Dubai. In this group were twenty-former GE-ites. 'If GE Money had not shut, we may not have been created,' Sanjiv admits candidly. Sanjiv's admiration, however, did not encompass buying parts of GE Capital in India as each part was sold off—even if this meant facing new, and possibly more aggressive, competitors.

The NBFC Blueprint

At Bajaj Finserv, by this time, both its commercial lending and business lending were established. His team was now ready to kick off financial services businesses in consumer lending and insurance by creating a one-stop shop for all financial needs for retail and SME customers throughout their life cycle via loans, insurance, savings, wealth management, business capital and retirement planning.

'Our Finserv mobile application which we brought out in 2015 for example,' says Sanjiv, 'made it possible for a borrower to get a loan sanctioned even before they enter the shop. The front end of the app is fairly simple, but the back end is connected to credit information bureau, our fraud detection systems and the 20,000 retail chains with which we have relationships.'

The RBI divides and subdivides NBFCs in a cascade of categories. Two definitions are important. One, the conditions that separate those allowed to accept deposit from the public from those that cannot. Two, size. NBFCs with assets of Rs 5 billion and above are labelled 'systemically important' and RBI treats them with the same stringency as small banks. Bajaj Finance is a deposit-accepting NBFC and 'systemically important', i.e., a NBFC-D-SI in RBI terminology.

Banks offer a set of financial services as a package deal. NBFCs tailor their services. By unbundling, targeting, and specializing, NBFCs promote competition within the financial services industry. NBFCs may specialize in a specific sector to gain information advantage. An NBFC does not have a full banking licence, nor can it accept deposits from the public. It can, however, provide services not necessarily suited to banks, serve as competition to banks, specialize in sectors or groups, and offer multiple alternatives to transform an economy's savings into capital investment.

India has been cautious with its NBFCs. Austerely regulated since 1992 by the RBI, the central bank provides oversight of NBFCs similar to its oversight of high-street banks. The strict regulatory regime ring-fenced India during the 2007–2008 global financial crisis, and the several major corporate scandals which erupted in the early twenty-first century. In December 2015, for example, the RBI cancelled the licences of fifty-six NBFCs. Regular pruning continues.

What Is Luck?

'I like building businesses focused on excellence through differentiation to the customer,' shares Sanjiv. 'We focus on products that have a transparent incentive structure linked not only to sales volume but also persistency. Our operations have clear and quantified targets on issues related to quality, policy or loan turnaround times, customer service and cost. As we keep improving on these, we build an overall superior customer experience.'

'Luckily, I am born in a group where I have both the opportunity and the responsibility to build our financial services businesses, including Bajaj Finserv, Bajaj Finance, Bajaj Allianz Life and Bajaj Allianz General, with long-term value in mind,' muses Sanjiv. 'Profit is not a driver but the result. Else, it would set you on a wrong path. Our management is tasked to identify clear value drivers for each business and focus on delivering the same consistently to our customers. Why should someone come to buy insurance or take a loan from Bajaj and not someone else? There are enough other options available.'

'At the same time, when I look at brands, there are two very clear roles that a brand has to play,' Sanjiv continues. 'Bajaj stands for certain basic values of longevity, credibility and trust. So when somebody asks Bajaj, he knows he is getting a good deal, that the company is fair and transparent in their dealings, and that the company is there for the long term. Secondly, you need focused brands for that particular part of the business. While the parent brand gives the comfort, the product brands tell you what to expect from the product. Finserv wealth management, for example, focuses on the wealth management side.'

'We keep seeking ways to serve customers better than others, to provide innovative disruptive financial solutions,' says Sanjiv. 'We hope to increase the stickiness of our relationship with them and that is all that needs to be done. There is no rocket science here. You need to be honest. You need to be transparent. For us, as part of integrity, it is important that people follow the culture we have set down: a culture of transparency, a culture of selling honest products to customers.

The Last Word

'Growth is not a challenge. Growth is in building the right business in a healthy, profitable manner,' points out Sanjiv.

34

From Allianz Bajaj to Bajaj Allianz: 2001–21

Head of Allianz Asia Pacific Heinz Dollberg, Bajaj and head of Allianz SE and Insurance Growth Markets Werner Zedelius in New Delhi on 12 March 2007.

The room was packed. Bajaj stood up, cleared his throat, and adjusted the mic. 'Given the outlay of your company in insurance, we believe that it will be a profitable investment in the medium to long term,' he told shareholders at Bajaj Auto's fifty-sixth AGM on 28 July 2001.

'Bajaj Allianz General Insurance Company issued the largest number of policies among all private players in the non-life segment in 2001–2002, and instantly became the number one in this line of business,' he shared with the media. 'Allianz Bajaj Life Insurance began its operations a few months later. Two plans were launched: the Child Care Plan and Invest Gain. And we did an additional capital infusion of Rs 49.37 crore. In its first full year of operations, we issued more than 1,15,000 policies with a gross premium of Rs 69.17 crore. We opened branches in thirty-three cities with a sales force of 9500 people.' The insurance business was, no doubt, an exciting opportunity which Bajaj did well to grab with both hands, shareholders nodded their approval.

The Revolving Door

Allianz operates in seventy countries, Bajaj in a country of 19,500 languages. In a nascent sector, hiccups are unavoidable. At Allianz Bajaj Life, Mark J. Purslow quit after a year. His successor, James Walton, quit in less than a year. At Bajaj Allianz General Insurance Company, Graham Norris quit and left India. The foreigners were haemorrhaging.

Allianz was quite used to revolving doors, as was Pamnani from his Citibank days. But neither Bajaj nor the Bajaj organization were accustomed to western hire-and-fire style of thinking, be they managers or workers.

Before arriving in India, Norris was Allianz's Hong Kong CEO for almost seven and a half years. Access to the huge Indian market as an Allianz country manager responsible for establishing general insurance was seen as a big step up by his cohort. He lasted all of eight months in India.

In Singapore, Purslow had headed Allianz Life's reinsurance business. In India, he was the Allianz vanguard to find joint-venture partners, obtain life and general insurance licences, and open the shop. The legwork done and licences granted, Purslow was appointed Allianz Bajaj's CEO for the life insurance business.

After the exciting work in the hubbub of New Delhi and Mumbai was over, the firangs trooped into Akurdi. A few weeks later, both Norris and Purslow lobbied for Mumbai as the headquarters of the insurance companies. Bajaj, however, insisted on Akurdi with its lower manpower costs, greenery, and expansive facilities.

The buzz reached Michael Diekmann. The troubleshooter arrived in Pune in April 2001. Could Allianz consider replacing Norris with Sam Ghosh? In Hong Kong, possibly an authoritarian style of management was acceptable but may not be quite suitable for Indian business, hinted Ranjit Gupta. Hong Kong was minuscule. Did Graham have the mental bandwidth to establish from scratch an insurance company in a continent the size of India?

'Ghosh's role in the pre-licencing period was significant,' Gupta pitched to Diekmann. Ghosh had acclimatized as easily to the local culture as he did in Australia. That he was a UK-qualified chartered accountant with a degree in mechanical engineering from Imperial College added a special cachet. Diekmann was on the same page when the Puneites suggested creating a country manager position for Sam Ghosh, with Kamesh Goyal as group CEO. Time to roll up sleeves and build the business instead of grumbling.

A Rose by Any Other Name Would Smell as Sweet[1]

'We are not only acquiring a new name effective from 3 August 2004,' Sam Ghosh addressed the media, 'we have put in motion a new level of energy and commitment to delivering the best products. The name change coupled with aggressive strategic market initiatives to reach and service customers better, will give us an unbeatable position in the insurance market in India. Bajaj Allianz Life and Bajaj Allianz General together can unleash the "Power of One" and be the leader in the insurance industry.'

'The switch in the name of the two companies,' continued Ghosh, 'comes in conjunction with research findings from existing customers, business associates, prospective customers and other stakeholders indicated higher comfort level and ease of recalling the Bajaj name first and then Allianz, and hence the name Bajaj Allianz. Bajaj Allianz General Insurance and Bajaj Allianz Life Insurance will now

---

[1] William Shakespeare in *Romeo and Juliet*.

have a common logo and branding which will help in increasing visibility and familiarity, creating a much larger awareness and a greater mindshare.'

Reading the morning newspapers were Life Insurance Corporation of India (LIC) and General Insurance Corporation of India (GIC).

The Invincible LIC

Parliament passed the Life Insurance Corporation Act on 19 June 1956. LIC sprung to life on 1 September. One of India's more powerful organizations, some whisper that even a union finance minister or the sector's regulator would hesitate long and hard before turning down a suggestion by the LIC chairman. Its board has one chairman and four managing directors—a structure gladiatorial by design. Aspirants need political savvy, luck and the right networks in ample measure. Given this background, naturally, the chieftainship of LIC is one of the most sought-after jobs in India.

LIC has demonstrated over decades that it can keep its grip on its formidable market share through upheavals. Nine chairmen whizzed through the organization between 2000 and 2014, for example. One chairman was kicked upstairs to be the insurance regulator after being kicked downstairs to be a managing director. Interim chairmen filled three pauses as the government pondered on whom to appoint.

In the private sector, Sanjiv and Allianz quietly climbed the insurance ladder at a remarkable clip. Allianz Bajaj entered in ninth place with sales of Rs 7.14 crore in 2001–2002. Rebadged as Bajaj Allianz in 2004, it steadily moved up in the league table to third place with sales of Rs 3133.58 crore in 2005–2006.

LIC was way ahead of both at Rs 90,792 crore, and the difference between ICICI Prudential and Bajaj Allianz slim at roughly Rs 1000 crore. The three-year period between FY 2011 and FY 2014 demonstrated LIC's vigorous capacity to withstand competition. This period saw the private sector's year-on-year (YOY) growth plummeted into the red to −4.52 per cent (FY 2012). It fell deeper the next year to −6.87 per cent (FY 2013) before pulling itself together with a loss of −1.35 per cent (FY 2014). In contrast, LIC's YOY growth pattern is remarkably dissimilar. It briefly dropped into negative territory but only by -0.29 per cent (FY 2012) before climbing back into the black to 2.92 per cent (FY 2013) followed by a stout growth of 13.48 per cent (FY 2014), which enabled LIC to recover 75.39 per cent of its market share.

At some point LIC's market share will whittle down simply because of market expansion and less because of loss of customers. Nobody expects its leadership position to be seriously challenged for a long, long time.

The Richest Man in the World

Berkshire Insurance opened its office in India by not opening an office. It was only a website[2] with a shaky lifeline, but it made headlines: individuals who bought a Bajaj Allianz motor insurance policy through its site would get a chance of a lifetime to meet one of the wealthiest individuals in the world.

'A new policy purchased through berkshireinsurance.com will qualify for an invite,' shared Kara Raiguel, a Berkshire India director, in an email, adding generously that 'the price to insure a Maruti Suzuki India 800 built in 1996 would cost Rs 2163 ($48). Warren Buffet, the chairman and CEO of Berkshire Hathaway will meet policyholders on 25 March 2011 between 6–8 p.m. in New Delhi's Taj Palace Hotel.'

IRDA was not amused. 'It is not correct. In insurance you can't give incentives. It is against the principles of insurance. It is like an insurance agent giving a Diwali gift,' sniffed a senior official. 'We Insure Just About Everyone' is a favourite Warren Buffet tagline. In India, it just didn't work.

After the hubbub, lucidity. In a clarification to the stock exchange, Bajaj Finserv stated that 'it did not have any plan, at present or in the foreseeable future, to sell equity to Berkshire Hathaway. Berkshire Hathaway will enter the Indian insurance business as a corporate agent for BAGIC, a 74 per cent subsidiary of Bajaj Finserv.

---

[2] www.berkshireinsurance.com

The tie-up will help BAGIC expand its customer base. BAGIC has about forty corporate agents.'

To give Buffet his due, the feisty eighty-year-old was in India to play the role of a grandfatherly philanthropist alongside Bill Gates, who was on the same journey.

The Unravelling

India's Reliance Life sold 26 per cent of its equity to Japan's Nippon Life for Rs 2948 crore. US-based New York Life sold its 26 per cent in Max New York Life to Mitsui Sumitomo for Rs 2731 crore at three times the embedded value. Aviva India dropped to thirteenth place in the league table and itched to be free of its partner Dabur.

Head offices across London, Europe, the US and the Far East were feeling as battered as Indians. China and India had been identified as 'high priority' and 'must win' markets. A decade later, with small profits and big government restrictions, the results were not in line with the expectations.

There will always be contrarians in such situations. One of them was Rajan Raheja, founder of a diversified business group including realty. Raheja held a 50 per cent stake in the Indian arm of ING, a Dutch firm, acquired in 2005 for Rs 231.6 crore. The embedded value of a life insurance company is the current value of future profits plus adjusted net asset value. The March 2013 rumble enabled Raheja to acquire 26 per cent of ING for Rs 550 crore, and picked up 24 per cent from Vysya Bank and assorted other investors. ING Vysya Life Insurance Company became Exide Life Insurance Company. ING Netherlands sold its stake in India at a loss.

LIFE INSURANCE COMPANIES GROWTH, 2001–2006

(Rs CRORE)

	2001–02		2002–03		2003–04		2004–05		2005–06	
LIC	49821.91	1	54628.49	1	63533.43	1	75127.29	1	90792.22	1
ICICI Prudential	116.38	2	417.62	2	989.28	2	2363.82	2	4261.05	2
Bajaj Allianz	7.14	9	69.17	8	220.80	7	1001.68	3	3133.58	3
Birla Sunlife	28.26	5	143.92	4	537.54	3	915.47	4	1259.68	5
HDFC Life	33.46	4	148.83	3	297.76	4	686.63	5	1569.91	4
SBI Life	14.69	7	72.39	7	225.67	6	601.18	6	1075.32	6
Tata AIG	21.14	6	81.21	6	253.53	5	497.04	7	880.19	7
Kotak Mahindra	7.58	8	40.32	9	150.72	9	466.16	8	621.85	9
Max New York	38.95	3	96.59	5	215.25	8	413.43	9	788.13	8
ING Vysya	4.19	10	21.16	10	88.51	10	338.86	10	425.38	11
Aviva	-	-	13.47	11	81.5	12	253.42	11	600.27	10
Reliance Life	0.28	12	6.47	13	31.06	13	106.55	12	224.21	12
Met Life	0.48	11	7.91	12	28.73	14	81.53	13	205.99	13
Sahara							1.74	14	27.66	14
Shriram									10.33	15
Total (LIC+Private)	50094.46		55747.55		66653.75		82854.8		105875.8	

Adapted from www.irdaindia.org. p. 19 and Shodhganga. 'Market Share of Life Insurance Companies 2001–2006'. 09_chapter 1.pdf. Both retrieved on 14 September 2020.

35

Unlocking Shareholder Value: 2004–08

A hard day's night.

At the heart of every business are three cores: the shareholding, the businesses, and the returns. Opportunities in the auto, finance and insurance sectors were growing. Concentrated focus would further strengthen the group and empower its growth. The exercise of unlocking shareholder value took four years. How did Bajaj manage the challenges, the contradictions, and the politics so smoothly?

The first step was to peer into the future. Bajaj Auto had a modest auto financing division for its two- and three-wheelers, a subsidiary incorporated on 25 March 1987 to promote sales during a lean period. Bajaj Auto Finance became the nucleus of Bajaj's demerger strategy. In an interview to *Business Today's* Nevin John, Bajaj acknowledged that the move to delink the lending business from Bajaj Auto was the game changer. 'It was the toughest and yet the most successful decision of my life.'

Bajaj Auto was, and is, one of India's most cash-rich companies. In the 2000s, it held cash and cash equivalents of roughly Rs 8000 crores. FIIs, analysts, large investors and the media were always curious to know as to how the surplus funds were going to be used or invested by the company. They were concerned about the diluted return on capital employed, which according to them was due to the less-than-ideal utilization of the surplus funds. From the investor point of view, the demerger had two significant benefits. They could hold separate focused stocks. And they could benchmark Bajaj companies with peers in their respective industries.

The Valuation Meisters

Debating with Pamnani on whom to pick as his external financial advisers for the demerger, Bajaj narrowed his options to the 3K troika: Nimesh Kampani, Uday Kotak and Hemendra Kothari. With razor sharp minds combined with joie de vivre personalities, all three are formidable. Bajaj chose Kampani.

Financial Times's correspondent, Khozem Merchant, once dubbed Kampani as India's rainmaker. In 2005, when Kokilaben, the Ambani family matriarch, wanted to end the acrimony between her two sons and help them arrive at a settlement, she turned to Kampani. Kampani crunched the numbers to arrive at a valuation acceptable to both brothers Mukesh and Anil—crucial not least because of the conflicting figures the brothers assigned to Reliance Infocomm Limited.

Coincidently, Kampani himself was going through a split when Bajaj approached him. Global players were keen to strike out on their own in India's fast-expanding M&A market. The USA's Morgan Stanley suggested it buy out its partner of ten years. JM Morgan Stanley Securities offered $425 million for Kampani's 49 per cent holding. Kampani offered $20 million for Morgan Stanley's 49 per cent holding. Deal done. J Sagar & Associates acted as the legal advisers for the restructuring.

The Formula

For the best outcome, Bajaj decided that Rajiv should continue to run the auto manufacturing business as managing director and chief executive officer. Sanjiv would hand over the international market function to Rajiv in the next twelve months. Sanjiv would oversee the finance business and the new strategic businesses.

Both sons would sit on all boards, and Sanjiv would continue as executive director of Bajaj Auto. Rajiv would join Sanjiv's boards as each was created. Bajaj Auto's board structure should remain unchanged, and Bajaj would serve as the chairman of the two new boards. A couple of cousins from the Ramkrishna's side of the family would be good. In the throes of a legal battle with his nephew Kushagra, there was no point in inviting Shishir.

In 2007, Bajaj Auto's stock roughly stacked up as 30 per cent promoter holding, around 20 per cent with foreign institutional investors, and with the public holding about 26.50 per cent. It also had a tangled legacy. Shards of managing agencies promoted during the British raj found niches in core family investment firms such as Jamnalal & Sons for example, which traces its history to a colonial era of managing agencies. Bajaj Holdings was established in 1926. Bajaj Auto antecedents go back to 1945 as Bachhraj Trading. These slivers completed the total.

Untangling the knots was a Herculean assignment, and a swarm of experts were brought in. Nimesh Kampani and his son Vishal, a fresher from the London Business School who joined his father in 1997, rolled up sleeves and got to work. It was the youngster's idea to rename Bajaj Auto as Bajaj Holdings and vice versa. Complicated as it sounds, the switch worked well, and made life easier for the team.

The Bajaj-Kampani game plan was to ensure that Bajaj Auto could concentrate on auto manufacturing; Bajaj Finserv on wind energy, insurance and financial services; and Bajaj Holdings as the family's primary investment firm and holding company. The remaining assets and liabilities, including investments in group companies and balance cash and cash equivalents, would be retained in Bajaj Auto but Bajaj Finserv and Bajaj Holdings would be able to tap (on an arm's length basis) into the cash pool of the investment company to support future growth initiatives, if required. 'It was necessary to ensure that there were adequate flows to allow the group to start new businesses,' said Nimesh at the time.

In order to achieve the game plan, the team dug into the paperwork required for Bajaj Auto to transfer to Bajaj Finserv the wind power project, the agreements and contracts of the insurance companies (BALIC, BAGIC) along with the relevant assets and liabilities, and Rs 800 crore in cash and cash equivalents.

Another set of paperwork dealt with internal swops of shareholding. Bajaj Auto, suggested the team, should purchase 43.5 million shares of Bajaj Holdings for Rs 43.5 crore, and 43.5 million shares of Bajaj Finserv for Rs 21.75 crore. The auto business, along with all assets and liabilities including investments in PT Bajaj Auto Indonesia and a few vendor companies, were to be transferred to Bajaj Holdings. Agreed upon and actioned, the final step, as mentioned earlier, was for BAL to become BHIL and BHIL to become BAL.

A one-to-one share allotment policy was developed for every shareholder of Bajaj Auto, internal and external. A Bajaj Auto share would have a face value of Rs 10, a Bajaj Holding share of Rs 10, and a Bajaj Finance share of Rs 5. Once the new shares were issued, the team calculated that the existing shareholders of Bajaj Auto would hold about 70 per cent shares in the new companies in the same ratio as their current holding, with the remaining approximate 30 per cent held by Bajaj Holdings.

The merger plan was approved by the board, the stock exchanges, the Bombay High Court, SEBI and shareholders and a shoal of other regulatory authorities.

More than a decade after the event, the Bajaj Auto demerger of 2007–2008 remains an amazing case study. The outstanding success lay in management's careful examination and assessment of every minutia in the transfer of assets, contracts—and people. Sticking to his tenets, Bajaj ensured the demerger teams never strayed from boundaries.

To tame the media's frenzied interest in the team's activities and decisions, Bajaj would occasionally drop a nugget or two. He would 'be the chairman of all the three companies'.

—'Please understand, It is not a split of Bajaj Auto. It's a demerger. The two are very different.'

—'The boards of the two new entities—Bajaj Holdings and Investment Ltd and Bajaj Finserv Ltd—would have Rajiv Bajaj, Sanjiv Bajaj and Madhur Bajaj as directors.'

—'Initially, the board members of the new entities would not get any salary for their roles as directors.'

Bajaj's efforts did not go in vain. At least a couple of reporters swallowed the management line. The more seasoned journalists smiled at their juniors. The meat was missing.

Bajaj Auto Board Meeting, 17 May 2007

On the morning of the day before the critical Thursday, 17 May 2007 board meeting, the *Business Standard* reminded its readers (i.e., gunning squarely at the board) that 'sibling rivalry in India is not new and has more often than not been good for minority shareholders.' It continued, 'This time, the sum of the parts of Bajaj Auto should definitely be greater than the whole.' The board obliged.

At this juncture, the demerger was carefully positioned as 'India's second biggest motorcycle maker set to restructure the company to unlock the value of its growing insurance business'. By the end of the meeting, the board signed off on three core items.

Existing shareholders would hold 70 per cent in the new companies, with the balance 30 per cent held by the holding company, BHIL. This would be done through the issue of new shares. The board also approved the transfer of Rs 1500 crore cash and cash equivalents to Bajaj Auto, and Rs 800 crore cash to Bajaj Finserv. This was out of Bajaj Auto's Rs 8500 crore cash reserves. And existing shareholders would be issued shares at a ratio of 1:1 in each of the new companies as described above.

The board's decisions failed to cheer investors. Bajaj Auto shares plunged 10 per cent intra-day before closing down 6.7 per cent at Rs 2500 in an otherwise bullish market.

Bajaj Auto Finance, Chairman's Report, 16 May 2007

Nor was the mood particularly chirpy at Bajaj Auto Finance, as Pamnani discovered in his first meeting as BAFL's new vice-chairman. BAFL depended on Bajaj Auto's performance. As Bajaj pointed out, 'January to March 2007 witnessed the beginnings of slackening domestic demand for two-wheelers . . . I wrongly hoped that this slowdown (was) a temporary aberration.'

'The RBI maintained a very tight monetary policy,' continued Bajaj, 'which raised interest rates on consumer loans to exceptionally high levels. Moreover, banks and finance companies significantly reduced their exposure to auto loans, and severely curtailed the supply of credit. The twin effects of higher interests and lower credit availability hit the two-wheeler industry very badly. Thus, after a decade of spectacular double-digit growth, two-wheelers suddenly faced a slump. For the first time in over ten years, the industry as a whole witnessed negative growth. From 8.47 million in 2006–2007, overall two-wheelers' sales fell by 4.8 per cent to 8.07 million in 2007–2008. The decline in motorcycle sales was sharper still: by 7.8 per cent, from 7.1 million vehicles sold in 2006–2007 to 6.54 million 2007–2008.'

As May segued into August, ICRA, a watchdog credit rating firm, kept Sanjiv's companies—Bajaj Finserv, BAFL, and the two insurance collaborations—in its sights. But the markets were agog, and the gossip racy. 'Marketmen of course raised expectations that the financial assets from the demerger would be spun into Bajaj Auto Finance, and later be used to acquire a small bank,' recalls *DNA*'s Satish John.

Regulatory approvals began to trickle through. SEBI gave its nod. The Bombay High Court sanctioned the demerger scheme between BHIL and Bajaj Finserv, and their respective shareholders and creditors, effective from 31 March 2007, the close of the Indian financial year. In Pune, the local Registrar of Companies smoothly filed the high court's instructions.

Simultaneous listing ceremonies took place on Monday, 26 May 2008: Bajaj Auto on the BSE, and Bajaj Finserv on the National Stock Exchange (NSE).

Transmitting Shareholder Value

The demerger worked exceedingly well for Bajaj shareholders. The total market cap of the three companies upped to Rs 26,165 crore, a 24 per cent increase over the market capitalization of the original Bajaj Auto. On the last day before its delisting, 13 March 2008, it was Rs 21,042 crore, based on data from the Bombay Stock Exchange. These figures didn't include Bajaj Auto Finance.

Bajaj had identified unlocking shareholder value as one of the reasons for separating the firm's automotive and financial services businesses, though it was also driven by the need to accommodate the separate corporate ambitions of Bajaj's two sons. And he delivered.

There was one fly in the ointment. At the 18 August 2007 shareholder meeting, about 95 per cent of the shareholders had voted in favour of the scheme. Of the 3 per cent shareholders who voted against the scheme, Shishir held 1.8 per cent, reckoned J. Sridhar.

'Mr Bajaj often jokes that he prefers "cash under his pillow for enjoying a blissful and peaceful sleep",' shares Sridhar. Kevin D'sa nods in agreement: 'The chairman doesn't believe in unrelated diversification unlike a number of industrial groups. Focus and core competence are his mantra. Even at the risk of being called hyper-conservative and orthodox and risk-averse, he does not engage in acquisitions, takeovers or capital expenditure merely because of our surplus or to be fashionable. Nor does he believe in returning cash to shareholders just because there is a surplus in hand. But as I recall, he did once yield to a buyback in the year 2000.'

The Last Word on the Demerger

The shares of Bajaj Auto and Bajaj Finserv surged. The markets celebrated. Overworked teams finally went home to their families. In his own inimitable self, Bajaj harrumphed to the world, 'I am proud of my sons. They have done a wonderful job for the company. They are individuals in their own right, and if you call it differences, so be it.'

'One of the things I managed to do right is succession planning,' smiled Bajaj at the ET Awards Lifetime Achievement Award ceremony, 'and I am receiving this award because the next generation—and that doesn't just mean my elder son Rajiv but his entire team at Bajaj Auto—has started to deliver. In business as in the movies, timing is very important. In that sense, this ET Award is well timed. Come April 2005, I shall cease to be the managing director of Bajaj Auto, but will continue as its chairman. It is better to step down when people ask, why are you leaving!'

'Comparisons are the death of joy,' Bajaj shares with reporter Aveek Datta. 'I am not interested in comparing Bajaj Auto with Bajaj Finance any more than I am interested in comparing myself with another auto company. How does that help me? But when the immigration officer in a Latin American country looks at my passport and recognizes that I am from the company that makes the tuk-tuks in his country, it is priceless. No market cap can compare with that.'

36

From Kon'nichiwa to Sayōnara: 2003–17

Bajaj and Shinichi Morita at the Wind 25 launch in 2003.

The two elderly gentlemen posing in front of a battery of cameras were unabashedly proud. Eyes dancing, Bajaj swung a leg over the new Wind 125 bike, gripped the handlebar, and flashed a megawatt smile. Being Japanese, Shinichi Morita's demeanour was more circumspect, but the crinkles around the eyes behind his round spectacles gave away his excitement. Both had invested financially and emotionally in the making of a world bike from India.

The bike had to be perfect. For Shinichi Morita, president of The Consumer Products & Machinery Company (a member of Kawasaki Heavy Industries), the stakes were higher than for Bajaj, and the mission challenging. At an awkward moment, Morita had to convince his board and the larger umbrella organization, headed by Masamoto Tazaki, Kawasaki Heavy Industries president, to extend the relationship with Bajaj outside India.

The turn of the century saw Kawasaki Heavy Industries enter three years of losses. By 1999, the Japanese economy was compressed by two developments in its biggest market, the US. A slowdown in America triggered a recession in the world economy. And the al-Qaeda's 9/11 attack[1] on New York had both immediate and long-term economic impacts.

In what came to be described as 'Japan's Lost Decade', her exports declined significantly and local private sector capital investment weakened. The Japanese government's structural reform policies placed restraints on public works spending, triggering another rollover adverse impact on its economy. De-growth registered at 21.81 per cent in December 2000. 'Owing to this confluence of unfavourable factors, economic conditions in Japan were extremely challenging,' acknowledged Tazaki. Kawasaki limped to a return to profitability in 2002. Morita's presence at the launch and the media meet indicated just how important the initiative was back in Japan.

The Wind under My Wings

The bike, one of the first in its cusp segment in India, breezed into the local market in July 2003. Positioned between the 100-cc commuter and the higher-powered 150-cc plus segments, it offered

---

[1] 11 September 2001.

the advantages of both extremes. This was Bajaj's opening at a four-stroke 125 cc bike. In India, Bajaj expected a large shift in buyer preference in favour of this segment in the long run. Around 1,00,000–1,20,000 bikes would be offered in India. Kawasaki pitched the Wind 125 as an exclusive world bike made by Bajaj in India for the domestic and export markets. 'The Wind 125 was designed keeping the world market in mind,' Morita shared with local Indian journalists at the launch. 'We have plans to export this bike to South-East Asia, Mexico, Brazil and countries neighbouring India, but we will check the response here first.'

'We were looking at setting up a joint marketing company with a small equity base, maybe on a 50:50 basis, purely for exports,' added Bajaj. 'Kawasaki Bajaj motorcycles made in India would be sold through Kawasaki channels internationally.' Exports were planned to countries such as Thailand, Brazil and Argentina. Trials were scheduled in the Philippines.

The Wind 125 launch laid four new milestones. The expansion of the Bajaj-Kawasaki partnership beyond India gave new momentum to a nineteen-year history of collaboration. The Waluj plant was designated as a global hub of Kawasaki Heavy Industries. Earlier, Kawasaki was largely in the background, working jointly with Bajaj Auto on engine technology for bikes. In international markets, the relationship reversed with Kawasaki opening up the export market, and Bajaj production in the background. The last and the best: the dreams Bajaj had in the mid-1980s of exporting two-wheelers, albeit bikes and not scooters, were finally fructifying.

In India, and at the launch of the Wind 125 in August 2003, Shinichi Morita was at his polite best. Back in Japan for the thirty-seventh Tokyo Motor Show a few weeks later on 31 October 2003, he was less reticent in his conversation with Press Trust of India's Rakesh Hari Pathak.

'Quality is the most crucial issue,' Morita pointed out to Pathak. 'At the moment Bajaj may be satisfied with the domestic market. We are talking to Bajaj for improving quality in order to export successfully.' Asked about Bajaj's response to higher investments, Morita was suave. 'It was both yes and no,' he said. 'Yes, because we talked as collaborators. And no, because Bajaj is an independent entity and they make their own business decisions. Bajaj is a strong partner with a good production base . . . we are fully satisfied with our association.'

The Idea of India Kawasaki Motors

In Kobe and Tokyo, towards mid-2005, a thin-edge-of-the-wedge discussion emerged in the ranks of Kawasaki's senior management: should we continue with Bajaj or go it alone? Its bikes were facing competition from KTM, which brought in more profits for Bajaj than the JV. The eight-year-old alliance was due to end soon anyway. How about establishing IKM as a 100 per cent subsidiary of Kawasaki Heavy Industries, Japan?

'How important is the formation of the India subsidiary?' asked the *Mint's* Shally Seth to Hiroshi Takata, president, Kawasaki Heavy Industries. 'With every other global motorcycle maker having already established its presence in the country, do you think this step is rather late?'

Takata's response was measured: 'The co-operation with Bajaj started in 1984. Kawasaki gave them technical assistance and Bajaj gave us low-cost sourcing. We were able to sustain our relationship for a very long time. The formation of India Kawasaki Motors is indeed very important for Kawasaki as we can see the demand for large motorcycles increasing. We don't think it's too late because the demand for mid-to-large motorcycles has just started picking up. Now that Bajaj has the expertise to make motorcycles on its own, we want to take our relationship to the next level and study where we can strengthen our cooperation in countries other than India.'

The Bikers Lament

For a quarter century, Bajaj's infrastructure, expertise and perspicacity had made it easier for Kawasaki to engage with the Indian market, acknowledged the Japanese. Would Bajaj agree to becoming a sales and service agent for Kawasaki bikes? The Pro-Biking dealerships and showrooms, for example, that Rajiv had developed with KTM was an extremely tempting sales channel, prominent in all major Indian cities. Would the two Bajajs be willing to continue the marketing, selling and service of imported Kawasaki bikes through the Pro-Biking franchise?

After discussion with Rajiv, the answer was a thoughtful yes. The Indo-Japanese relationship stepped up a notch. Kawasaki gained access to 300-plus Probiking showrooms, which until then had been KTM's exclusive patch. In August 2013, the Ninja 300, with its host of features and priced at Rs 3.5 lakh (ex-showroom Delhi), appeared in Pro-Biking showrooms.

Worryingly for IKM, KTM's offerings were well received by local bike enthusiasts. Several KTM products manufactured and sold by Bajaj Auto in India began to compete directly with Kawasaki models. Between 2012 and 2017, KTM bike sales grew at a compounded annual growth rate of 48 per cent. Not only did Kawasaki feel KTM's heat in the market, but KTM also brought in more profits for Bajaj. It was inevitable that KTM would win this battle.

An aggrieved biker community went for the jugular. 'The Kawasaki-Bajaj split is causing terrible inconvenience to almost all Kawasaki motorcycle owners,' moaned bikeadvice.in. 'With the partnership speculated to end next month, Bajaj's Probiking dealerships have hard-stopped the sale and servicing of Kawasaki motorcycles,' groaned another. 'Spare parts have disappeared off the shelves particularly in tier two cities,' whinged a third. 'The way Bajaj has stopped providing cover in this transition phase is pretty cut-throat,' wailed a fourth. A ménage à trois rarely works for long, and Kawasaki began to feel like an outsider.

IKM Chakan

It took Yuji Horiuchi, the expat head of India Kawasaki Motors, and his managers three years to clear legal formalities for the 10,000 square metres plant, but by 1 July 2010 these were mostly over and done with, and Kawasaki launched its Chakan operations in September. From the sidelines, dealers and bikers watched the official solo entry in the Indian market for hints of a possible launch of bigger and better bikes from the Japanese international portfolio, which would likely include sports bikes, tourers, cruisers and more. They were destined to be disappointed.

Earlier, in an October 2009 internal beauty parade, Kawasaki chose the Ninja 250R for its test launch. In its projections for India, Kawasaki hoped to sell 5000 motorcycles a year, about as many as it sold in China. Though the new Chakan plant was geared for models of various sizes, including the 1000 cc Ninja, Kazuo Ota, head of Kawasaki's motorcycles and engines division, suggested models with displacements of around 200 cc and not large bikes, adding that the Indian plant now had the capability to develop new models in India.

The Ninja 250R generated an impressive response despite being close to the Rs 3,00,000 on-road tab. Encouraged, Kawasaki set a sales target of 1000 Ninjas for the Indian market in 2010. The first locally assembled Kawasaki motorcycle to roll out was the top-of-the-range Ninja 1000. A stream of Ninjas followed: the Ninja 300, Ninja 400, Ninja 650, Ninja ZX-6R, Ninja 1000, Ninja ZX-10R and Ninja Z650. IKM's unit inside the Chakan plant began smoothly assembling CKD packs made in Japan and imported into India. 'The bike generated a great response despite the high on-road tab,' blogged Saad Khan and Kannan, 'but rival Honda promptly cocked a snook at Kawasaki by making an affordable 250 cc for half its price.'

An in-house R&D centre grew to thirty engineers, with several Kawasaki engineers from Japan 'permanently' assigned to India. The goal: make Kawasaki more competitive in India. Their task: find ways to incorporate locally manufactured, low-cost components into models targeted at emerging markets.

Interest in what Kawasaki Heavy Industries would do with its Indian twig grew in Tokyo, Kobe and Akurdi. 'Kawasaki is currently finalising ten new dealerships,' shared an IKM manager with *Autocar*. 'Kolhapur, Bhubaneshwar, Ludhiana, Nagpur, Vizag, Calicut, Mangalore, Kolkata, Dehradun and Goa are expected to be up and running by the end of 2017, taking our total to twenty-two. Kawasaki has a concept of soft opening for a new dealership where bookings are accepted so that customers don't need to wait until full-fledged services commence. At present, each existing dealer has its own service centre and additionally eight dealers run a mobile service van in selected cities.' The word from Tokyo came: raise Kawasaki-only dealers to thirty by 2020 end.

The partnership expanded to the ASEAN region where Bajaj-branded motorcycles formed part of a joint retail strategy. For example, teaming up with Kawasaki helped Bajaj Auto increase its market share for the Pulsar and Discover brands in Indonesia and the Philippines. The revitalized relationship also enabled the Ninja 250 cc CBU[2] to be priced attractively around Rs 90,000, the local ex-factory price in Thailand. For Bajaj, after paying Indian custom duties, the ex-showroom price still came at an attractive Rs 2 lakh.

Going forward, the partners hoped to jointly explore more regions in the Asia-Pacific region and other parts of the world where the Kawasaki brand was strong. 'We are considering the markets of South-East Asia, Latin America and China. However, so far, we do not have any concrete idea on how we want to go about it,' admitted Bajaj. 'Trials are scheduled in the Philippines.'

Sayōnara but Not Quite the End

As scheduled, the thirty-three-year-old Bajaj-Kawasaki alliance ended on 1 April 2017 in India. Both parties quietly agreed that jointly selling their motorcycles to the rest of the world made better sense than sniping at each other in India. Undercurrents were there, but the Bajajs are good at retaining relationships.

---

[2] CBU: completely built-up bike.

37

The Rajya Sabha: 2006–10

Rajya Sabha in New Delhi in 2006.

Settling his large frame into Air India's deep-red bucket seat, exchanging a comradely glance with the portly Maharaja icon pasted on the aircraft's walls, accepting a drink from the pretty air hostess and making sure his wife, Pratibha, was comfortable, Sharad Pawar finally relaxed. India's minister of agriculture was on his way to

274

Washington and New York for the second meeting of the US-India Agricultural Knowledge Initiative Board to be held on 6–7 June 2006. Besides a meeting with Nobel laureate Norman Borlaug, the American agronomist who scripted India's Green Revolution, Pawar had a packed two days ahead. Not nearly as packed, or as contentious, as his campaign to get his friend Bajaj a seat in the Rajya Sabha. But he would be back well in time for the counting of votes—and any cajoling that might be required, reckoned Pawar as he drifted into sleep.

Forty-four days earlier, a murder created a vacancy in the Rajya Sabha when Pravin Mahajan shot dead his elder brother Pramod, a talented BJP leader, in Mumbai. According to the Indian constitution, a new member must be promptly elected from the same state as the deceased for the remainder of a predecessor's term of office. Four years in this case.

Pramod Mahajan succumbed to his injuries on 3 May 2006. Almost from the moment he was shot, long lines of hopefuls for his Rajya Sabha seat formed outside and inside Delhi's 24, Akbar Road,[1] 10, Bishambar Das Marg,[2] 11, Ashoka Road,[3] and Mumbai's Sena Bhavan.[4] Telephone lines sizzled, hopes ran high, but it would be Bajaj who breasted the finish line. He won the Rajya Sabha election on Thursday, 16 June 2006. His term started on 20 June 2006 and ended on 4 July 2010.

Bajaj's near future began with four phone calls.

'On Sunday, at the behest of Sharad Pawar, I phoned Rahul bhai,' recalls Praful Patel, a talented politician. 'Would you like to join our club, that is the Rajya Sabha, I asked Rahul bhai. Characteristically, he said, "*Soch lo*, don't regret your decision later, because once I agree and step in, there will be no chance of backing off". That's Rahul bhai—gritty, determined and a fighter, especially for a cause.'

'Actually, I did not think it would be possible for me to join the Rajya Sabha,' remembers Bajaj. 'Sharad Pawar's phone call from London before leaving for New York came as a surprise because which party would take me in as I will not want to be a party man?'

[1] Office of the Sonia Gandhi-led Indian National Congress (the Congress).
[2] Office of Sharad Pawar's Nationalist Congress Party (NCP).
[3] Office of Rajnath Singh of the Bharatiya Janata Party (BJP).
[4] Office of Bal Thackeray of the Shiv Sena.

'By this time, Sharad was in London, and Praful on an Alaskan cruise. They talked the next day (there was not much time left) and both came up with my name. The rest is history. I made it very clear to Sharad that I would only come as an independent and not otherwise,' shares Bajaj. 'I spoke to Praful on the same day. Arrangements needed to be finalized because the last date to file the nomination was only five–six days away. Then, I spoke to some senior people in the BJP and the Shiv Sena with whom either Sharad or Praful had already suggested and accepted my candidature. In brief, I spoke to Advaniji and one or two others in the BJP, and Uddhav and Balasaheb in the Shiv Sena. All these people (obviously they were being polite!) said that the moment Sharad Pawar and Praful Patel suggested my name, they gave their consent very readily and happily.

'I had nothing to do about positioning myself as an independent candidate. All I had to do was to file my nomination (for which Praful's man in Mumbai helped me). Sharad and Praful had explained to me the arithmetic: that out of the 288 MLAs, I will get about 190 votes and it would be a clear victory. This was made all clear to me before I filed my nomination.'

The Arithmetic

The trick in such situations is to get the math right. Lok Sabha members are elected directly by voters across the country. Rajya Sabha members are elected indirectly by the states and their MLAs.[5]

The party position in the 288-member Maharashtra state Assembly was the Indian National Congress—seventy-three, the Nationalist Congress Party (NCP)—seventy-one, the Shiv Sena—fifty-eight, the Bharatiya Janata Party—fifty-four, the Jansurajya Party—four, the Communist Party of India-M—three, Peasants and Workers Party (Bharat Ki Kisaan Mazdoor Party)—two, Bharipa Bahujan Mahasangh—one, Republican Party of India (Athawale)—one, Swatantra Bharat Party—one, Akhil Bharatiya Sena—one, Independents—nineteen. Plus, one nominated member. Bajaj needed a minimum of 145 votes to sail through.

Members of a state's Legislative Assembly vote in the Rajya Sabha elections in what is called proportional representation with

---

[5] MLA—member of the Legislative Assembly.

the single transferable vote (STV) system. Each MLA's vote is counted only once. MLAs don't vote for each seat. If that were the case, then only the ruling party representatives would make it through. Instead, the MLAs are given a paper with the names of all the candidates. They have to give their order of preference for each candidate, marking 1,2,3 . . . against their names. If ten or more members choose a candidate as their first choice, s/he gets elected.

Carefully positioned as an Independent candidate, Bajaj distanced himself from party politicking and the nitty-gritty of campaigning, trusting Pawar's well-honed skills.

Going by the arithmetic, Pawar's job was simple. His NCP had seventy-one MLAs. Add the Shiv Sena's fifty-eight and the BJP's fifty-four, and Bajaj could romp home with 183 votes. Life is never that simple.

Sonia Gandhi

Technically and officially, the NCP and the Congress were allies in Maharashtra. Naturally, the Congress expressed reservation over Pawar's party joining hands with the Shiv Sena-BJP combine for the sake of his friendship with Bajaj. And there was history.

Pawar exited the Congress on the issue of Italian-born Sonia Gandhi's right to lead the country. 'It is not possible that a country of 980 million, with a wealth of education, competence and ability, can have anyone other than an Indian, born of Indian soil, to head its government,' wrote Pawar, P.A. Sangma and Tariq Anwar in a 15 May 1999 letter to Gandhi. The trio left the Congress and founded the NCP a few days later.

Time compressed for the rebels. Voting for the thirteenth Lok Sabha opened on 5 September 1999. The BJP won, the Congress lost, and NCP managed to capture a mere eight seats. The tumble generated a reconciliation between Pawar and Gandhi to challenge the BJP in the Maharashtra State Assembly election of 2004. The Congress-NCP alliance won.

A frustrated Congress protested against the NCP's tie-ups with the BJP and the Shiv Sena combine. Pawar nonchalantly declared that Bajaj's contribution to Maharashtra was immense and the state needed business icons like him. 'We do feel that people like him should be there in the Parliament,' Pawar blandly told reporters. 'He is not a party candidate, he is an Independent candidate.'

'Bajaj's father, Kamalnayan Bajaj, and grandfather, Jamnalal Bajaj, were both Congress stalwarts,' Pawar reminded everyone. 'His father was a three-term Member of Parliament from the Congress party. His grandfather was a colleague of Mahatma Gandhi, a member of the Congress Working Committee, and the treasurer of the Congress party in pre-Independence India.'

A seething Sonia Gandhi promptly plucked out Avinash Pande from the Congress fold to challenge Bajaj. Local, well-educated, Maharashtrian, Pande was a qualified Nagpur lawyer who had made a name for himself as one who helped *mathadi* (unprotected manual workers, usually male) and bidi workers (mostly women). The NCP's state president, Arun Gujarathi, valiantly tried being pacific. 'The NCP has sponsored Bajaj's candidature. It is a coincidence that the BJP and the Shiv Sena are supporting him,' he insisted. No one was taken in. In 2010, Gandhi would ensure Pande's appointment to the Rajya Sabha.

The Shiv Sena

But perhaps observers should have tried to be taken in, or at least tried to understand the curious friendship between the maverick Marathi manoos, Balasaheb Thackeray and a conservative Marwari bania with a Padma Bhushan conferred by the Atal Bihari Vajpayee government in 2001.

Born and bred in Poona, a shy and timid Thackeray moved to Mumbai in the early 1950s to work as a cartoonist in the *Free Press Journal (FPJ)*. 'We were all proud of him,' wrote Behram Contractor, India's foremost satirist and Thackeray's colleague at the time. 'Two of his works had been included in a British anthology of cartoons. Laxman's[6] had not.'

The rise of the Communist Party of India (CPI) in the run-up to the second Lok Sabha election of 1957 brought together Ramkrishna Bajaj and Thackeray. 'Both Balasaheb and my uncle were anti-communists,' explains Bajaj. 'Though the ideologies of the

---

[6] R.K. Laxman, India's foremost cartoonist, illustrator and humourist. Laxman and Thackeray were contemporaries, born and dying within years of each other.

Congress and the Shiv Sena were not common, they maintained a good rapport.'

In 1960, Thackeray quit his job. According to Contractor, who stayed on at *FPJ*, 'Either behind that timid front a volcano had been raging, or everything that happened afterwards happened by chance and accident. Mr Thackeray left the paper in a rage, or at least as much rage as his then gentle nature could command. An American newspaper had reproduced one of his cartoons and sent him a cheque. The management kept the cheque, claiming that the cartoon was its property.

Skint but determined, Thackeray, along with his younger brother Shrikant, promptly launched *Marmik*, a sort of Marathi *Punch*. The *FPJ*'s 'management was south Indian and his first attack was against south Indians,' continues Contractor. The Gujaratis were attacked next, then the Muslims. The basic thinking was that non-Maharashtrians (non-Marathi-speaking) were the haves of Bombay, and the Maharashtrians, to whom the city geographically belonged, were the have-nots.

A political agenda developed. The new party needed a name. Ramkrishna suggested Shiv Sena. Thackeray accepted. On 19 June 1966 Thackeray launched a far-Right regional political party, with its ideology based on pro-Marathi ideology and Hindu nationalism (Hindutva). However, the initial linchpin of the Thackeray-Bajaj relationship was B.K. Desai, Ramkrishna's secretary.

'We made a threesome,' recalled Sharad Pawar. 'B.K. Desai (was) a very well read and intellectual person. He took to writing articles in *Marmik* under an assumed name and later was Balasaheb's adviser and totally behind his setting up the Shiv Sena . . . We began meeting regularly, along with a few others on the second or third floor of Elphinstone College, (located) in those days opposite Kala Ghoda. The first few meetings of the Shiv Sena were unremarkable—it was Ramrao Adik who first addressed the first meeting of the Shiv Sena.

'Balasaheb shot to prominence when he took up the Maharashtra-Karnataka border issue and decided to blockade Morarji Desai for anti-Maharashtra remarks. That was when I was first affected by his politics—I was in Baramati and travelling towards Mumbai when my car was attacked in Lalbaug by stone-throwers. I escaped unhurt, but my windshield was broken and a senior Congress leader travelling with me broke his jaw.'

'After my uncle passed away in 1994, I came more in touch with Balasaheb,' recalled Bajaj. 'He was always in favour of development of industry. I remember, many years ago, in Bajaj Auto's Akurdi plant, when the wage agreement was up for renewal, our management was in dialogue with the Bharatiya Kamgar Sena. At the time of wage negotiations, there used to be disagreements, strong bargaining from both sides, but there was never any violence. I was never asked for any money.

'I went to meet Balasaheb in Mumbai after one of the union agreement meetings. I clearly remember, after discussion, he told the Kamgar Sena, "Bajaj Auto will consider your demand for higher wages favourably, but you must ensure that you will do nothing to harm the company by going on strike and you should improve your productivity". He would argue in favour of workers but never ignored the interests of the company. Balasaheb was always in favour of building industry.'

Given the multiple layers of the fifty-year Bajaj relationship, Thackeray naturally agreed to Sharad Pawar's solicitation for their mutual friend and directed his fifty-eight Shiv Sena MPs to vote for Bajaj in the 2006 Rajya Sabha by-election.

Shiv Sena-BJP Alliance

And what about the third spoke in Pawar's strategy wheel?

With Mahajan initiating and Bal Thackeray concurring, the Shiv Sena and the BJP had formed an alliance in 1989. At the time, the BJP had been in existence for only nine years and had negligible influence in Maharashtra. Mahajan recognized and exploited the identity crisis the Shiv Sena was going through. When Thackeray founded the Sena in 1966, it was a political organization that championed the cause of the local sons-of-the-soil but did not wield any significant influence beyond Mumbai city. In the 1980s, the party seemed to be losing its relevance as support for its Marathi chauvinism weakened.

Mahajan saw an opportunity for the two parties to unite on the Hindutva platform. A year after they tied up for the Maharashtra Assembly and the Lok Sabha, their political presence in Maharashtra skyrocketed. Earlier, the BJP and the Shiv Sena won a handful of seats each in assembly elections. After the alliance, even though they lost the 1990 election to the Congress, the two parties won an unprecedented ninety-four seats: fifty-two for the Sena and forty-two for the BJP.

Nonetheless, the Shiv Sena was the big brother of the alliance, keeping a larger share of seats for itself. In 1995, with communal friction high in the state after the 1993 Bombay riots, the Sena-BJP alliance won and came to power for the first time in the Assembly. The Sena made Manohar Joshi the chief minister, but with neither party experienced in governance, they stayed in power for just one term.

Even though they lost the Assembly elections for the next fifteen years, the alliance helped both parties expand their influence in Maharashtra. In 1999, the alliance won 125 seats; in 2004, they won 116. Although they could not generate the numbers on their own, together they served as a consistent opposition to the Congress-NCP alliance.

Until his death in 2006, Mahajan was the glue that held the BJP and the Sena together. 'The alliance came close to breaking up several times, particularly because Thackeray was not very fond of Vajpayee or Advani,' wrote Sujata Anandan in her book *Samrat*. 'Mahajan was always the one sweeping up the tensions and patching things up.' But after Mahajan, Pawar was there to patch things up for his favourite industrialist.

The Caste Factor

For Bajaj's Rajya Sabha candidacy, Pawar initially foresaw little to fear in terms of communal politics but caste issues are never far in any Indian election. Both Bajaj and Pande came in for flak.

Congress president Sonia Gandhi received a complaint from Castribe, an organization of state government employees belonging to backward classes. Castribe drew Gandhi's attention to an alleged assault by Pande on the Nagpur district collector while he was an MLA.

Meanwhile, some OBC (Other Backward Class) bodies sent out a call to MLAs not to vote for Bajaj for his 'anti-quota' stance. A few responded. Suresh, alias Pappu Kalani, of the Republican Party of India-Athawale faction, Haridas Bhade of Bharatiya Republican Party led by Prakash Ambedkar, and the Shiv Sena's Gulabrao Gavande did not vote. Gavande apparently could not make it as his flight was delayed. Kalani and Bhade's gestures were a support for OBC organizations.

Clarifying his position on the quota issue after his victory, Bajaj said he did not believe in caste, and his stand against reservations was limited to the OBC quota and the proposed reservations in the private sector. 'I won't change my opinion and they (the reservationists) won't change theirs. About 37 per cent of my workforce in Bajaj Auto belong to backward castes. I recruited them on merit, not caste,' he said.

On Thursday, 15 June 2006, Bajaj defeated Pande by a margin of 105 votes. Vinay Kore stepped in to be the first signatory to Bajaj's Rajya Sabha nomination paper.

The Parliamentarian

'In becoming a Rajya Sabha MP, has he found his true calling?' wondered Rupa. 'It is clear he relishes the challenge. Maybe it is the genes expressing themselves. For Jamnalalji was a Treasurer of the Congress in the 1930s and Kamalnayanji, a three-time member of the Lok Sabha between 1957–1972. In fact, there are old timers in the Parliament who still remember Kamalnayan ji.'

'The bonhomie Rahul generated in the House was palpable with MPs from the entire political spectrum,' Rupa continued. 'Even MPs from the Left came to consult Rahul! An MP from Himachal who did not know him earlier, told him, "When you came in, we thought here comes another money bag, but you have broader concerns." On another occasion, after Rahul spoke in the house, a MP from the DMK sent a chit saying, "Only Rahul Bajaj could have said this!" This cross-spectrum appeal and acceptance is possibly his greatest strength.'

'I knew that the Rajya Sabha members expected an industrialist to speak about industry. I did not want to do so,' reminisces Bajaj. 'Farmer suicide was a major issue. Coming from Vidarbha, where many farmers' suicides were taking place, it was appropriate as the title of my speech was "Farmers' Suicide in Vidarbha". Incidentally, Sharad Pawar was in the house when I spoke.'

'Both of us were elected from Maharashtra as Independents in the Rajya Sabha,' recalled Padinjarethalakal Cherian Alexander (aka P.C. Alexander), 'and as Independents, both Rahul and I could therefore take a non-personal stand on issues which came up for discussion.'

'Independent members have certain limitations regarding the time allotted to speakers,' continued Alexander, 'and the order of being called to speak. At Rahul's initiative, a few of us Independents used to occasionally meet and discuss ways and means of getting more opportunities and time to participate in debates. He always came up with practical solutions to achieve our objective without causing any friction to others. And whenever Rahul bhai did choose to intervene in a debate, etc., he was listened to with great attention as he always spoke with great clarity and conviction.'

'The Question Hour gave members a good opportunity to ask the government about subjects troubling them,' continues Bajaj. 'Of course, no one, including me, was interested in all the questions. Hence, either I used to leave the Chamber for the Central Hall when I was getting bored or kept trying to understand the questions and answers. I very much enjoyed chatting with people in the Central Hall. Many of them, including those from the Lok Sabha, became at least acquaintances if not friends. We discussed political, legal, industrial, agricultural, the behaviour of the government and the opposition.

'I remember a particular discussion in the Central Hall on the problems of the sugar industry, especially in Uttar Pradesh (UP)—all our sugar mills were in UP. While I was not managing the sugar companies, obviously I was interested. There were some controversies between industry and the government on the pricing of cane. Industry felt that specially in UP, the state government used to fix a very high cane price to get farmer votes. However, in one such discussion, various angles came up which gave me a much better idea about the sugar industry at least in UP, in terms of the views of industry and the government.'

Bajaj's term ended in 2010. Pande got another stab at a Rajya Sabha seat. On Rahul Gandhi's recommendation, the Congress-nominated the staunch supporter of the Gandhi-Nehru family; Pande won easily.

Kudo Confetti

Some came from Manmohan Singh, for example, when he was prime minister, and Bajaj in the Rajya Sabha. By nature, Singh is rather a reticent man. But not always, as one discovers in a personal letter to Bajaj dated 2 May 2008:

'I have always enjoyed my conversations, my arguments and my debates with Rahul,' wrote Singh. 'I learnt a lot from him and continue to do so, but I have also disagreed with him on issues. What I valued, however, is his generosity of spirit, his civility and his forthrightness. These features of his personality made him a public figure and he fulfils that role admirably as a Member of Parliament.'

Continuing the unusual garrulity, Singh adds, 'I have always had the highest regard for his business acumen, his entrepreneurial leadership, his deep abiding patriotism and his commitment to our national development . . . he has stood tall as one of our most respected business leaders.'

Singh's finance minister, P. Chidambaram, was even more candid. 'Although he was regarded as belonging to the infamous Bombay Club, I do not think he was against globalization: in my view, Rahul was expressing a legitimate point, one which ought to be always kept in mind as India integrates with the global economy . . . As a person, he is warm, friendly and self-deprecating. I have enjoyed his humour even if, on occasions, I was at the receiving end.'

'I love to provoke Rahul,' chortled BJP leader Arun Jaitley, who passed away in 2019, 'and he responds! Evenings get enriched and exciting with his presence. That's the reason why we continue to have mutual respect and affection for each other.'

'He interacts with everyone in the Parliament including the Watch and Ward staff, and never stands on ceremony,' admired newspaper baron Vijay Darda. 'I have personally benefited from his thinking. We began *Lokmat* from Nagpur in the 1970s, and we found that Bajaj advertisements were appearing in our competitor's newspaper. I remember writing to him that our rival was getting all the *moolah* and we were left high and dry despite our family bonds. His response was instructive. He wrote to me that business and personal relations are to be treated on different footings. Once *Lokmat* comes up to the mark, all Bajaj advertisements would naturally flow to us. The message was clear. He wanted us to work hard to beat our rival. That is how it turned out to be.'

Bimal Jalan dubbed him simply as 'Rahul: The Inimitable'.

38

GRüß Gott:[1] 2007–21

Rajiv Bajaj and Stefan Pierer.

---

[1] 'God Bless', a greeting.

'Rajiv and I met for the first time at the Geneva Car Show in March 2007 where we presented our X-Bow,' recalled Austria's Stefan Pierer to reporter Alan Cathcart, 'and the chemistry worked immediately.' An impressed Rajiv promptly acquired a 14.5 per cent equity stake in KTM.

A few months later, in August 2007, a financial crisis engulfed the US, drawing the world into its wildfire. In India and Akurdi, fears were initially muted and the hoary saying, *'Dilli Dur Hai'*, active. Not so for Pierer. Rajiv bailed out the distressed Austrian by picking up a near 40 per cent equity stake in KTM AG, which would grow to 48 per cent. On a stronger financial footing by 2019, Pierer negotiated the transfer of Bajaj's stake in KTM AG to KTM Industries AG.

Quizzed by the press in India, Rajiv was at his urbane best: this wasn't an equity investment or a game of ownership. 'Such financial investments are not sustainable in the future,' he pointed out, adding, 'the basis of the relationship between KTM and Bajaj is the integration of two kitchens cooking together, and what binds them is equal purpose not equity.'

Experimental synergy led to the successful launch of the KTM Duke 125 in India. In 2012, the Bajaj-KTM partnership launched its first co-developed product, the KTM Duke 200, offered in select world markets, including India. A KTM 390 Duke appeared alongside the addition of two superbike models, the RC 200 at Rs 1,60,000 and the RC 390 at Rs 2,05,000, expanding the portfolio and improving profitability at dealerships. By FY 2014, Bajaj Auto had sold over 11,050 KTMs in India and exported 24,016 KTMs. KTM's market share in India in this segment grew by 28 per cent. In 2020, Chakan produced 1 lakh KTM bikes.

'KTM is a racing champion and Bajaj has a brand like Pulsar that makes a million Pulsar bikes every year,' said Pierer, 'and Bajaj is focused on ramping up production to meet the increase in demand. Everything is from the Chakan factory and is jointly developed and designed with Bajaj. That is something Bajaj can be proud of, and it is a benchmark for the Japanese.'

'We needed partners,' recaps Pierer. 'Honestly, the alliance and joint development with Bajaj performed beyond our expectations.

I didn't expect the rapport on a personal level to be that good. And that has translated nicely into executives at both sides and R&D as well.'

Ditto for Bajaj. 'KTM's focus was almost entirely on the US and Europe. On our own, it would not have been possible to participate in markets of KTM,' admits Rajiv. Together, they want to become the biggest sports motorcycle company in the world.

'The tie-up with Bajaj Auto was key for us to become a global company,' admits Pierer, 'especially to penetrate deeper into emerging markets and take on Japanese companies. In order to make it big in emerging markets, you need smaller displacement bikes at competitive prices. KTM managed to go to China with India-designed and developed bikes and through the CKD route to Malaysia. The bikes were selling in Columbia, the Philippines, Indonesia and Brazil. We started getting a third of our global sales from India which then became the third biggest market for KTM after the US and Germany. Over two years, KTM sold 30,000 units in India. In 2020, KTM grew 46 per cent in India. In fiscal 2021, it grew at 120 per cent at a time when the motorcycle industry in India was growing at 10 per cent.'

Say Welcome to the Electric Bike

France's Peugeot in 1996 produced the world's first electric scooter for consumer purchase, featuring a 3 horsepower DC motor powered by three nickel-cadmium batteries.

In Chakan, Rajiv knew he had to get his electric products into the marketplace by 2030, before the ban on combustion-engined two-wheelers kicked in.

'For sure the electric bike is coming big time,' agrees Pierer, 'and we were one of the pioneers in that segment, firstly with a high voltage concept before all the disadvantages of that became clear, with the various safety issues relating to logistics, warehousing, dealerships and so on. It necessitated a big battery pack and then you are losing your profitability. But now we've finally recognized how it works best commercially, with a low voltage 48V 15kW powerpack—that's quite enough.

'We are quite closely collaborating with Bajaj on the small displacement, low voltage electric products,' continues Pierer, 'so we have jointly developed a 4kW and 8/10kW electric motor, and that the powertrain platform can be used for multiple brands from a scooter to a motorcycle.

'Our first interpretation of the scooter using the Husqvarna brand is 100 per cent based on the Bajaj Chetak scooter which is already in the market in India, where we're using the rolling chassis and doing our own design interpretation. But for sure we're working on our own Husqvarna e-motorcycles—we are convinced in the potential of the so-called small displacement class from the electric equivalent to a 50 cc two-stroke up to around 125 cc.

'We will also have a huge increase in production in India because Bajaj is building the small displacement Husqvarna for us there. They started in February 2020, shortly before Corona showed up, and they're selling quite well everywhere, including in India. Last December, 8000 KTMs and Husqvarnas were sold there—that's a serious number. So, we expect next year around 1,60,000 or even up to 1,80,000 units will be coming from India,' described Pierer.

The China Factor

'In India, Mr Narendra Modi is betting big on electric vehicles. But does he need China's help?' asked *South China Morning Post*'s Vasudevan Sridharan, pointing out that 'the South Asian nation wants to become a 100 per cent EV nation by 2030, despite teething problems implementing the switch. But China controls the bulk of components essential to the manufacture of EV batteries, so the prime minister's dream is dependent on Beijing's blessings.'

The above planning took a sudden back seat with the 5 May 2020 Galwan valley skirmish between India and China. By 15 June, Indian companies started boycotting Chinese products. Action on the economic front included cancellation and additional scrutiny of contracts with Chinese firms; and calls made to stop the entry of Chinese companies into strategic markets in India. By November 2020, the Indian government had banned over 200 Chinese apps, including apps owned by Alibaba, Tencent, Baidu, Sina and Bytedance.

'We like to believe that we are a global company,' says Rajiv, 'and therefore from a cultural point of view and an operational point of view, the organization demands completeness and inclusiveness not just of employee gender, but also of working with dealers, distributors and suppliers from all over the world. And that is why I believe that we must continue to trade with China because if we conduct our business at the exclusion of such a large country, such a large market, we will find ourselves incomplete over time, and we will be poorer for the loss of that experience.'

'In a supply chain, commitment is important,' Rajiv continues. 'A sense of mutuality and reciprocity is indispensable to build the kind of intricate supply chain that the auto industry needs in order to deliver the final product to the customer. I say this in the context of what happened when our government, for whatever reasons, suddenly came down hard on imports, especially from China. Now, to my mind, doing something like that is to cut your nose to spite your face. Because overnight, how can one source components that are simply not made in the domestic market yet need to be delivered to domestic and export customers?'

'Maintaining continuity is the second important aspect of the holistic view of supply chains,' he added. 'If it is cheaper to make something out of China or procure something from Thailand, we must always procure stuff from wherever it is most competitively available.'

'We did an elaborate comparison based on five metrics: land, labour, electricity, logistics and the legal system for an exhaustive comparison of India, Vietnam, Indonesia, Thailand and Malaysia,' Bajaj continued, 'and to be honest, in the "ease of doing business" analysis, we were not very pleased with the conclusion we drew for India. Operating in one of the ASEAN countries is easier than what we encounter here in India.'

The Last Word: Stefan

'I learnt two things in India,' shares Pierer, 'and one is patience, which I admit is not really my strength! But I have finally learnt it, and if you stick at doing some things, sooner or later it works. And secondly, I've had a little bit of a special education in renegotiating something if some part of it is not quite clear. Yes, I've learnt a lot, and I appreciate that the size of the company, and where we are standing right now, comes in combination with Bajaj as a partner. People like Honda are looking at us in a different way after the combination with Bajaj, and we are really hitting the emerging markets with outstanding products and new designs at affordable prices. From whom else should I obtain market share?'

The Last Word: Rajiv

'The company's sharp focus on the motorcycles category, and its unwavering commitment to strategies of differentiation as well as the practice of Total Productive Maintenance (TPM) combined with global ambitions made Bajaj the most valuable two-wheeler company across the globe. This inspires us even more to serve and delight customers all over the world,' says Rajiv.

39

Bajaj Finance: 2003–21

Sanjiv and Bajaj.

NBFCs typically charge higher interest on loans than high-street banks. Why then would anyone go to an NBFC for a loan? Those who have been turned down by banks or those who know they won't meet a bank's eligibility criteria. Before Bajaj Finance came on the scene, the standard option were moneylenders on the fringes of the grey economy.

'So, we asked ourselves: what is it about us that can be special to our customers?' Sanjiv shared with *Mint*, 'and why should anybody come to us to take a loan in a very competitive space? The transformation of BFL from 2007–08 for a couple of years was the toughest period in my career so far.'

From 2003 onwards, the retail finance market saw rapid expansion driven by large private sector banks. Like others, BFL aggressively grew its retail finance book consisting primarily of captive two- and three-wheelers and some consumer durables. Assets under management trebled from Rs 784 crore in 2002–2003 to Rs 2613 crore by 2007–2008. 'However, growing in an intensely competitive market, BFL—a small player—we did not adequately budget for the risks,' recalls Sanjiv, 'nor was the team equipped to support this pace of growth, resulting in adverse customer selection. Further, a lion's share of the lending book was loans for purchase of two and three-wheelers offering very little diversification. The stress began showing in the financials through higher non-performing asset (NPAs) and loss provisions.'

'Nothing is as easy as it looks or as difficult as it seems. We did not have a strong technology platform,' continues Sanjiv. 'The credit policies and underwriting processes needed improvement. The expansion of our branch network and manpower had added significant fixed costs, while the operating models needed complete restructuring. Most importantly, we needed a young new team to rebuild the company. All this had to be done while ensuring that the business did not collapse since the losses from loans written in earlier years were sure to hit the financials in the next few years. I believed in our businesses and favourable demographics. I requested Pamnani to help me rebuild the organization and diversify our portfolio for greater stability.'

By the end of 2008, Sanjiv had a new CEO and a younger team develop the new businesses in a systematic manner. 'We built a strong fee-based model to ensure steady profitability. We laid an IT backbone and a sensible outsourcing strategy to keep us focused on our core strengths, including building a strong relationship with our customers. With all these efforts, our businesses, profits and share price started rising steadily.'

Mind the Gap

Monday, 30 June 2014. The financial community woke up surprised. Bajaj Finance introduced India's first end-to-end, 100 per cent online, unsecured loans for business expansion. In a completely automated process, the offering allowed an entrepreneur to apply for a business loan online with minimal form-filling. The offering was designed for small businesses in manufacturing, trade and services in need of a loan between Rs 0.8 million to Rs 3 million; for the self-employed; and for professionals such as architects, doctors and chartered accountants.

Depending on the authenticity of information provided, the customer could get immediate approval of the loan amount. On receipt of the relevant documentation, the company undertook to disburse the loan to the customer's account within seventy-two hours, a timeline substantially quicker than the then current industry average of thirty days.

'If banks can operate in different lending segments, so can we,' said Rajeev Jain, CEO. 'We say to our investors we will deliver 18–20 per cent sustainable RoE. Private banks generate RoE of 15–16 per cent, and NBFCs in a single line of business generate 24 per cent RoE. With 18 per cent RoE, we provide the agility of the NBFCs and the risk management strengths of banks. We feel our diversified presence helps in mitigating risks while growing at a reasonable pace. Investors did not believe our story then. Every company takes time to be discovered.'

Adds Sanjiv, 'When we started transforming Bajaj Auto Finance to Bajaj Finance, we decided to be multi-line. There were many mono-lines[1] like Mahindra Finance which focused on tractors or Muthoot Finance on gold. When we looked at private sector banks,

---

[1] Key players: Shriram Transport Finance Company in asset finance, Muthoot Finance in gold, Edelweiss Broking Limited in investment, IDFC in infrastructure, Ujjivan Small Finance Bank in microfinance, Capital First Ltd in finance, Mahindra & Mahindra Financial Services Limited in rural, and Sundaram Finance Limited in vehicles.

we saw that if one is mono-line, the associated risks could wipe you out in a down cycle.' Foresight proved prescient. SBI, for example, started aggressive lending to the farming community challenging Mahindra Finance, and HDFC Bank turned the heat on the market leader in gold loans, Muthoot Finance.

Bajaj Finance's model was a breakout innovation. Imitation being the sincerest form of flattery, several NBFCs and even a few banks jumped onto Bajaj Finance's ideas, further opening up the market. 'Along with some of my colleagues, we started studying the financial services opportunity in India from FY 2008,' recalls Sanjiv, 'and the team spotted demand gaps which we could innovatively fill.' Banks perceive lending to small businesses as a relatively risky proposition. Inadequate collateral and documentation make underwriting difficult. Banks end up adopting conservative policies to minimize their credit risk and the cost of delivery.

Sanjiv recalls, 'In those days, when someone wanted to buy a TV and get finance, they were asked to complete some hefty documentation and apply for approval. This process could take a week or more. We realized that anyone who was willing to go through this hassle to buy a small-ticket item like a TV is likely to be desperately in need of finance. This process would likely lead to adverse selection. The opportunity was obvious—can we give loans on the spot to better credit customers? Thus was born Bajaj Finance's three-minute loan—which was later to become a game changer in the financial sector.'

But to do this, one needed access to credit histories. This area was just starting in India. Millions from the middle and lower middle class had never taken loans from the organized financial sector, and therefore had no credit histories. India's first credit bureau to open shop was CIBIL[2] in August 2000. Netherlands' Experian, US-based Equifax and Italy's CRIF High Mark entered in 2010.

BFL embraced CIBIL wholeheartedly and the three-minute loan became a success as Rajeev and team were able to tie together the technology platform that married the CIBIL score, the deduplication engine (to check whether the customer had borrowed before) and the application engine which had the credit approval and scheme

---

[2] Formerly known as Credit Information Bureau (India) Limited.

algorithm. This integrated process was able to spit out an approval or specific offer to the customer at the dealership.

Bajaj Finance made a strong push to disseminate information among customers on how to build credit histories and became the largest contributor of CIBIL trade line information. Fifty per cent of its customers were first-time users of a formal credit system. The numbers ballooned. By 2015, the customer base had increased to 12.9 million people across 304 cities and 497 rural locations. By FY 2020, Bajaj Finance had 42.6 million customers in 2392 locations, 1357 of which were in rural markets.

In 2011, BFL launched another first in India—the existing member identification (EMI) card. Rajeev recalls, 'Once the three-minute loan became a hit with customers, we had to think ahead. If a customer comes for the second time—should he or she wait for three minutes and resubmit KYC (know your customer) documents? The EMI card was a limit given to an existing customer once he or she had paid at least three instalments on a loan. The card enables the holder to purchase consumer durables and lifestyle products using a pre-approved loan simply through "swipe and sign".'

A Start-up Feel. Always

In Sanjiv and Rajeev Jain's minds, the original four-point plan they had put together was crystal clear: focus on repeat customers; be in a perpetual state of beta; invest deep in technology; and build partnerships with the best in the world.

After almost a decade and a half into operations, Bajaj Finance continues to feel and behave like a start-up. The mood at its head office was buoyant, riding the wave of expansion of consumer credit. Perhaps it was the velocity of product introduction, and the management's promptness in terminating promising products, which didn't do well in the market. Or because analytics and business intelligence drove the organization, giving Bajaj Finance the edginess of an IT company. Or because of the sheer number of new hires, infusing the NBFC with fresh faces and fresh ideas, varied experiences and expectations.

'Our competitor is ourselves,' says Sanjiv. 'We will not be hesitant to discard an idea that has worked for us well in the past if we feel there is a better way forward. Each one of our long-range planning processes starts by questioning status quo. That has become the basis for disruptive thinking,' he adds.

Sanjiv focuses on one or two big ideas every couple of years. These start as pilot projects, gaining momentum as the company learns. Expanding on the success of the interest-free loan model of consumer durable financing where apart from a nominal processing fee the interest on the loan amount is funded by the manufacturer, Bajaj Finance capitalized on expanding this model of financing to other product categories. This enabled it to attract more customers as well as offer its existing customers a diverse product range. From TVs and white goods, it quickly moved into mobiles and other digital equipment, home furnishing and so on. For a good creditworthy customer, BFL thus created a platform where they could use their limit to spend on a variety of items using the interest-free financing model.

Successful initiatives became building blocks for a new round of experimentation and diversification. Bajaj Finance's product portfolio began to grow steadily, balancing size, risk and profit.

As leverage risk improves with quality of consumer creditworthiness, Bajaj Finance's model of offering interest-free loans enabled it to attract customers who sought to acquire aspiring products as the outgo is distributed over a period rather than upfront payment in other payment channels. These customers had other cards and better credit history which helped in having a customer base with low leverage.

The willingness to experiment, to continuously roll out new products and create innovative customer experiences is combined with the willingness to terminate. Unpopular offerings face quick deaths, ensuring no 'long tails'. This somewhat bold strategy succeeds on the back of analytics and business intelligence, operational excellence and risk controls.

'We already had a small to medium-sized enterprise (SME) strategic business unit (SBU). It just needed a bit of digital tweaking,' shares Jain, 'Bajaj Finance stepped neatly into an underserved segment growing consistently at a quicker pace than India's GDP. By 2020, Bajaj Finance had served over 3,60,000 SMEs in 1431 cities and towns, with both lender and borrower growing side by side.'

'We wish to dominate the consumer business where entry barriers are high,' Jain continues. 'In SME lending, we wish to consolidate, while in rural lending we want to accelerate growth. At present, we are nimble and can move with agility. On a sustainable basis, in a large market like India, there are always opportunities to grow if a win-win value proposition is created. We are the most profitable NBFC as per the published data, but we are not the largest. So, I think, the growth horizon for the next five, seven, ten, fifteen years remains very large. We have to make sure we deliver in a sustainable and low-risk manner. That's what really drives the business.'

The rural initiative started as a concept project in January 2012 and was launched eighteen months later in June 2013. The target for three years down the line was just 5 per cent of the book, but internally seen as an important business in the long term. 'We wanted to build Bajaj Finance as a truly national lending business,' recalls Sanjiv. 'We started EMI-based rural lending in thirty villages. On 1 June and in the first month itself, we sold high-end plasma TVs. Villagers get irregular hours of electricity, but their aspirations are no different from urban ones and business owners. Hence we need to deliver our best service to all customers to build a truly meaningful business.'

The Whistle-blower

In a business where money is the raw material, risk has many avatars. White-collar crime is one. In the summer of 2014, a whistle-blower emerged.

Consider for a minute what it takes for an employee to blow a whistle. All too often, whistle-blowers face considerable backlash and retaliation from peers, juniors and seniors in the organization, ranging from having significantly altered responsibilities to being bullied, fired or even quitting under duress. S/He also face the whistle-blower's quandary: will reporting a misdeed be an act of heroism or betrayal?

S/He stumbled on a misrepresentation in the mortgage department when some senior officials cut a deal to mask a loan default. Irregular transactions began to surface aimed at showing a borrower's account to be well-behaved even when EMI loan cheques bounced.

The practice to mask the default was simple. The staff who perpetrated the misrepresentation collected an EMI cheque from the customer a day or two before the end of a month to ensure the default did not surface on the thirtieth, when the company checks the level of delinquency in different businesses. As the cheque was dishonoured on the first or on the second of the following month, two cheques were collected from the customer and once again deposited towards the month-end. Thus, despite no fund flow taking place from the client's bank account to the company, the loan account showed as 'current' or standard on the thirtieth of both months. The misrepresentation continued for almost ten months. Two senior managers were asked to leave and three other employees resigned.

Two years earlier, in August 2012, Bajaj Finance, in line with the Bajaj Group companies, had introduced a whistle-blower policy. Guidelines of the policy, its processes and procedures were clear and online on the websites of all group companies. Top management and heads of the HR department had taken time and care to explain the policy to all employees. It worked.

Yet the reality is that whistle-blowing brings two moral values into conflict with each other. For example, doing what is fair (e.g., promoting an employee based on talent alone) often conflicts with showing loyalty (e.g., promoting a long-standing but unskilled employee). Human nature prioritizes one over the other. Gandhian thinking and culture help bridge the two values, obviating conflict by emphasizing the need for acts of both fairness and the greater good.

Of equal importance is the manner in which Bajaj Finance handled the situation. First, it ensured the privacy and protection of the whistle-blower's identity even as it briefed employees of the consequences of wrongdoing. In parallel, the leadership vacuum was immediately filled. The sensitive approach ensured nil disruption. As news of the incident spread, Bajaj Finance's share price barely blipped. It dipped a few basis points momentarily when the news hit headlines but recovered, ending slightly higher on the same day.

The Last Word

'Sanjiv always asks two questions about any fresh business proposal,' muses Rajeev Jain. 'Can it scale to become a billion-dollar business? And how will it be different from and superior to others in the same field? Once the broad goals are set, he gives the operating CEO a free hand.'

40

CII: 1979–2021

Bajaj and Tarun Das.

'Rahul became President of the CII in 1979,' penned Rupa, 'and he used that platform for stating the business case. The CII has been his enduring commitment.' During (former US) President Bill Clinton's March 2000 visit to India, Bajaj was CII President for a second time. The 'twice' broke hallowed CII convention. According to CII protocol, the presidentship is decided a year in advance.

'Vijay Kirloskar had to step down for personal reasons at the end of his term as Vice President,' wrote Tarun Das. 'CII was in a crisis and members turned to Rahul. As the debate raged, it became necessary to reach out to his "home" boss, Rupa, to get her consent. She was very supportive.'

'Few know this, but it was Rahul who gave us the name CII,' continues Das. 'By 1986, we had already changed our name to Confederation of Engineering Industry (CEI). The very next year he said we should become a pan-Indian industry body. It took us four years to overcome strong internal opposition to change our name in 1991. We started out as metal bashers, after all. We were also clear about two things: one, we would not take on the government; at least not publicly. Whatever was unpalatable, we would convey behind closed doors. Two, we will provide platforms for the government where we don't ask for anything.' This approach served CII well.

The organization was often tested under the Indira Gandhi administration, recalls M.V. Subbiah. 'In my year as president of AIEI, the times were difficult for the country and AIEI, thanks to our then Prime Minister Indira Gandhi. We were asked to call a meeting of industrialists by our then industries minister, Mr Narayan Dutt Tiwari. Also present was Mr Rajiv Gandhi, then an MP from UP, and also the chief minister of UP. Mr Tiwari started appealing to the Indian industrialists in chaste Hindi. And there I was sitting blankly, not knowing what to do.

'From the audience, in his inimitable and characteristic way, Rahul suddenly said that the president of AIEI and some of your industry friends have gone to sleep as they did not understand the language. This naturally broke the ice and there was thunderous laughter from all. At that point, Rajiv Gandhi asked for a parallel mic and started parallel translation and the meeting went on,' Subbiah ends.

'Rajiv Gandhi was perhaps not comfortable with FICCI and ASSOCHAM because they represented the old world of Indian business—Modis, Birlas, Shrirams and others,' reminisces Das. 'Less than a year after he became prime minister, Gandhi decided to take us with him on his first overseas state visit to Russia in May 1985. At the end of the tour, he introduced us to a sceptical Indian ambassador in Moscow (Saiyid Nurul Hasan) saying grandly,

"I want you to meet the people who will shape the future of India."
Our jaws dropped.'

'Rahul's contribution was constant,' admits Das, 'and he was
involved in *all* the internal debates and differences which emerged
when framing the policy, be it foreign investment, opening of the
economy, indirect and direct taxes, trade policy, etc. His lifetime
involvement included several occasions when his view was not
accepted in CII, but he always accepted the consensus.'

Below, five very different challenges reveal the bandwidth
required of CII leaders.

Three Banks and One Second-time President

At the fag end of the twentieth century, a Lok Sabha debate on
Wednesday, 22 December 1999:

> SHRI T.M. SELVAGANPATHI (SALEM): Sir, I would like to
> raise a very serious issue about the Task Force Committee set up by
> the Confederation of Indian Industry, the CII.
>
> Sir, the CII had recommended to the government closure of three
> nationalised banks, that is, the Indian Bank, the UCO Bank, and the
> United Bank of India. This report has created a panic and uncertainty
> among the general public, the borrowers from the banks and the
> depositors in particular. It is going to create an adverse impact on the
> people who have deposited money in these nationalised banks. This
> report is going to have a run on the nationalised banks in this spectrum.
>
> Sir, now, the cat is out of the bag. Fearing exposure in the hands
> of the Bank Employees' Union, the CII has come out with the
> withdrawal of the Report. There is something hidden in this episode.
> The Task Force consists of certain corporate sector industrialists,
> mainly, two members, Shri Rahul Bajaj and Shri Bharat Ram, both
> of them owe Rs 500 crore and Rs 350 crore, respectively to these
> nationalised banks. Fearing exposure, they have recommended
> liquidation of all the three nationalised banks.

Trade unions reacted immediately and purposefully. The main
reason for the huge losses of these banks was on account of corporate
loan defaulters, they emphasized. The corporate sector owed more

than Rs 500 billion to the banking sector and if these were made good, there would be no question of banks becoming sick. The All India Bank Employees Association threatened to release the list of companies that had defaulted on payments to state-owned banks, unless CII immediately withdrew its report. The unions and its lawmakers specifically called out CII president Rahul Bajaj and its vice-president Arun Bharat Ram among the defaulters.[1]

An anxious CII reacted by: 'keeping the sentiment of the banks, its employees and management in mind, we asked the government not to consider these recommendations,' Das told reporters.

Bajaj, in contrast, told the media that the chamber stood by its earlier recommendation to close down the banks. Denying being a bank loan defaulter, he declared his readiness for the disclosure of the list of corporate defaulters. 'It's unfortunate that the controversy is overshadowing the twenty-six other suggestions in the sixty-nine-page report,' added Bajaj.

The report, submitted to the finance minister on 13 December and released a couple of days later, was prepared by a task force headed by ICICI's K.V. Kamath. It included Bajaj, Jamshed J. Irani, Das and Omkar Goswami. Speaking to the media, Kamath pointed out that the closure of the three banks would cost an estimated Rs 9800 crore. 'Any further injection to these banks is akin to artificial respiration and will continue to soak up scarce payer funds from a fiscally constrained exchequer,' he warned. Indian Bank, UCO Bank and United Bank of India were systemically weak banks in spite of having received Rs 6740 crore of government funds.

Support for CII came from many sources, including the secretary of the All India Congress Committee (AICC), Jairam Ramesh. Speaking for himself, and not the AICC, Ramesh chipped in with, 'Let there be no illusions. Bank reforms will be resisted by the million-strong, white-collared employees. But at some stage, we have to bite the bullet. Core reforms are possible only when banks are converted into companies under the Companies Act and government equity is reduced to below 50 per cent. After insurance, this is the next battle waiting to be fought in the Parliament.'

[1] India Abroad, 'CII Proposal to close 3 banks sparks controversy', New York, December, see https://search.proquest.com/docview/362758770?acccountid=13042.

The JV Brigade

'It was in March 1996 that this issue hit the headlines through a debate on joint ventures that brought huge media coverage to the CII,' recollects Das. 'Joint ventures concluded in the early 1990s were falling apart and the CII Secretariat spoke of the "cowboy" approach of MNCs to joint ventures and the "short-termism" which was leading to break-ups.'

Javed Sayed of the *Economic Times* led with a strong front-page story that created a perception that CII was anti-foreign investment. The very next day, Ambassador Frank Wisner of the US came to the CII headquarters for a meeting with the secretariat leadership to clarify CII's position.

Later that evening, the Ambassador had a conference call with US companies in New York and Washington DC to address their concerns about the CII's position. 'He was key in calming their apprehensions that the CII had made a U-turn on foreign policy,' said Das. The CII clearly had not.

The idea was to caution both Indian and foreign companies to be careful in concluding joint ventures. Shotgun marriages clearly had not worked. MNCs were seeking Indian joint venture partners to rapidly access the Indian market. 'Indian companies were seeking new products and technology through the JVs. Neither was doing due diligence, hence divorces were the new development on the industrial scene,' described Das.

Says Das, 'The difference in approach came into CII discussions and there were strong differences in-house. "Ratan Tata vs Rahul Bajaj" was one situation faced in the Steering Committee. One seeking a slower pace of opening, the other advocating speedier opening. The CII kept a balance in pushing for steady deregulation but was sensitive to all points of view.'

The issue had resonance in India with its history of 200 years of colonial rule and the still remaining vestiges of insecurity, low self-confidence and some resentment against the 'East India Companies' of the 1990s. But there could be no question about the plus points of MNCs coming into India. They brought with them several pluses:

1. higher wage levels
2. customer care of a higher order
3. quality of products
4. technology levels
5. management capability
6. competitiveness and efficiency
7. research and development

Indian companies learnt from MNCs, adapted themselves and became competitive in India and globally. 'It was an essential process of learning and competing,' stresses Das. 'The restrictions on MNCs remained supposedly for "political" reasons but essentially because of the pressure on the government from Indian companies. This impacted banks, insurance, retail and other areas, but not engineering and manufacturing where customs duties were reduced and 100 per cent FDI was allowed.'

The Rahul Bajaj Report

It was an exciting thought—why not design a proper corporate governance code? Business life would be so much more peaceful without shades of grey. The only squiggle was that so many had the same thought.

Still, Bajaj was an early bird. 'The first corporate governance initiative in India came neither from the Securities and Exchange Board of India (SEBI) nor the Ministry of Corporate Affairs (MCA) nor shareholder activists, but from an industry association,' remarks Goswami, Bajaj's co-author. Bajaj gathered and chaired the twelve-member task force. Work began towards the end of 1996. Finance minister, P. Chidambaram, released 'Desirable Corporate Governance: A Code' aka The Rahul Bajaj Report in April 1998. 'The press lapped it up,' Bajaj grins. 'Some of the more progressive companies started to voluntarily adhere to the CII code.'

How could SEBI and MCA be left behind? Given below is a meagre sample of the more interesting report. In 1999, a SEBI committee under Kumar Mangalam Birla drafted a code of corporate governance remarkably similar to the CII's. The MCA produced the J.J. Irani report in 2005, the Naresh Chandra report in 2009, and the Companies Act, 2013. SEBI's turf saw Infosys's N.R. Narayana Murthy's 2003 report, and Uday Kotak's on 5 October 2017.

Snuggled inside the Uday Kotak report was a dynamite stick. It wanted to snip the position of chairman-cum-managing director.

'The roles and offices of Chairman and CEO should be separated, as far as possible, to promote balance of power,' mandated the regulator. 'Separation of the two posts may be regarded as good practice, as it can help to achieve an appropriate balance of power, increase accountability and improve the board's capacity for decision making. To prevent unfettered decision-making power with a single individual, there should be a clear demarcation of the roles and responsibilities of the Chairman of the Board and that of the Managing Director/Chief Executive Officer (CEO).'

'If we compare our key governance requirements, as well as our accounting and financial disclosure standards with those of listed companies in Britain, the US, Australia, France, Germany and other OECD (Organisation for Economic Co-operation and Development) nations, we are in the top decile,' says Bajaj.

'In the US, the chairman is often the CEO. There is little hard evidence to suggest that one works better than the other. I am completely against it for Indian conditions,' grumbled Bajaj to anyone and everyone willing to hear his case. 'Here is another insufficiently thought-out recommendation: for listed entities where public shareholding is at least 40 per cent of the voting stock (and for all listed companies from 1 April 2022), the chairperson must be a non-executive director.'

'Micromanaging didn't stop here,' quibbled Bajaj. The Kotak Committee recommended the topics to be discussed at the board such as strategy, succession planning, risk management, environment, sustainability and governance. 'Good boards discuss all of these subjects at length. Bad boards don't. But what purpose does this serve, other than to have companies make a meaningless disclosure in their annual reports that these have been indeed discussed?' he questioned.

Bajaj groused, 'Do our regulators inherently distrust the promoters and directors? If that were so, it would be a terrible bias. Moreover, do they believe crafting a "perfect" set of regulations that can invariably ensure that everything shall occur exactly in line with what is designed? That hasn't happened anywhere in the world.'

TVS Group's Venu Srinivasan jumped in. 'India's joint family system distinguishes it from European businesses—and Western concepts should not be imported blindly,' he pointed out. 'In the US too, power gets concentrated when the same person, with insignificant holding, becomes the chairman and CEO of a company. But in India and Asia, in general, families own significant holding in companies. They are committed to create wealth. You cannot import Western rules in an unrelated system.' The sprawling TVS family, at this time, had between 40–70 per cent shareholding across group companies.

The regulator set the pace. 'From 1 April 2020, the top 500 listed companies by market value will be required to separate the post of Chairperson, CEO and MD and ensure they are not related.'

'We don't want to return to the control and permit raj. We need corporate development, not an increasing burden of controls. The new law, while improving some areas of governance, also carried several draconian provisions and restrictions,' said Bajaj resignedly. 'In any event, it became the law of the land for Indian companies.'

The Godhra Situation

The 6 February 2003 CII session in Delhi for its members to interact with Narendra Modi, Gujarat's chief minister at the time, didn't go quite as Das had planned. On the stage with Narendra Modi were Jamshyd Godrej, Das, with Bajaj as Chair. 'The speakers chosen for the day were men who can't be controlled,' reported Surajeet Das Gupta, Sohini Das and Dev Chatterjee in *Business Standard*.

The backstory is that two pogroms took place—one anti-Hindu, the other anti-Muslim. The burning of a train in Godhra, a small town in Gujarat, on 27 February 2002, caused the deaths of fifty-eight *karsevaks* (Hindu pilgrims) returning from Ayodhya. Rioting broke out. According to official figures, the riots ended with 1044 dead, 223 missing, and 2500 injured. Of the dead, 790 were Muslim and 254 Hindu.

Wipro's Azim Premji and N.R. Narayana Murthy condemned the violence, Deepak Parekh pointed out that India's image as a secular country was damaged. But it would be Anu Aga of Thermax who asked, 'Why did Modi do so little to stop the rioters?' And received a standing ovation for her impassioned speech. Quietly,

Aga started keeping aside 1 per cent of the company's profits for the social sector. After the storm, Aga invested Rs 450 crore on a new plant at Vadodara, opening another door for workers of all faiths.

'When the genocide took place in Gujarat, I, as the chairperson of the CII western region, spoke out against it,' recalls Aga. 'Some people did not like what I said and within the CII, there were members who were against my very vocal stand. One day during that period, Rahul took me aside and said I should stop talking about this cause, and he assured me that he would write an article against what was happening. True to his word, he wrote a forceful and thought-provoking piece condemning the killings in Gujarat.'

Backtracking to the CII's 6 February 2003 meet in Delhi: if Godrej was relatively low-key, Bajaj was to the point. The year 2002 was a 'lost year' for Gujarat on the economic front. Bajaj said, 'Why don't we get investment in Kashmir, the North-east, or Uttar Pradesh and Bihar? It is not just the lack of infrastructure, but also the sense of insecurity. I hope this won't happen in Gujarat as this comes to mind because of the unfortunate events.'

Then, Bajaj turned to Narendra Modi directly: 'We would like to know what you believe in, what you stand for, because leadership is important. You are today the undisputed leader of your party and government in Gujarat, and we want to know you better . . . We are prepared to work with governments of all hues, but we also have our own views on what is good for our society and what works for it.'

Narendra Modi's turn came. 'I feel the CII has been unfair to Gujarat last year. In the last eight months, we attracted Rs 8000 crore of investment. So why are you asking me about law and order?' Narendra Modi asked. He added, 'There is no need to give Gujarat a bad name. You and your pseudo-secularist friends can come to Gujarat if you want an answer. Talk to our citizens. Gujarat is the most peaceful state in the country. I know there are people in this country with vested interests. But what is your interest? Gujarat is the only state which can produce a Gandhi but when required, it can also produce a Patel. I think you understand what I mean.'

No meeting can end without Bajaj having the last word. Wrapping up the meeting, Bajaj said, 'We may have our differences but that is what a democracy is all about. There is nothing personal in what Jamshyd or I said, nor were we passing a value judgement.

We were just expressing the apprehensions of our members. In any case, it is best not to rake up history, but better to look forward. Personally, I was very impressed by something you (Narendra Modi) said that one should not use one's authority without responsibility.'

Speaking to reporters after the meeting, his outburst was provoked, said Narendra Modi, by 'the *teekhi* language used by Rahul Bajaj and Jamshyd Godrej'.

Dissecting the event, the author of *Narendra Modi: The Man, The Times*, Nilanjan Mukhopadhyay, wrote, 'One route for (Narendra) Modi to improve his image was by wooing businessmen—practical people who don't carry ideological baggage.' As he points out, 'A poll showed that people were keen to move on. That's where he got his clue.' Supportive prominent businessmen—Gautam Adani, Karsan Patel and Anil Bakeri—launched the Resurgent Group of Gujarat.

The next CII meet was in Ahmedabad in April 2003 with Narendra Modi as chief guest. Godrej opened the floor by referring to Delhi meet on 6 February 2003, where sharp questions were put to the then Gujarat chief minister. Meetings should not be disrupted, pointed out Godrej, and he hoped that (Narendra Modi) would use his huge mandate to ensure the safety and security of all Gujaratis.

Das's Dilemma

Back at the CII office after the fracas, Das had a major situation to resolve ahead of him. 'We had about 200 worried members in Gujarat,' writes Das in *Crossing Frontiers*. In Delhi, CII saw its access to the BJP-led government curtailed, blunting CII's edge in its core business of lobbying.

'I didn't know anyone in the BJP,' Das continues. 'Hari Bhartia, then chairman of the CII's national committee on technology and innovation, facilitated the meeting with Jaitley. He was at home. A cricket match was on. We sat in his house watching Tendulkar and talked for two hours. Jaitley wanted to know everything: who I was, what CII was, who the office-bearers were, what was their thinking. At the end, he told me (Narendra) Modi was coming to Jaitley's home for dinner and he would talk it over.'

'Some days later, we spoke again and Jaitley told me that (Narendra) Modi wanted an apology,' Das continues. 'That was out of the question. Urgent meetings of CII presidents were held under the chairmanship of Ashok Soota, the then president of CII, to discuss and approve.'

A solution was worked out. 'I offered to draft a letter at the end of which we would say that CII regretted the misunderstanding. The letter was faxed to the CM. It was not an apology, but we were sure that the media would make out it to be one. And it did. This was followed by a visit to Gujarat, a "photo op" for the media to convey to the industry in Gujarat that the CII and the State government had settled the issue. Very importantly, each step had been agreed through prior consultation with the (then Gujarat) chief minister.

'The evening I was leaving to meet (Narendra) Modi, my wife accosted me. "You just can't do this . . . Among our close friends are Anu Aga, Azim Premji, Jamshyd Godrej and several from the Parsi and Muslim communities." My answer was that I had two options: I could quit and say I will not do this. Else, I had to look after our members.

The next year, Narendra Modi agreed to attend another CII function in Delhi. All went well till a glitch was discovered: the television channels were playing tapes of the previous year's acrimonious meeting. 'Modi was livid,' recalls the man who had to bear the full brunt of his verbal volley.

Rapprochement finally happened in October 2008. The Tata Motors factory to make the Nano at Singur in West Bengal barrelled into the Mamata Banerjee zone. An exasperated Ratan Tata declared he was prepared to relocate the factory. It was a prestigious project. Offers were received from the chief ministers of Uttarakhand, Maharashtra and Karnataka. '(Narendra) Modi won the race with Usain Bolt-like speed,' is how the *Business Standard* team describes the race.

The site chosen was Sanand, near Ahmedabad. Kevin and Jackie Freiberg, in their book *Nanovation*, say the memorandum of understanding for the factory was inked within ninety-six hours of Tata's announcement to quit Singur. A happy Tata remarked, 'Usually, a state takes ninety to 180 days for land and other clearances. Gujarat took just three days. It has never happened before.' He started to refer to Narendra Modi as the 'good M' and his Singur tormentor the 'bad M'.

Pragmatic as always, Narendra Modi's attitude was, 'Look, we can keep harking back to those days or we can move on. I choose not to get stuck in time.'

41

World Economic Forum: 1977–2021

Bajaj at the WEF meet in India.

'Rahul started attending the annual meeting of the World Economic Forum (WEF) at Davos from 1979, well before globalization became a buzzword,' wrote Rupa. 'In 2003 he became the first Indian to be a co-chair of the Annual Meeting.'

'I had recently become president of CII,' remembers a nostalgic Bajaj, 'and I was among the earliest to join the WEF from India. I was the first Indian member of the WEF's International Business Council, the first Indian to co-chair a Davos meeting and now I am honorary director of the foundation board, the first and its only honorary member. These things take time.

'India did not really figure in the calculations of most foreign companies in view of our policies and regulations. Even at the annual meetings at Davos in Switzerland, not many participants were interested in India. Since July 1991, however, the changing economic and industrial policies of the Government of India made foreign companies sit up and take a fresh look at India's potential as far as their business is concerned.

'One other factor which influences the decision of foreign companies is political stability. We, the Indian industrialists, are trying to convey to our foreign counterparts that these are two localized problem areas, and India is probably a safer place to live in than many other countries of the world.'

The Backstory

August 1984 saw Rajiv Gandhi, the then general-secretary of the ruling Congress party, visit Davos at the invitation of Klaus Schwab and the European Management Forum (EMF), the WEF predecessor.

Rajiv Gandhi's interest lay in learning about problems faced by overseas companies in doing business with India. His forty-five-minute address at the EMF on 'Social, Political and Economic Perspectives of India' portrayed India as a stable political entity, nearly 80 per cent of whose national income came from private enterprise. When the EMF mooted the idea of an India Economic Summit in Delhi, Rajiv Gandhi promptly agreed to request his mother to inaugurate it.

History had other intentions. With Indira Gandhi's assassination on 31 October 1984, the Congress Party chose Rajiv Gandhi as its leader, and in the general elections that followed, garnered 404 of the 514 seats. The new prime minister's immediate task was to restore order to a shocked and fractured nation and the world. The dust settled. The first EMF-CII India Economic Summit meeting would be held as scheduled, on 15–16 April 1985 in New Delhi, with Rajiv Gandhi delivering the inaugural address.

'Planning the first meeting was not an easy task for the EMF,' recalls Das. 'Uncertain of the ins and outs of India's complex functioning, it needed a partner to support them with the right skills for their international business members and help bring in a fair representation of the top business and political leaders from India.' For the first meeting, the four prominent chambers of commerce and industry in India partnered with the EMF, with the understanding that it could select one of these associations as its long-term India partner, depending on its initial experience. The smallest of these, AIEI (now CII), stood out.

'The first EMF India Meeting was well-attended by 200 or so companies from across the world,' continues Das. 'For Indian corporates who had little interaction with the outside world and faced many regulations in travelling abroad, this opportunity to discuss issues concerning India and get outside perspectives was unprecedented.' The event model was based on the Informal Gathering of World Economic Leaders (IGWEL).

The IGWEL

The IGWEL became a useful place to launch and test new ideas. To integrate business leaders into high-level discussions, a World Economic Brainstorming (WEB) session preceded each IGWEL. 'Many initiatives that were later officially undertaken by international organizations or governments were in fact "born" in Davos,' described FT's Jonathan Carr.

A large number of small tables are arranged. About a dozen participants can exchange ideas, concerns and suggestions informally with politicians, ministers and heads of international organizations. A rotation system, with three prominent people spending forty minutes at each table, ensure a useful variety of conversation partners. This new event style at Davos was presented with the motto: 'Don't miss the opportunity of speaking your mind!'

'Entrepreneurs were delighted to have the opportunity to talk economics with a prime minister, a finance minister or an industry minister,' pointed out Schwab. 'An interesting aspect of the WEB was that public figures put questions to business leaders, thus obtaining a first-hand, direct feedback on their policies and gathering suggestions of needed actions.'

Le Reconnaître

'Nelson Mandela attended the WEF in 1992,' says Bajaj. 'The South African anti-apartheid leader and head of the ANC had been released from prison two years earlier. He made a joint appearance—the first outside his country—with South African President F.W. de Klerk and Chief Minister of KwaZulu Mangosuthu Buthelezi.'

'India arrived in Davos at the same time, on 3 February 1992,' continues Bajaj, 'with Prime Minister P.V. Narasimha Rao's visit. Before that, India did not really figure in the calculations of most foreign companies, and whatever Indian participation there was, was limited to a few industrialists and ministers. That the Indian prime minister attended the annual meeting was a signal to foreign businessmen that the Indian government had changed its outlook and is progressively liberalising its policies and deregulating the economy. The prime minister's speech at the plenary session made it clear that the government wanted to welcome foreign technology, foreign investment, and favoured a step-by-step approach.'

'Rao came, saw, but didn't conquer,' reported *India Today*'s Aroon Purie, 'he merely left his calling card. It wasn't his fault. He came with the wrong generals and ill-equipped foot-soldiers. When hard-nosed businessmen asked, "What's the bottom line?", India had no carte blanche to announce. Rao, in the end, had to rely on a personal assurance: "I request you to believe a man with twenty-five years of experience in government and a half-century in public service, that India's reforms will not only be carried out but accelerated".'

After the plenary, the briefing session where a panel of experts or individuals open themselves for questions. Several briefing sessions are held simultaneously and are meant for delegates who want detailed answers. The turnout at the sessions indicated the degree of interest in the subject.

At Rao's briefing topic, 'India: Changing Course for Globalisation', attendance was excellent. 'But India blundered,' noted Purie, 'Rao should never have taken the briefing session as the questions predictably required detailed knowledge about the economy which Rao confessed he was not an expert.'

When asked about privatizing telecommunications, Rao burst out with: 'Don't ask me the nitty-gritty details. I have so many things on my mind. While I'm talking to you, my mind is in the South of India (Cauvery).' Not very inspirational for a foreign investor. It was followed by a question on rupee convertibility. Distinctly uncomfortable, he leafed through a folder and read out an answer related to the latest amendments to FERA. 'The Pakistani finance minister quietly chuckled and said, "he's reading the wrong answer".' The session went downhill till it ended twenty minutes early, unheard of at the WEF.

'Where was the great intellectual power India keeps boasting of?' queried Purie. 'This session should have been handled by Manmohan Singh or Commerce Minister P. Chidambaram, assisted by Montek Singh Ahluwalia or Ashok Desai. Especially after Rao set the stage so well in the plenary session. But there was nobody from these ministries.'

India Everywhere

There was no way that international delegates arriving at Zurich airport for the opening of the WEF conference on 26 January 2006 could miss the huge billboard and its message: 'The World's Fastest Growing Democracy', and its slogan, 'Fifteen Years, Six Governments, Five Prime Ministers, One Direction'.

A billboard is a billboard. What does it actually take to make a statement at Davos? Two years of planning, $6 million,[1] an elaborate marketing and PR campaign, with a bit of camaraderie within a powerful elite is the quick answer.

The 2006 WEF kicked off with India's Mukesh Ambani sharing the honours with Switzerland's Nestlé, Peter Brabeck-Letmathe; the UK's WPP, Sir Martin Sorrell; Spain's Banco Español de Crédito, Ana P. Botin; and Harvard University of the US, Lawrence H. Summers. 'The interest in India was huge,' recalls Bajaj.

'India played host to more than 600 business, political and civil society leaders from thirty countries at the WEF's twenty-second Economic Summit,' reported Mythili Bhusnurmath of the *Economic*

---

[1] A $4-million campaign was funded by contributions from twenty-two Indian companies. The Manmohan Singh administration chipped in with another $2 million via the India Brand Equity Foundation.

Times. Of this, 110 were Indian business leaders and government officials. They participated in more than 200 meetings and spoke in sixty sessions. The total Indian force was about 300, including print and broadcast media representatives, a dozen chefs, support staff, artisans and musicians. A far cry from the fifty delegates who participated in sixty meetings in 2005.

India's prime minister, Manmohan Singh, couldn't make it. Nor could Sonia Gandhi or the leader of the Opposition. The government initiative was led by Finance Minister P. Chidambaram, Commerce Minister Kamal Nath, and Deputy Chairman of the Indian Planning Commission Montek Singh Ahluwalia. Delhi Chief Minister Sheila Dikshit, Rajasthan Chief Minister Vasundhara Raje and Kerala Chief Minister Oommen Chandy brought state-level perceptions. 'We wanted to project India as the fastest-growing free market economy in the world,' said Nath. Thematically, business was 'Credible India'; in tourism, it was 'Incredible India'.

Attendance for 'The Big Debate' was strong, covering five issues: the emergence of China and India, changing economic landscape, new mindsets and changing attitudes, growing future jobs and regional identities and struggles. Within each of these themes were multiple subset questions. The audience was grouped around these themes on separate tables; and there was voting at the end on the key concerns of these segments.

'The voting outcome was revealing,' noted Kunwar Natwar Singh, economist and former Indian Foreign Service officer. 'On the emergence of India and China, the maximum concern was the sustainability of development and orderly integration of these economies in the global economy. On a changing economic landscape, the issues were of growing global and structural imbalances and business sensitivity to climate change. Two linked concerns were job creation and the global educational framework. Job creation was considered vital to create an educational system designed to respond to changing skill requirements. On regional identities, the rising economic disparities occupied centre-stage.'

The high point was the closing night: 650 delegates on the dance floor, swinging to Bollywood songs until early morning. 'Had we done these five years back, people would have laughed,' reminiscences Bajaj with a gleam in his eye. 'The entire flavour at Davos was about hearing India, tasting India, smelling India.'

The Great Reset

The fiftieth WEF annual meeting in Davos was held on 21–24 January 2020. COVID-19 arrived in Switzerland on 25 February 2020.

'A better economy is possible. But we need to reimagine capitalism to do it,' Schwab told *Time* magazine. 'Like most people, I was constrained to observing the situation from inside my home and the WEF's empty offices, and I relied on video calls to know how others were doing. The pandemic represents a rare but narrow window of opportunity to reflect, reimagine, and reset our world.'

'We received a letter of support from Prime Minister Narendra Modi, about the principles of global equitable access to COVID-19 vaccines, and this was very important,' shared Schwab with *Business Today*. 'This new mechanism could take the form of a large multi-country contract manufacturing network to be built, with the goal of increasing the global manufacturing volumes to an additional capacity in line with the enormous global demand. India should be the essential hub of this network.'

To reset the future, Schwab's mind map had four building blocks: change our mindset—if we made it up once, we can make it up again; create new metrics—measuring what matters will change everything; design new incentives—you get what you pay for; and last, build genuine connections—distance is the danger. 'Though clear and down-to-earth, the WEF recovery plan was interpreted as sinister,' wrote Naomi Klein, 'first by fringe conspiracy theory groups on social media, and then by prominent conservative commentators—prompting tens of thousands of interactions across Facebook and Twitter.'

The Last Word But One

'Rahul, we love holding your hand in Davos on the snow and ice to make sure you do NOT fall and break your leg. BUT isn't it time you bought a really good pair (expensive!) of non-skid shoes?' reminded art historian, environmentalist and writer Pheroza Godrej.

The Very Last Word

What are the perks of being a regular at Davos for almost four decades? Alpha status in Davos for a billionaire means AA car access. According to a *Bloomberg* report, Bajaj enjoys a car pass that allows entry into private entrances to which only heads of states and leaders of the world's biggest corporations are entitled.

The 25th anniversary of WEF's partnership with India:

'The World Economic Forum and the Confederation of Indian Industry (CII) have had a very long and productive relationship. At twenty-five, it is a relationship that is both youthful and mature. I have had the privilege and pleasure to see this relationship blossom from its inception.

The Annual Meetings at Davos and the India Economic Summits have been India's window to the world. Much of what is now the establishment view in India was, and is often, uttered with vigour at the World Economic Forum Annual Meetings in Davos and especially at the India Economic Summits, organized annually by the Forum and the CII in New Delhi. A lot of the thought leadership for the Indian government and also for Indian industry has come from the fertilization of ideas at the India Economic Summit.

I believe that the patient and untiring work that has been done at the India Economic Summit over the last quarter century is now paying dividends. India is no longer a country with a future potential, but one of *the* countries. There is now an unstoppable momentum taking the country forward.

The focus of the Indian Economic Summit has always been the future. So, its content and format have constantly evolved to deal with a changing economy and society. Both, Davos and the India Economic Summit, have been and will remain permanent fixtures in my calendar.

Incidentally, I may add that my association with the Annual Meeting in Davos started in 1979 and has continued uninterrupted ever since. Klaus Schwab presented me with a World Economic Forum award in 2008.'

—*Rahul Bajaj*

42

The Iconoclast: 1977–2021

Sanjiv, Nanoo Pamnani, Amit Shah and Rajeev Jain on 30 November 2019.

It is a beautiful moment and Bajaj savours it to the full. Giving him company in the front row, sitting on his right is old friend, Adi Godrej, and on his left, Shefali Bajaj. In front of him, on the stage, are Sanjiv, Pamnani and Rajeev Jain. With a beaming smile, Amit Shah confers on the trio one of the biggest honours of corporate India: the *Economic Times* 'Company of the Year' award.[1] The audience, from Mukesh Ambani, Sunil Bharti Mittal and Kumar Mangalam Birla to the Bajaj Finserv team propping up the wall, bursts into applause.

The open house Q & A follows. On stage, chairs are swiftly brought in for Piyush Goyal, Nirmala Sitharaman and Amit Shah. 'Someone came up to me,' recalls Bajaj. 'I was in the front row only because of Sanjiv and Nanoo. "Sir, Bodhisatva Ganguli[2] is asking if you would like to ask a question." I shook my head, indicating a "no". But he kept requesting me. From the stage, Piyush spoke directly to me. "*Rahul bhai, kuch toh boliye!*".[3] I couldn't now not speak.'

A mic is handed to him. Bajaj stands up. He is a tall man. Everyone can see him. Within seconds, expectations ripple. Bajaj switches frequently between English and Hindi in order to make himself intelligible to the larger audience. He does his best to soften his voice, words and body language, for his messages will be bitter. He has crossed the age of eighty, officially retired, and with no Rupa to restrain him.

To reduce the temperature—or rather, to give notice on what is about to come, Bajaj prefaces his remarks by wryly noting that he was born 'anti-establishment' and his concerns as 'minor things'.

Bajaj raises three apprehensions: the ability of the Narendra Modi government to accept criticism, its lack of action against mob lynching; and the glorification of Nathuram Godse, Mahatma Gandhi's assassin, by the BJP MP Sadhvi Pragya Singh Thakur.

'Nobody from our industrialist friends will speak, (so) I will say openly,' begins Bajaj, 'an environment will have to be created. When the United Progressive Alliance-II was in power, we could criticize anyone. You are doing good work, but despite that we don't have

---

[1] Jury members: Anu Aga, Bhavish Aggarwal, Cyril Shroff, Kalpana Moraparia, Nandan Nilekani, Pawan Munjal, Sadhguru, Sunil Mittal, Uday Shankar.
[2] Editor and journalist
[3] 'Please do say something'.

the confidence that you will appreciate if we criticize you openly. Intolerance is in the air. We don't see any convictions . . .'

Referring to Thakur, Bajaj adds, 'Today anybody can be called a patriot. You know the man who shot Gandhi ji, or is there any doubt about that, I don't know. No one knew her (Thakur). You gave her the ticket, she won. That's all right. She won because of your support. Then you brought her into the consultative committee. The prime minister had said that it would be difficult, still you brought her into the consultative committee. (Yet) for this session, this small session, she doesn't have permission to attend. This is one example.'

In full control of the live situation facing him, Shah responds in Hindi.[4] 'Several media organizations regularly criticize (Narendra) Modi and the current government, even then, if you say that there is a certain kind of atmosphere, we will have to make efforts to improve the atmosphere. But I would like to say that there is no need for anybody to fear. No one wants to scare, and we have done nothing to be concerned about any criticism. The government is run in the most transparent way, and we have no fear of any opposition, and if anyone does criticize, we will look at the merit of the same and make efforts to improve ourselves.'

On incidents of lynching, Shah adds:[5] 'Lynchings happened earlier too, probably more than now . . . But it is not correct that there have been no convictions. Several cases of lynching have been concluded and there have been punishments, but the media does not

---

[4] Amit Shah (in Hindi): '*Magar phir bhi aap jo keh rahe hain ki ek atmosphere banaa hai, hamein bhi atmosphere ko sudhaarne ka prayaas karna padega . . . but main itna zaroor kehna chaahta hoon ki kissi ko darne ki koi zaroorat nahi hai . . . Na koi daraana chaahta hai . . . Na kuchh aisa karaa hai jiske khilaaf koi bole to sarkar ko chinta hai . . . Most transparent way mein ye government chali hai, aur hamein kissi bhi prakaar ke virodh ka koi dar nahin hai, aur koi (virodh) karega bhi to uske merits dekh kar hum apne aap ko improve karne ka prayaas karenge.*'

[5] *Amit Shah:* '*Lynching pehle bhi hota tha, aaj bhi hota hai—shaayad aaj pehle se kam hi hota hai . . . Par ye bhi theek nahin hai ki kissi ka conviction nahin hua hai. Lynching waale bahut saare cases chale our samaapt bhi ho gaye, sazaa bhi hui hai, par media mein chhapte nahin hain . . . Vineet ji yahaan par hain, agar dhoondh ke chaapenge to hamare liye thoda achchha hoga.*'

publish them. Vineetji[6] is here, if he looks for them and publishes them, it will be good for us.'

On Thakur, the home minister stresses that neither the BJP nor the Centre support any of her statements on Godse and that they condemn them. Adds Shah quickly, that there may have been some confusion over whether the Bhopal legislator had meant Godse or the revolutionary, Udham Singh.

Frank and Fair

'To be fair to Piramal Group chairman Ajay Piramal,' said Bajaj, 'it was he who first mustered up the courage to tell the government in September that all was not well in the relationship between industry and the ruling dispensation. And that mistrust between government and businesses was growing due to frequent raids, searches and lookout notices by various agencies on corporates. Today, I see there is a gap. There is mistrust between the people who are in power and the people who are wealth-creators.

'For once, it was the "silent Prime Minister" Manmohan Singh, now a vocal opposition member—who did the talking on behalf of those who blamed him for "policy paralysis" and criticized him while he was at the helm for being weak, indecisive and silent,' adds Bajaj.

Writing in *The Hindu* on 18 November 2019, Dr Singh commented on 'the palpable climate of fear in our society today'. 'Many industrialists tell me that they live in fear of harassment by government authorities,' the former prime minister pointed out. 'Bankers are reluctant to make new loans for fear of retribution. Entrepreneurs are hesitant to put up fresh projects for fear of failure attributed to ulterior motives. Technology start-ups, an important new engine of economic growth and livelihoods, seem to live under a shadow of constant surveillance and deep suspicion.' But who was listening?

---

[6] The managing director of Bennett, Coleman & Co. Ltd.

43

The Fourth Karta: 1994–2021

En famille.

'We have a legacy that can very easily be broken, but one that's very difficult to rebuild,' mused Bajaj. And, as is the Indian way, respect flowed from being the oldest of his generation in a very traditional family. 'In time this ripened into respect for a very competent businessman and a senior member of the family who went out of his way to ensure that the family stayed together through thick and thin,' noted Sumantra Ghosal.

'We five brothers[1] grew up together as a very close-knit joint family,' agrees Niraj, 'and we considered ourselves lucky to be part of this legacy.' The turn of the century, however, would become a pivotal moment for the clan. Kushagra, Shishir's eldest son, returned to India in 2000 after graduating from Carnegie Mellon University's Tepper School of Business.

'Kushagra wanted a position in the group similar to his eldest cousin Rajiv, who was so much older and so much more experienced with proven performance,' recalls Niraj. 'Kushagra claimed this as his birthright. For Rahul bhai, merit and the interest of the company and its shareholders are primary over the desires of family members. Kushagra also felt that we were, as a group, maybe too conservative, too ethical and not dynamic enough. He was possibly over ambitious by our standards and wanted growth at any cost. We were totally shocked when Kushagra, supported by his parents, wanted a separation. All of us, especially Rahul bhai, tried very hard to change their minds, but to no avail.'

'Once it was clear that there was no option but separation from Shishir,' continues Niraj, 'we started talking of an amicable parting. Put simply, their group would get control of two companies managed by them (Bajaj Hindusthan Sugar and Bajaj Sevashram). This would be done by transferring shares to each other and the difference would be given by us to them by cheque. Seems simple but in actual practice this required hundreds of transactions.

'We were shocked when in 2003 they suddenly filed a 1000-page case against us in the Company Law Board. We thought cordial talks were on to find an amicable answer. We could not imagine that Shishir, our brother, would file a court case against us. Painfully for both sides, this went for over five years. We finally settled. They withdrew the Company Law Board case in 2008, once, we believe, it was clear to all that the decision was going absolutely in our favour.

---

[1] Kamalnayan's sons: Rahul and Shishir. Ramkrishna's sons: Shekhar, Madhur and Niraj.

Stakes on both sides were very high. Possibly they took the services
of about ten leading lawyers and counsels in the country. We also
had about the same number advising us at different times during this
five-year period.

'In the separation of an approximately eighty-year-old business
group, each side wanted to study every word of the approximately
thirty-two agreements,' Niraj continues. 'It was very complicated.
I represented the four brothers under Rahul bhai's guidance. From
our point of view, we came to a settlement many times. However,
during that period, shares of companies managed by us under Rahul
bhai's leadership, kept appreciating. Their side kept wanting more
and more, and kept renegotiating.'

'Shekhar, Madhur and I thought this was just not fair, but
Rahul bhai is always soft and ready to give more to settle amicably.
Ultimately, it was, I believe, Rahul bhai's big heartedness that led to
the settlement. We four brothers had significant promoter majority
to control every company, but we never took advantage of this fact.
It was possibly the most stressful five years of my life, exhausting and
emotionally draining. I am sure it was a difficult time for Shishir and
his family too. They may have their own point of view. However,
what had they gained from this painful separation? After twelve
years of separation, what are the results today? If we had continued
being together, they could have been one of the promoters of the
third largest family business house in the country today,' asks Niraj.

Aryaman's Nana

The first thing that comes to my mind when I think about Rahul
Nana is his wit. He is sharp as a tack and always hits you with a
playful comment or a well-thought-out argument whenever you try
and refute him. He never fails to provide deep insights into almost
any topic you talk to him about. But these are things everyone knows.

Nana has a keen sense of humour. He will never let an opportunity
to poke fun at you pass by. He brightens the mood wherever he goes.
But these are things everyone knows.

Nana will always speak his mind. He never holds back and
doesn't know his limits, something that I'm sure has dismayed many

people in the past. I think it's one of his finest qualities. But these are things everyone knows.

You might wonder, then, what are these mysterious qualities that not everyone knows? It's his intense love for family that no one talks about. He is just as devoted to us as he was to his career. I spent a week in Pune with him while interning at Bajaj Auto in 2019. It was then that I discovered the softer side of Mr Rahul Bajaj.

We spent every evening together and enjoyed watching Jason Bourne movies. We ate chola-bhatura and pizza for dinner. We spent hours talking about his childhood and his journey through Cathedral, the school I currently study at.

Nana is truly a unique individual. I know he is always there for me whether I need counselling or consoling. I could never hope for a better grandfather.

Deepa's Light and Shade

After a somewhat tumultuous courtship lasting seven years, Rajiv and I finally married in December 1994! Often during those roller-coaster years my parents and I were told that 'Rahul Bajaj would never let his son choose Deepa'.

Nothing could be further from the truth. Papa is never intrusive, always supportive. He is as understanding and objective an in-law as a father can be. And he always gave my parents the feeling that this was an equal relationship in every sense.

That's not to say that my initial days of marriage were all honey and roses. I was brought up in a nuclear family with no idea of the complexities that a joint family entailed. I was completely unprepared for the adjustment that it called for. In large measure, Papa's patient demeanour and liberal attitude helped me to eventually settle in.

Papa naturally has a larger-than-life persona and I was very intimidated by him in the early days. However, I soon realized that he is the most approachable and open-minded person in the family. Perhaps he got it from his mother whom I quite adored for being amazingly so. As I saw the softer side of him post the birth of my son Rishab in 1998, I grew a little bolder. I was able to go to him unhesitatingly with my concerns and his advice was always unfailingly available to me.

While Papa is very forthcoming with his views—and he has an opinion on everything!—he never imposes them, at least not on me. He is staunchly vegetarian but never once asked me to be so. He isn't especially fond of dogs but is accepting of our desire to have them all over the house. This, I feel, is his greatest human quality.

I feel that today after twenty-six years as part of the Bajaj family, if I'm a better version of myself, then significant credit for that goes to him. I feel blessed to have lived a life of plenty, shielded as much as is possible from all that is inimical, by the shade that he provides us all.

Kiran's Test of Time

'I was eighteen years old and fortunate to get a grand tour of the Bajaj Auto factory, Pune, riding pillion with the chief himself! As we zipped in and around the premises on a Bajaj scooter, I got a glimpse of who he really was,' remembers Kiran. 'He knew each and every nook and cranny, every aspect of the operation; he even knew the names of his factory workers. In spite of being a busy man, he had the time and patience to explain the business to me, a mere novice and new addition to his family. Success came not from spending time in swanky offices and sporting top-end brands: he was on the factory floor at the crack of dawn, late until evening. He visited his office and talked to his staff. He was in the centre of all the action. You could say he lived and breathed his work.

'Rahul bhaiya is transparent, gifted with foresight, and the cherry on top is his ability to connect with all his people. He has an analytical mind and always looks at a situation or problem in great detail from every angle before coming to any conclusions. As a result, his decisions are well balanced and rational. Some of our family members owe much to him for helping them out in difficult situations with his impartial and logical thought process.

'Coming from a very different work culture in Calcutta, I was impressed and influenced by his approach. When I got an opportunity to run Hind Musafir Travel Agency, I tried to emulate him and so, inadvertently, he became my first management guru and my mentor. Rahul bhaiya taught me by example to never to be afraid to speak the truth. "If you are right, you can be bold"!

'At home, he is always very disciplined. There is no room for negotiation. He follows the same rules he set for his children when they were young. He still lives an uncomplicated life. He doesn't believe in buying extravagant gifts nor does he expect anything from others.

'At work, he makes sure his managers refrain from accepting favours that would compromise their integrity. Yes, he is strict from the beginning, but his stringent methods helped build his reputation as a truthful, courageous, and fair leader.

'Some have commented on his apparent tightfistedness, his inclination to play safe rather than take huge risks. Some also say his style is more managerial than entrepreneurial. Well, to them I can say— Rahul Bajaj has stood the test of time. He has the fortunate combination of his mother Savitri Bajaj's discipline and father Kamalnayan Bajaj's patriotic principles and business acumen. Even today, he stands tall on this very robust foundation and guides us all. Once I asked him what his favourite pastime was. His response? My work is my hobby!'

Kriti's Tauji

The first thing I think of when it comes to Rahul Tauji, is amazement. I am constantly amazed by his intellect, his attention to detail, his obsession with the truth, his many business achievements, and alongside that, such a deep affection for his family and zest for life with his endless arsenal of witty comments for any situation.

Even though I am his youngest niece, he will make sure to ask me hundreds of questions about my life. And then somehow remember all my answers! I have no clue how he has the time or the brain space to make me feel so important. If I am in Pune, he is never too busy to sit with me and chat, making sure I am taken care of properly to the point where he will even know exactly what I have eaten for every single meal while I am in his home.

At the same time, he will always challenge me. He insists on being true to oneself, when it comes to himself, or anyone else. If I try to deny something about myself, or make excuses, he will always catch it. He will insist that I face reality. And while the truth is often harsh to accept in the moment, I have always found myself making an effort to grow and improve after every one of these conversations with him. He always strives to help people around him to be the best that they can be. And I often find myself looking back on these more difficult interactions with gratitude.

Tauji is also first in line to congratulate me on any milestone or achievement, no matter how small. He even flew all the way to California for my college graduation! He shows as much pride and joy towards me as he does for any of his own children. And takes the time to make me truly feel like a part of his family.

Ultimately, he is someone who I have no choice but to admire and respect, not because he has asked me to, but because he has earned every bit of it.

Madhur, Kumud and Waluj

'The year 1985 was a big milestone,' shares Kumud, 'when the then biggest Bajaj Auto plant came up in Waluj (Aurangabad), and Madhur was given the responsibility of looking after it. We had just shifted to Aurangabad, and within a couple of months the inauguration function of the Waluj factory was announced. Many important dignitaries, including the President of India, business associates, friends and families were to attend. Since Madhur had a lot of work to do, he gave me the responsibility of beautifying the entire stretch from the entrance to the venue. I took up the challenge, though Rahul bhaiya was not in favour of leaving this big responsibility on a lady (in this case, me).

'I decided to do the whole place in another way. Instead of the huge pandal which was being suggested, I thought it would be preferable to do the main function in one of the big industrial sheds, much against the preference of some of the key people. The materials I chose included scooter scrap, fabric flags, potted plants and our own marigold to add colour. This was also in tune with Rahul bhaiya's thinking of using the local materials as far as possible.

'We managed to make the entire place look very festive and colourful: unlike a wedding yet apt for an industrial opening. The experience of hard work and out-of-the-box thinking paid rich dividends and every rupee spent was totally "Value for Money", Bajaj Auto's motto. The entire place looked ethereal and was much appreciated.

'After the function, an overjoyed Rahul bhaiya gave me a big hug and a bigger "thank you". This was a huge reward for me. More importantly, this gave him the confidence that women can shoulder higher responsibilities if given the opportunity. From then onwards, he entrusted the other ladies in the family and me with a host of responsibilities with positive results. In the last few years, in fact, he encouraged us to take up more and more challenges. It just goes to show how open-minded he is to change and to acknowledge our work.'

'Being in an industrial belt, the Waluj plant developed well,' shares Madhur. 'However, being a backword, sleepy and inactive town, people from Pune and other cities were reluctant to settle down in the extremely poor social infrastructure that existed. While we were able to attract local labour and junior level staff, it was difficult to attract executives at senior levels, even from Bajaj Auto's Pune plant.

'Together with my friends and relatives, we decided to develop a good social environment that included a good hospital (Kamalnayan Bajaj Hospital), a good school (Nath Valley School) and good cultural events like music, dance and plays. We also showcased Aurangabad with a "Maha Expo". All this had the intended effect of attracting crucially needed talent at senior levels not only at our Waluj plant, but also our ancillaries and units set up by other industrialists and entrepreneurs.'

'Building the social infrastructure, negotiating pay rise with the Shiv Sena union, were no easy tasks,' continues Madhur, 'as negotiations that took place every three and a half years went on for five to six months, which was quite stressful to say the least. But the evenings were spent with friends and relatives playing croquet in the vast lawns of our bungalow or introducing many first-time activities (for Aurangabad) like husbands cooking for their wives and children, treasure hunt via cars, etc. All this combined, I dare say, transformed a drowsy town to an alive and kicking city. Kumud and I were in Aurangabad from 1985–1994. Indeed, these were the best years of my working life.'

Manish, the Son-in-law

We had the fortune of taking so many holidays together—whether it was a cruise in Scandinavia, numerous trips to Davos, Austria, New

York, Goa and even Ireland. Papa's love for Italian food and his ability to organize the entire day around various meals is legendary. I still remember when Sanjiv and I were scolded and made to sit at the edge of the table when we ordered lamb shanks during a visit to a winery in Tuscany. He would meet my friends in New York when we were on vacation and had the ability to impress and be liked by each and every individual. His ability to live it up and dance till the wee hours of the morning in Davos but still get up in time for the 9 a.m. meeting is difficult to forget.

I still remember when Papa asked me to be the emcee for both his fiftieth anniversary in Pune and his seventieth birthday at the Taj in Mumbai. In both cases, the number of his friends who came up to share stories of Papa were amazing—strong bonds of friendship and memories. Whether he was a small dealer from rural India or the finance minister of India, Papa never differentiated between them—his warmth and ability to engage remained consistent and he interacted with each of his guests. He is also a great sport—when we poked him or teased him a bit while interviewing him, he took it in great spirit and would give it 'back to us'.

Having served on various boards of the group, it is very clear to see the value-add that Papa provided. He would always raise the one issue no one had thought of. Even when there were many 'functional experts' in the room, Papa's ability to 'rise above it all and provide a bird's-eye view' while not missing any detail at all is what we all remember. I recall two–three specific examples where he displayed this:

o   Chakan Plant: I recall many discussions and arguments at home on whether a new plant should be set up in Chakan instead of further increasing capacity in the existing plants at Akurdi and Aurangabad. The brilliance in Papa's approach was his ability to violently disagree if he wasn't comfortable with a certain approach but then have the humility and wisdom of trusting the decisions made by others in his team. The transition at both Bajaj Auto and at Bajaj Finserv were probably the smoothest generational transitions that I have witnessed in any family-owned or professional company.

o Demerger of Bajaj Auto to create Bajaj Holding, the new
    Bajaj Auto and Bajaj Finserv: I recall numerous discussions
    with Papa to really push him on segregating the finance
    business from the two-wheeler business during the 2007–08
    time period. While initially he was hesitant, he soon saw the
    logic/implications and took full ownership and allowed us to
    form a core working group to 'make it happen'.

o I really appreciate all Papa did to support the 'birth' of
    Kedaara Capital. For the first few years, he willingly
    attended our AGMs in places like Hyderabad and Udaipur.
    Our investors loved their interactions with this 'doyen' of
    Indian industry and to get his varied perspectives on the
    political and economic climate in India—he was such a sport
    and so willing to attend these events even when there was
    no need to.

Equally at home in Bombay or Delhi: Papa is always at home
whether discussing stuff about the grandkids or the next five-year
plan for one of the companies in Mumbai as he was challenging a
new government initiative or law in Delhi. I recall helping him file his
papers for his Rajya Sabha seat—the years that he spent there were
some of the most exciting for him. He thoroughly enjoyed his time
at the Upper House, forming close links with many of the ministers
and lawmakers in Lutyens' Delhi. His interactions are always based
on intellectual equality and he never asked for a favour from any
of the 'powers that be'. I still remember how affectionately Jaitley
hugged him at a dinner in Delhi and how Pranab Mukherjee would
not let go of his hand when they were sitting together and discussing
a few things before an awards function. I still recall how he stood up
to and asked (the Home Minister) Amit Shah some very challenging
and uncomfortable questions at the ET Awards function—when no
one else in the audience had the guts to do the same.

All in all, our Papa is a truly special individual—and truly one in a
million! Those of us who have had an opportunity to interact closely
with him will remember those moments very fondly in the years
ahead (despite surviving and showing some scars from those very
same interactions). He is a proud Indian but a humble individual, a

very successful businessman but with a very human heart, someone who will argue his perspective till the sun sets but is flexible enough to recognize the wisdom in the views of others . . .

Minal's Look-see

'My first meeting with Rahul bhaiya was a memorable one,' recalls Minal. I had met all the other members of the Bajaj family except him before saying "yes" to Niraj for marriage. He had undergone a throat surgery. I went to the hospital to meet him. What amazed me was the simplicity. No one, nor did he, expect me to be dressed in formal clothes. I was in my daily, normal outfit. His smile as soon as he saw me made me feel so comfortable. As they later said that I was lucky he wasn't allowed to speak else he would have grilled me there and then!

'Rahul bhaiya has an uncanny ability to correct drafts, letters, etc. I had begun looking after the Jamnalal Bajaj Foundation. I must have sent him hundreds of letters after perfecting them from my point of view. Yet in every one of them he would find some corrections, including commas, etc. It has been a great learning for me to look into the minutest of details. In any discussion, I thought I was fully prepared, but his sharp mind would ask something which would make me wonder why I didn't think of it.

'His curiosity amazes me. Not only concerning us but my family also. He wants to know every detail about everything, whether it is about a celebration or health related. His concern is rare to find. This is his way of showing his love for us. I have found it even with some of our employees. He will spend an hour talking to them if they are unwell to see if every aspect has been considered and will go the extent of even talking to the doctor. This makes them loyal for life.

'His zest for life, simplicity, ethics and transparency have been a huge inspiration for me. In my initial years, I was scared of him but my first holiday with him changed that. Niraj and I have had the good fortune of going on many holidays with Rahul bhaiya. He is a totally different person on these trips, full of fun and laughter. He would be involved from day one of the planning with tremendous enthusiasm and with a keen eye for detail. His simplicity is such that he would find as much joy in sitting in a roadside cafe as fine dining.

When we travel with our children, the focus is on sightseeing and shows. Eating is secondary. With him, lunches and dinners would be planned first and all other events around it. His energy was unbelievable during the WEF in Davos.'

Naresh Jain's 'Dear Friend'

My earliest memories of Rahul really begin with my engagement to Suman. Whenever he visited Delhi, we always spent an evening together. Since then, he is more of a dear friend than a brother-in-law. We spent many holidays together in India and abroad, and I have special memories of my holiday at Kodaikanal in 1974 with both our families.

Straightforward, very affectionate and very supportive, Rahul has a very good sense of fairness. His giving a business opportunity to my two sons can never be forgotten by me. I wish Rahul all the very best in health and happiness.

Nimisha's Tauji

When I think of Bada Papa, I can only think of this larger-than-life personality who has carried this whole family together, who has never been afraid to speak his mind, who has given priority to fairness over favouritism, and who has always stood for what he believed was right no matter the consequences.

As a child, I remember feeling a bit daunted by him. I didn't spend much time with him then, but whenever I did see him, he had a very commanding personality with his height and strong voice and the only person who could overrule him was Badi Ma. But I also admired him immensely—I remember thinking that since we share our birthday, some of our habits are the same, including our taste in food. Maybe some of the other stuff will rub off on me too.

Over the years we have spent much more time together, whether it is the multiple holiday cruises taken together or living in NCPA Apartments whenever he came to Mumbai. I got to better know the fun-loving person who loved life and made the most of it. Of course, he still kept us on our toes with his eye for detail. If he decided to quiz you on a topic (which you were supposedly proficient at), you better have known all facts and figures because he would catch you on your smallest mistake.

Even after forty years I get amazed by his words and his actions. He recently resigned as the chairman of Bajaj Holding and Bajaj Auto, the companies he built, and made sure that the succession line is clear, and everything is sorted in his lifetime. While he doesn't need a particular post to command, the respect and status he has earned, it's not easy to let go of your baby and the fruits of your labour that you have spent a lifetime building. It takes a very secure, a very fair and a very forward-thinking man to do that.

I do wish to learn a lot from him and look forward to many more moments to share together.

Nirav's Tauji

When I think of Rahul Tauji, I can think of only one thing . . . learning.

Spending time with Tauji during Diwali, on holidays, family gatherings and dinners, I've gotten a chance to learn how to be disciplined, focused, determined, respectful, detail-oriented, uphold integrity, be hard-working yet be family oriented without forgetting to enjoy life a little.

I remember being inspired to be like him when I saw how detail-oriented he was when it came to Badi Ma's health. I was amazed as to how he could understand a subject completely outside his wheelhouse, just to ensure Badi Ma was getting the best medical care.

I remember his multiple lessons on being disciplined, punctual and respectful without compromise. Initially I used to think he probably doesn't live by these principles but as I spent more time with him, I realized, on the contrary, that he never wavers from these principles.

I remember times where he taught me to not back down just to conform to a herd mentality. It is okay to go against the grain as long as it is logical and with good intentions. His actions, be it on a public platform or private, are a testament to always doing the right thing despite heavy opposition.

Tauji is a workaholic, yet I remember so many times when he put family above anything else. I believe that working for the unity of the family and the business drove him. I remember a conversation with him post my MBA where we spoke about my career. He has always pushed me to work hard, but that conversation was different. I felt, for the first time, that he had confidence and belief in me (in a professional sense) and that sparked a fire within me.

Despite all these serious aspects of Rahul Tauji, I've always admired his ability to enjoy life, let loose and make everybody laugh. There is never a dull moment around him.

These are just a few of the countless memories I have with him. But as we all have experienced with Rahul Tauji, no matter whether it is one story or a million, each one leaves an impression.

Rishab's Dada

Growing up, I was always told you are not a true Bajaj if you don't think about food 24/7 and have the prominent 'Bajaj nose'. Fortunately I was spared the latter, though my belly is evidence that I couldn't escape the former! It wasn't long before I learnt why Dada was truly 'the head of the family'.

Growing up in Akurdi might be boring for some kids, but not when you had grandparents like I did. One of my fondest childhood memories is sitting with Dadi in her room and jumping off the bedposts and landing on her bed. Each time I did this, her heart would stop as the last strand of my hair kissed the ceiling, but when Dada would be there, he would smile at me and encourage me. He takes far greater risks every day, and lives for them. This was evident most clearly in how he took charge of Bajaj Auto when all of thirty-two and overcame all the hurdles that appeared before him to build it into the world's biggest scooter company.

The phrase 'strong and silent type' is often used to describe people. However, this doesn't apply totally to him. Strong indeed, but silent never. I remember watching him do his 'walk the talk' interview with a journalist in the garden of our home. He was very animated in his expressions and it was not until a few weeks ago that I watched the interview again and truly realized why.

Despite being in his office for the most part when I lived with him, never did he fail to keep the grandfather–grandson bond as strong as could be. Even though he is one of the most powerful industrialists in the country, he never made anyone around him feel small.

Dada always aims to be the best in whatever he does, be it scooters or politics. This aspect of his nature is seen in his fondness for the best food wherever he goes. He is generally very fixed in his ways, except when it comes to his food. He'll never say 'no' to anything you put in front of him!

A few years ago, when Dada was admitted to hospital, I remember calling him to check up on him, only to be greeted with the words, 'Rishab, please ask Deepa to send aloo-sabji and sooji-poori for dinner.'

Unfortunately, my Nana, Nani and Dadi couldn't see me go to college. Dada, however, made up for all of them. The interest he's shown in my education over the past four years and discussions for my future studies and work have been second only to my father's. I guess they are more similar than they would like to admit!

A man of many wise words, with a calm and collected personality, yet one of the kindest people I have come across, you are an inspiration to millions around the country, myself included, and I am very proud to be your grandson!

Sanjali's Dada

As someone who has always lived in the same house as Dada, it's not easy to put down a few memories. While growing up I didn't see Dada as often due to his work and travel, but he always made it a point to be there for my birthday and other events like grandparents' day and annual day at school. My brother and I often had dinner with Dadi on the weekends, and if Dada was in town, this is when we usually spent time with him. He would come home around 9 p.m. after we were done with dinner, give us big hugs and sit down to watch whatever we were watching—whether it was a Disney show, a Bollywood movie or, after some complaining, a Hindi serial that Dadi was watching. This is when we would talk to him about school, exams, extracurricular activities or just how our day had been in general. We would then sit and watch him have his drink and eat an entire plate of Budhani wafers and ketchup—his go-to evening snack.

Dada has always said he's glad he has at least one granddaughter out of his five grandchildren and has never differentiated between my brothers and me. While everyone sees him as this strong, outspoken businessman, as his only granddaughter I always see the softer side of my Dada. I remember playing with my dolls on the floor in his bedroom as a child and needing some help. Without thinking twice, I turned to ask Dada to hold one of my dolls and he happily did. This made my mother and Dadi burst out laughing and take a picture of this moment.

As we grew up, and especially after Dadi passed away, our interactions with Dada started on a daily basis. We started having dinner together every day, and soon he knew about everything we were doing. There has never been a quiet moment at our dinner table, be it discussing schoolwork, college plans, a little bit of business and politics, movies, TV shows and, of course, food! It is something we're both extremely passionate about and never get bored talking about. As I started learning how to cook and bake over the last few years, he has always been an enthusiastic supporter—willing to try everything, but also an honest critic whenever needed. I don't think there is anyone more of a foodie than Dada is. You can see his eyes light up when his favourite food is made—chaat, pizza or cheese in any form!

We were once on a holiday together with the entire family in Italy and staying at a villa that didn't have any Internet connection. On our day out sightseeing one day, we decided to stop at a café. Everyone was excited when they realized the café had Wi-Fi and immediately took out their phones, but Dada was more excited about the hot chocolate and French fries he had just ordered! When he goes on holidays, Dada is very particular about having an itinerary in advance, but what is more important is knowing where each meal is going to be. This is something I've learnt from him, and whenever we have been on holidays together, we always plan our days around the meals!

Sargam's Man of the Word

He is Mr Rahul Bajaj to the world, Bada Papa to me.

Bada Papa is a man of his word. When I was six, I went on a holiday to Darjeeling with the family. On day two, I got chickenpox and was sent back immediately. On the way to the airport, Bada Papa promised me that wherever he goes the following year, he would take me.

The following year, holiday plans were made for the US. In those times, our family had a rule that children below twelve didn't go abroad. But Bada Papa said if I don't go, he won't go either, and of course the rule was kept aside for a bit. It would have been so easy for him to simply discount what he said to a six-year-old, but he didn't. I will never forget, and I try to imbibe and follow it in all that I do.

I spent a major portion of my school life with Bada Papa and Badi Ma. We went to the school in Akurdi, the same school all the employees' children went to. He insisted we take the bus. When we started working at Bajaj Auto, he insisted that punctuality was key. At 8.41 a.m. thrice in a month, we were called to the CMD's office. I saw him make Rajiv and Sanjiv, both starting their careers on the shop floor, earn their way up.

At various stages, I didn't understand the value of these actions, but when I look back, this is home schooling that will stay with us for life and hold us in good stead. A lovely by-product of this grounding is to be happy and grateful for the small things in life.

Bada Papa is a man with the largest arms for the warmest hugs. He carries the entire family with him, effortlessly and happily. You see . . . you just can't beat my Bada Papa!

Shefali's Second Father

Sanjiv and I had been dating for three years in 1993, when I remember he called me one Sunday morning and told me his father wants to speak to mine. Naturally my immediate reaction was, 'Why?' Papa spoke to my father and in his own style said, 'Let's save on our telephone bills and train tickets and get these two married.' That's the first time I realized my future father-in-law was cool! The first few years of our marriage I didn't have many interactions with him as he was travelling a lot and had very long working hours. When he visited us in Boston, where Sanjiv was doing his MBA, he was very happy partying with our friends and spending quality time with us.

While he continued to stay busy, once Sanjali and Siddhant were born, he always knew what was happening with each one of them through Ma. He made a point to be there for their birthdays and school functions as long as he was in Pune.

I started interacting with him on a daily basis after Ma passed away in 2013. I remember thinking to myself, 'Now I'm responsible for him' and honestly, I was quite nervous about it.

The first thing I changed were his eating habits, much to his dismay. His timings were breakfast at 11.45 a.m., lunch at 3.45 p.m. and dinner at 9.45 p.m. His meals consisted of chaat, samosas, chips and anything fried. To be fair to him, he took all suggestions very openly and tried his best to change. If he was getting late, one phone call from the kids to him in the office at 7.45 p.m. saying, 'Dada, we are hungry' would suffice—he'd be at the dining table soon after.

Dinner-time discussions revolve around work, studies, basketball, travel plans and, of course, food. We've had a number of great holidays together in the US, Kashmir, Goa, Mussoorie and Dubai, but he's always made sure he doesn't impose on us. Since food is such an important part of our family, he's always enjoyed a meal out, whether it was a Sunday brunch, Japanese dinners, or a simple south Indian lunch at Vaishali.

Papa loves going to the theatre to watch a good movie and, during most visits, is happiest when someone asks him for a photograph or autograph. He always obliges and, much to the other person's delight, is willing to start a conversation—often making us late for the movie. Another thing he always enjoys is spending time with our friends. Although he gets into discussions with them, he never imposes his views or opinions on anybody, often agreeing to disagree. Always young at heart, he insists they call him Rahul instead of 'Uncle' and has spent many evenings with our friends dancing into the wee hours of the morning together.

Papa has a very caring side to him which people don't often see, and he is always there for us. If any of us is unwell, he will always call to check on us and a visit to our rooms every day is a must. Recently, when the kids and I had COVID, he could only see us from a distance, but we got a call every morning and evening checking on us and our symptoms.

To the whole world he is Rahul Bajaj—the outspoken, extremely successful businessmen, but to me he is Papa—my second father.

Shekhar's Three Principles of Life

Rahul bhai is always very passionate, dedicated, and energetic towards anything he does. Even if I send him a casual note, he will study it in detail and respond very sincerely. Any subject or note which goes to him, whether it is official or personal, he will always respond to—which used to always amaze me. Then I realized that he cannot respond casually. Therefore, I decided I will not send him any query unless it is very important because I realize it takes lot of energy out of him.

He was always ready to respond to any query when he was chairman of Indian Airlines. As Indian Airlines was not doing well, there were, therefore, lots of complaints that continuously came to him through mail. He used to answer each and every mail or letter, which is practically unthinkable for anybody.

He has always followed three principles in his life: first, never overate; second, never worry (do *chintan*, not *chinta*); and third, never miss medicines.

I remember when we were young, we were unhappy with his strictness. Nonetheless, Madhur, Niraj and I were always treated as his brothers (including getting shouted at). Only because of Rahul bhai's great leadership, style and vision, Bajaj is one the leading groups in India.

We were fortunate to have our founder Jamnalalji. He passed away in 1942 at the age of fifty-three. Thereafter, Kamalnayanji, the eldest son, took over active responsibility of the Bajaj Group companies from 1942 to 1972. He passed away at the age of fifty-seven. From 1972 to 1994, my father Ramkrishnaji took over the business responsibility. My father passed away at the age of seventy.

In 1994, Rahul bhai took over control of the Bajaj Group and established one of India's largest conglomerates. He has been able to keep the Bajaj group and family with full harmony. Normally, family groups tend not to survive for more than three generations. With the grace of God, we are very fortunate to be together, and all of us are looking forward for our fifth generation to enter the business very soon.

Siddhant's Dada

'Sidd, do your best but never be overconfident.' This is one thing I always remember Dada saying to me, whether it is before exams, basketball matches or, recently, before my test for a driving licence.

As a child, I didn't spend a lot of time with my grandfather as our timings were very different and he travelled a lot, but whenever I got a chance, I would drop him to the office and spend a few minutes with him there. Although he had a very busy schedule, he always knew what was going on with us in school, with sports or anything in general. This was because we were very close to Dadi and she always kept him up to date. The one thing I will never forget is that as long as Dada was in Pune, he always made it a point to come for my birthday parties, school events, and in recent years, some of my basketball matches. I particularly remember the time he surprised me at my school's annual day when I was in the eighth grade, because I was felicitated for being selected to play basketball at the national level.

In the past eight years, after Dadi passed away, I became closer to Dada because Mamma changed his meal timings and we started spending a lot more time together. We also went on fun holidays together. During these years I've had many funny and interesting conversations with him and learnt his opinion about various topics, from business to politics and even sports. A lot of evenings spent over meals, cricket matches, watching movies and sports showed us a side of him we had never seen as children. Very often Mamma asks us what we want for a meal since we are both foodies, and he always leaves it up to me, saying, 'I'm sure you'll have something fun and unhealthy made'.

He is always happy and proud when I achieve something significant, like doing well in my board exams, being selected for the Maharashtra basketball team and becoming head boy of my school. He always encourages me to work hard and do my best. After each of these achievements, he makes it a point to celebrate with some good food and a lot of dessert!

I've always looked up to Dada and learnt a lot from him, but recently realized there is one topic I can teach him about—that is technology. From showing him how to send his first WhatsApp message many years ago, teaching him how to use Netflix, and more recently navigating his Zoom meetings—we have spent many afternoons together. He always notes down every detail of the instructions I tell him, because he is keen to learn and do everything himself even at his age of eighty-two.

While I'm fortunate to be born into this family headed by my outspoken, hardworking, and extremely successful grandfather, to me he will simply always be my caring and loving '*Dada*'.

Sunaina's Hero

I did not spend too much time with Papa during my growing years as he was always travelling or working late. Hence the few memories that I have with him are very vivid—he would take us for a drive whenever he bought a new car (which wasn't so often!), and he would take us zigzagging through the sleepy, narrow roads of Akurdi at night. This always had us in squeals of joy and was something we always looked forward to.

Sometimes, Papa would pretend to be asleep, and I and Neelima would climb on his back and he would suddenly start shaking and throw us off! We so enjoyed it! My father has never raised his voice at me, but I was so scared of him that on the few occasions where he did so with my brothers, I had tears in my eyes. It soon became a joke in my family.

Being a Gandhian family, my father was not, and is still not, into receiving or giving gifts; and so, we never got anything whenever he returned from his work trips abroad. In those days, getting anything from abroad was 'WOW!' He got me only two things on two separate trips—a Swiss clock pendant and a Caran d'Ache colour pencil set. They are my most cherished possessions and I have them with me even today. I still remember the joy I felt when I received them.

I started interacting more and more with him as I grew into my teens. I saw his dynamism, his hard work, how driven he was and how open he was to anything. We started going on holidays abroad then and I saw the real him. He could let down his guard and was so much fun. He was such a charmer and great on the dance floor—he had the moves! Soon it was time for me to look at prospective grooms for marriage and he fully gave me the space and time to arrive at a decision I was comfortable with. This was quite unusual in a traditional Marwari family in those days. Even though I was emotionally closer to my Mom, it was Papa whom I could freely speak with. Through my early married life, Papa kept a discreet check on how I was settling in. What I appreciated was that he never intruded, but I always felt that he was right there behind me like a rock to support me if I ever needed it.

I subconsciously married someone very much like Papa. And it is a delight to see him and Manish interacting and getting on like a house on fire. Papa used to come to Mumbai very often and we always met up for a meal. It was during these numerous dinners and late-night coffee get-togethers that I really got to know him. I learnt so much from Papa: his foresight, his forthrightness, his sense of fairness, his pride in being Indian, his fearlessness and most of all, his ability to take criticism and to apologize immediately if he felt it was valid. I have seen him go through so many tough situations where he had to take a tough stand for a resolution. Even if it hurt him, he did it if he believed it was the right thing to do. These were huge learnings for me, and even today, if I face a difficult situation in my life I always think—'what would Mummy or Papa do in this situation?' Often, I have an answer: I know they will be my guiding stars forever.

Mummy's and Papa's was a love marriage and he was smitten with her from the beginning. Not that they didn't fight or argue, but both were so strong, well-matched and intellectually compatible individuals that I believe they were true soulmates. They were a combination of fire and water. Mummy was Papa's sounding board, and just her being there calmed him. She was like the sun and his world revolved around her more than he realized.

During her last year, he left no stone unturned and became half a doctor himself in trying to choose the best place and the best kind of treatment for her. I don't think most people could do the kind of extensive and exhaustive research, and medical interactions which he did for her. He wanted to be certain that he had chosen absolutely the best option for her. He was totally committed to her and in her passing, a part of him went with her.

Papa always regrets not having spent time with us in our childhood, and is enjoying his grandchildren so much that he jokes that if he knew it would be so much fun, he would have had his grandchildren before he had his children! He makes an effort to spend time with them, do masti with them, and is much more lenient with them than he ever was with us! He gets most concerned if any of them are sick or have hurt themselves. Playing with them brings out the child in him which is a pleasure to watch. A year ago, he and my nine-year-old had a hotline going on. They would call and message each other very often, with my son mostly complaining about me, and Papa totally agreeing with him and being his partner in crime!

44

Jamnalal's Legacy

Jamnalal Bajaj at the Karnavaton-ka-bagh detention centre in 1939.

Friday, 26 July 2019. The seventy-fourth AGM of Bajaj Holding & Investment Ltd., at Akurdi in Maharashtra.

Niraj Bajaj looks distinctly edgy as he takes his place in front of the mic. The large, high-ceilinged room is packed with shareholders and employees. The stage is stacked with the board of directors. The sequence of events will be filmed for prosperity. In a moment, Niraj will announce that the board of Bajaj Holdings & Investments Ltd has elected him chairman of one of the oldest companies of the Bajaj family.

From the dais, Niraj looks down at Bajaj, seated in the audience. Bajaj gives his cousin an encouraging nod. By stepping down and appointing Niraj as chair of the company that holds the promoter shares of key companies in the Rahul Bajaj group, Bajaj is signalling his desire to keep family bonds strong.

Later that evening, Bajaj explained why he did what he did. 'It's simple. Jamnalalji was the founder of our group, and I want to uphold his legacy.' The vote of confidence in Niraj—the youngest of Ramkrishna Bajaj's three sons, and with whom the eighty-year-old Bajaj has had many boisterous arguments—was Bajaj's intent to keep united as many male descendants of the two branches for as long as possible.

APPENDIX

1

Rajya Sabha: 23 August 2006[1]

Thank you, Mr. Vice-Chairman, for giving me this opportunity to make my maiden speech. My family comes from Wardha and Shri Janeshwar Mishraji, who is not here, mentioned about the Ashram of Gandhiji which is Seva Gram and that is where my late grandfather Jamnalalji invited Gandhiji in the early 1930s from Sabarmati near Ahmedabad. Mr. Vice-Chairman, Sir, a lot has been said about this subject. I would try not to repeat it and one of the ways, I will do it is by concentrating on my region which is Vidarbha and which is the cotton bowl of the country. So, I will talk about cotton, Vidarbha and then, later on, a little bit about the economy and the society.

We have heard that suicides primarily are by small and marginal farmers. It is very correct. We have also heard that like any commodity, Mr. Vice-Chairman, industrial commodity, in the services sector, IT or otherwise, only way one can be sustainable and one can survive is when the selling price exceeds the total cost of production. Keeping in mind States like Maharashtra and Vidarbha where less than five percent of the land is irrigated, the chances of crop failure are obviously very high. So, if you take the cost of production of cotton in Maharashtra and Vidarbha, it is much, much higher than other places including a State like Gujarat.

---

[1] All texts in this section have been reproduced in original.

Wherever a human life is lost unnaturally, it is a tragedy. But when someone takes his own life, in my view, it is a catastrophe. And yet, in recent years, we have seen thousands of farmers taking their lives with numbing regularity. What should be done? Costs have to come down or selling prices have to go up. For the time being, I would not worry about the consumer and the customer; though on onion prices, Governments have changed. But let's leave it aside because here, we are not talking of the production of an industrial commodity, we are talking of 65 per cent of the population of this country. They are consumers as well as producers. We have heard enough that if you don't take care of the farmer, how will India move forward? I fully share that view because we are all inter-dependent.

The Minimum Support Price for cotton in some States, has been lower than the cost of production. As Shri Arjun Senguptaji was rightly saying, MSP is fixed to ensure that a farmer, at least, gets something more than his cost - cost-plus approach. Mr. Vice-Chairman, the 2004-05 report of the Commission for Agricultural Costs and Prices estimated the cost per quintal of cotton – I won't give too many figures, only three figures at Rs.1643 in Gujarat, Rs.2229 in Karnataka and Rs.2216 in Maharashtra. But there was naturally only one Minimum Support Price and, in that year, that was Rs.1960. Cost being above MSP does seem to explain and, at least, it is one major reason for the distress in Maharashtra and Karnataka. In Gujarat, because the cost was lower than the MSP, we have not heard of that many or, if any, suicides from there.

So, the first point I am making, Mr. Vice-Chairman, is that you can take care of debt items — and I will come to that in a moment — but all those are temporary measures of help today, tomorrow. If you are to keep selling your product, in this case, cotton, or any other agricultural product, at a price lower than the cost of production, no amount of debt can take care because ultimately, the debt has to be repaid. *Ek bar maf kar denge, do bar maf kar denge, interest ko bhi chod denge, lekin paise kahan se ayenge? Chahe budgetary support yeh kam kare, bank kare, ooper se to paise nahi ayenge kyon ki yeh to tax payers ka paise hein.* So, ultimately, the farmer must make a profit. Yes, I will talk a little about the private moneylender, about whom much has not been said except some passing reference by a few speakers.

I may also mention, Sir, that in 2004-05, the Maharashtra Government offered prices of around Rs.2,500/- per quintal. Very good. But, then, it became unsustainable for their budget. Sir, in 2005-06, they reduced the price to Rs.1,980/-. I have already referred to the cost of production, in Maharashtra, of cotton, which was higher than Rs. 1,980/-. And the result is for all of us to see. Of course, Sir, I cannot say to my Agriculture Minister that he has been unfair to Vidarbha and partial to Western Maharashtra! That would be a very unfair comment, Sir, because I come from Vidarbha and he comes from Western Maharashtra! But that is a fact of life. Even when we have had a Chief Minister like Vasantrao Naik, who was from Vidarbha, probably not much was done because he did not have that strength.

Private moneylenders, Sir, when do they lend money? When the banks and the cooperative societies do not lend. The marginal farmer has not paid his loans. He cannot get loans elsewhere. Also, the moneylender is not only supplying inputs. He is also now buying the output. So, he has a stranglehold on the farmer. I understand that, nowadays, they are charging as much interest as 60 per cent per annum. Sir! I think, Manohar Joshiji or someone else mentioned 30 per cent. Sometimes, they charge 60 per cent. At 60 per cent, even the best-run industrial establishment will fold.

Whether he charges two per cent, four per cent or six per cent, is not the point. The question is — I don't understand it, Sir; maybe, the Agriculture Minister will tell me — that there is the Bombay Moneylenders' Act. 1946. Our Agriculture Minister was probably four years old then, Sir, and I was a little older! Now, that Act says that if the moneylender is not licenced, he cannot recover his loan; he cannot go to courts, and if he is licenced, the total outstanding amount cannot be more than twice the loan. And it also specifies the rate of interest. I do not know why my State Government is not taking advantage of that Act. There must be some reason for that.

Rajnathji rightly referred to the WTO. I do not want to take too much time on that. I would only say this. When we talk of market prices, we talk of normal market prices. The international cotton prices are not normal. US$4 billion dollars, Rs.18,000 crores, is the subsidy provided by the US alone to just its cotton farmers. The total subsidy for farmers by the OECD countries is US$ ¥ 350 billion. Cotton farmers get Rs.18,000 crores there. My farmer, in Vidarbha also, maybe, can compete with the American farmer, but he cannot compete with the United States Treasury. Kamal Nathji, in some other context, rightly said that he can compete with the wheat imported, or any other commodity, in the agricultural area, but he cannot compete with the subsidies which a country like the United States provides.

And because of this, I come to my recommendations, Sir.

In the short-term recommendations — Mr. Arjun Sengupta said about the import duty — first of all, Sir, I am referring to the import duty on cotton which is not produced in this country. If it is not produced, nobody gets hurt. And the textile mill people are very influential people. You know, industrialist, big industrialist, not people like me, small industrialists, Arjunji. But when cotton is produced in this country, if we import cotton from a country which subsidises its cotton farmers, then we must have an anti-dumping duty. I don't understand why it is not there. It would be WTO compliant. If there are no cotton imports from such countries, fine. I am just saying, if there is cotton import, which is a subsidised variety, then I must have a countervailing duty.

Sir, why don't we hear about suicides from Gujarat? One reason is that, obviously, 40 per cent of the land is irrigated. In Vidarbha, it is four per cent. It is important that in Gujarat farmers normally also have some other income from dairying, vegetables, etc. which they supply to the nearby industrial centres. That does not exist in Vidarbha.

Sir, I believe that the relationship between agriculture and industry is symbiotic. A prosperous agriculture develops industry and a prosperous industry develops agriculture incomes. I strongly believe that India can't move forward, unless its farmers move forward; and the growth is only of value, when it is inclusive.

Sir, the irony of the fact is that the cotton economy in our country has good growth in demand ahead of it. The domestic market is growing and with the end of Multi-Fibre Agreement, though China has benefited quite a bit, a very large market has opened abroad for us also. Our exports of cotton clothes are growing and we have further potential to grow.

Mr. Chairman, Sir, may I suggest six short-term measures and two medium-term measures? I am not referring to the long-term measure because John Maynard Keynes said," In the long run, we are all dead". My six short-term measures — some of them are being implemented or will be implemented or have been announced by the Government — are:

One, a one year moratorium on repayment of dept owed to private money-lenders. This has been done for six months or so by the Andhra Pradesh Government. A two-year moratorium — I am saying only a moratorium because I don't want to start a bad example of non-payment of loans — on repayment to cooperative institutions and banks, especially, by small farmers whose holdings are below two hectares and whose loan is below Rs. 1 lakh. But the banks must step in to help such farmers.

Two, Immediate disbursal of, at least, Rs. 1 lakh to the families of each farmer who has committed suicide. I don't want this to be misused. However, if you ask ten kinds of questions like whether he has committed suicide or whether he was murdered or whether he died in an accident, he will never get this money.

Three, there should be a declaration that private money-lenders and the private sector man can't charge interest above a certain rate, whatever the Government thinks fit, I would even say 20 per cent.

Four, all land transfers that have been made in the last two or three years should be reviewed, and if the cause of such land transfers was exorbitant interest rate, then it should be considered, within the laws of the country, whether that transaction can be invalidated; and, of course, the lender should be repaid his loan.

Five, a review of the Minimum Support Price of cotton and the appointment of the Maharashtra Cotton Procurement Federation, in addition to the Cotton Corporation of India, as an agent to procure cotton at the MSP. Six, anti-dumping duty—I referred to it already—should be levied on cotton, if cotton, which is subsidized, is imported.

Sir, the two medium term proposals are: One, to increase irrigation in the region through irrigation schemes and villager level initiatives to conserve rain run-off. Mr. Sitaram Yechury and

Shrimati Brinda Karat are not here. Two, as I said, the relationship between agriculture and industry is symbiotic. So, we must encourage industrialization in these areas.

Sir, we have 60 per cent of the population living on agriculture. America has only two per cent of its population living on agriculture and it produces more than what it needs. Today, we are employing 60 percent in agriculture. But we can't continue to absorb 60 per cent in agriculture. It may not be two per cent. It may come down to 40 per cent or 30 per cent or 20 per cent. Where will the surplus persons go? They have to go to industry and they have to go to the service sector which are complementary to each other. So, I would suggest that we must encourage industrialization in these backward areas by providing infrastructure. This is what is required. Industry does not want fiscal incentives. In fact, that distorts our decision-making.

In Himachal and Uttaranchal, I was against extending the benefits given by three years; that distorts the situation. Even I am going there. I didn't want to, but there are such benefits that you cannot ignore them. Sir, in these backward areas, if we provide the right infrastructure, and, my friends may not like it, a flexible labour policy – don't give them in areas where I am already there, but only in these backward areas – then, a lot of industries will come up in these areas, and both agriculture and industry would benefit.

What we need are a few, but effective measures. In our governance, we have come to be obsessed sometimes with the form, and we are unmindful of substance. There are, for example, 29 Government Resolutions of the Maharashtra Government on Cotton as of 24th May, this year. I don't know whether they are only on paper. I may add that someone has to be responsible to implement all these plans. Right now, everyone from PMO downwards is responsible which means, perhaps, no one is responsible. I would suggest, especially for Maharashtra, that a Cabinet Minister level or a Deputy Chief Minister level person is appointed, and this position be created in Maharashtra with the sole responsibility of improving the state of agriculture in Vidarbha. A young and a dynamic person—he is not here; otherwise, he will shout at me – Shri Praful Patel, who is considered to be one of the best Ministers in the Centre, should be given this responsibility.

Sir, since this is my maiden speech, I seek your indulgence in saying a few words to outline my broad perspective on our economy and society.

We pledged at our independence to take India forward. We have taken it forward, but nowhere near as much as it can be taken, or where it was capable. The glass is still only half filled. We still have unspeakable poverty, which was referred to by Dr Arjun Kumar Sengupta, where 28 per cent of our people, that is, 300 million people, are living on less than one dollar a day, a poverty which crushes human dignity, stalking our land. Our poor governance, in my view, has, by and large, been a drag on our development. It is the tenacious spirit of India, alive in the hearts and minds of every Indian, whether he is a worker, farmer, businessmen, entrepreneur, or, I do not know whether I should say, politician, and their spirit, hard work and entrepreneurial ability which have taken and continue to take our country forward.

I believe that we stand at a propitious moment in the history of our nation. While we acknowledge the challenges, – there are many challenges – a world or opportunity also awaits us. As you know, in the world, India is not just a flavour of the week or the month or the year. We are the flavour of the times. Previously, it was only China. Now it is China and India. Both in the services and manufacturing sector, we are poised to gain from the developments in the world economy. We are becoming internationally competitive despite the serious handicaps of lack of infrastructure, right from social infrastructure, health, education, drinking water, sanitation and of course, physical infrastructure. The key reason, however, for my optimism, as I said, Sir, is the quality and entrepreneurship of our people.

Though low as a percentage of our population, we must strive to increase this. We have the world's largest pool of smart, hardworking manpower, be it in IT, manufacturing, or finance. And, this is very important and we are conscious of it that demographically, we will remain a country of the young even in 2025. We have to ensure that we encash this demographic dividend by investing in their education and their skills. With education and skill, India will become a great country; we shall capture the world in the next 25 years. But if our youth are not educated, are not skilled, instead of becoming a great asset, they will become a great liability.

Sir, we need good governance to achieve these goals of inclusive economic growth. This will come from changes at the top and pressures from below The pressure from below will increase, as economic and social development make our people more self-assured and more articulate. The reopening of the Jessica Lall and Mattoo cases, under intense public pressure, bodes well for our democracy. Democracy is not just elections. Democracy is active participation by every citizen in the affairs of the state, and the state exists essentially to provide public goods and services to its citizens.

In this connection, in passing, Mr Chairman, Sir — I have no time to go into details – I would like to add that to ensure that we can take hard decisions, the Lok Sabha and all the State Assemblies should go to elections simultaneously; co-terminuously, and only once in five years. We should also ensure that a vote of no-confidence in the Leader of the House, the Chief Minister or the Prime Minister should be, like Germany, which is a democratic country, accompanied by a vote-of-confidence in an alternate party and person.

Sir, quality of leadership is crucial in determining outcomes. Leadership is not just a matter of charisma or showmanship or public relations. But it is of understanding today, it is of envisioning a better tomorrow and having the confidence in oneself and of one's team to make our future happen. Leaders are those that deliver better outcomes. Occupying a chair does not make us a leader.

Sir, Gandhiji occupied no chair but led the country from subjugation to freedom, striding like a colossus in our hearts and minds. We will do well, may I say so, Sir, in all humility, to remember Gandhiji's teachings of the seven social sins – wealth without work, pleasure without conscience, education without character, commerce without morality, science without humanity, worship without sacrifice and politics without principles. In my view, precisely, because we have ignored these teachings that we have underachieved.

In this august House, I will endeavour in all humility to play the role that the Constitution envisaged each Member to play. That is, on behalf of the people of India, hold the Government accountable. No more, no less. We have enough good laws. What we lack is speed and justice in their implementation. I would like to consider myself as representing a large political spectrum. Three of the major parties in Maharashtra supported me as an independent; and my family is steeped in the Gandhian culture, and this gives me a lot of pride. So, I will try to be even handed as an independent, with right and wrong for the country being the sole yardstick for holding an opinion, though I may be mistaken at times.

In conclusion, Sir, coming into this august House, I am conscious of my responsibilities to the nation. Panditji's 'Tryst with Destiny' reverberates inside my mind. I have come here to try to help in all humility redeem the pledge that was taken by our founding fathers. So, may God give me the strength to make a difference! I get a strong feeling, Sir, that I can bank on the support of both sides of this august House.

Thank you, Sir.

2

Requiem

By Rajiv Bajaj

25th February 2014. It is now nearing 3 p.m. in Leipzig, almost exactly a year since we were given the heart-rending news about Mummy. I have missed her every single day of this last year, just as I had thought that I would.

When I clean my ears, I remember how she would layer
an earbud with a little Nivea cream to clean them so that
there wouldn't be the slightest pain!
When I brush my teeth, I can hear her saying
circular motion, not straight!
When I shave, I remember her watching nervously as
I shave for the first time, telling me to mix some water
with the aftershave so that it would not sting my cheeks!
When I clip my nails, I can hear her again - fingernails
along the finger, toenails straight!
When I wash my hair, I remember her massaging *nimbu*
and coconut oil into my scalp every weekend!

And when I have a bath I can image her watching me as I began washing my feet in the shower, telling me, wash from top to bottom, not bottom to top!

And when I'm getting dressed I hear her saying, see what Papa does, how he holds his shirt and pulls his pants up. That's how you are supposed to tuck it in!

These are everyday chores that I will do till I die and so I will remember mummy every day till I die. But beyond these little gems, she taught me the most important lesson that I've ever learnt.

We were gathered on the balcony outside our room - mummy, Sanjiv, our maid Hirabai, and me. Anxiously Mummy watched in the direction of Papa's office, which had been set on fire by some workers. Hirabai too looked that way - her son was employed as a worker, she was worried for his safety. Perhaps she was conflicted. I certainly was.

I asked Mummy - why is this happening? Who is right? Who is wrong? As softly & surely as she always spoke, she said whenever you're in doubt just listen to your conscience, it is that little voice inside you through which God speaks to you.

That's the sign of a great teacher - they don't give you the answer, they tell you how to think about the problem. I have not been able to follow Mummy's advice in my life. But I think that I shouldn't be too hard on myself for that.

It's easy to think like her, tough to act like her.

It's easy to talk like her, tough to walk that talk.

Perhaps that is why she left the noble impression that she has on so many, many people. As Maya Angelou said, people will forget what you said, they will forget what you did, but they will never forget the way you made them feel.

Unknown to either parent, as a child, I read many letters that Mummy wrote to Papa, as couples do when all is not well.

It told me that her commitment to him matched her courage for herself. It told me that she carried his heart in hers, always & forever. So much so that before she finely left, she left her spirit behind him.

Papa, you have been unbelievably strong this last year.

You have not let your grief tinge our lives.
It has confused me.

I know that you're not that strong.
And you've also been softer, quieter.
You've been patient, listening.
You've been warm, thoughtful.
I'll tell you why.

It's not you, it's the mummy that lives in you now.
I believe this is true because my conscience told me so.
If you will be happy & well, mummy will be happy & well.
More than ever before.

Because, as Bollywood tells us, *Baba Moshay, maut sirf naam se badnam hai, varna taqleef toh zindagi hee deti hai....*
I'm sure that you've heard the Yiddish proverb - God couldn't be everywhere, so he made mother. Mummy certainly lived her life accordingly.

* * *

Rupa's mortal remains were flown to India on Friday March 3, 2013. She was 74 when she passed away in a hospital in Germany, where she was undergoing treatment for a prolonged illness. The last rites were performed at Pune's Vaikunth crematorium at 4.30 p.m.

3

Chats with Mom

By Sanjiv Bajaj

My formative years were at the Bajaj Auto Akurdi campus. While growing up, many conversations—formal and informal—revolved around manufacturing, the scooter business and the motorcycle business. As a youngster, it is always exciting to be in an environment where you make your own bikes and ride them. It was only natural for me to get into that business.

After obtaining my mechanical engineering degree from Pune in 1991, I joined Bajaj Auto on the shop floor and worked there for eighteen months, after which I signed up for an MSc in Manufacturing Systems Engineering at the University of Warwick in the UK. It was a great learning experience and helped me when I started working with our manufacturing improvement teams in Akurdi. And then, in September 1995, I went to Harvard for my MBA. From making scooters to working in a manufacturing industry, Harvard was a very different experience for an engineer like me. The case study method of teaching taught us how to look at various business issues in a complex world, think both deep and fast about alternate solutions and then argue your point of view in class discussions. It was a great snapshot of business through more than six hundred real-life cases over two years. We had regular speakers, including stalwarts like Warren Buffett and Alan Mulally, who headed and presented to us the Boeing 777 manufacturing programme. The Harvard MBA was, in hindsight, a major turning point in my career.

When I returned from Harvard, my father and I decided I should complement the expertise and skill sets of my elder brother Rajiv who was working in manufacturing. So I started focusing on the finance side of the business. However, I soon felt the need for a more direct business role and saw the opportunity to build exports at Bajaj Auto. From FY2005–08, when I ran exports, the annual volumes went up from about 15,0000 to 62,5000 vehicles as we consolidated our presence in existing markets and expanded into new ones around the world.

My relationship with my mother was very disciplined, as she was with all of us until I was probably seventeen or eighteen. She was a strict disciplinarian, and informal, friendly conversations at home were few. When we were growing up, all the masti we used to do happened with aunt Kumud and uncle Madhur who lived with us for many years and then moved to a place nearby. At sixteen, when I wanted a glass of beer, it was with them. When I wanted to learn to drive, it was again with them—much before I was eighteen. My father was not very happy about this, so all the little things we wanted to do, happened with my aunt and uncle.

My mother was serious and disciplined but hugely supportive. She was always there for us, our rock. As children, in the morning when we woke up, she would come to our room and sit with us till we left for school. During exams, she supervised our studies and never went out of town with my father. She was solid, but in a strong, quiet way. It was around the age of seventeen when we got more free with one another and built a friendly and more informal relationship.

Our relationship over the next twenty-five years became a lot more casual and equal, where I would discuss all kinds of thoughts, including work. She would listen intently, always give her advice in her own patient, mature and sensible way. The relationship, I would say, really flourished after my teenage years right to the end. For example, I started eating meat after the age of seventeen. I didn't know my mom was a non-vegetarian until I was probably fifteen or sixteen. Of course, we never ate meat at home.

Between 2004–2005, in my first year running exports, my father started putting pressure on me to perform. 'So far you were the finance head. Now you have to build success in the exports business. This is now yours, you are driving it; the success or failure is yours,' he would say to me. He would push hard. I understood that he was doing this for my success. I used to tell him, we are building the foundation blocks and this will take time, but we will see the results soon.

Once in a while, he would tell me, 'But you know, I was talking to so and so in the company, and they were telling me export volumes should grow more. Otherwise it will not be seen as a success for Sanjiv.' From FY2006, the volumes started growing, and we had dramatic results in coming years. From then onwards, that pressure went away.

The other thing my father used to watch was our attendance punching cards. If you are not in office for ten to eleven hours a day, then you are not working. Whereas for me, what is important is to get my work done and then do other stuff like my workouts and spend time with the kids. I would be home normally by 6 p.m., and then work after dinner for a couple of hours. He wouldn't understand that initially. In his eyes, visibility was very important, which I can partly understand. 'What would other people say? What would other people feel? They will think you are not working,' he would insist.

I knew my style was more balanced and would get me results. I didn't feel the need to get involved in and approve every small decision. I preferred building an empowered but accountable way of management. Mom was the balm. 'Look, don't worry, you know your father, he only wants the best for you.' None of that bothered me, but I used to say yes to her. Mom felt the responsibility and need to make up.

There was a time when Rajiv won a whole lot of awards in 2009 or 2010. It was very well deserved. In her own way, as a mother, she used to tell me, 'Don't worry, I know you are doing good work, your time will also come.'

After I moved to financial services towards the end of FY2008, she knew there was a lot of work to be done as these were smaller businesses and there would be no recognition of performance for some years. She knew the pressure was there. She played a very strong support role, listening, discussing and encouraging me.

Whatever recognition I was fortunate to get was after my mother's death in 2013. It's a big regret. She should have seen at least some of my work.

4

Evolution: 1926–2021

Sr. No.	Date of Incorporation	Name of the Company
	Bajaj Group Companies **17 September 2020**	
(A)	**Private Companies**	
1	27 August 1926	Bachhraj Factories Pvt. Ltd.
2	12 January 1927	Bachhraj & Company Pvt. Ltd.
3	5 March 1938	Jamnalal Sons Pvt. Ltd.
4	14 February 1941	Baroda Industries Pvt. Ltd.
5	9 March 1941	Bajaj International Pvt. Ltd.
6	6 January 1953	Bajaj Sevashram Pvt. Ltd.
7	16 July 1979	Nirlep Appliances Pvt. Ltd.
8	31 January 1992	Kamalnayan Investment & Trading Pvt. Ltd.
9	31 January 1992	Rahul Securities Pvt. Ltd.
10	31 January 1992	Madhur Securities Pvt. ltd.
11	31 January 1992	Niraj Holdings Pvt. Ltd.
12	3 February 1992	Shekhar Holdings Pvt. Ltd.

Bajaj Group Companies 17 September 2020		
Sr. No.	**Date of Incorporation**	**Name of the Company**
13	3 February 1992	Rupa Equities Pvt. Ltd.
14	13 April 1994	Sankalp Resorts Pvt. Ltd.
15	18 April 2006	Emerald Acres Pvt. Ltd.
16	17 August 2006	Adore Traders & Realtors Pvt. Ltd.
17	31 March 2008	Sanraj Nayan Investments Pvt. Ltd.
18	9 June 2008	Rose Realtors Pvt. Ltd.
19	26 July 2014	Simply Cheqit Pvt. Ltd. (Under process of being Struck Off)
20	30 July 2014	LazyTech Online Pvt. Ltd.
21	30 July 2014	Rapidkart Online Pvt. Ltd.
(B)	**Listed Companies**	
22	27 February 1934	The Hindustan Housing Company Ltd.
23	29 November 1937	Mukand Ltd.
24	14 July 1938	Bajaj Electricals Ltd.
25	29 November 1945	Bajaj Holdings & Investment Ltd.
26	15 June 1962	Hercules Hoists Ltd.
27	11 June 1975	Maharashtra Scooters Ltd.
28	30 January 1987	Mukand Engineers Ltd.
29	25 March 1987	Bajaj Finance Ltd.
30	30 April 2007	Bajaj Auto Ltd.
31	30 April 2007	Bajaj Finserv Ltd.
(C)	**Unlisted Public Companies**	
32	23 November 1937	Jeewan Ltd.
33	30 April 1951	Hind Lamps Ltd.
34	24 August 1962	Hind Musafir Agency Ltd.
35	6 January 1966	Bombay Forgings Ltd.

Bajaj Group Companies 17 September 2020		
Sr. No.	Date of Incorporation	Name of the Company
36	1 July 1971	Vidyavihar Containers Ltd.
37	26 February 1979	Bajaj Auto Holdings Ltd.
38	23 June 1979	Mukand Global Finance Ltd.
39	15 December 1993	Sidya Investments Ltd.
40	4 July 1995	Starlite Lighting Ltd.
41	17 October 1995	Stainless India Ltd.
42	20 May 1998	Hospet Steels Ltd.
43	19th September 2000	Bajaj Allianz General Insurance Co. Ltd.
44	12th March 2001	Bajaj Allianz Life Insurance Co. Ltd.
45	16th March 2007	Bajaj Allianz Financial Distributors Ltd.
46	13th June 2008	Bajaj Housing Finance Ltd.
47	7th April 2010	Bajaj Financial Securities Ltd.
48	1st August 2012	Mukand Sumi Metal Processing Ltd.
49	7th February 2014	Bajaj Finserv Direct Ltd.
50	15th January 2015	Mukand Sumi Special Steel Ltd.
51	16th March 2015	Bajaj Allianz Staffing Solutions Ltd.
52	5th July 2019	Bajaj Finserv Health Ltd.
(D)	Section 8 Companies (Private)	
53	6 February 1991	Bhoopati Shikshan Pratisthan
54	6 February 1991	Mahakalp Arogya Pratisthan
55	6 March 2014	Bajaj Electoral Trust

Acknowledgements

The writing of this book has been one of the most pleasurable periods of my career. More than a decade ago, I had promised myself that I would write Rahul's biography. Time flew. I jotted notes, gathered fodder, crafted the vignette style, but didn't chew. During India's COVID-19 lockdown, time became irrelevant. Voilà, dear reader! It's now in your hands.

Given that this book was so long in the making, I would like to first thank the subject of this book for never asking me 'why' – not even when 'why' could, and, should – have become 'when?'. In the writing process were some amazing bonuses: Rahul's incredible memory, his immense capacity to ferret out the tiniest detail, nor bother me.

Chatting with Oxonians opened several unexpected horizons. The Bodleian Library helped me re-shape my words and their usage. The seminars I attended, in particular at Somerville College and the Saïd Business School, left indelible marks as also a taste for curiosity in different colours.

A most wonderful aspect of Oxford is the ease in making friends in a world inside a world. I take this opportunity to thank each of you: Abdur Razzak, Alastair Colin-Jones, Alex Rogers, Alfred Gathorne-Hardy, Alice & Franklin Prochaska, Andrew Parker, Andrew White, Annette & Colin Mayer, Anthony Evans-Pughe, Benjamin Thompson, Bhaskar Choubey, Bridget Kustin, Chris McKenna,

Daniel Anthony, Donna Seymour, Eve Carpenter-Smith, Faisal Devji, Frances Caincross, George S Yip, Hanan Yanny, Helen Fletcher, Hiram Samel, Jan Royall of Blaisdon, Janine Nahapiet, Jeff Sampler, Joanne Ockwell, Julie Hage, Kate Roll, Lalit Johri, Linda Scott, Mallica Kumbera Landrus, Mary Johnstone-Louis, Nick Bostrom, Patrick Clibbens, Paul Collier, Paul Francis, Pegram Harrison, Peter Tufano, Marc Ventresca, Ngaire Woods, Richard Bryant, Roger Hood, Roy Westbrook, Salil Tripathi, Saphire Richards, Sara Kalim, Steve Rayner, Steven 'Steve' H Simon, Tarun Ramadorai, Tim Morris, Tim Royal, Usha Prashar, Vijay R Joshi.

I was born in Muzaffarpur and grew up in London. As I write these words, I surprised myself by the friendships which evolved over the decades. Here too, I take the opportunity to thank each of you: Andrew Likierman, Angela Graham, Ayad Khajanji & family, Balwant Patel, Bhaskar Choubey, Camellia Panjabi & Ranjit Mathrani, Charles and Elizabeth Handy, Clive Crook, Colin Blake, Costas Markides, Dominic Houlder, Donald L Sull, Emma Duncan, Eva Goldenberg, François Ortalo-Magné, Gary Hamel, Gay Haskins, Jay Conger, Hanna Klein, Henrietta Royle, Herminia Ibarra, Kamini and Vindi Banga, Joan & Peter Darbyshire, Julian Birkinshaw, Laura D'Andrea Tyson, Lynda Gratton & Nigel Boardman, Lukas Kroulik Jakub, Mariam & Nasheed Faruqi, Michael Hay, Nigel Andrews, Nirmalaya Kumar, Nishit Kotecha, Paul Zuckerman, Rajesh Chandy, Richard Bryant, Saeb Eigner, Salil Tripathi, Santosh Golecha, Saul Estrin, Sharon Wilson, Shirley Cramer, Silvia Millor, Simon Long, Stella Afnaim, Subniv Babuta, Susan 'Suzie' Balch, Suzanne Davis, the late Sumantra Ghoshal and Christopher A Bartlett, Tarun Ramadorai, Thomas Lauda, Tirthankar Roy, Tobsha S Learner, Toni Bouteldja, Tracy Rose, Varun and Shibani Purandare, and Wendy Payton.

1972 was a seminal moment for Indians in the UK. Early August 1972 saw the Kothari family turn up in London as refugees after Idi Amin, the President of Uganda, ordered the expulsion of his country's Asian minority withing 90 days. Anyone who could pitch in to help, did so. Very soon, the Bagris, the Kotharis and my family provided support to each other. The same year, I returned to

India, adjusted to a Marwari culture, absorbed the history of India's freedom movement from my in-laws, made new friends, learnt what to do, and what would not be appreciated in the local culture, but the real discovery was getting to know Bombay (the city switched to Mumbai in 1995). Best of all, I unknowingly stepped into a truly liberal joint family.

Used to an active life, I turned to journalism. The city's hotbed seethed with rumours and farce: all of which was grist for the daily production of an article. I was lucky to be in a metropolitan city that never sleeps. For more than three decades, I was a free-lance reporter with long stints with India's *Economic Times* and the UK's *Financial Times* and some grist from *The Economist*. While putting together this acknowledgement, I went back to my old notes, and what you will read in this book are strands from both my published and unpublished work.

Further, this acknowledgement would be incomplete without Bajaj managers and teams in the picture. Writing is a solitary affair. Your interest and support in the making of this biography offered interesting twists and turns. Somehow, every time I thought I had completed a chapter, new, relevant, and critical data would arrive, and I would have to reboot – but it was always worth the effort. I take this opportunity to thank each one of you in the shaping of the book in your hand. Similarly, I would like to thank Radhika Marwah and the Penguin Random House India team for their support.

I save the best for the last. Aparna and Amit, Radhika and Amanda, Mukesh and Ruchi, Amartya and Agastya: no words I can say or write are a match for your smiles and encouragement.

A brief note on names, organizations, dates and format. Throughout the book, the time period of each chapter, the names of buildings, roads, people, activity, dates, spellings and more, is based on the event date of its chapter. For example, if a chapter is based on an event in 1960, the city name will be Bombay. In a chapter after 1995, it will be Mumbai. Bajaj Electricals will appear at its right time, in the right chapter, as Radio Lamp Works.